Centrally Planned Economies

Offering a retrospective view of how the system operated in Communist Czechoslovakia, this book is an important voice in the discussion about the systems of central planning. The unique features of the book include in-depth research comprising both archival records and analyses of around 75 interviews conducted with period managers across a wide range of management levels. They provided evidence of pervasive inefficiency resulting in appalling economic outcomes.

The book begins with a background to the politico-sociological system in Czechoslovakia and proceeds to describe the Marxist-Leninist ideological foundation of the regime, which underpinned the formal setting of the Czechoslovak model. These initial chapters set the context for the subsequent analysis of the real functioning of the system. The book explores the economic outcomes that must be understood as a natural consequence of the ways in which this system operated. The author finishes by answering the important question of why centrally planned economies trailed behind the market economies.

The book's unique use of the interview research format brings a vivid, close-up view of the everyday economic life in the centrally planned system. This will be a valuable contribution to the discussion surrounding the day-to-day reality of the system, which was found to be more colourful than is generally deemed. The book will appeal to both economic historians and students of economic history. A warning against repeating past mistakes, this book will also be of interest to those seeking a greater knowledge of the realities and consequences of centrally planned economies.

Libor Žídek, Associate Professor, has lectured at the Faculty of Economics and Administration at Masaryk University, Czech Republic, since 1997. He specializes in economic transformation with a particular focus on the Czech economy. He also has a keen interest in planned economy, particularly in Czechoslovakia and generally in economic history. His doctoral thesis focused on the impact of globalization on economic policy and his habilitation thesis on the transformation process in the Czech Republic. He teaches courses on World Economic History, Economic Transformation and Macroeconomics. He has lectured on the topics of central planning and transformation in a number of countries, including the USA, Canada, Japan, Germany, the UK, Poland, Finland, Ukraine, and Jamaica. He has presented at conferences and published several books and a number of chapters and journal papers.

Routledge Studies in the European Economy

When Ideas Fail
Economic Thought, the Failure of Transition and the Rise of Institutional Instability in Post-Soviet Russia
Joachim Zweynert

Economic Crisis and Structural Reforms in Southern Europe
Policy Lessons
Edited by Paulo Manasse and Dimitris Katsikas

Crisis in the European Monetary Union
A Core-Periphery Perspective
Giuseppe Celi, Andrea Ginzberg, Dario Guarascio and Annamaria Simonazzi

Rethinking Economic and Monetary Union in Europe
A Post-Keynesian Alternative
Philip B. Whyman

Central and Eastern Europe in the EU
Challenges and Perspectives Under Crisis Conditions
Edited by Christian Schweiger and Anna Visvizi

Greek Employment Relations in Crisis
Problems, Challenges and Prospects
Edited by Horen Voskeritsian, Panos Kapotas and Christina Niforou

Centrally Planned Economies
Theory and Practice in Socialist Czechoslovakia
Libor Žídek

For a full list of titles in this series, please visit www.routledge.com/series/SE0431

Centrally Planned Economies

Theory and Practice in Socialist Czechoslovakia

Libor Žídek

Routledge
Taylor & Francis Group
LONDON AND NEW YORK

First published 2019 by Routledge

2 Park Square, Milton Park, Abingdon, Oxon, OX14 4RN
605 Third Avenue, New York, NY 10017

Routledge is an imprint of the Taylor & Francis Group, an informa business

First issued in paperback 2020

British Library Cataloguing-in-Publication Data
A catalogue record for this book is available from the British Library

Library of Congress Cataloging-in-Publication Data
A catalog record for this book has been requested

ISBN: 978-1-138-61438-3 (hbk)
ISBN: 978-0-367-72862-5 (pbk)

Typeset in Bembo
by Apex CoVantage, LLC

Contents

Figures and diagrams

Figures

Diagrams

Tables

Boxes

Acknowledgements

I would like to give my thanks foremost to Lucie Coufalová, who enormously helped with the whole book, she is the author of the first chapter, provided feedback and tagged nearly all the interviews. My thanks go to other members of the research team as well – foremost Hana Lipovská (who made interviews and contributed to some parts of the book), Václav Šebek (interviews and invaluable feedback to the draft of the book), Vladimír Handl (interviews and a great job on the functioning of the Communist Party), Tomáš Nigrin (interviews and topics about transport), Štěpán Mikula, Zuzana Richterková and Zdeněk Rosenberg, who contributed to the monograph mainly by conducting the interviews. Magdalena Šuterová provided a highly contributing feedback and helped enormously with formalities. I would like to thank to Lubor Lacina for his feedback and everlasting support. My great thanks go to our respondents, who were willing to share with us their time and memories. My other acknowledgements go to team member Michaela Stejskalová, who helped us with the methodology of the interviews; students, who transcribed the recorded interviews; Robert Švábenský, who helped with the English; and members of my department for their support. Moreover, I would like to thank a lot to Routledge, namely Kristina Abbotts for her kind support of the entire book concept and her patience with me and Christiana Mandizha for the formal setting of the manuscript.

Introduction

Reality of the central planning in socialist Czechoslovakia

The weakness of the centrally planned economies in comparison to the market economies was proved by the collapse of the Soviet Bloc and the fall of the iron curtain at the end of the 1980s. By the 1970s, it was clear that the systems were inefficient, unstable, and significantly lagging behind the performance of the market economies. The arms race during Reagan's presidency just accelerated such development. In the book, we reveal microeconomic reasons for economic performance in socialist Czechoslovakia by presenting the results of our unique research that was based foremost on interviews with top managers from the 1970s and 1980s. We concentrate on the last two decades of the system mostly for practical reasons, namely ability to reach respondents. The main goal of the book is to give the readers an idea about everyday economic reality in the socialist totalitarian system. The authors continue in previous research into central planning, but the novel method of research interviews brings a new insight into the functioning and development of the system. The results generally break the common view that individual companies (at the bottom of the hierarchical pyramid) without hesitation followed the orders of the centre. The everyday reality was more complicated and foremost full of paradoxes, pretence, and negotiations. The practice was far remote from textbook theory dealing with central planning.

Our research approach was based on oral history methods – for example Vaněk, Mücke, and Pelikánová (2007), and Vaněk and Mücke (2015). In qualitative, semi-structured interviews conducted between 2015–2017, a total of 75 accounts were collected. Data analysis was carried out at the same time as they were collected (field research). Three different methods were used to contact potential respondents. Firstly, the successors of the original companies were contacted, but the discontinuity created by the economic transformation has led to the fact that today's companies have seldom contacts with its former managers. In order to achieve a satisfactory number of testimonies, we made use of personal contacts and partially also used the snowball method. In order to get an unbiased picture of the then practices, the interviews were focused on rather technical topics. The respondents stay anonymous to the readers. Each of them is assigned a unique identification number ID (e.g., <ID001> belongs to respondent number 1), which identifies him or her in the text.

The respondents had held mostly important managerial posts in companies from diverse branches, such as mining, power industry, construction, engineering, transport, textile industry, agriculture, and food processing, as well as positions in the planning apparatus in the 1970s and the 1980s. All respondents had access to some (but various) level of the planning process in the given period and were familiar with day-to-day business operations of their companies. Appendix Table A contains the characteristics of the narrators. Ninety-one percent of them had higher education, and there were only two women among all the interviewed respondents. Apart from the two interviews done with a couple of respondents, the rest were done individually. All the narrators worked in different companies. The structure of the Czechoslovak economy was almost monopolistic with few large companies in all industries. Consequently, providing detailed information about the companies could jeopardize the anonymity of the respondents.

Most of the respondents had generally critical attitudes towards the socialist economy. They complained about omnipresent shortage and praised the functioning of the market economy. Some of them stated that they had to somehow muddle through and deal with the "rules" of the system. Many of them had a humorous approach and laughed at the nonsenses of the system. They were often very positive about interpersonal relationships at the workplace, when asked to summarize the pros and cons of the system. Only one of the respondents strongly defended the functioning of the system and considered the interview to be an attack on socialism. Some of the potential respondents changed their minds at the very last moment before the interview. Generally, the respondents pointed out the negative aspects of the functioning of the system, which in their view did not work and from present perspective they consider it amusing.

The oral history methods cannot be a substitute to quantitative research methods. They have natural limits because they cannot achieve "objective" results. They deal with people and their memories that could certainly be selective as well as the respondents might lie. Moreover, the respondents were, for natural reasons, mostly elderly people and we were not able to embrace the whole economy. In results, our sample of respondents was not and could not be overall representative and we do not aspire to generalize our results to represent the entire population. However, the team members during the interviews did their best to emphasize a neutral attitude towards the topic and allow the respondents to freely express themselves to achieve the most valuable outcomes for the readers. In the interpretation of the interviews, we considered the context and naturally the historical period.

However, we are well aware of the shortcomings of the oral history methods and thus these main methods were supplemented by research in archives (including archives of the former secret police StB and materials of the top bodies of the Communist Party), stenographic records from Parliament, quantitative research and foremost broad review of literature on the topic including memoirs (from the Czech sources we build on the theoretical works of Lubomír Mlčoch and Zdislav Šulc). It should be emphasized that the functioning of the socialistic society and economy has fascinated several generations of researchers and there exists an indefinite number of sources on this topic. Thus, we did not and could not seek absolute complexity of our analyses and had to select the materials. However, we tried to provide the readers with vivid analyses of the everyday functioning of the centrally planned system in socialist Czechoslovakia by using a novelty approach. Throughout the text, we support our arguments with figures and tables. Furthermore, we illustrate some behavioural patterns in boxes, which are foremost short case studies.

The monograph is divided into six chapters. It proceeds from describing the environment in Czechoslovakia, via theory and formal model of the system of central planning to everyday reality of the planning and to conclusions. Chapter 1 is dedicated to the description of the socio-economic environment in the country. The general goal of this chapter is to provide readers with a picture of the functioning of the society. Without this general introduction, readers lacking personal experience with the totalitarian system would find the surreal reality of the centrally planned system difficult to understand. Chapter 2 shortly deals with economic applications of Marxism-Leninism that constituted ideological background of the overall system. We consider for example Marxian surplus-value and conceptual reasons for nationalization. The third chapter is interconnected with the previous one because the formal settings of the planning mechanism in Czechoslovakia were supposed to be based on the Marxist-Leninist ideas (Chapter 2). In this chapter, the reader will find, for example, an analysis of the formal models of corporate structures, different forms of plans or more specifically the role of the Státní plánovací komise (State Planning Commission). The first three chapters are preparatory for Chapter 4, which contains an analysis of the real functioning of the system in the selected period based primarily on the interviews from our research. This chapter is the core of our work. We show the contrast between theory and everyday practice of the centrally planned system from the inside. Our respondents told us about their everyday economic life in the planned system, among others about the setting of the plan or dealing with scarcity. The real functioning of the economic system resulted in economic outcomes that are summarized in Chapter 5. In the final Chapter 6, we show that the typical features of centrally planned systems foremost the overall inefficiency of the system were only logical and inevitable conclusions of the settings of the model.

This work was supported by the Grant Agency of the Czech Republic, Real functioning of the centrally planned economy in Czechoslovakia (No. GA15–09404S).

1 Formal and informal institutions of the socialist era

Lucie Coufalová[1]

The general intention of this part is to show the main characteristics of the environment in which the companies in the centrally planned system in Czechoslovakia operated. We describe the main features that constituted this environment. The chapter deals with the settings of the institutions (broadly a description of the socio-economic environment) in the socialist era. In specific, we describe the political development including the role of the Communist Party (1.1). Next, we concentrate on some aspects of the legal system and functioning of the judiciary in the country (1.2). In the following section, paternalistic and repressive aspects of the state are analyzed (1.3) and the last section is dedicated to informal institutions – values in the society (1.4).

The socio-economic environment can be defined by institutions. We should distinguish between institutions that are understood as sets of rules (for example the legal system) and institutions in the form of organizations (for example the central bank or the planning commission). In this chapter, we pay attention only to the former. Economics treats institutions as "humanly devised constraints that shape human interaction" (North 1990, p. 3). Rules make a person's and government's behaviour more predictable and in effect reduce uncertainty. Institutions are therefore something one needs to consider in the decision-making process. For example, low property rights protection and high risk of expropriation make people not invest in their businesses and rather pursue other investment objectives. The effects on social life are analogical. If trusting behaviour increases the chances of being punished – for example because of being reported by a colleague or a neighbour – people tend to reduce their far-reaching social ties and isolate themselves in their families (Boenisch and Schneider 2013).

Institutions are often divided into two subgroups: Formal and informal. Formal institutions are generally codified by an authority – the state – they involve those specified and enforced by the government; for example, the legal system or courts of law. Informal institutions are not defined by the state or enforced by the government but they are built in the society in the way of thinking and acting. These involve customs, morals, level of corruption and respect to the law. Informal institutions evolve spontaneously, they are more stable and change only over long periods (generations). On the contrary, the legal system can be changed relatively quickly.[2]

The mutual interaction between formal and informal institutions is complicated. People tend to behave according to informal institutions regardless of the formal ones. Or to put it in another way – even top-quality formal laws will not convince people to behave accordingly if they do not intend to abide. For example, the Eighteenth Amendment to the US Constitution was legally perfect – it was a clear formal institution which prohibited production and sale of alcoholic beverages (valid between 1920 and 1933). However, it was also "a period of time in which even the average citizen broke the law" which made it the only case in the history of the USA when the Constitutional Amendment was repealed (Rosenberg 2017).

The specific impact of institutions on the economy is unclear but most economists believe that institutional environment is one of the key factors influencing a long-term ability to grow because institutional environment affects factor productivity or the long-term potential growth of the economy (see, e.g., North 1992). If there is, for example, low level of respect for the law, the costs of the functioning of the market subjects' increase. This determines their profitability in the long run, and thus also investment and growth. Institutions are difficult to quantify or measure in general and therefore any attempt at measurement during the centrally planned economy (CPE) period was even more complicated. All in all, the state of both formal and informal institutions under socialist rule is generally seen as an obstacle for economic growth (see for example Tříska et al. 2002).

In the following text, we concentrate on the state and development of formal and informal institutions during the CPE period that affected functioning of the economy. They partly overlap, but we separate, among others, the political and legal systems, paternalistic state and behaviour of people (informal institutions) in this period.

1.1 Political system and development

The Czechoslovak political system after 1948 was totalitarian. We consider totalitarianism in accordance with Heywood as:

> *An all-encompassing system of political rule that is typically established by pervasive ideological manipulation and open terror and brutality. It differs from autocracy, authoritarianism and traditional dictatorship in that it seeks "total power" through the politicization of every aspect of social and personal existence. Totalitarianism thus implies the outright abolition of civil society: the abolition of "the private".*
>
> *(Heywood 2012, p. 207)*

In Czechoslovakia, the basic concepts were authoritative governing, and enforcement of the pervasive communist ideology officially based on Marxism-Leninism.

Historically, the Communist Party was relatively strong already in pre-War Czechoslovakia. It gained around 10% of the votes in the interwar period and it was one of the strongest Communist parties in Europe at that time. This state was deepened by the political shift to the left that took place after World War II.

This phenomenon appeared not only in Czechoslovakia but in several other countries as well – for example in Italy and France.[3] It was, among other reasons, caused by admiration and gratitude towards the Soviet Union (SU). There were three main reasons for this attitude – the fact that the SU avoided the suffering of the Great Depression in the 1930s (due to the economy's disconnection from the world markets), admiration for winning the war and gratitude for liberation of Czechoslovakia. The consequence of this political shift was that the Czechoslovak Communist Party won the first election in 1946 and gained 114 out of 300 seats in parliament. The Communists had the highest support in the Bohemia part of Czechoslovakia (see Table 1.1) and especially in the borderlands with Austria and Germany from where the ethnic Germans were expelled.[4] From the total of 156 electoral districts in Bohemia and Moravia, the Communist Party won in 137 of them, and in the borderlands it reached absolute majority in 43 districts (Čapka and Lunerová 2012).

Table 1.1 Results of the first post-war election to the Czechoslovak Parliament (Ústavodárné Národní shromáždění), May 26, 1946

	Communist Party
Bohemia	43.25%
Moravia	34.46%
Slovakia	30.48%
Czechoslovak Republic	40.17%

Source: Žaloudek (2004)

Political competition by democratic parties was at that time already restricted because all legal political parties were associated in the so-called National Front (Národní Fronta) – a group of political parties with a monopoly on political power (see Box 1.1). Several political parties were not allowed to re-establish after World War II. Due to proportional settings of the electoral system in Czechoslovakia the Communists created a coalition government and they (and their allies) were able to control "power" ministries. The Ministry of the Interior as well as the Ministry of Information were held directly by the members of the Communist Party. The Ministry of National Defence was held by the war hero of the eastern front, general Ludvik Svoboda (in those days with no party affiliation), who only became a Communist Party member in 1948 and later on was elected president (1968–1975). This made it easier for the Communists to get the whole country under control following their coup in February 1948.

Box 1.1 The National Front

The National Front was established in April 1945 when the Czechoslovak government was created in the already liberated town of Košice in easternmost part of Slovakia. It consisted among others of the Communist

Party of Czechoslovakia and the Communist Party of Slovakia, the Czechoslovak People's Party (a form of a Christian-Democratic Party) and the Czechoslovak Social-Democratic Party. Several political parties were banned for alleged collaboration with the Germans – among others the Slovak People's Party and the Republican Party of Farmers and Peasants. The National Front was dominated by socialist parties foremost the Communists. Competition among political parties was thus limited. Later on (in the 1970s and the 1980s) the Front co-opted many other specific (and sometimes even obscure) organizations (e.g., the Czech Union of Beekeepers).

The political regime in the following years was extremely harsh. There were political processes, executions, and people were sentenced to long imprisonment in de facto concentration camps. The first emigration wave took place as well. This situation slightly relaxed only after Stalin's death in 1953. Klement Gottwald, the long-standing leader of the Czechoslovak Communist Party since 1929 and perpetrator of the February coup, died just 10 days after his Bolshevik mentor Stalin when he had returned from Stalin's funeral in Moscow.

The role of other authorized political parties during the whole period was only formal and their goal was to pretend political pluralism. In fact, their practical influence was minimal. In reality, the National Front was fully subordinated to the needs of the Communist Party and any competition among the political subjects was unthinkable. Political freedoms in Czechoslovakia did not exist. The regime tried to increase its legitimacy by extremely high voter turnout at parliamentary elections (see Table 1.2).

Table 1.2 Voter turnover in Czechoslovakia, 1954–1986 (in %)

	Nov. 1954	*June 1960*	*July 1964*	*Nov. 1971*	*Oct. 1976*	*June 1981*	*May 1986*
National Front ballot	97.89	99.86	99.9	99.96	99.39	–	–
House of the People	–	–	–	–	–	99.81	99.97
House of the Nations	–	–	–	–	–	99.77	99.97

Source: Žaloudek (2004)

The voters were presented with a single list of the National Front preapproved candidates – in reality, there was just one candidate on the list. It meant that the voters could just approve or disapprove the candidate of the National Front. At the same time, taking part in the election was compulsory, and the citizens had little chance to avoid voting should they want to express their dissatisfaction with the regime this way. It was difficult even to put blank ballots into ballot boxes because going behind the divider was considered as an expression of informal disapproval with the regime. Quite to the contrary, manifestation voting was supported by the regime (see Box 1.2). Regardless of the non-existence of choice, the regime pretended that it held real elections.

Box 1.2 Practice of communist exercise of law

The communist legislation after the implementation of the Socialist Constitution of 1960 was formally very similar to the legislation of any democratic state. The Election Act No. 44/1971 Coll. stated that the elections were secret. Candidates could be nominated not only by the Communist Party, but also by "any other political party or social organization under the National Front," there could be more candidates in each constituency. The reality was different. Even though the regime presented its election as the only true democracy in contrast to the "bourgeois" democracy that Lenin had described as "Restricted, truncated, false and hypocritical, a paradise for the rich and a snare and deception for the exploited, for the poor" (Lenin 1974, p. 243).

What was then the difference between Communist elections and elections in a democratic country? Firstly, the difference after 1960 was embedded in the Constitution, which proclaimed the leading role of the Communist Party. But secondly and foremost, the law was democratic in theory, but it was not observed by the regime in practice. The regime tried to pretend that everything worked as in a normal democratic society including election campaign. For example, the chronicle of the town of Letovice mentions the following:

> *Agitation centres of the National Front were created for the elections purposes; the town radio was broadcasting pre-election agitation on daily basis; shop windows were used for information of the successes of the local companies and about electoral districts. The radio was broadcasting interviews with the candidates. Music bands played in front of polling stations.*
>
> *(Municipal Council of Letovice 1971)*

But there was always just one candidate in every constituency, which meant that the voters merely confirmed the choice made by the National Front and they did not vote in reality. The elections were thus de facto a farce. Mr. Votoček, who was the mayor of the town of Olomouc said that he had intended to obtain an MP position in the federal parliament or at least in the Czech chamber together with the mayor position, to be able to defend interests of the town. However, he was told that the candidate and de facto the MP had to be a woman 35 years old or younger and a worker (Vaněk and Urbášek 2005).

The only option was not to elect or to cross out the nominated candidate. Such strategy was however very difficult to implement in practice especially because the citizens were forced to vote in a manifestation way/openly. Voting decisions of the citizens were often written into their "cadre" dossier. Rudé Právo (a daily of the Communist Party) after the elections proudly declared that "all candidates of the National Front have been elected" (Rudé Právo 26th May 1986).

At the same time, there were economic consequences of the elections. One of the respondents in our research who worked in a managerial post in catering industry (<ID052>) said: "Jesus, it was the time before the elections, we had to make sure that bread was available for sale till the end of the opening hours, not to make people angry. I say, the state holidays, May Days, elections and this, they all were carefully watched, carefully watched."

The leading role of the Communist Party in Czechoslovakia was codified in a new constitution approved in 1960. At the same time, the Communist Party officially declared that the society had reached the phase of socialism (see Box 1.3).

Box 1.3 The development of the politico-economical stages

In the view of the communist ideologists, there were several stages of the political-economic development to follow (as they believed) the inevitable fall of the capitalist society (see Chapter 2). The first stage was called people's democracy, the second socialism and the third communism. These different stages were supposed to reflect a different level of development. The main characteristics can be expressed in the dominant slogans of the period. The slogan of the socialist period was "to each according to his/her contribution." In communism, it was supposed to be "to everybody according to his/her needs." Socialism was considered by its proponents to be a rationally governed society that stood against Hayek's spontaneous orders (Hayek 1982) and was supposed to remove instability, waste, frustration, and unjust policies of the capitalist society (Bottomore 1990). Hába et al. wrote that "the characteristic feature of advanced socialism is complex and balanced development of all parts of the economy" (Hába et al. 1988, p. 100). But in socialism, scarcity was supposed to still exist and a strong state was required (Gregory and Stuart 2014). The lower stage (people's democracy) in Czechoslovakia was formally proclaimed as completed in 1960, which was expressed by change of the official name of the country to the Czechoslovak Socialistic Republic. The regime believed that: "Socialism in our country has won!

We have entered a new era of our history and we are determined to move on to new, even higher goals. Instigating socialist construction, we are moving towards building a socialist society and gathering forces for the transition to communism" (Act No. 100/1960 Coll., Constitution of the Czechoslovak Socialist Republic). This formal change of the name was meant to underline the progress of the country on the way to the highest development stage – communism – that was planned to be reached in (near) future. Communism is characterized by the absence of markets and money, abundance and withdrawal of state control. Its condition was increase in workers' productive capacity (Gregory and Stuart 2014).

The practical behaviour of the already socialist-proclaimed regime started gradually to change towards a slightly higher level of freedoms in the respective decade. This trend culminated in the short period known as the Prague Spring in 1968. At the beginning of the year, the Communist Party started internal party reconstruction and replaced its leadership. Censorship was abandoned, citizens were allowed to travel abroad and there were even attempts at founding/re-establishing of political parties. These liberation trends were abruptly ended on 21 August of the same year when armies of the "friendly" countries (meaning other socialist countries under the leadership of the SU) invaded Czechoslovakia. The Communist Party, under pressure by the SU, altered its policy and declared the previous changes and reforms as a counter-revolution. The invasion was in this respect presented as "fraternal-assistance." The party leaders expressed gratitude to the "friendly" armies for saving socialism in Czechoslovakia. The nation, which was in majority shocked by the invasion and opposed it, was forced to accept these changes. The consequence was another wave of emigration and sharp decline in membership in the Communist Party (partially by exclusion and partially by walkout). The following period is labelled as "normalization" which is an euphemism for a period that was characterized by an effort to get rid of everything related to the previous reforms, reapplying of strict control of thinking, and economic centralization (Dillon and Wykoff 2002). The key political representatives of the Prague Spring were forced to withdraw under pressure of the hardliners. The new prominent politicians who were selected by Moscow to serve in the following decades were Gustáv Husák (Secretary General of the Communist Party 1969–1987; President 1975–1989) and Lubomír Štrougal (Federal Prime Minister 1970–1988). They were later replaced in the posts of Secretary General of the Party by Miloš Jakeš (1987–1989) and the post of Prime Minister by Ladislav Adamec (1988–1989) before the end of the communist reign.

One of the few lasting formal achievements of the reform period was establishing of a federation between the Czech and Slovak Socialist Republics at the beginning of 1969. The consequence was, among others, the creation of national parliaments for each of the Republics – the Czech National Council (Česká národní rada – ČNR) and the Slovak National Council (Slovenská národní rada – SNR). The implication was that Czechoslovakia had three parliaments. In addition to the two national councils, the federal parliament (Federal Assembly) was composed of two chambers; the House of the People (Sněmovna Lidu – SL) and the House of the Nations (Sněmovna národů – SN). There were at the same time three governments – the federal, the Czech and the Slovak. By far, the most important role played the federal government (in the following text the term "government" refers to the federal government if not stated otherwise). However, all of them were in practice subordinated to the Communist Party structures. The everyday functioning of the parliament was described by our respondent, a long-serving MP <ID075>. He told us that all draft laws in the period 1986–1989 were adopted unchanged. All of them were proposals by the government, none by the "legislators." The Parliament committees did not interfere with the proposals. The MPs were obliged to appear in the Federal Assembly to "contribute to discussion" about the law proposals applying experience from their district (for example MP – a milkmaid from a cooperative). However, most of the deputies did not (were not able to) write such papers. They were thus prepared by a special team of lawyers/committee experts and the MPs only read these papers in the Chamber. Whenever someone wrote it by themselves, they had to have the text approved in advance by this body. Because of the location of the Federal Assembly and the (insignificance) of its members, a joke circulated: What is the Federal Assembly? This is something between a museum and a theatre.

The election period in socialist Czechoslovakia was five years long. The parliaments were not overly active because parliamentary sessions took place quite rarely and the number of approved acts was relatively low (see Table 1.3).[5]

Table 1.3 Number of parliamentary sessions and number of discussed acts 1971–1989*

	Federal Assembly			*ČNR*	*Number of discussed acts*	
	SL+SN	*SL*	*SN*		*FS*	*ČNR*
1971–1976	23	5	6	22	43	27
1976–1981	21	5	5	19	25	12
1981–1986	21	5	5	20	83	29
1986–1989*	17	4	5	16	31	26

Source: ČSSR. Joint Czech and Slovak digital parliamentary library 1971–1989

*till November 17, 1989

The parliament was naturally fully under the control of the Communist Party. The average share of Communist MPs was more than 70% (see Figure 1.1). The MPs formally without any affiliation constituted the second biggest share in the parliaments. The role of the smaller political parties was negligible.

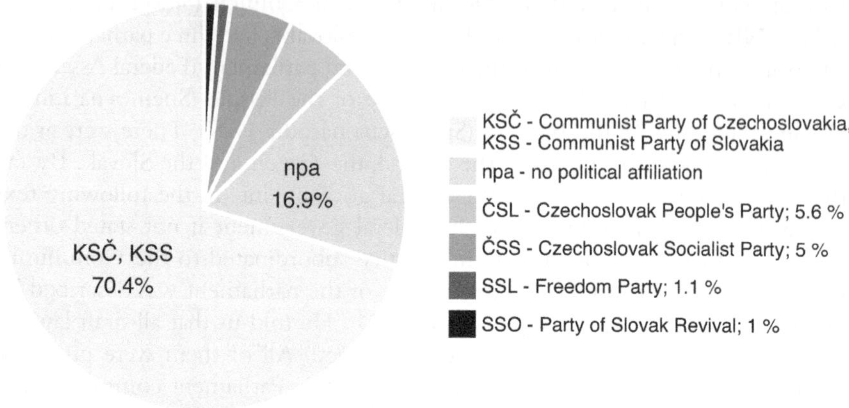

Figure 1.1 The average share of MPs political affiliation in the House of the People during the period of 1971–1986

Source: ČSSR, Joint Czech and Slovak digital parliamentary library (1971–1989)

Only a small portion of the population – dissidents – exercised active (non-violent) resistance against the regime and strived for the plurality of political options and freedom of expression. The prominent figure of the opposition in the 1970s and 1980s was playwright Václav Havel, whose anti-regime political activities resulted in his multiple imprisonments (five years in total). The dissidents grouped into several opposition organizations. Opposition strengthened after the Communist Party purges in the early 1970s when former leading communists, including the members of the party's Central Committee (e.g., Zdeněk Mlynář or František Kriegel), joined these movements. The most important of the dissident organizations was Charter 77, which was founded as a non-political group. The dissident movement became more active when Czechoslovakia signed the Helsinki Declaration of 1975. The Declaration among others guaranteed respect for human rights and fundamental freedoms, including the freedom of thought, conscience, religion, and belief. The dissident movement consequently pointed out that the Czechoslovak socialist government was breaking its own obligation by not granting these basic rights to its citizens.

Very strong tool for the regime against any opposition was a criminal offense about the subversion of the republic under Section 98 of the Criminal Code (Act No. 140/1961 Coll., Criminal code). Pursuant to this paragraph, one should be punished who, "from hostility to the socialist and state constitution of the republic, subverts its social and state establishment, its territorial integrity, its defence or autonomy, or its international interests." This law was highly flexible. and was abused by the regime to punish dissidents as well as emigrants. An example of a practical application of this act could be the following:

> *For example, a man was sentenced for the subversion of the country for four years, claiming he was robbed by the regime, he defamed people in the border regions,*

> *threatened progressively thinking citizens, and claimed that the system in the CSSR would not last. He expressed his vulgar views of the SU, its technology and culture, and boasted of having been a member of the German Army. The impetus of his hostile attitude was the fact that he was prevented from running a business. [The Appeal] Supreme Court ruled that alliance with the Soviet Union and irreconcilable fight against fascism and similar movements belong to the basic principles of the socialist state system.*
>
> *(Černý 2008, p. 44)*

The general political stalemate in Czechoslovakia lasted well into the second half of the 1980s when Gorbachev's Perestroika allowed liberalization of the political as well as economic environment in the CPEs. However, Czechoslovakia was a laggard in these aspects. Mainly because the very same people – hardliners – who were responsible for the suppression of the Prague Spring reforms were still in power. They were naturally unwilling to promote new reforms, similar to the ones of 1968, regardless of the fact that they had to formally follow the Soviet example.[6] The overall practice was that the word "Perestroika" was used, but it did not have any specific meaning, as it was interpreted differently by different people. The economic reforms were in most cases planned for the period after 1990. Czechoslovakia was thus a laggard in liberalization in the 1980s. The other socialist countries, namely Hungary or Poland, progressed more towards freedoms. Adam writes that, for example, travelling restrictions in Czechoslovakia, as well as freedom of expression and research, were much stricter than in Poland or Hungary in this period (Adam 1995).

The socialist regime in Czechoslovakia collapsed in November 1989 after a long-lasting decay. It was surviving as one of the last socialist regimes in Central Europe. The collapse on its own was de facto a matter of several weeks and took place without violence. Due to this, it became known as the Velvet Revolution.

To sum up, contrary to other socialist countries, the overall political environment remained highly conservative until the end of the communist regime in the autumn of 1989.

1.1.1 *The Communist Party of Czechoslovakia*

The decisive political force in the country was naturally the Communist Party of Czechoslovakia. We consider its structures, membership and impact on the society on the following pages.

The highest authority of the Communist Party was the Congress. It took place every five years (in the research period in years 1971, 1976, 1981, and 1986) and lasted several days. It discussed and approved a report of the Central Committee of the Communist Party; it determined the line of the Party; discussed and solved the questions of the further development of the socialist society; vote for the Central Committee, etc. The program and discussion posts of the delegates, who arrived in the capital of Prague from all over the country, were approved or consulted in advance. The Congress was generally more of a "show" than a real work session or discussion about real problems.

The organizational structure of the Communist Party was organized on the territorial principle combined with institutional principle. It was headed by the Central Committee, via County and District Committees to basic organizations (see Diagram 1.1). The power was in the hands of the Presidium of the Central Committee of the Communist Party (Ústřední výbor KSČ – ÚV KSČ) with the Secretary General (generální tajemník) as formally the highest representative of the party and the most powerful person in the country. In the 1970s and 1980s, this seat was held by the Czechoslovak president Gustav Husák and, since 1987, by Miloš Jakeš. The Central Committee delegated power to a hierarchy of National Committees (Národní výbory KSČ): 12 County Committees (Krajské výbory KSČ – KV KSČ) and 127 District Committees (Okresní výbory KSČ – OV KSČ), and subordinated Local Committees (místní výbory KSČ), each with their own secretariat. Furthermore, there were basic organizations (základní organizace KSČ) in each of the districts – factory, local, and village.

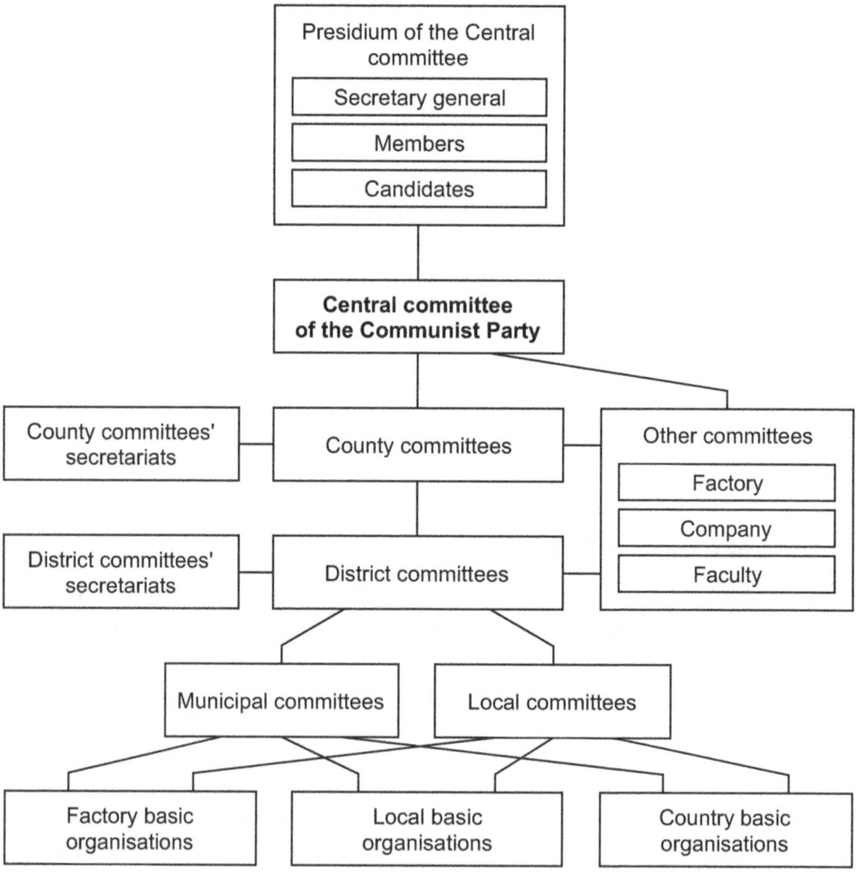

Diagram 1.1 Organization structure of the Communist Party of Czechoslovakia

The communist structures were pervasive, which can be seen from the example of heavy industry in 1987. There existed an all-company committee (celozávodní výbor – CZV) and eight basic organizations (základních organizací – ZO) of the Communist Party functioning in the Federal Ministry of Metallurgy and Heavy Industry (FMHTS). These included 715 employees (out of that 153 in managerial positions) and 63.4% of the employees were members of the party (97.8% of the management). The middle segment in the planning hierarchy was represented by the General Directorate (Generální ředitelství VHJ hutnictví železa – GŘ VHJ HŽ). They had their own basic organizations of the party. The GŘ VHJ employed 373 people (79 in managerial posts) and membership in the Communist Party was generally 41.5% (84.8% among management). One of the main companies in the sector was Nová huť Klementa Gottwalda (NHKG). It housed one all-factory committee of the Communist Party, 11 all-company commitees and 64 basic organizations. The NHKG had 21,300 employees. The general share of party membership was 22% (68.44% among the management). Some 97 candidates became members of the Communist Party in the NHKG (out of that 75 workers) in 1987 (ČSSR. Předsednictvo ÚV KSČ 1988).

The governing inside the Communist Party was expected to work on the organizational principles of so-called democratic centralism. This system was supposed to give a chance to party members to participate in discussions about the political course of the party and at elections nominate party candidates. But they were at the same time supposed to conform to the views of the majority and follow and enforce the decision of the party centre. It meant that party members could present their own opinion publicly only if it was in compliance with the political course of the party. In practice, the decisions were made by a small circle of the party management (Žaloudek 2004). The official slogan was that Czechoslovak society was "led by the Party and the Government" (Kabele 2005) and there was obviously a lasting influence of the brotherly SU and the brotherly Communist Party of the SU. In fact, key personnel and policy decisions were actually made in Moscow because Czechoslovak communists had to conform to democratic centralism within the entire Soviet Bloc as well.

Individual membership in the Communist Party was in most of the cases a condition for promotion to higher managerial posts (Mlčoch 1990). Devotion to communist ideology of the majority of these managers in the period of late socialism was at minimum doubtful. For aspirants to higher posts, the pressure to join the Communist Party was pervasive, including, for example, firemen, as described by a respondent in Vaněk and Krátká. He said:

> *I, for instance got to a situation in 79 that they told me very clearly that if I wanted to become a Chief, I had to join the party. But they would say – "we are not saying you have to, but if you don't, you'll stay at the prevention department, we'll find someone else." It took me a long time to decide – my wife's family had been persecuted by the communists. In the end, my colleagues persuaded me, because they*

> *said – "for God's sake do it, because if we get someone who does not know anything about it, everything you've done here will go down the drain." So, I just said "OK."*
> *(Vaněk and Krátká 2014, p. 68)*

Winiecki quotes a survey conducted in the socialist period, according to which 74% of the Communist Party members in Russia thought that people entered the Party in order to get a better job and promotion (Winiecki 2000). Možný writes that all white-collar workers were appointed to post by the Party decision, and the same was true for any other higher position – for managers in companies, rectors, deans or even bishops. A company director who wanted to change a deputy had to consult this managerial step with the secretariat of the Party as well (Možný 1991). The membership in the Communist Party was thus often seen as a formal prerequisite for career upswing.[7] This corresponds with Vaclav Klaus' statement that people tried to maximize their benefits as in capitalism but subordinated their behaviour to existed limits of the socialist society (Klaus 2009). Information about membership in the Communist Party was not officially publicly available but a sharp decline in the number of members after 1968 can be seen in Table 1.4. This was a result of purges inside the party as well as subsequent voluntary withdrawals.[8] However, the personal experience at the level of companies varied. One of our respondents – a worker in one of the biggest metallurgy companies <ID027> – told us that in case that a manager was expelled from the Party s/he could return to a technical position but not to

Table 1.4 Membership in the Communist Party of Czechoslovakia and the share of its members in the population, 1949–1981

Date	*Members*	*Total number of inhabitants*	*% of population*
1949	2,300,000	12,782,002	18.0
1954	1,489,234	12,675,096	11.7
1958	1,422,199	13,343,750	10.7
1962	1,680,819	13,823,956	12.2
1966	1,698,002	14,271,547	11.9
1967	1,689,207	14,271,356	11.8
1968	1,690,977	14,333,176	11.8
1969	1,671,637	14,388,603	11.6
1970	1,535,537	14,349,557	10.7
1971	1,194,191	14,418,969	8.3
1976	1,382,860	14,973,723	9.2
1981	1,538,179	15,344,346	10.0
1986*	1,675,000	15,552,827	10.8

Sources: Bieliková, Dějiny KSČ v datech, 1984; Kvasil, Malá československá encyklopedie, 1986.

*members plus candidates

a managing position. Directors and deputies in the company had to be members of the Party. However, another respondent, head of production in heavy industry <ID035>, said that in his company even the position of foreman and even technical positions were conditioned by membership in the Party in the 1980s. He added that basic organizations tended to refuse politically untrustworthy cadres (for example people active in 1968) and blocked their appointments. However, the level of restrictions varied in different organizations. At the same time, leaving the party would not be without sanctions. One respondent in Vaněk and Krátká even recalled a joke: "What is the difference between a ship in a storm and the KSČ? none – everyone feels like throwing up and no one can leave" (Vaněk and Krátká 2014, p. 256).

Interestingly, one of our respondents (non-member of the party) told us that in the 1980s more people started to enter the party not only for promotion but because they believed in possible changes from within the party. In his view Perestroika played a role in this trend (<ID020>, a head of technical department in engineering).

The communist ideology was implanted in the citizens from childhood. There were several steps. The relationship between the regime and children started already with propaganda in kindergartens. For example, the directors of kindergarten and teachers in the 1970s had to swear their loyalty to the Communist Party in the following way:

> *I hereby promise to work in the interest of the working class and to implement the Communist Party policy. I will be faithful to the Czechoslovak Socialist Republic and will defend and consolidate its socialist system. I promise to preserve the Constitution of the Czechoslovak Socialist Republic and other laws and regulations, I will vigorously carry out my duties and the instructions of the executives and observe confidentiality in the working matters. According to the principles of Communist education, I will cultivate love for the socialist country, I will lead them [children – authors comment] to respect for the working class and the Communist Party. I will educate them in the spirit of Marxist-Leninist theory and worldview. I commit myself to developing international feelings and deepening friendship with the socialist countries, especially the Soviet Union. I am aware that in my personal life, attitudes, and participation in public life, as a socialist teacher, I have a major influence on the children's behaviour and as well as on behaviour of the nearest public. I will always prioritize the benefit of the Czechoslovak Socialist Republic and its people. I am aware of the consequences that would result from my failure to fulfil the promise.*
>
> *(Drda, Mlejnek, and Škoda 2010, p. 8)*

Then pro-regime attitudes were further cemented by children participation in the Jiskry Organization (first and second year of basic school), and the Pionýr Organization – officially Pioneer Organization of the Socialist Youth Union (the rest of the primary school) up to the Czechoslovak Socialist Union of Youth (Socialistický svaz mládeže – SSM) (15–25 years old). The membership in these organizations was close to compulsory and non-participation was considered as a form of resistance, with possible negative impacts, for example a ban from university enrolment. At the same time, the communist ideology was indoctrinated by the educational system regardless of age and specialization.

Higher education in the communist ideology was provided by the Evening University of Marxism-Leninism (VUML). The students were regularly employed people and the study lasted for three years. The students were not necessarily members of the Communist Party but they were considered as "cadres" (i.e., people considered as loyal, reliable, and politically conscious) or people in preparation for a higher position in industry or other spheres of the society – education, healthcare, agriculture, trade, or transport. This form of political education was often a condition for job promotion offered to people who refused to enter the Communist Party. They accepted it as lesser evil. Možný writes that intellectuals had to "bend the back" and study "nonsense" at the VUML to be allowed to do their jobs. He expressed it as "a self-humiliating ritual of a neurosurgeon to save his word" (Možný 1991, p. 24). The curriculum included among others history of the working-class movement and the Communist Party, Marxism-Leninism, scientific communism, political economy and study of experience from the SU.

The highest political education in Marxism-Leninism was provided by the Political University of the Central Committee of the Communist Party of Czechoslovakia (Vysoká škola politická ústředního výboru Komunistické strany Československa – VŠP). The intention was to educate scientific cadres for the Communist Party. The graduates gained the title RSDr. (Doctor of Social and Political Sciences). For example, in the Federal Ministry of Metallurgy and Heavy Industry, the rate of graduation from the VUML or from post-gradual studies at the VŠP reached 33% among the management, at the GŘ VHJ HŽ it was 53.2% and in the NHKG 86% of the management and 39.2% of foremen in 1987 (ČSSR. Předsednictvo ÚV KSČ 1988).

Employees were formally organized in monopolist trade unions – Revolutionary Trade Union Movement (ROH). But these trade unions were often toothless because the organization was subordinated to the needs of the Communist Party. ROH followed foremost the interests of state and not the employees, oversight of work safety, health insurance etc., it was supposed to be convincing the masses about the importance of building socialism and creation of requirements for transition to communism (Havelková 2009b). More than half of the ROH local board members had to be communists. Representatives of the ROH took part in various committees and participated in meetings of the management in the companies. Their main practical activities were in collecting membership fees, giving away confectionary at Christmas and organizing holiday activities. In some of the companies, however, they played a role for example in negotiating working conditions.

Generally, we can agree with Možný who writes that the Party was omnipresent, it intervened in all levels of the society and economy and was informed about everything in the country (Možný 1991).

1.2 Legal and enforcing system

The legal system under democratic conditions creates safeguards for the operating of the system. It was the same in the totalitarian system where the legal system after 1948 was designed with the aim to keep the Communist Party in power. Montesquieu's system of separation of power was eliminated. Nominally, there was the legislative power (held by the Federal Assembly), executive power (in the hands of the government) and judicial power. However, members of the Federal Assembly were chosen by the National Front, where the Communist Party had the leading role. The Prime Minister was also a member of the Party's Central Committee and judges were likewise elected by the Federal Assembly. Similarly controlled by the Party, the media failed to act as watchdogs.

One of the key areas were property rights. The Communist coup d'état of February 1948 brought about a dramatic change in the conception of the state and the law in the society. The Communist Party policy fundamentally altered codification of property rights in the new legal system which was crucial for functioning of companies. The "Two-Year Plan for Law" of 1949–1950 restructured the existing legal system.

A new Constitution was passed on 9 May 1948. It included provisions securing basic human rights and freedoms. Even though these respective sections of the Constitution were never formally amended in the following years, legislative, administrative, and political interventions and regulations turned them into empty, powerless declarations (see Jánošíková, Knoll, and Rundová 2010). The Czechoslovak economic system was defined as based on nationalized natural resources, industry, finance, and banking, and land ownership according to the proclamation "the land belongs to those who work on it." It also codified protection of private and medium-sized enterprises and inviolability of personal property. The Constitution also guaranteed private agricultural land ownership up to 50 hectares. However, these parts were never observed in practice.

The 1960 Constitution defined socialist property (state-owned, namely national, property) and cooperative property as basic forms of property. The Constitution granted rights of small-size entrepreneurship (mainly agricultural) based on the owner's personal labour and provided it did not exploit other persons' labour. Personal property rights (income-generated savings, consumer goods, items of personal and household use, and family houses) were declared as inviolable. The Constitution made no amendments regarding private property.

In summary, the Communist takeover marked fundamental changes in prop erty rights in Czechoslovakia. The new legal regulations codified and pushed forward socialist property (state, cooperative, and municipal enterprises). Other forms of property (personal and private) were legally marginalized – for more about the property rights see Chapter 3.

1.2.1 Administration of justice

Law execution was fully under the control by the Communist Party as well. Independence of the judicial power and division of power in the overall system did not exist. Nearly all judges and prosecutors were members of the Communist Party. There are probably no official data about membership of judges in the Communist Party before 1989. However, we can estimate it according to notes from a parliament session taking place on 18 May 1990. MP Holomek mentioned that 95% of the members of the judiciary in the South Moravia region were members of the Communist Party before 17 November 1989 (ČSSS. Czech National Council 1990). Judges were expected to serve the socialist establishment, which was even embedded in the law. Act No. 36/1964 Coll., among others, stated explicitly: "One of the basic goals of judges is protection of socialist state, socialist regime and relationships with the world socialist system. Not sustaining these goals from the judges' sides is evident violation of their obligations" (Act No. 36/1964 Coll., on the organization structure of courts and election of judges).

Schönfelder describes the functioning of the judicatory in socialist countries. He emphasizes that court rulings were in fact politically motivated and dictated by the Communist Party. He uses a term "telephone law" – meaning that verdicts were based on telephone calls "from above" (Schönfelder 2016). The formal principle of the presumption of innocence was not applied in practice as documented in countless trials with dissidents. Dolejší writes about the deteriorated state of lawyers at the end of the 1980s, who were affected by ideology and formalism (Dolejší 2015). The same was true for the education of lawyers.[9]

Litigation between companies was uncommon, which was partly because the centre made the key decisions and played the role of an arbiter. Note, that the term "centre" is used in the book in the meaning of the central governmental institutions. They kept the executive power but were subordinated to the Communist Party. Thus, for example the respondents talk about the "centre" but they, in fact, mean their superior institutions.

The second reason was that companies were mutually dependent and in constant communication with each other, which greatly reduced troublesome surprises. It was not common to take another company to court, for example for not delivering some products, among others, because the initiator would risk that the contractor would not deliver anything in future.

1.3 Paternalist and repressive state

The regime had two faces – one cherishing and the other repressive. These faces in practice reflected the well-known policy of carrot and stick. Both of these strategies were applied with an intention to keep the communists in power. We follow this division in the inner structure of this section.

1.3.1 Paternalist state

A striking aspect of the socialist era was lack of independence and omnipresence of the paternalistic state. People thus lived their lives convinced that the state should protect them and should take care of them "from the cradle to the grave." The regime/state promised everyone everything. Women were promised to be liberated from domestic servitude and to achieve economic independence. Craftsmen and small entrepreneurs were supposed to enjoy the security of employment and be free from competition pressures. Peasants enjoyed fixed working hours and free Saturdays, workers access to clerical jobs, the youth job placement (umístěnka), tenure, inexpensive meals in the companies, kindergartens for their children, etc. (Možný 1991).

The economic dependence on the state was strengthened by the relatively low wages and highly subsidized basic goods and services. Tanzi comments on this topic as follows:

> *The financial wage is much lower than the total reimbursement. A large portion of the total income comes in the form of subsidized rent, free education and healthcare, subsidized transport, food and vacations. In other words, numerous individual consumer decisions are made by the state (or the state company for which he/she works).*
> *(Tanzi 1995, p. 158)*

The dominant role of the government was expressed by the level of redistribution as well. The share was generally high even for the standards of the centrally planned economies (see Table 1.5).

Table 1.5 Government incomes and expenditures 1989 (% of GDP)

Country	*Income*	*Expenditures*
Czechoslovakia	62.1	64.5
Hungary	61.3	63.7
Poland	46.8	48.7
Rumania	45.7	40.7
Bulgaria	57.7	60.1
Soviet Union	43.8	50.7
USA	34.3	36.5
Germany	45.7	45.9
Canada	40.3	43.9
France	46.2	47.8

Source: Jonáš (1997)

The government provided (supposedly free of charge) education, healthcare, and other social services (for example pensions). The regime considered these free services as one of its greatest achievements which were often used for propagandistic goals. But the measurable results were questionable. Social progress materialized, among others, in a long-run decline in infant mortality. However, life expectancy at birth stayed static for decades – the indicator was 67.92 years in 1960 and 67.58 years in 1990 for men and the respective numbers for women were 73.40 and 75.41 (Arltová, Langhamrová, and Langhamrová 2013). The numbers meanwhile significantly improved in the western countries (for long-term development see Figure 1.2). On the other hand, the paternalistic state was manifested in a relatively soon retirement age. In the 1980s, men in socialist Czechoslovakia had the right to a pension at age of 60, but physically demanding professions, like miners, received theirs earlier at 55. Women retired at the age of 57, but this age was further decreased according to the number of children a woman raised – a mother of five children retired as early as aged 53 (Act No. 121/1975 Coll.). In the developed countries, the retirement age at that time was, on average, 63 for men and 61 for women (Gendell 1998).

The country lagged behind in share of inhabitants with university education as well. Bálek states the number of university graduates per 10,000 inhabitants in 1989: Czechoslovakia 119, Belgium 260, Denmark 247, Finland 313, France 284, West Germany 284, the Netherlands 282, Austria 264, Sweden 219, USA 560, Japan 218, the SU 185 (Bálek 2007). The overall university system worked on the so-called reference numbers – quotas. These quotas determined quantity of students that were allowed to enrol in respective specializations according to the center's view of the needs of the economy (Urbášek 2008). These quotas were notoriously extremely low, especially for humanities. On the other hand, Czechoslovakia had a long tradition (dating back to the interwar period) of apprenticeship provided by large companies – for example ČKD Praha, Škoda Pilsen, Tatra Kopřivnice etc. – that was considered as high-quality secondary education (e.g., Kalinová 2012).

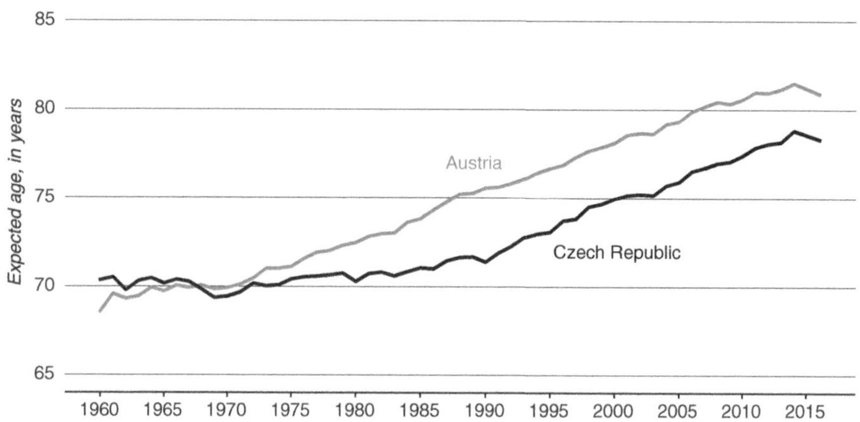

Figure 1.2 The average life expectancy in the Czech Republic and Austria (in years)

Source: World Bank (2018)

The regime presented itself as having achieved the state of equality and rich society but in practice many people lived in poverty. For one of the estimations, see Table 1.6. The table shows that more than a million people (out of the total of 15 million inhabitants of socialist Czechoslovakia) lived below the social minimum at the end of the 1980s. And foremost that there were 400 thousand children living below this benchmark.

Table 1.6 Share and numbers of households, persons, and children below social and living wage in Czechoslovakia

	Social minimum			*Living wage*		
	1980	*1985*	*1988*	*1980*	*1985*	*1988*
In percent						
Households – sum	9.46	7.68	7.30	1.12	0.95	0.72
Without children	10.70	8.22	6.46	1.14	0.77	0.43
With children	8.04	7.22	8.31	1.09	1.16	1.56
Persons						
Sum	8.15	6.82	7.06	0.93	0.93	0.78
Without children	8.20	6.06	4.88	0.94	0.62	0.34
With children	8.13	7.20	8.23	0.93	1.09	1.01
Children	9.27	8.25	9.38	10.8	1.26	1.16
In thousands						
Households – sum	506.0	406.2	402.0	59.9	59.4	39.2
Without children	305.6	224.0	192.8	32.6	21.0	12.8
With children	200.4	182.2	209.1	27.3	29.4	26.4
Persons						
Sum	1232.5	1038.7	1082.7	141.1	142.2	118.8
Without children	424.7	306.8	261.1	48.5	31.6	18.3
With children	807.9	731.9	821.3	92.6	110.6	100.5
Children all together	422.8	385.6	427.1	49.1	59.1	52.9

Source: Hiršl (1992)

1.3.2 Repressive state

At the same time, the regime had its repressive face. The state/the Party was trying to control all the inhabitants. It used all possibilities to get information about behaviour and thinking of individual people. It amassed "cadre" dossiers on everybody from childhood to retirement, and these included information about the persons' political stands and activities, family background and civic obedience. Various institutions (schools, street committees of the Communist Party, employers, etc.) contributed to individual "cadre" dossier. A cadre department was a part of each institution from factory to hospital. It was guarding and managing the "cadre" materials. Kádrovák (the person in charge of the dossiers) was a key person in the institution and on his or her views depended the future of the employees. Vaněk and Krátká quote an interview with a person who gained an attractive job in one of the authorized foreign trade companies (PZO) (Vaněk and Krátká 2014). The respondent did moonlighting jobs for the General Director of Transakta. The situation developed in the following way:

> *After some time, I came to him [the General Director] and asked him if he could find me a job in his company. And he said – come anytime. So, it was on the second or third of January, 1976, I came to Transakta and guess what? They got me a job! Well it is true that in the meantime, my friends in the Benešov company, where I worked, replaced all the reports and references on my name which, up to then, were all spotless. The only thing was that there was this one and only line that said that my attitude towards the socialist system was not positive.*

In some cases, the secret police force, State Security (StB) collected materials on people who were supposed to be dangerous for the regime. People did not know who was a friend and who was an informer and could not trust anyone.

Similarly, to the judiciary, the police (the official name was Public Security – Veřejná bezpečnost) were used by the Communist Party to achieve its political goals, in addition to dealing with common criminal acts. In practice, the Party, not the state, controlled the police. Police forces, among others, suppressed underground political opposition. There was no power to control it, and when a policeman for example abused the power of a public official there was no possibility to call for rights in the system of the malfunctioning of the legal state.

However, this was the main task of the secret police force. At the end of the 1980s, the organization had around 15 thousand employees and a net of around 30 thousand secret informants. The StB's main objectives were to investigate any activities that could possibly be considered as anti-state or western influenced, and to persecute dissident movement. However, the specific scope of the StB activities was broad and it included, for example, investigation of companies failing to meet the central plan, as it also could be considered as an anti-state activity. StB agents came into companies and inspected the meeting of the plan and behaviour of people in certain professions as well as the reasons for defects or wrong storage. There were permanent informants inside the companies too. This view is documented by one of our respondents who told us:

> *The StB came regularly. I mean to our company . . . I guess they were from the district or regional department and they had their own person taking care of our company. This . . . this guy would come to see and talk to the director, I knew him. The company actually had two people who were like the ones to deal with the StB. One of them was the head of the special department and the other a man in charge of the telex and similar kinds of stuff.*
>
> *(assistant to the director in engineering <ID043>)*

Vilímek writes that the co-operators in the companies were mostly mid-level technical staff that dealt with partners, subcontractors, and participated in meetings of the top management (Vilímek 2012). However, the directors had their cooperation with StB as part of their work. Moreover, sometimes the secret cooperation was even terminated when someone was appointed director because the directorial position was demanding enough even without the burden of cooperation with the StB (Vaněk and Krátká 2014). Admittedly, at the same time the strict police control of the society contributed to a relatively low level of criminality in the country in international comparison.

The Czechoslovak People's Army was another repressive power in the country that helped the Communist Party retain its power. Army officers were, together with police officers, strongly favoured by the regime – for example in wages or other benefits, like access to scarce housing. The Czechoslovak People's Army was integrated into the Warsaw Treaty Organization of Friendship, Cooperation, and Mutual Assistance – informally called the Warsaw Pact (1955–1991). Estimations say that the army expenditures consumed on average around 6% of Czechoslovak yearly national income between 1969 and 1989 (Krč 2000) or around 8% of GDP (Turek 1995). But the numbers must be taken with a pinch of salt because, for example, Ivan Kočárník (Deputy Minister of Finance in 1990) writes that the official defence expenditures in 1988 were 29 billion CSK but the real figure was 49 billion (Kočárník 1990). Regardless of the real volume of finance flowing to the army, even Lubomír Štrougal, Prime Minister of that time, mentions in his memoirs that the defence expenditures for the 200-thousand-large army enormously blocked economic development (Štrougal 2009). The size of the army was a result of compulsory two-year military service for all men above 18 years of age.

Additionally, the Communist Party had its own armed force too – Lidové milice (People's Militia). They were formed as a combat unit of workers affiliated to the Communist Party just before the coup in 1948. The chief commander of the Militia was the Secretary General of the Communist Party. The main goal of the force was to intimidate political opponents – it was known as the "armed fist of the working class." In practice, it was used to suppress public unrest and protests. The People's Militia existed throughout the entire communist era without being legally enshrined.

At the same time, the regime tried to keep information flow under absolute control. Nearly any information was potentially secret – partly because the regime felt to be in permanent danger and information could be possibly abused by enemies. Censorship (and foremost self-censorship) was pervasive, and the government controlled all forms of mass media and entertainment (see Box 1.4).

Box 1.4 Life of musicians in socialism

Art was under strong control by the regime. Multiple artists were not allowed to perform their art and the most famous dissident organization – Charter 77 was created in defence of an underground band – Plastic

People of the Universe. Plocek (at that time a member of a popular folk band Poutníci) writes about the situation in the official music sector. A musician or a band had two possibilities, either to stay amateur or to try to become professional. In the first option, the musician had to be firstly registered with an official agent. Then, the second condition was taking part at an official test rehearsal where the musician had to perform his or her repertoire in front of a commission. The repertoire had to be ideologically acceptable and the commission evaluated the artistic "quality" of the performance. The bands often pretended to be obedient and for example played in suits and silently even though at concerts they played in jeans and loudly. The third condition was a "bandmaster exam" from music theory and from "political knowledge." After passing the exam, the band was allowed to give concerts and the musicians received a 30-crown fee per a performance (at that time worth of 12 bottles of beer or 3 blocks of butter).

If a band or an artist were popular, he or she could apply for a professional test rehearsal and a professional agent – usually County Cultural Centre (Krajské kulturní středisko). Another condition was a political part of the exam including ideologically motivated questions with no relevance to music. Plocek writes that the typical question was, e.g., "On which Siberian river is located the biggest Soviet hydro-powerplant?" He adds that it was necessary to stay calm, to not oppose, and to accept possible advice from the committee. The successful result was that the artists could become freelancers with fixed performance program that covered not only music but even the accompanying speech that had to follow the officially arranged and approved scenario as well (Plocek 2015).

The County Cultural Centres were subject to Pragokoncert – an agency representing the most famous pop music singers. Plocek writes that obtaining a contract with this agency required bribes and other corruption mechanisms. The artists under Pragokoncert received a minimum fee of 600 crowns per performance. And it was the only agency allowed to organize concerts abroad. However, a permission to have a concert abroad was a privilege of only senior artists and the agency could demand up to ¾ of their income on levies (Plocek 2015). It was even speculated how much the most famous Czech singer Karel Gott (highly popular in both German countries) earned for the government in convertible currencies for concerts in West Germany. Rumours during the socialist era said that it was more than the whole export of Škoda automobiles.

Meanwhile, the system tried to isolate the citizens from the outside world. The regime formally tried to prevent the society from negative influence of the western world (that was often presented as hostile to socialist regimes) but in practice it kept people in almost universal ignorance. Fences along the borders with Germany and Austria were justified as an attempt at preventing capitalist spies and intruders from crossing the border, although in practice it prevented people from emigration.[10] Simultaneously, the regime exposed the citizens to widespread pervasive propaganda (including education). Propaganda was everywhere even in technical publications like the Medical Yearbook (Ústav zdravotnických informací a statistiky & Ústav zdravotníckej štatistiky 1981). Its foreword contained, among others, this paragraph:

> *January 22 was the 110th birthday of V.I. Lenin, the founder of the Communist Party of the Soviet Union and the Soviet state. The name of Lenin relates to the historic victory of the Great October Socialist Revolution, which opened a new era of world development. Lenin, in his scientific work that followed the revolutionary teachings of Marx and Engels, gave scientifically grounded developments from the overthrow of capitalism to the realization of the socialist revolution and the establishment of socialist social order. The outstanding meaning of Lenin's teaching is that his findings and conclusions are of general application. This general validity of his teachings was verified in practice, not only in the Great October Socialist Revolution, but also in many other countries where the transition to socialism occurred.*

However, the results of this political brainwashing were limited partly because the propaganda was unconvincing and partly because people had access to foreign radio and TV broadcasting (despite the broadcast signal intrusion). Kabele quotes a survey that was realized on the requests of the Communist Party in May 1989. The results said that one quarter of Czechoslovak inhabitants watched German or Austrian TV broadcasting. Radio stations such as The Voice of America, Free Europe, and BBC were followed, at least occasionally, by 43% of the inhabitants (Kabele 2005).

International contacts on personal or business level were very scarce.[11] More or less "normal" travelling was limited to several socialist countries (East Germany, Hungary, Bulgaria, Romania, and Yugoslavia). For individual travellers it was difficult to go even to Poland or the SU because an invitation letter was needed in the 1980s. Applicants for approval for a journey to capitalist countries had to have a passport (the regime prevented some people from obtaining a passport and its confiscation was a way of punishment). Then they had to obtain the permission to buy foreign currency (devizový příslib). And finally, applicants came under intense scrutiny to receive the so-called exit clause (výjezdní doložka). In this final step, the police examined the request and the applicant had to have approval of the director of school or the employer (including the Communist Party organization at they workplace). However, Rychlík writes that the centre complained that the approval process in the companies was just formal instead of it granting the permission to meritorious workers (Rychlík 2007). Nevertheless, the whole process lasted several months.

The isolationist attitude was only one of the reasons of this policy. Another was obvious worry that people would not return – for example, the reason for revoking the exit clause at the border just before departure was that the officials discovered hidden certificate of university graduation or apprenticeship certificate (Rychlík 2007). However, there were economic reasons as well – foremost was a lack of convertible currencies (see Chapter 5), and it is not surprising that the first official request to be made was for permission to purchase foreign currency. An option to individual tourism were organized package holidays. There were just five travel agencies in Czechoslovakia that organized foreign tours. Not all of them provided excursions to capitalist countries. These tours were generally rare. It was necessary to wait up to several days (with a sleeping bag) in front of the travel agency to be allowed to purchase this kind of trip. The exit clause was still necessary to obtain and costs were extremely high – for example a ten-day trip to New York with the Čedok travel agency at the end of the 1980s cost 50,000 crowns (average month salary was around 3,000 crowns) (Drda, Mlejnek, and Škoda 2010).

The overall state of travelling could be demonstrated by average expenditures on foreign tourism per a person and year. The amount was, in the case of Czechoslovaks, just USD 20 in the 1980s in comparison to USD 431 for the Austrians, USD 329 for the Germans, USD 306 for the Dutch, and USD 529 for the Swiss (Zeman 1990). The limits on travelling were mutual and relatively few foreigners visited Czechoslovakia (see Table 1.7).

On one hand, the state provided "free of charge" services and behaved in a paternalistic way. But otherwise, it was pervasive, and the Communist Party maintained a tight grip on the society by using its repressive forces. The regime tried to control flow of information into the country as well as personal contacts with abroad.

1.4 Informal institutions: behaviour of individuals

The last subtopic deals with informal rules (values and morals) in the society. The citizens had to deal with many formal as well as informal constraints. The totalitarian state limited not only political freedoms but also freedoms of speech, assembly, and religion. The overall behaviour in the society was based on an informal rule that "what is not allowed is forbidden" instead of "what is not forbidden is allowed" that is characteristic of free societies. The educational system led students to conformity. Individuality was suppressed, and collectivist aspects were promoted – for example bonuses at work were conditioned, to a significant degree, by production of the whole collective. Everybody was exposed to communist ideology. Independent and critical thinking was not supported. The only forms of approved criticism were those adhering to principles of socialist ideology.

We deal with three specific subtopics – working habits (1.4.1), morals and religion (1.4.2) and everyday economic incentives (1.4.3). At the end of the section we present a conclusion about the impact of informal institutions on the behaviour of citizens.

Table 1.7 Tourism to and from Czechoslovakia (number of tourists in thousands)

CAPITALIST COUNTRIES

Average in years	*ACTIVE (incoming foreigners)*					*PASSIVE (outcoming ČSSR inhabitants)*			
	Number of tourists	*Average length of stay (days)*	*Purpose*			*Number of tourists*	*Average length of stay (days)*	*Purpose*	
			holiday	*business*	*transit*			*holiday*	*business*
1970–1974	828*	6	563	123	132	202	21	75	127
1975–1979	996	5	604	223	169	363	11	161	202
1980–1984	1,101	5	642	264	195	497	17	221	276
1985–1989	1,509	5	955	290	264	613	16	309	304

SOCIALIST COUNTRIES

Average in years	*ACTIVE (incoming foreigners)*					*PASSIVE (outcoming ČSSR inhabitants)*			
	Number of tourists	*Average length of stay (days)*	*Purpose*			*Number of tourists*	*Average length of stay (days)*	*Purpose*	
			holiday	*business*	*transit*			*holiday*	*business*
1970–1974	7,373	6	6,536	352	485	3,278	7	3,089	189
1975–1979	16,067	5	12,441	311	3,315	8,934	5	8,446	488
1980–1984	15,003	5	9,425	593	4,985	7,174	6	6,716	458
1985–1989	20,741	3	10,876	939	8,926	6,742	6	6,229	513

Source: Statistická ročenka Československé socialistické republiky (1971–1989)

* Ten thousand people travelling for health purposes included in the total number of tourists; data for health purposes discontinued later on

1.4.1 Working habits and inequality in income

The socialist system hoped to change the behaviour of its citizens and their values. This goal is sometimes expressed as an attempt at creating "New Socialist/Soviet Persons" who were supposed to work hard for a better future of all citizens without any direct personal reward. There is no unambiguous definition of the New Person (see Nečasová 2018). They were expected to be honest, comradely, and heroic and idealistically working with a view to building socialism (Gregory and Stuart 2014; Fučík 1951) (see Box 1.5). He or she was expected to replace Homo Economicus that is motivated by material reward. These values were expressed in "socialist morals." The question to consider for the proponents of the regime was how to achieve this desirable state. Havelková writes that the regime oscillated between unlimited trust in employees on the one hand and a feeling that it was necessary to educate and force them (Havelková 2009b) on the other. The restrictive side was already mentioned in the previous section. The motivation side was supposed to be achieved by politically inspired public awards (for example the Hero of Socialist Labour, which was awarded to miners, milkmaids, assemblers, but also to company directors or to soviet astronaut Jurij Gagarin) or honorary degrees and certificates of merit.

Box 1.5 New Soviet Person

Idealistic attitudes toward the soviet/socialist person can be read in the following article (fictitious conversation) from the communist daily Rudé Právo (Kraus 1961, 17 September).

Son: "Have you read that people in the Soviet Union will travel free of charge in the following years?"

Father: "Of course, who would not read the draft program."

Son: "Does it mean that there will be no train and bus conductors anymore?"

Father: "Of course. It is possible to arrange already by self-service. And wait for what is coming. The profession of a conductor will disappear. And ticket inspectors as well."

Son: "But it is impossible. Who would keep an eye on order, on passengers? Who would curb them and reprimand them? You know how it sometimes looks on a tram or train."

Father: "For sure. But don't forget that it will not come at once but gradually. By that time, all people will be different than today."

Son: "How different?"

Father: "Totally different. Soviet, communistic. Foremost, they will not need any official supervision. They will know on their own in any situation how to behave to be a merit for everybody. It will be astonishing progress . . . despite the well-known fact that it can never be totally excluded that a post might obstruct reason. But it takes time."

Son: "I wish it would run very fast, as fast as possible. You also wish for it, don't you?"

Competition (at all levels and forms) was felt as an alien aspect in the society that was supposed to be based on principles of comrade cooperation among people for a better future of the community (Bottomore 1990; Hába et al. 1988). But a special "cooperative socialist competition" was supposed to exist. The idea was that the "new socialist/soviet people" would soon prevail. But in reality, the expectations of creating a "new," better person generally did not come to fruition and the experiment with changing people's behaviour and motivation failed. Later on, the notion of a "new person" became perceived more as a caricature of itself.

The behaviour of people was indeed affected by the system and the following part of the text describes these changes. One of the examples could be popular slogans like: "We pretend to work, and the state pretends to pay us." It generally expressed the weak working morals (Mlčoch 1990). Motivation problems were deepened by the non-existence of unemployment. The communists promised to eradicate unemployment and they were formally successful with this goal. They took pride in zero unemployment that was supposed to be one of the greatest achievements of the system. It was often glorified by the regime propaganda as a straight difference to market economies/capitalism.

The regime tried to improve the motivation of employees by application of the so-called chozrascot (or at minimum features of the chozrascot system). These were motivation principles that were supposed to interconnect individual performance with personal reward. It was in fact attuned with the theoretical principles of socialist economy that was (in contrast to communism) still supposed to keep interaction between performance and reward (Hába et al. 1988). But the regime's egalitarian instincts were much stronger. The regime was proud of its formal equality among the people. The practical consequence were efforts to minimize differences among people including the level of income inequality. This struggle was, unlike seeking western living standards or technologies, successful. Czechoslovakia had the highest degree of levelling in the whole Eastern Bloc (Havelková 2009b), and thus in the whole world – the Gini coefficient[12] amounted to just 19.7 in 1986 (Gros and Steinherr 2004). Inequality was so low that the last communist prime minister complained that wage levelling supported mediocrity and damaged the talented, and as such it was a source of criticism by young specialists (Adamec 1989). For example, a doctor's monthly income was only 100–200 crowns higher than the average wage (Kalinová 2012). However, high-ranking members of the Communist Party were paid well. The monthly income of the Secretary General of the KSČ was 18 thousand crowns gross with additional 8,000 crowns in tax-free recompense in 1989 (the average wage was approximately 3,000 at that time). Income of a regional party secretary was 10,000 crowns with tax-free recompense between 3,000–5,000 crowns (Drda, Mlejnek, and Škoda 2010).

However, the everyday practice was obviously far from the officially declared equality and fair treatment of all citizens. The differences among people stemmed from several aspects. Foremost the members of the Communist Party had preferential treatment and especially senior Communists had numerous privileges including special hospitals, shops, recreational centres and extra pensions (Turek 1995). In addition, there were favoured occupations – generally workers and particularly workers in heavy industries and mining, because these were supposed to be the vanguards of the socialist society and thus supporters of the regime. These privileges were among others expressed in wages. An example of the wage distribution in the economy can be seen in Table 1.8. The table shows that the low-qualified labour force earned relatively high incomes. Workers in the mining, metallurgy, and energy industries earned an average of 30% higher income than a skilled workforce in healthcare or education. The main reason for the relatively low salaries of healthcare professionals and teachers was the fact that the regime assumed that their low income would be compensated by the inner satisfaction from their work (Havelková 2009b).

Table 1.8 Wages of workers by main occupation groups in 1984

Job groups	*Average wage (in Kčs)*	*Wage relations (in percent)*
Workers processors	3,086	100
Agriculture workers	3,170	102.7
Workers in mining, metallurgy, and power engineering	4,174	135.2
Construction workers	3,177	102.9
Operational and service workers	2,564	83.7
Technicians	3,708	108.5
Management and administration staff	3,116	104.2
Education, culture, and health workers	3,011	97.5
Workers in science, research and development	4,052	131.3

Source: Kalinová (2012)

Employees' wages did not reflect the differences in qualifications needed to practice the profession. This was mainly the result of different working conditions which were the main cause of higher wages in the mining industry than of workers in science and research (Kalinová 2012). "My brother was an ordinary worker and I worked in high management, but he earned twice as much as I did. Workers were a real power. And miners too, you know," said a respondent from an engineering company (foreman <ID015>). As far as education and salary evaluation were concerned, in 1984 qualified workers and those with higher secondary education earned 24% more, labour force with secondary education 20%, and university graduates 56% more than people with basic education (Průcha et al. 1988).

On the other hand, there were obviously discriminated persons – often labelled as "class enemies" – dissidents or people with a wrong "cadre profile" – meaning for example children of ex-entrepreneurs or proponents of the 1968 reforms and religious people. They were punished in extreme cases by imprisonment or forced emigration. But more common punishments were material – e.g., not being allowed to work in their profession. Some university professors were only allowed to work for example as boilermen. They had difficulty accessing decent accommodation, their children were not allowed to study, etc.

It can be surprising that even though the workers were favoured by the regime, they still accounted for half of the poor people in the country (see Table 1.9).

Table 1.9 Share of the people below the social minimum on the overall number of poor people according to social categories. The sum = 100.

	Workers	*Employees*	*Peasants in cooperatives*	*Pensioners*	*Others*
1958	27.2	13.0	12.5	23.2	24.1
1965	45.6	7.8	4.5	31.3	10.8
1970	49.2	10.7	2.4	33.9	3.8
1973	48.1	10.2	1.4	37.5	2.8
1976	50.7	11.7	1.6	33.3	2.7
1988*	48.3	25.5	1.9	21.7	2.6

Source: Hiršl, Analýza struktury chudého obyvatelstva v Československu v roce 1988, 1992

* Several worker professions were re-classified as employees in 1980.

The regime declared that it was historically the first system that secured equal positions for men and women. The equality was even enacted in the 1960 Constitution – "Men and women have the same status in family, work and public activity" (Act No. 100/1960 Coll., Constitution of the Czechoslovak Socialist Republic). The system tried to demonstrate this equality for example by the relatively high level of women among the MPs (see Table 1.10). These numbers were quite high for that period. We can compare them to the share of women MPs in the British Parliament in the respective period that varied between 3–6.5% (House of Commons Information Office 2010). On the other hand, there was not a single female Minister in any Czechoslovak federal government between 1970 and 1989.

Table 1.10 Number of MPs (men and women) in different parts of the parliament

Elections	*House of the People*			*House of the Nations*			*Czech National Council*		
	women	*men*	*women (percent)*	*women*	*men*	*women (percent)*	*women*	*men*	*women (percent)*
November 1971	53	147	27	37	113	25	50	150	25
October 1976	59	141	30	41	109	27	57	143	29
June 1981	56	144	28	43	107	29	56	144	28
May 1986	63	137	32	44	106	29	55	145	28

Source: ČSSR. Chamber of deputies (1971–1986)

Moreover, the differences in wages were persisting. Jechová states that women's wages were on average 35% lower than those of men (Jechová 2012). According to Večerník, the differences between male and female wages were stable during the whole period (Večerník 1992). In some cases, it was a result of the fact that men held physically more demanding jobs, had the opportunity/obligation to travel to remote workstations or worked in three shifts. In many businesses, however, men took much higher wages for identical work (often with the same level of education and qualification), as they were still considered to be the breadwinners (Jechová 2012). Even the then Federal Prime Minister expressed his disapproval of the common practice that women's wage was 10–20% lower than men's for the same work and in the same qualification class (Adamec 1989).

The truth was that women participation in the labour market enormously increased, partly as a reaction to the redeployment of men to (heavy) industries (Kalinová 2012) but mainly due to the omnipresent scarcity of labour force (see Box 4.4 in Chapter 4).

1.4.2 *Morals and religion*

Moral values in the society were expressed by relatively widespread slogans like "those who do not steal from the state, steal from their families." These values were affected by the political development as well. People were forced to demonstrate their loyalty to the regime for example on the May Day. Regime-loyalty manifestations were compulsory and people had to shout out slogans about the superiority of the socialist system and economy that they often did not believe. Shop windows had to be decorated at multiple occasions during the year, public buildings were bedecked with slogans, people had to attend ideological-political trainings, etc. Možný writes about "ritualized everyday small self-humiliation" that symbolically affirmed social relationships (Možný 1991). Frequent anonymous reporting about people's "misbehaviour" (for example about a critical attitude towards the regime) directed to communist institutions, the police or the StB was common.[13]

The dismal moral state was deepened by the official attitude towards the intervention of the Warsaw Pact armies in 1968. Ordinary people (non-dissidents)

who disagreed with the official interpretation (that approved of the invasion) were forced to lie (Havel writes about life in a lie, see his essay "Power of the Powerless" – Havel 1985) or at minimum be silent. The whole nation was due to this forced to dissimulate their true feelings and thoughts. Openly expressing one's own opinions did not pay, since one could have his or her career ruined (a better scenario) or be imprisoned. Most people did not care about politics or tried to avoid it by any means. In the Czechoslovak environment, the phenomenon of cottages is often mentioned (e.g., Bálek 2007) as a place where people tried to escape from everyday reality. To sum these aspects up, the moral decline resulting from 50 years of totalitarian regimes left indelible marks on the population. Havel argued in an open letter to Dr. Husák (the then Secretary General of the KSČ) that this state had long-term negative consequences on the nation when he wrote:

> *What I am afraid of is something else. The whole of this letter is concerned, in fact, with what I really fear – the pointlessly harsh and long-lasting consequences which the present violent abuses will have for our nations. I fear the price we are all bound to pay for the drastic suppression of history, the cruel and needless banishment of life into the underground of society and the depths of the human soul, the new compulsory deferment of every opportunity for society to live in anything like a natural way. And perhaps it is apparent from what I wrote a little way back that I am not only worried about our current payments in terms of everyday bitterness at the spoliation of society and human degradation, or about the heavy tax we shall have to pay in the long-lasting spiritual and moral decline of society. I am also concerned with the scarcely calculable surcharge which may be imposed on us when the moment next arrives for life and history to demand their due. [. . .] So far, it is the worst in us which is being systematically activated and enlarged – egotism, hypocrisy, indifference, cowardice, fear, resignation, and the desire to escape every personal responsibility, regardless of the general consequences.*
>
> *(Havel 1975)*

Religion did not play an important role in the society. There were long-term historical reasons for the relatively high level of secularity (especially in the Czech part of the country). The communist regime deepened these trends and religiosity was nearly totally suppressed. Open faith was a reason for discrimination or for blocking of promotion or study. For the state of religion (after the fall of the communist regime when people were allowed to express their attitudes) and the differences between the parts of the country, see Table 1.11. At the same time, the society suffered from a high divorce rate and a high number of abortions (Stevens 1985).

1.4.3 Everyday economic incentives

Other incentives for the behaviour of individuals were the consequences of the shortage economy. The natural consequence was a high level of petty corruption

Table 1.11 Population by religion in 1991 (as of 3 March)

Religious beliefs, Church	*Czechoslovakia*		*Czech Republic*		*Slovak Republic*	
	number	*%*	*number*	*%*	*number*	*%*
No religion	4,628,415	29.7	4,112,864	39.9	515,551	9.8
Roman Catholic	7,208,768	46.3	4,021,385	39.0	3,187,383	60.4
Slovak evangelic	330,548	2.1	4,151	0.1	326,397	6.2
Other	825,367	5.3	498,198	4.8	327,169	6.2
Not identified	2,583,452	16.6	1,665,617	16.2	917,835	17.4

Source: Češka (2013)

that appeared on an everyday basis even with purchasing fruit or books. Fassmann quotes surveys among Czechoslovak citizens. The shares of people that admitted to giving a bribe in the previous 12 months were as follows: 1979 – 34%, 1981 – 32%, and 1989 – 52%. At the same time, even the relative volume of bribes to wages was increasing. In specific, people complained foremost about corruption in retail (58%), healthcare (45%), services (34%), and education (13%) in the 1980s (Fassmann 2007). Insufficient supply contributed to unethical/criminal behaviour of shop assistants too. Winiecki (2000) writes that random inspections in Czechoslovakia in the mid-1970s found out that shop assistants were cheating customers in 40% of the cases. In the next decade, the number increased to 45–65% (he mentions that these numbers were still significantly lower than in other centrally planned economies). At the same time nepotism, connections, and favouritism were common ways to get the "right" job or enrol children to schools.

Acquaintances were also invaluable even in business for obtaining raw materials or semi-manufactured goods for the companies (Kabele 2005) – see Chapter 4. Možný emphasizes the omnipresent and prevailing system of counter-services (Možný 1991). These practices were criticized (however rarely) even in the communist parliament. Such criticism was surprising because critical comments hitting the system were generally not accepted by the regime, which makes it a fact reflecting the seriousness of the problem (and courage of the respective MP). A Member of Czech National Council, Václav Zýka in 1977 said at the parliamentary session among others: "There is substantial discontent among people, who are unable to easily satisfy their justified needs of proper citizens of the socialist state without bribes"; "lifestyle and property of some citizens, who live 'beyond their means,' absolutely rule out a possibility of honest acquisition" and a "relatively large part of the nation is accepting corruption as something common, and their view of the people living without justification beyond their means is not that they are thieves but that they are skilful" (ČSSR. Czech National Council 1976–1981).

The consequence of all these incentives was a real change in behaviour. Some authors argue (for example Zon 2000) that instead of creating a "new socialist person," a different creature with totally different values was created. The new people did not express a spirit of initiative, because standing out was potentially dangerous and because they were used to merely listening to orders. They tried to avoid any responsibility for the same reason or because they felt that it did not pay off (ibidem). People generally did not trust each other, possibly with the exception of family members (Možný 1991), and the general level of trust in the society was significantly lower than in developed countries (e.g., Raiser, Haerpfer, Nowotny, and Wallace 2001).

Interestingly, the Prime Minister from the 1970s and 1980s Lubomír Štrougal mentions in his memoirs that the regime never carried out any public survey about the satisfaction of inhabitants (however there were probably surveys which were never published). Neither the party nor the state apparatus were concerned with what ordinary people thought, their dissatisfactions, or their views of life and future of the country. The leaders did not have true and needed information about the state of the country (Štrougal 2009). But the conservative wing was at the same time convinced that everything was all right and that the majority of people were satisfied (ibidem).

The description of the functioning of the society would not be complete without some aspects that could be considered as positive, at minimum, for some of the inhabitants. On the pros side can be foremost that the system was extremely stable. People generally dislike changes and the system provided a change-free environment with a very high level of social security for the citizens. For example, it was extremely difficult to lay off an employee, and people had secure jobs. The social status of some professions – for example miners – was high in comparison to market economies. If people did not want to express their own opinions, they abstained from expressing critical political views, and were generally obedient to the socialist state (Winiecki 2000 writes about extreme opportunism), they were rewarded with cheap basic foodstuffs, utilities and services and "free of charge" education and healthcare. The society was highly homogeneous, and the level of criminality was low. Generally, life in the socialist society was predictable, to some degree casual and with minimal changes. Such characteristics were favoured by a significant part of the society (e.g., Pullmann 2011). At the same time, there was generally little knowledge about the functioning of democratic countries (including market economies). Life in capitalist countries (and goods from these markets) was often, in spite of everyday massive propaganda, glorified and idealized among the ordinary people in Czechoslovakia and the general view of the west could be often described as naïve. The main reason was that common people could not access it.

This first chapter provided basic information about the functioning of society in socialist Czechoslovakia. Now we turn our attention towards the ideology that was the pillar of the centrally planned model.

Notes

1 Department of Economics, Faculty of Economics and Administration, Masaryk University, Czech Republic.
2 This attitude is in compliance, for example, with German sociologist Dahrendorf's view of the consequent transformation process. He wrote already in 1990, after the fall of the

Communist regimes, that "formal change of the constitution would take six months; positive views of changing economy would hardly appear sooner than in six years; but building solid foundations of society that would work under good as well as bad weather would last sixty years" (Dahrendorf 1990, p. 99).

3 In the first post-war general election in 1946 the Italian Communist Party came third with 18.9% of the votes and the French Communist Party won the general election in October 1945 with 26.1% of the votes.

4 After the expulsion of the nearly entire 3 million German minority after the War the country became more homogenous with two dominant nations – Czech and Slovaks. In 1948, 3.4 million people lived in the Slovak part and 8.9 million in the Czech part of Czechoslovakia. In the following decades, the consequent population growth was significantly higher in Slovakia than in the Czech Lands. In 1989, 5.3 million people lived in Slovakia vs. 10.4 million in the Czech Lands (Vintrová 2008). It means that the population ratio was broadly 2:1 in favour of the Czechs in the 1980s.

5 For comparison, the current Czech election period is only four years long but, for example in the 2013–2017 period, there were 58 parliamentary sessions. The Federal Assembly discussed 83 acts in the 1981–1986 period. The Czech Parliament debated 643 acts in the 2013–2017 period.

6 Mikhail Gorbachev was elected General Secretary on the 11 March 1985. The first clear declaration of Perestroika in the Czechoslovak Parliament was introduced immediately after the general election in June 1986 (Digitální knihovna PS PČR).

7 The Communist Party tried to keep the membership share of different classes in some proportions. Jan Vrba (later on director of *Textilana*) said in an interview for IPPKID that he was offered a membership in the Communist Party as a condition for his promotion, which he was offered for his organization skills in the 1960s. He was told that seven workers were prepared to enter the Party together with him because the required proportion between higher-post and lower-post workers at that time was one to seven (IPPKID 2015).

8 489,648 members and candidates of the Party were expelled from the KSČ between 1969 and 1975. From the offices of the Federal government 1,041 people (9.9%) and from the offices of the Czech government 683 people (10.3%) had to leave. The economic sphere suffered in a similar way (Hradecká and Koudelka 1998).

9 Dolejší quotes professor Cepl, who after 1989 became one of the respected judges of the Constitutional Court, who was supposed to have said that "the whole Prague Law Faculty should be pulled down and powder[ed] by unslaked lime" (Dolejší 2015).

10 Interestingly, Štrougal (the Prime Minister in the 1970s and 1980s) argued that such regime at the borders was necessary due to Czechoslovakia´s obligations to the Warsaw Pact (Štrougal 2009). However, Hungary was a member of the Pact, too, and the physical obstacles were removed in the 1980s.

11 There were even complaints in the parliament about declining the amount and quality of information about world development of technologies that experts in research were able to acquire – MP Benda in a parliament session on 20 of October 1987 (ČSSR, Federal Assembly of the Czechoslovak Socialist Republic 1986–1990).

12 The Gini coefficient ranges between 0 and 1 (100). Zero means absolutely equal income for all inhabitants in the country. Higher numbers mean higher inequality.

13 Interestingly, Mr. Votoček, who was the mayor of the town of Olomouc, said that he had an obligation to provide throughout analysis of each anonymous letter within three days after receiving it (Vaněk and Urbášek 2005).

2 Marxist-Leninist economic theory

The goal of this chapter is to shortly describe the pillars of the Marxist-Leninist thinking with emphasis on those relevant parts that were important for practical functioning of the centrally planned economic systems. The authors of this text are well aware of the fact that the ideas of the eponyms of socialist thinking did not provide a coherent ideological universe. In addition, problems appear because the followers of Lenin's ideology began introducing the ideology into practice and it is sometimes difficult to distinguish between the ideology itself and instructions for everyday practice.

It must be noted that literature about Marxism-Leninism (and its criticism) is gigantic. For example, Lenin's Collected Works only comprise 54 volumes in the original, each about 650 pages. They were translated into English in 45 volumes by Progress Publishers, Moscow. The intention of this chapter (and this book) is not to provide a thorough analysis of the Marxist-Leninist philosophical thought. Instead, the authors concentrate on a brief analysis of the main theoretical aspects of the thinking that consequently reached fruition in the centrally planned theory (Chapter 3) and practice (Chapter 4). This chapter is thus preparatory for the analysis presented in the following chapters.

The authors of this text deem essential the attitude of the ideologists of socialism towards capitalism (2.1). Marx's economic thoughts are based on the idea of the surplus-value which is acquired unjustly by private owners of the capital and which should (as he claims) belong to the workers. The ideologists label this behaviour of the private owners as exploitation. The second section (2.2) shows how Marxism-Leninism dealt with problems of capitalism by introducing socialism. Socialism was regarded by its proponents as an unavoidable historical development. The very first step of socialism was nationalization, which addressed the core capitalist problem of ownership. The linear logic follows with application of the centrally planned system because the government somehow had to deal with the companies it nationalized. Due to this, these two topics constitute the main part of the second section. Marx and Engels concentrated on the criticism of the capitalist system and they did not contemplate the functioning of socialism much. Thus, the rest of the section is based, to a significant degree, on the works of their successors, who tried to answer the theory's practical questions, but the chapter concentrates on the theory itself and it tries to avoid comments on economic practice. The third section (2.3) briefly analyzes criticism of the ideological aspects of the centrally planned model.

2.1 Capitalism

The starting point of our analysis must be Marxist criticism of capitalism. Two key terms in Marxian economic attitude that are needed to be considered are ownership and surplus-value. These two terms are in Marxism naturally interconnected. Marxian theory was created as criticism of the capitalist economic system. This system was, in Marx's eyes, inherently and inevitably sentenced to the exploitation of workers by capitalists, which was deemed as gratuitous appropriation of somebody else's work. Worker's labour was considered as merely a kind of "goods." This exploitation was enabled by capitalists' ownership of the means of production. Marx believed that workers produce "surplus-value," meaning surplus of the overall value of the production above the value of their labour force (wage) (Marx 1887). In other words, in a capitalist society, the necessity of reproduction of the labour force determines the value of the labour force. The reward is kept on the subsistence level and it can be even lower if unemployment is widespread (e.g., Robinson 1942). Robinson further points out that the main cause is the industrial reserve army of labour, which refers to the unemployed and the under-employed in the capitalist system (Robinson 1942). In Mandels' words: "It is nothing but the monetary form of the social surplus product, that is to say, it is the monetary form of that part of the worker's production which he surrenders to the owner of the means of production without receiving anything in return" (Mandel 1973, p. 9). This surplus-value is appropriated by the capitalist, as it is enabled by the capitalists' ownership of the means of production, and this way the exploitation takes place. The workers can produce new value only by working on machinery that is provided by the capitalist. A form of the surplus-value is thus the capitalists' profit that enables some section of the society to become a ruling class and to emancipate them from the need of the working class and for its own subsistence (ibidem). To sum it up, in Marx's view, the surplus-value is not created by exchange. And it is not produced by the capital or land means of production but only by labour force (Veszeláková et al. 1972). Mandel writes that "It is consequently inaccurate to say that it is the capitalist who creates employment, since it is the worker who produced the surplus-value, which was capitalized by the capitalist, and used, among other things, for hiring more workers" (Mandel 1973, p. 44). In fact, factories, machines, etc. are in consequence just the product of the surplus-value materialization that has been transformed into private ownership into the capitalist capital, it is, in other words, "a colossal proof of the continuous exploitation undergone by the working class since the origin of capitalist society" (ibidem). In consequence, and because of this private ownership of the means of production, the capitalist system is considered as unjust and leads to the pauperization of the working class.

On the other hand, Marx believed that capitalism had positive features because it solved the problem of production. However, it did not solve the distribution problem and was therefore destined to decline (Osterfeld 1993). The reason was that capitalist economic crises were not crises of scarcity, like all the previous ones, they were crises of overproduction: "The unemployed die of hunger not because there is too little to eat but because there is relatively too great a supply of foodstuffs" (Mandel 1973, p. 52). In this period of crises, the capitalist cannot sell all his or her production and the unsold goods do not materialize their surplus-value. The capitalists do not get back their invested capital, which results in production restriction and the laying off of employees. The workers have no savings (because wage is on subsistence level) and can only manage while working.

Mandel writes that:

> *The factor of periodic economic crises is inherent in the capitalist system and remains unsurmountable. [. . .] Crises are the clearest manifestation of the fundamental contradiction in the system and a periodic reminder that it is condemned to die sooner or later. But it will never die automatically. It will always be necessary to give it a conscious little push to effect its demise.*
>
> *(Mandel 1973, p. 53)*

The little push was supposed to be provided by the starving working class.

2.2 Socialism

Marx's answer to the previous unjust state was in the coming of socialism. This development was, according to the Marxist-Leninist theory, inevitable. Marx concluded this necessity from the evidence based on his historical materialist method. He detected several imperative stages of the mankind development by application of this method. And they were further appropriated and modified by Lenin. Their socio-economic formations were the following:

1 Primitive communism – prehistory based on cooperative tribes.
2 Asian production means.
3 Antic production means. The second and third productions means were unified to slave production means by Lenin.
4 Feudalism – aristocrats were the ruling class.
5 Capitalism – capitalists were the ruling class. Lenin (1964) identified the highest (monopolist) stage as imperialisms.
6 Communism. Lenin identified the first stage as socialism. Communism will be characterized by the absence of markets and money, abundance and the withering away of the state.

(Gregory and Stuart 2014)

In the eyes of the theorists, it is the conflict between the classes which causes progress among the stages. Societies have always taken on the form of an oppressed majority living under the thumb of an oppressive minority. In capitalism, the conflict takes place between the bourgeoisie and the proletariat. The proletariat will irreversibly grab power (under the leadership of the Marxist-Leninist party) in a revolutionary action because the bourgeoisie is not willing to surrender voluntarily. In Marx and Engels' view the decline of capitalism is inevitable because the system is developing its own contradictions up to an unsolvable state (Hába et al. 1988). It creates conditions for the appearance of a new, classless socio-economic system – communism – which will be created on the ruins of capitalism. As Lenin expressed: "The proletariat seizes state power and turns the means. [. . .] But thereby it abolishes itself as the proletariat, abolishes all class distinctions" (Lenin 1964, p. 400).

Marx emphasized that the rule by the working class must be a dictatorship (Gregory and Stuart 2014). In specific, he believed in the idea of the dictatorship of the proletariat (Marx and Engels 1969), which was deepened by Lenin (1964). He believed that the state will "wither away" and because democracy represents the state it will evaporate as well. Toppling of the bourgeoisie and abolition of private property was supposed to liberate the man from the domination of others (Havelková 2009b). It was meant to result in a situation when everybody is supposed to be an owner. This is based on the principle that, as a member of the society, in which everybody works for everybody, each member of the society is de facto an owner. His or her work is not "goods" and the reward is not the consequence of exchange but a share of the overall outcomes (Havelková 2009b). Marx described the situation after nationalization of the means of production and eliminations of the goods production in the following way:

> *Accordingly, the individual producer receives back from society – after the deductions have been made – exactly what he gives to it. What he has given to it is his individual quantum of labour. [. . .] He receives a certificate from society that he has furnished such-and-such an amount of labour (after deducting his labour for the common funds); and with this certificate, he draws from the social stock of means of consumption as much as the same amount of labour cost. The same amount of labour which he has given to society in one form, he receives back in another.*
>
> *(Marx 1970, p. 15)*

Marx believed that he revealed the principles of human development and that downfall of capitalism was inevitable. At various times, Marx appeared to associate this downfall with the tendency of the rate of profit to fall, with tendencies to overproduction, underconsumption, disproportionality, and overaccumulation with respect to labour, without ever clearly championing one or the other theory. Engels consistently referred both to the contradiction between the tendency of capitalism to increase production without limit and the limited consumption power of the mass of the population; and to the anarchy of the market, in his explanation of the crisis tendencies of capitalism (Clarke 1994).

These theories gave rise to a scientific discipline – political economy of socialism. Engels wrote that "political economy, in the widest sense, is the science of the laws governing the production and exchange of the material means of subsistence in human society" (Engels 1947, p. 186). But Marx and Engels never specified the economic functioning of socialism (e.g., Carr 1966; Rozsypal et al. 1981). They considered it as a worthless and non-scientific approach because the specific settings of the system would depend on the historical conditions when socialism eventually develops, and these were not known in their time (Hába et al. 1988). Due to this, the practical consequences of the theoretical socialist system were based more on Lenin's thoughts and foremost on everyday practice of the communist governments.

The reality of socialism that was described (and in fact created) by the later ideologists resulted in omnipotent governments. Oliva, who was a proponent of the regime, points out that: "In a socialist economy nothing can be done without leadership and supervision of the state" (p. 8). He added that:

> *In socialistic economy, it happens that the planners wish to spread among inhabitants a higher volume of a certain type of goods than was the previous quantity. They plan to increase production of this type of goods and consequently reduce its prices. The intention is materialized and due to this the demand grows. Here, unlike in the capitalist economies, the will of economic policy makers prevails. It seems that what happens is powered by what people want regardless of the objective necessity and that the people's will is the key decision-making factor superior to (and denying the existence of) economic rules.*
>
> *(Oliva 1952, p. 10)*

The socialist economy was supposed to be based on basic statements that were considered to be unquestionable laws. They were expressed by Stalin and were required to be regarded as valid in all socialist economies. Pavlát and Vojtíšek write: "Economic laws – scientific laws are a reflection of such processes and contexts that take place in the objective world we recognize and which exists outside of us, independent of our consciousness and our will" (Pavlát and Vojtíšek 1959, p. 99). But the laws were supposed to be historically transient and different for various economic systems. Although the views of the laws varied among the authors, Stalin is considered their main author. The basic law in socialism was this: "The securing of the maximum satisfaction of the constantly rising material and cultural requirements of the whole of society through the continuous expansion and perfection of socialist production on the basis of higher techniques" (Stalin 1972, pp. 70–71). He continued:

> *Consequently: instead of maximum profits – maximum satisfaction of the material and cultural requirements of society; instead of development of production with breaks in continuity from boom to crisis and from crisis to boom – unbroken expansion of production; instead of periodic breaks in technical development, accompanied by destruction of the productive forces of society – an unbroken process of perfecting production on the basis of higher techniques.*
>
> *(ibidem)*

At the same time, it was believed that socialism would be, on the contrary to capitalist economic system, without economic crisis, as the authors of the main socialist textbook wrote:

> *In capitalist society, proportionality is fortuitous, and the economy develops cyclically, by means of crises which recur periodically. In contrast to this, socialist economy develops uninterruptedly along an ascending curve and at rapid rate, on the basis of proportions laid down by the Socialist State in conformity with the requirements of the law of planned development of the national economy and the basic economic law of socialism. Socialist economy is free from economic crises, which break up the economy, do colossal material damage to society, and periodically throw it back.*
>
> (*Academy of Sciences of the U.S.S.R. 1957, p. 408*)

There were, however, other laws. Their substance was well known and possible to use in the development of the socialist society and economy. They were the following:

1 Law of socialist industrialization (increasing role of industry in economy).
2 Law of collectivization of agriculture (creating of cooperatives).
3 Law of rewarding people according to work, elimination of the exploitation of man by man.
4 Law of planning (law of planning development).
5 Law of socialist accumulation.
6 Law of distribution of production of means.
7 Law of increasing living standards.

(Doležalová 2009)

Earlier, we analyzed the socialist system globally. Now we progress to the description of specific theoretical settings of the system. The necessary precondition was the leading role of the communist party that was executed via the state (2.2.1). The key ideological pillar of the socialist economy was nationalization of property (2.2.2). Nationalization then led to central planning (2.2.3) and partly to other specifics of the system (2.2.4). The centrally planned system was in fact unavoidable once property was nationalized, as the economy had to be somehow governed. The practical specific attitudes depended on the level of centralization (the system varied from highly centralized systems – e.g., in Czechoslovakia – to more decentralized systems, such as in Hungary, or ones with self-management socialism for example Poland in the 1980s). The other aspects of the system like monopolization naturally resulted from the state ownership as well. We can compare them with Eucken, who provided an interesting insight into the functioning of the directed economy of Hitler's Germany. He argued that the whole directive system was founded with an attempt at providing jobs and securing the position of the working class. The other steps including fixed prices or intervention into ownership were just natural consequences of this effort (Eucken 1948). It means that one political decision naturally (and unavoidably) resulted in other economic measures. However, a strictly controlled economy appealed to the Nazi ideology because it emphasized the rule of the party over the economy and society in general (Tooze 2007). We might say that both the ends and the means were in line with authoritarian ideology. Socialism followed the same logic.

2.2.1 Leading role of the communist party and role of state

The road to socialism needed a ruler. Lenin insisted on a role of a vanguard party that would fight for the revolutionary program. He wrote: "Without revolutionary theory there can be no revolutionary movement [. . .] the role of vanguard fighter can be fulfilled only by a party that is guided by the most advanced theory" (Lenin 1961, p. 370).

What was then needed was a body that would execute the communist party's will – the state. However, Marx and Engels firstly, as well as Lenin, did not believe in the positive role of the state. Engels wrote:

> *The first act by virtue of which the state really constitutes itself the representative of the whole of society – the taking possession of the means of production in the name of society – this is, at the same time, its last independent act as a state. State interference in social relations becomes, in one domain after another, superfluous, and then dies out of itself; the government of persons is replaced by the administration of things, and by the conduct of processes of production. The state is not "abolished." It dies out. This gives the measure of the value of the phrase "a free people's state," both as to its justifiable use at times by agitators, and as to its ultimate scientific insufficiency; and also of the demands of the so-called anarchists for the abolition of the state out of hand.*
>
> *(Engels 1947, p. 94)*

But, being confronted with reality, Lenin changed his opinion on this issue and the state thus became the executor of the communist party's will. Nevesely for example comments:

> *In the conditions of the victorious socialist revolution, the socialist state – the dictatorship of the proletariat – promotes the aims and interests of the working class, their allies, at the expense of the defeated bourgeoisie and their allies. The socialist state, in its complex structure, is used fully to accomplish the building of socialism. In this respect, the role of the state and its institutions is irreplaceable and extremely important. In the concept of Marxist-Leninist theory, state and state power have never been understood to be self-serving for power itself, but state power has always been and is always seen as a decisive means in implementing the program and goals of the victorious working class and its allies.*
>
> *(Neveselý 1977, p. 40)*

The conclusion is that the communist party was supposed to play the decisive role in the building of the socialist society, including the economy. The realization of its policy was supposed to be ensured by the state, which would, however, cease to exist later on after reaching the developmental stage of communism.

2.2.2 Nationalization

The very first and ideological step in the Marxist construct (that was supposed to be carried out by a revolutionary party) was nationalization. The theorists expected that in the new socio-economic system – socialism – the means of production would at first be in the state ownership. This view was an elaboration of Marx and Engels's statement: "The proletariat will use its political supremacy to wrest, by degree, all capital from the bourgeoisie, to centralize all instruments of production in the hands of the state, i.e., of the proletariat organized as the ruling class; and to increase the total productive forces as rapidly as possible" (Marx and Engels 1969, p. 26).

Lenin considered as the only alternative to state ownership (after appropriation of the capitalist property) ownership by working collectives, and he strongly refused it. In specific he wrote: "Just think: on August 5th, when numerous decrees on the nationalisation of factories in Russia had been issued – and not a single factory had been 'appropriated' by the workers but had all been converted into the property of the Republic" (Lenin 1974, p. 316). Elsewhere he wrote that only state ownership can guarantee the elimination of exploration of man by man and, without it, it would not be possible to appropriate surplus-value and ensure the permanent growth of living standard (Lenin 1964).

Robinson contributed that "under socialism income from property will be abolished and each individual will receive a share in the total product corresponding to his own contribution to it" (Robinson 1942, p. 32).

Note that the original document – the *Communist Manifesto* – already expected the use confiscation of property as a violent political tool with a view to eliminating the opposition, as one of the requirements claimed: "Confiscation of the property of all emigrants and rebels" (Marx and Engels 1969, p. 26). Here, proponents of socialism followed the well-established practice introduced by previous struggles and revolutions carried out since ancient times, e.g., during the Confessional Wars or the French Revolution. Confiscation and other, often violent, changes of property rights were by no means the novelty of socialism. However, complete nationalization of the economy and its centralization under the state was.

2.2.3 Planning process

Widespread state ownership had to be governed somehow and in fact the only and natural possibility was via central planning – when the centre organizes the economy. Lenin stated:

> *To organize the whole economy on the lines of the postal service so that the technicians, foremen, and accountants, as well as all officials, shall receive salaries no higher*

> *than "a workman's wage," all under the control and leadership of the armed proletariat – that is our immediate aim. This is what will bring about the abolition of parliamentarism and the preservation of representative institutions.*
>
> *(Lenin 1964, p. 432)*

Oliva considers planned economy as one of the laws of socialism. He writes that those who own the means of production also decide about the economy. He adds that planning is possible only in societies where the whole society is the owner of the means of production, which is possible only in the socialist society. The socialist system is, in his view, not only a possibility but a necessity form to take advantage of all the opportunities and to achieve concord (Oliva 1952).

Theoretical considerations about planning were possible to find already in works by Marx and Engels. Rozsypal et al. write about planning opposed competition and anarchy, which characterize capitalism (Rozsypal et al. 1981) – see 2.2.4. But it was Lenin who developed the first practical planning system considering a unified state-wide plan as a base of the entire economic activity of the Soviet State (Průcha 1988). According to Sitárová and Kliment: "Leninism considered central planning not only as a precondition for implementation of the societal goals but as a means of mobilization of all strength and its involvement in the building socialism as well" (Sitárová and Kliment 1981, p. 440). We should note that Lenin was forced to deal with the situation of War Communism and planning was considered as the key tool. The idea of socialism embraced the concept of a non-monetary centrally planned rationing economy (Doležalová 2009). The conclusion is that the planning was the next and unavoidable step in a situation of nearly absolute state ownership.

At the same time, the ideologists deemed central planning and planning of production as a scientific way to govern the economy. The way was considered as superior to the chaotic markets (Hába et al. 1988). The whole system was supposed to be governed as a single company. Lenin wrote: "The transformation of the whole of the State economic mechanism into a single, huge machine, into an economic organism that will work in such a way as to enable hundreds of millions of people to be guided by a single plan" (Lenin 1972b, pp. 90–91).

Lenin pointed out that it is impossible to work without having a plan intended for a lengthy period and for achieving serious success. He stated that "the plans of the various branches of production must be strictly co-ordinated, combined, and made together to constitute that single economic plan of which we stand in such great need" (Lenin 1965, p. 511).

Simultaneously, it was believed that the planning system would be highly efficient: "By planning, the Socialist state ties together the production of different enterprises and brings about the most rational location of socialist production" (Academy of Sciences of the U.S.S.R. 1957, p. 409). At the beginning Lenin admitted possible mistakes in the planning process but they were expected to be later corrected:

> *In view of the difficulties of the present time, we shall have a programme in which there will be many mistakes, but that does not matter – the next Congress will correct*

> *it. [. . .] Our Programme now will be constructed not so much according to the books as from practice, from the experience of Soviet power.*
>
> (*Lenin 1972b, p. 142*)

The practical feasibility of the central planning was advocated by Lange's theoretical concept (1936). His basic idea was that production factors can be allocated rationally even in the absence of the market. A central body should determine their prices. As far as the prices of consumer goods and labour are concerned, they should be determined on the relevant markets. The pricing structure may be functional due to the fact that they are set by the centre and managers are obliged to respect them when deciding on the volume of production and the choice of resources. Prices should be determined using the "trial and error method," similarly to the market economy. In the event of a mismatch between supply and demand, the planning authority is obliged to adjust them in order to achieve the equilibrium. There is a single point where prices of products and factors of production are balanced and therefore clearly identified. These prices determined by the central authority have the same objective validity as the market ones (Lange 1936).

Generally, the founders of socialism intended to (or de facto had to) apply the planning process in the economy. They considered this scientific way of governing as more efficient to disorganized markets. The crucial role was supposed to be played by the state (the economic centre). The companies were assumed to play just inferior role in the global mechanism.

2.2.4 *Specifics of central planning environment*

The very foundations of the socialist economic system were nationalization and central planning. It featured, however, other attributes that stemmed from the ideology as well. In this (sub)section, we discuss the key economic topics – the role of labour force, monopolization of the economy, ideas about abandoning money and attitudes towards world integration. These topics will appear also in the following parts of the text.

General labour duty and dealing with the labour force

Theorists of socialism usually commenced their argumentation by tackling the exploitation of labour. The worst aspect of capitalism was seen in the uncertain position of the employees that were ever in danger of being exploited by the capitalist and affected by a random impact of the business cycle. Unemployment was felt as a social illness that was unfairly imposed on the working class. The utmost goal of the socialist economy thus was in elimination of this uncertainty and providing employees with absolutely stable and secured jobs. One of the other features was the right to work, which at the same time meant labour duty. General labour duty was already mentioned in the *Communist Manifesto*. Lenin further elaborated this idea when he wrote:

> *What is universal labour conscription? It is a step forward on the basis of modern monopoly capitalism, a step towards the regulation of economic life as a whole, in accordance with a certain general plan, a step towards the economy of national labour and towards the prevention of its senseless wastage by capitalism.*
>
> *[. . .]*
>
> *But take the same institution and think over its significance in a revolutionary-democratic state. Universal labour conscription, introduced, regulated and directed by the Soviets of Workers,' Soldiers' and Peasants' Deputies, will still not be socialism, but it will no longer be capitalism. It will be a tremendous step towards socialism, a step from which, if complete democracy is preserved, there can no longer be any retreat back to capitalism, without unparalleled violence being committed against the masses.*
>
> *(Lenin 1977, pp. 363–364)*

The natural consequence of general labour duty was the elimination of unemployment. Additionally, labour force was supposed to be broadened by female workers, as Engels considered housework as unproductive and thus non-contributing towards creating surplus-value. Women were expected to join the work process after the removal of capitalism (Havelková 2009a).

At the same time, Pavlát and Vojtíšek point out that:

> *Socialist relationships [are supposed] to be relationships of comrade cooperation and mutual help of people deprived of exploitation and that are fully developed only on the basis of the socialization of the decisive means of production that is conducting the socialist revolution.*
>
> *(Pavlát and Vojtíšek 1959, p. 37)*

This view resonated with Engels who wrote that socialism "allows all members of society to develop, maintain and exercise their capacities as all-sidedly as possible" (Engels 1976, p. 257).

In theory, the labour force and generally all people were supposed to be highly motivated. The authors of the Brief philosophical vocabulary expressed this attitude:

> *Labour in communism is voluntary, free of rule and norm, labour conducted without the view of, or demand for, wages or other rewards. It is work done for the benefit of society and based on a conscious decision that it is important to work for the higher good of general welfare.*
>
> *(Rozental' and Judin 1955, p. 394)*

The theorists of the system expected the creation of a "new socialist person" who would work hard for the better future of everybody without personal demand for material reward (see Chapter 1). But this new socialist person was considered to be imperfect prior to the establishment of the communist stage of development.

State monopoly and competition

Inherited structure of the economy was supposed to be monopolistic because capitalism in the eyes of the ideologist inevitably led to monopolization. Lenin believed that this inherited structure of the economy was one of the advantages of socialism:

> *For socialism is merely the next step forward from state-capitalist monopoly. Or, in other words, socialism is merely state-capitalist monopoly which is made to serve the interests of the whole people and has to that extent ceased to be capitalist monopoly.*
>
> *There is no middle course here. The objective process of development is such that it is impossible to advance from monopolies (and the war has magnified their number, role and importance tenfold) without advancing towards socialism. [. . .] The dialectics of history is such that the war, by extraordinarily expediting the transformation of monopoly capitalism into state-monopoly capitalism, has thereby extraordinarily advanced mankind towards socialism.*
>
> (*Lenin 1977, p. 362*)

Simultaneously, the concept of competition was seen as incompatible with the cooperative socialist ideology. The definition of competition expected it only in the capitalist system as authors of *Příruční slovník naučný* stated:

> *Competition – in political economics, these are relationships between private manufacturers realized by means of fight over securing and maintaining more profitable conditions for production and distribution of goods. Competition is typical of production of goods based on private ownership of the means of production. In capitalism, competition is characterized by capitalists competing for higher profit. In socialist economic systems, which are based on nationalized ownership of the means of production, competition cannot exist.*
>
> (*Procházka 1962–1967, p. 593*)

Competition was considered as wasting of sources for non-productive activity instead of concentrating on real production (Teplý 1976). The socialist economy textbook quoted Lenin:

> *Capitalism is inconceivable without competition and anarchy in production, and the consequent waste of social labour; and in the same way socialism is inconceivable without planned development of the national economy, which enables social labour and its products to be utilised rationally and economically.*
>
> (*Academy of Sciences of the U.S.S.R. 1957, p. 398*)

Instead of (capitalist) competition, socialist competition was expected to develop: "It is a communist method of building socialism, which is based on maximal activity of the millions" (Stalin 1953, p. 113). Rozental' defined socialist competition as "demonstration of conscious, creative initiative of the working masses building a new, communist society" (Rozental' and Judin 1955, p. 455).

Banking and non-monetary economy

Already Marx and Engels believed that the state should fully control money and credit. One of the requirements in the *Communist Manifesto* was this: "Centralization of credit in the hands of the state, by means of a national bank with State capital and an exclusive monopoly" (Marx and Engels 1969). Doležalová adds that banks were supposed to be just a central accounting department and exchange among the subjects was supposed to be replaced by distribution (Doležalová 2009). Lenin wrote about controlling of the banking sector the following:

> *The big banks are the state apparatus which we need to bring about socialism, and which we take ready-made from capitalism; our task here is merely to lop off what capitalistically mutilates this excellent apparatus, to make it even bigger, even more democratic, even more comprehensive. [. . .] A single State Bank the biggest of the big, with branches in every rural district, in every factory, will constitute as much as nine-tenths of the socialist apparatus. [. . .] This will be country-wide book-keeping, country-wide accounting of the production and distribution of goods, this will be, so to speak, something in the nature of the skeleton of socialist society.*
>
> *(Lenin 1972a, p. 106)*

According to the ideologists, the socialist economy was supposed to be initially organized on non-monetary principles as one hierarchically organized unit with one economic outcome. Exchange and monetary relationships were supposed to be replaced by central planning and ex-ante coordinated natural streams. Bukharin and Preobrazhensky wrote:

> *The gradual abolition of money will also be aided by the enormous issuing of paper money, in association with the enormous reduction in the exchange of commodities caused by the disorganization of industry. The increasing depreciation of the currency is in essence its spontaneous cancellation.*
>
> *(Bukharin and Preobrazhensky 1969, p. 396)*

In the first stages, however, money was supposed to stay but it should play only a role of evidence and control. We can again note that stable environment was crucial for the planners and thus it was more convenient to plan in natural units instead of money, which is affected by changing price levels. The elimination of money can be considered as highly convenient or even a necessity in the system of central planning. On the other hand, Hába et al. write that the most important economic law of commodity production in socialism was the *law of value*. It stated that the exchange of goods is governed by amount of necessary abstract work needed for its production – it means according to their value. Value expressed in money terms is then the price of goods. The amount of value included in the goods is thus the most important aspect for the determination of price (Hába et al. 1988). Otherwise, profit and profitability were not important values in the socialist economy as the authors of the Political economy state:

> *The profitability principle of private capitalism is governed by the aim of acquiring the maximum profits. In contrast to this, the law of planned development of the national economy, and socialist planning, ensure a higher form of profitability: profitability considered from the point of view of the economy as a whole.*
>
> *(Academy of Sciences of the U.S.S.R. 1957, p. 409)*

International integration

From economic point of view, economic integration is a highly important aspect of the functioning of the economy. Marx expressed his positive attitude towards international trade in his speech in Brussels in 1848. He saw trade as a tool against national state and means of deepening of class struggle. At the same time, free trade in his view broke down traditional culture as a step towards the creation of world culture (Marx 1976).

Lenin argued in favour of the participation of the Soviet Union in the world trade with a view to obtaining maximum benefit from the world division of labour (Jones 2001). However, in the discussion in the 1920s among the Bolsheviks, he strongly supported monopoly of foreign trade (Lenin 1965b). He believed that this monopoly was the right form of protection that the country needed to develop its own industry (ibidem).

After analyzing the core ideological aspects of socialism, we turn our attention towards basic criticism of the socialists thinking.

2.3 Criticism of Marxist economic policy

Marxism has been subject to fierce criticism since its inception and these attitudes further developed in time. Research on this topic is enormous. This chapter mentions just the key criticism that deals with the functioning of the centrally planned system.

Among sharp critics of Marxism there are Ludwig von Mises and F. A. Hayek. They are critical of the overall concept. For example, Mises states:

> *Because his [Lenin's] blindness made it impossible for him to see the role the market and the consumers play under capitalism, he could not see the difference between freedom and slavery. Because in his eyes the workers were only workers and not also customers, he believed they were already slaves under capitalism, and that one did not change their status when nationalizing all plants and shops. Socialism substitutes the sovereignty of a dictator, or committee of dictators, for the sovereignty of the consumers.*
>
> *(Mises 1991, p. 25)*

Hayek generally believes that capitalism is a spontaneous order and socialism expresses humans' hubris. He points out:

> *So, priding itself on having built its world as if it had designed it, and blaming itself for not having designed it better, humankind is now to set out to do just that. The aim*

> *of socialism is no less than to effect a complete redesigning of our traditional morals, law, and language, and on this basis to stamp out the old order and the supposedly inexorable, unjustifiable conditions that prevent the institution of reason, fulfilment, true freedom, and justice.*
>
> *(Hayek 1988, p. 67)*

Friedman draws attention to the illusion of the ideologist to organize the whole economy because all tiers will apply a significant part of free will. In specific he mentions:

> *I have already suggested, the most obvious and extreme case of a command economy is an army in which the general supposedly gives an order to the colonel, the colonel to the major, the major to the captain, the captain to the lieutenant, and so on down to the buck private. At every stage the individuals who are responding to those orders have volition of their own and interests of their own, and they react in part in accordance with these. At every stage in that process they have some element of discretion.*
>
> *(Friedman 1981, p. 4)*

Their criticism is more specific as well. Mises generally argues that rational economic calculation is not possible in socialism. In his view, in the socialist economy under the conditions of social ownership of production means there is no market where capital goods would be exchanged. Due to this fact, their value cannot be determined in money. Therefore, calculation in monetary sense is not possible to be made. Subsequently, this makes it unreal to compare the relative prices and to choose between alternatives. The rational production is not possible if the prices of the means of production are not a consequence of the free market forces. Without an economical calculation, the economy can only work on paper, leading the author to conclude that a rational socialist society must be based on the same formal laws governing capitalism (Mises 1990). Similarly, Hayek argues:

> *As soon as the state takes upon itself the task of planning the whole economic life, the problem of the due station of the different individuals and groups must indeed inevitably become the central political problem. As the coercive power of the state will alone decide who is to have what, the only power worth having will be a share in the exercise of this directing power.*
>
> *(Hayek 2001, p. 111)*

Hayek, on the other hand, does not deny the theoretical possibility of replacing the market price mechanism by means of mathematical calculations (Kouba 1968). However, given the information intensity, this is completely unrealistic in practice, because the centre does not have detailed information about the production process and it is therefore beyond its ability to make decisions about it. According to Hayek, the centre does not have enough information and cannot effectively use the allocated resources. If the decision-making process is to be effective the decision must be left in the hands of those with the relevant information (Hayek 1948, similarly Friedman 1981). Likewise, for example Gregory and Stuart argue:

> *In theory, if planners know the objective function, the production technologies, and the resource constraints, they could solve a system of equations that would tell them what and how to produce. Intuition tells us why such optimal planning is virtually impossible in practice: economy produces millions of distinct products and factor inputs – nor the powerful computers can solve millions of simultaneous equations for optimal combination of inputs and outputs – there is necessary aggregation. However, it does not work in real-world infinite amount of information: suppliers of information might be tempted to game the information they pass up to the planners.*
>
> *(Gregory and Stuart 2014, pp. 167–168)*

The only possible planned society, according to Coase, is a firm. He questions Lenin's view of Russia being run as one big factory, arguing that a firm, a little planned society, could only exist as long as its function is conducted at a lower cost than could be achieved by market transactions. The planning is thus desirable in an efficient economic system, because it lowers the transaction costs, but only within organizations of the appropriate size (Coase 1991). In other words, as James M. Buchanan proclaimed: "If a fly were multiplied nine times in all dimensions, it would not be able to get off the ground and might even collapse under its own weight. There is a problem of dimensionality here" (Wagner 2014). Rothbard de facto concludes about lack of information for efficient investment:

> *Deprived of a free price system and profit-and-loss criteria, the government can only blunder along, blindly "investing" without being able to invest properly in the right fields, the right products, or the right places. A beautiful subway will be built, but no wheels will be available for the trains; a giant dam, but no copper for transmission lines, etc. These sudden surpluses and shortages, so characteristic of government planning, are the result of massive malinvestment by the government.*
>
> *(Rothbard 2009, p. 967)*

The famous Mises' debate with Lange about possibility of socialist calculation still continues; for example Nutter, who points out the impact of nationalization, writes:

> *If we now come full circle and return to Lange's model of socialism, we see how empty his theoretical apparatus is. Markets without divisible and transferable property rights are a sheer illusion. There can be no competitive behaviour, real or simulated, without dispersed power and responsibility. And it will not do to disperse the one without the other. If all property is to be literally collectivized and all pricing literally centralized, there is no scope left for a mechanism that can reproduce in any significant respect the functioning of competitive private enterprise.*
>
> *(Nutter 1968, p. 37)*

Hoppe emphasizes another aspect of common ownership. He argues that after socialization everybody becomes the owner of everything. This change does not solve the decision-making problem because it is impossible for everybody to decide about everything. Consequently, socialism creates elites (Hoppe 2010).

In addition, Mises (1990) draws attention to the loss of individual motivation, as there is no incentive for state-owned enterprises to innovate or adapt to the changes in the demand. The entrepreneur's initiative is based on his or her material interests resulting from the ownership of the business. This, therefore, fundamentally disproves Marx's assumption that individuals are trying to make the best for the whole society.

Mises emphasizes the role of entrepreneurs in capitalism as well and he points out that they do not have any substitute in socialism. He writes that entrepreneurs are "speculators, promoters, investors and moneylenders." He continues claiming that they are the driving force of progress and they would be missed in socialism: "Nobody has ever suggested that the socialist commonwealth could invite the promoters and speculators to continue their speculations and then deliver their profits to the common chest" (Mises 1998, p. 709). Kirzner agrees about the importance of capitalists for the dynamism of the economic systems:

> *The success which capitalist market economies display is the result of a powerful tendency for less efficient, less imaginative courses of productive action to be replaced by newly discovered superior ways of serving consumers – by producing better goods and/or by taking advantage of hitherto unknown, but available, sources of resource supply. The theory focuses on the concept of discovery.*
>
> *(Kirzner 1997, p. 20)*

He continues that "the justice of the system is often criticised on the grounds that profits have not been earned or deserved, that they are pure surplus captured at the expense of labourers and/or of consumers." He concludes that the profit is reward for the entrepreneurs' discoveries and it comes into existence as a result of acts of discovery (ibidem).

Rothbard generally summarizes that the central planners would have problems balancing the stationary system, and he mistrusts their abilities to achieve economic growth. He writes:

> *A centrally prohibited economy, irrational and inefficient enough for given ends and given means and techniques at any point of time, is all the more incompetent if a flow of inventions and new developments are desired in a society. Bureaucracy, incompetent enough to plan a stationary system, is vastly more incompetent at planning a progressive one.*
>
> (*Rothbard 2009*, p. 961)

To summarize, Marxist economic thoughts are based on the idea of surplus-value that is produced by the labour force and appropriated by capitalists. The main goal of the socialist economy was due to it elimination of this exploitation of man by man. In socialism, the means of production were supposed to be owned by all inhabitants (in practice by the state). The natural unavoidable consequence was the nationalization of the means of production. The next inescapable step was central planning. The ideological construct had several further consequences, such as the monopolization of the economy. Theory of socialist economy has been criticized since its inception. Critics of the socialist system mostly target the theoretical settings of the system. In this chapter, we created the ideological framework for the description of the formal settings of the centrally planned model in Czechoslovakia, which is analyzed in the following chapter.

3 Formal settings of central planning in Czechoslovakia

The socialist economy was supposed to react to negative aspects of the functioning of the capitalist economy and create an ideal society characterized by harmony and abundance. The respective socialist countries and societies had their specifics, and due to it their applied economic policies diverged although they generally were supposed to follow the SU model. The foundations were thus similar in all the countries.

The previous chapter described the theoretical/ideological Marxist-Leninist framework. This chapter answers the question of how this ideology transformed into a formal centrally planned model in Czechoslovakia (e.g. how the planning mechanism was organized). This chapter is thus closely tied with the previous one and prepares ground for the following chapter and its analyses of the everyday functioning of the system. The main goal of this chapter is to describe the formal model of the planning system that functioned in socialist Czechoslovakia. We follow the ideological framework and specific aspects of socialism that were described in Section 2.2. We start in an analogous way with the leading role of the Communist party (3.1). Then we concentrate on the theoretical attitude towards ownership development (3.2). Following the previous logic, we deal with the central planning system in Czechoslovakia in the next section (3.3), and the fourth is dedicated to more specific aspects of the system (3.4). The general attitude of this chapter is descriptive. These theoretical descriptions should help the reader to understand the practical aspects of the planning system (Chapter 4).

The text includes several citations from Czechoslovak constitutions and laws because the formal settings were naturally based on the legal system. We deem the language and message of the legal acts illustrative to socialist mentality.

3.1 The role of the Communist Party

The Communist Party played the key role in the communist ideology (Chapter 2) as well as in the everyday practice of the socialist regime (including functioning of the economy, see Chapter 4). Several aspects of this functioning were already mentioned in Chapter 1, which described the overall environment. The leading role of the party was codified by the 1960 constitution. The exact formulation was (Art. 4):

> *The guiding force in society and in the State is the vanguard of the working class, the Communist Party of Czechoslovakia, a voluntary militant alliance of the most active and most politically conscious citizens from the ranks of the workers, farmers and intelligentsia.*
>
> *(Act No. 100/1960Coll., Constitution of the Czechoslovak Socialist Republic)*

Naturally, the leading role of the Communist Party was not limited to society, but it was fully manifested in its directing of the economy as well. However, in Haba's words, the Communist Party implemented its leading role by political means. It meant that the economy was not governed directly by orders to economic institutions but throughout the Party's ideological, political, cadre and control activities. Moreover, the policy was carried out by communists working in state and economic institutions, and in mass and social organizations (Hába et al. 1988). In this respect, the Communist Party was hierarchical. Diagram 3.1 shows the interconnection of the economic units with state bodies. The role of the Party in the economic system is more deeply developed in the following chapter.

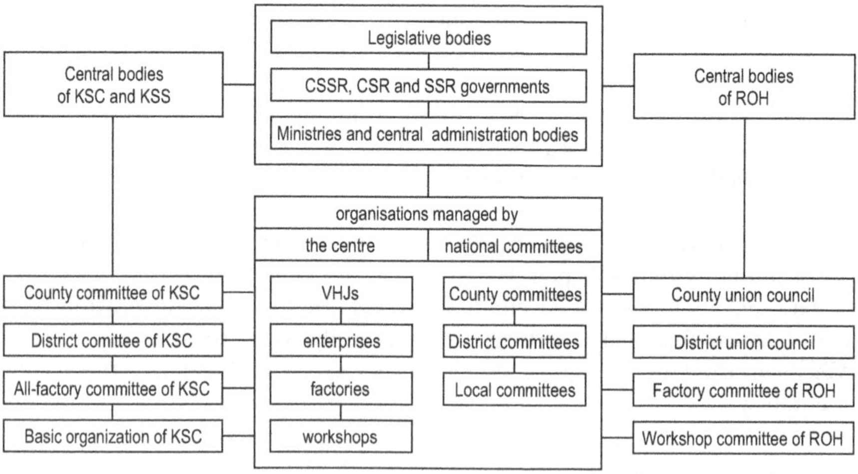

Diagram 3.1 Organizational arrangements of the unity of policy and economy for the national economy management

Source: Rozsypal et al. (1981)

3.2 Ownership – nationalization

The very core of Marxist ideology was in eliminating private property. This transition had to inevitably appear in the formal settings of the centrally planned model (as well as in practice). The spring of 1948 saw the second phase of post-war nationalization, according to Act No. 114 and 115/1948 Coll. The scale of industrial sectors where all enterprises were subject to nationalization significantly widened. In some sectors, expropriation criteria were based on the degree of technological equipment or the volume of yearly output (e.g., saw mills, brickworks, mills, etc.). In other industrial sectors, expropriation applied to enterprises with more than 50 employees. Among enterprises that were nationalized were wholesale companies, foreign trade companies, travel agencies, printing industries, and health resorts. Although the law offered compensation for the expropriated property, its claiming was hampered by such a complicated system of prerequisites that, in practice, there was no compensation granted at all (Půlpán 1993).

The common/state ownership in Czechoslovakia was anchored in the socialist constitutions. Already the first Constitution of 1948 stated in Article XII:

> (1) The economic system of the Czechoslovak Republic rests:
>
> On the nationalization of mineral wealth, industry, the wholesale trade and of finance;
>
> On the ownership of the land in accordance with the principle "The land belongs to those who till it";
>
> On the protection of small and medium-sized enterprise, and on the inviolability of personal property.
>
> (2) The entire national economy of the Czechoslovak Republic shall serve the People. In this public interest the State directs all economic activity by a Uniform Economic Plan.
>
> (Act No. 150/1948 Coll., Constitution of the Czechoslovak Republic)

The implementation of the land reform went hand in hand with what was termed the "socialization of the village," which was characterized by collectivization in agriculture. In its early stages, collectivization was voluntary, but as of 1950, agricultural labourers were forced to join the cooperatives. Collectivization was heavily propagated by the Communist Party. It is important to note that in legal terms a member of the cooperative was still the owner of the land that he or she brought to the cooperative. However, such ownership was in fact circumscribed and the owner was not allowed to carry out and benefit from his or her property rights, because the law allowed the cooperative to use the land as a building site for cooperative activities (Půlpán 1993).

The 1960 Constitution further cemented the common ownership in the Czechoslovak economy. It defined two main forms of ownership – state and cooperative. It formally allowed small businesses to be private, but this measure was not applicable in practice. All citizens were expected to protect socialist ownership. For more details, see Box 3.1.

Box 3.1 Ownership aspects in the 1960 Constitution

Article 8 declared:

(1) Socialist ownership has two basic forms: state ownership, which is ownership by the people as a whole (national property), and cooperative ownership (property of people\'s co-operatives).
(2) National property is particularly: the mineral wealth and basic sources of power; the main areas of forests, rivers, natural therapeutic sources; means of industrial production, public transport and communications; banks and insurance institutions; broadcasting, television, and motion picture enterprises, and the most important social institutions, such as health facilities, schools, and scientific institutes.
(3) Land joined for the purpose of joint co-operative cultivation shall be in the joint use of unified agricultural co-operatives.

The following Articles (9 and 10) specify the possibilities of other forms of ownership:

> Within the limits of the socialist economic system small private enterprises, based on the labour of the owner himself and excluding exploitation of another\'s labour power, shall be permitted.
>
> The citizen\'s personal ownership of consumer goods, particularly articles of personal and domestic use, family houses, as well as savings derived from labour, shall be inviolable.

Companies were supposed to be custodians of the national property (Article 11):

> The State shall establish economic organizations, particularly national enterprises, which shall, as independent legal persons, be entrusted with the administration of part of the national property.

The citizens had an obligation to protect socialist ownership (Article 35):

> Citizens shall be in duty bound to protect and strengthen socialist ownership as the inviolable foundation of the socialist social order and the source of the welfare of the working people, the wealth and strength of the country (Act No. 100/1960 Coll., Constitution of the Czechoslovak Socialist Republic).

The conclusion is that there were just two allowed forms of ownership of companies (or other bigger economic entities) in the centrally planned system – state and cooperative ownership. Oliva, as a proponent of the regime, added that the socialist state acted as an entrepreneur on behalf of society and that it was no longer private ownership but society (socialistic) ownership (Oliva 1952). Similarly, Hába, the author of à textbook about central planning, wrote about social ownership or in fact about "all-society" (celospolečenský) ownership. He believed that the pivotal characteristic was that social ownership unified the subjects instead of dividing them because in the socialist society the citizens were at one moment owners as well as producers (employees). All were supposed to be equal owners of the means of production. In his view, it was the way to avoid both the exploitation of man by man and class division of the society because there was no special class in the society that would differentiate by its ownership of the means of production (Hába et al. 1988). In socialism, the all-society ownership was expressed by state ownership.

The practical process of nationalization in Czechoslovakia is described in the following chapter, which deals with the everyday functioning of the economy. Private ownership of the means of production was totally eliminated and the state controlled everything. However, Doležalová mentions that the "transition of Czechoslovakia to socialism did not follow any coherent theory nor theory of Marxism (or Marxism-Leninism). [. . .] Establishing of common ownership of the means of production did not mean accomplishing of a theoretical postulate, it was a practical political step" (Doležalová 2009, p. 81).

3.3 Description of the planning model

Nationalization of the economy was accompanied by the introduction of central planning. The centrally planned models in nearly all major European socialist countries were founded on the Soviet model with five-year plans. This model was imposed on the countries when the communist parties came to power. The planning was globally based on the propositions of the system's ideologists (Chapter 2). However, the models in respective countries had specific settings that further diverged in time (for example the Hungarian case). Kornai defined the traditional model of centrally planned economies as a coherent system, with functioning causal relationships, where each component (tier) determined the next component (Kornai 1992).

The centre was expected to plan (at the minimum level) the main aspects of the whole production. Consequently, the goal of the individual companies was maximizing the effort to achieve these planned goals.

The 1960 Constitution of the Czechoslovak Socialist Republic defined the main characteristics of the economic system as well. The system was based on central planning. The plans were prepared for five-year periods. Moreover, all inhabitants and all companies were obliged to maximize their effort to meet the plans – see Box 3.2.

Box 3.2 Centrally planned economy characteristics anchored in the 1960 Constitution

Article 7:

The socialist economic system, in which the means of production are socially owned and the entire national economy directed by plan, ensures, with the active co-operation of all citizens, a tremendous development of production and a continuous rise in the living standard of the working people.

Article 12 continued:

(1) The entire national economy shall be directed by the state plan for the development of the national economy, which shall be drawn up and implemented with the widest active participation of the working people.
(2) The plan for the development of the national economy and culture, usually worked out for a period of five years, shall be promulgated as law and shall be binding for that period as the basis of all planning activity by state organs and economic organizations.

And the constitution undertook all participants to maximize effort to meet the plan:

(1) Every organization and every citizen who is allotted any task connected with the fulfilment of the state plan for the development of the national economy shall exert every effort and show the utmost initiative to carry out this task with the maximum success.
(2) All economic organizations shall systematically create the material, technological and organizational conditions for their activity, in accordance with the long-term plans for the development of the national economy, in such a way that their planned tasks may be fulfilled (Act No. 100/1960 Coll., Constitution of the Czechoslovak Socialist Republic).

The following subsections deal with the specifics of the planned system. We deal first of all with the general principles of planning (3.3.1), definition of the main entities in the planning system (3.3.2), different types of plans and their mutual relationship (3.3.3), the process of the plan's creation (3.3.4) and description of the use of the main balance method in the system (3.3.5).

3.3.1 Principles of planning

The planning process was supposed to be based on several principles of planning built on the Soviet pattern. The following seven principles were provided by Rozsypal in a textbook describing the planning process in Czechoslovakia (Rozsypal et al. 1981):

1. Partiality – the plan was the main condition for realization of the Communist Party program. A base on which the communists mobilized working masses to fulfil the goals of the construction of socialism to meet the goals of party congresses and goals of development of the communist society.
2. Scientism – findings by all scientific branches were projected into the plans.
3. Democratic centralism – declared division of power and responsibility, consolidation and deepening of central state planning governing, broadening of power of bodies of corporate sphere and participation of employees. The party conceived its program on the bases of the respect of objective needs of development of the socialist society and the interests of the working class and working people.
4. Obligatory state plans.
5. Complexity – the state plan had to embrace all aspects of the reproduction process.
6. Long range and continuousness of prognoses of the governing subjects.
7. Unity of state plans – factual and methodical interconnectedness of different plan levels:
   - five-year and one-year,
   - regional and branches,
   - material and value, and
   - state and plans of all socialistic institutions and authorities.

3.3.2 Definition of the main entities in the planning hierarchy

The planning hierarchy obtained (strategic) orders from the Communist Party. The government and, in practice, the State Planning Commission (SPK – Státní plánovací komise) were at the top of the planning pyramid. The SPK was responsible for preparation of the plans and checking of the planning and production processes. It passed the plans at the next level to other central institutions – to the responsible ministries. The middle planning units in industry were, until 1988, the so-called production economic units (Výrobně hospodářské jednotky – VHJ). There were several different models of this economic structure. At the bottom of the hierarchy were individual socialist enterprises. The alternative versions of the organization structures are depicted in Diagram 3.2.

The economic centre (Federal government, State Planning Commission, ministries)

The State planning commission[1] stood at the top of the planning hierarchy. It was founded by Act No. 41/1959 Coll., on the State Planning Commission, in June 1959. In practice, it acted as a ministry and its chairman/minister held

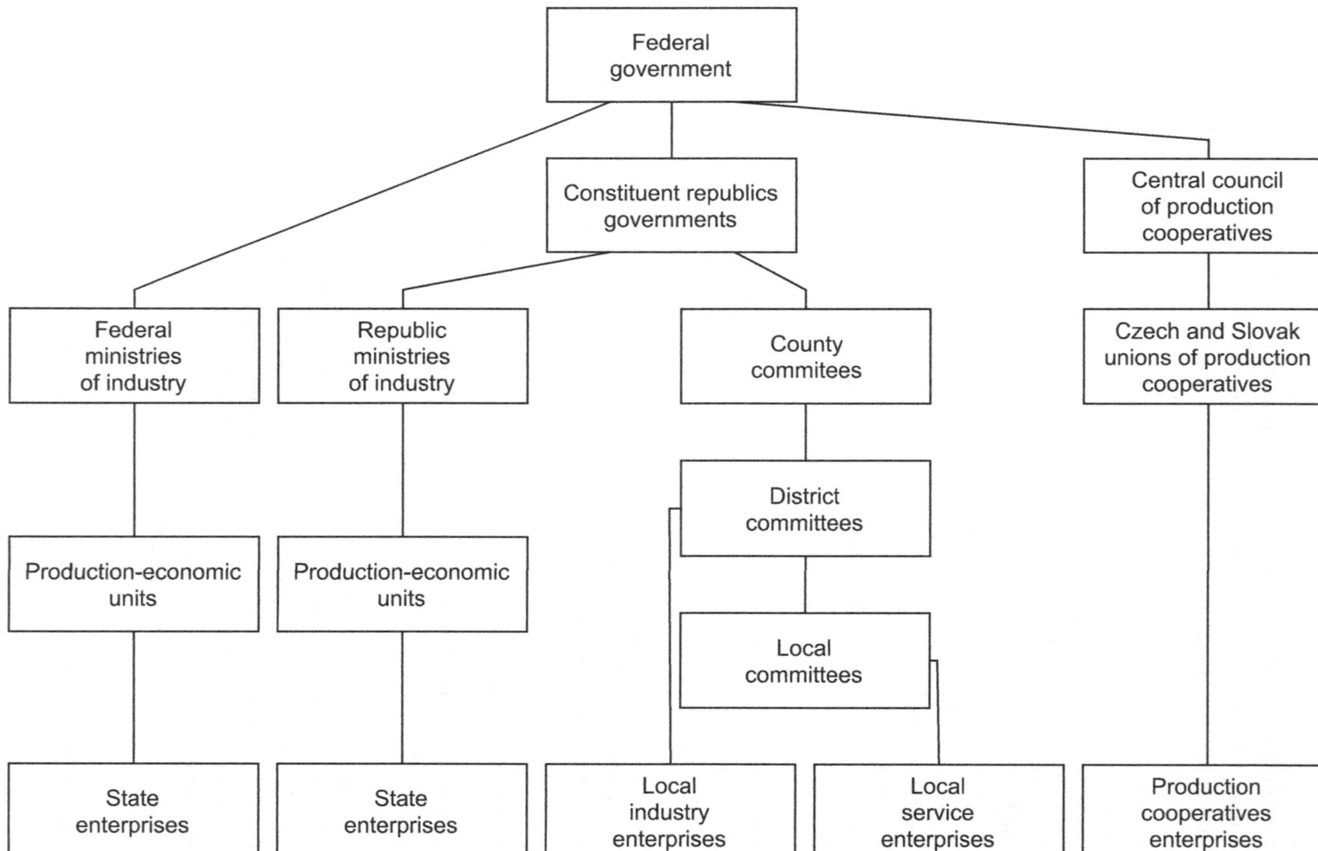

Diagram 3.2 Organization structures in the Czechoslovak economy

Source: Teichová (1995)

a post in the government. In addition to the chairman, the Commission comprised of deputies, several economic ministries, and important representatives of economic life, science, and technology. The members were named and removed by the president on the government's proposal. The planning activity itself was performed by the administrative apparatus. The main objective of the SPK was to devise a proposal of the plan for the development of the socialist economy (five-year as well as one-year operative plans). All plans in the economy had to go through this institution. The commission's plan proposals were consequently approved by the government. Apart from that, the Commission prepared substantial changes in the price system. Among other tasks, it checked the fulfilment of the plan and issued methodical instructions that defined the form and terms of the plans submitting process (Průcha 1988). The plans were subsequently passed via the Ministries to the production economic units.

Production-economic units (VHJ)

The middle elements in the planning chains (and in fact a third tier) in the planning hierarchy were called production-economic units (VHJ). They were supposed to play an elementary managing role above the companies and to divide the plans to individual socialist companies or more generally to the subordinated units. But at the same time, they played the middleman role in negotiations between the individual companies and the centre. Their purpose was to realize the goals of the technical, production, and economic character of the entrusted companies.

The VHJs were introduced into the planning system in April 1958. Until that time, hundreds of companies were subordinated directly to the respective ministry. The companies were joined according to their activity under a main company and its new directorate-general (generální ředitelství – GŘ). VHJ can be understood as a trust with different companies or divisions. The VHJs were directed by the ministry and organized into branches and main business syndicates (trusty podniků). Production of the same industry was joined into a VHJ (these were naturally easier to govern from the centre than individual companies). The VHJ was directly governed by its corresponding branch ministry. Generally, the VHJs existed in three different organization-legal structures after 1974: Specialized enterprise (oborovýpodnik), concern (koncern), and trust (trust podniků), as can be seen in Diagram 3.3. The differences were in the level of autonomy, legal status and in subordinated units.

For the overall organization structure of industry according to the VHJs at the end of 1985, see Table 3.1. The most common form was trust followed by concern. The number of specialized enterprises was much lower. The number of employees per VHJ was very high regardless of the organization structure of the VHJ (see the last column of the table). Federal or Republic Ministries managed all together 114 VHJs with 1,109 organizations (including GŘ) and 2,709 thousand employees. Additionally, there were 54 industrial organizations

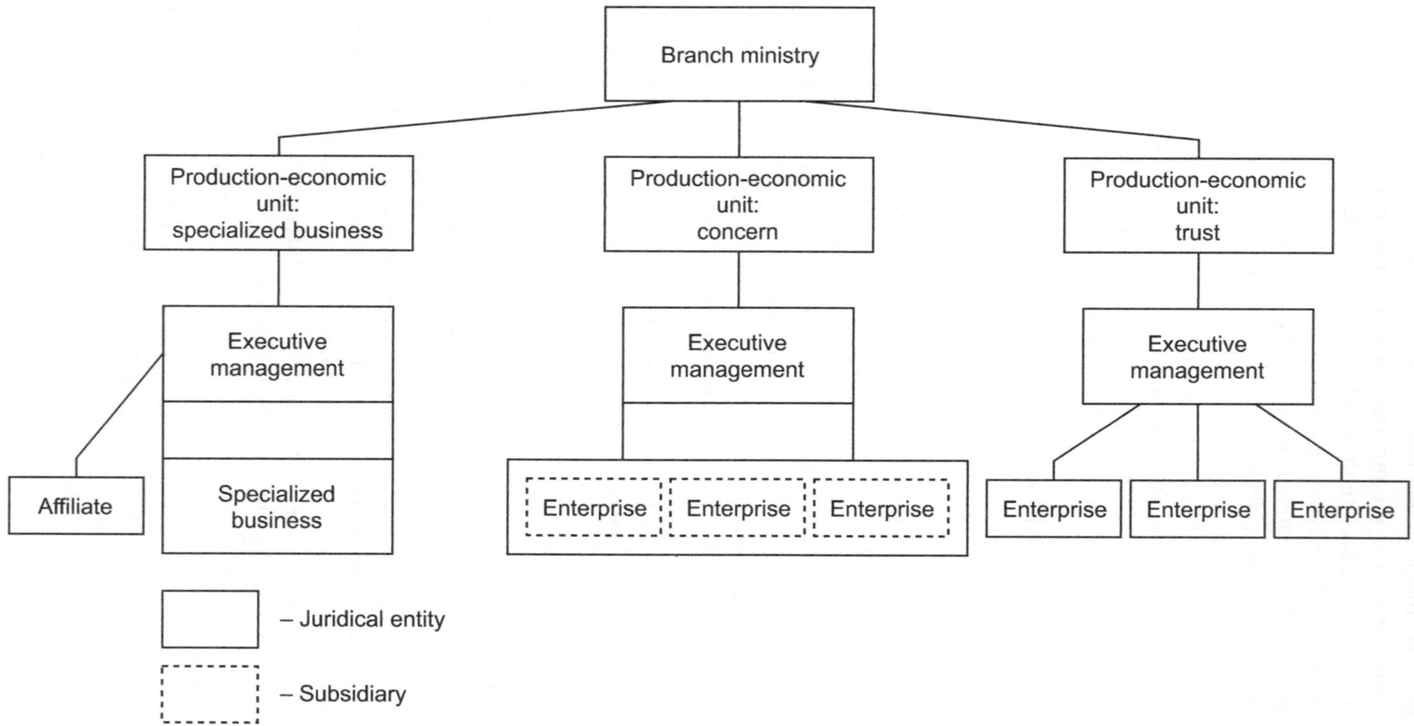

Diagram 3.3 Organization structure in different forms of production-economic units

Source: Teichová (1995)

Table 3.1 Organization structure of industry according to different forms of management (31 December 1984).

Level of management		*Industry altogether*	*Of which*			
			Trusts	*Concerns*	*Specialized enterprises*	*Directly managed organizations*
Federal	a	68	12	27	2	27
	b	538	182	352	4	–
	c	1,591	597	918	47	29
Czech government	a	62	19	11	17	15
	b	383	221	111	51	–
	c	801	432	205	151	13
Slovak government	a	35	18	1	5	11
	b	183	166	9	8	–
	c	352	328	7	10	7
County committees	a	–	–	–	–	–
	b	21	–	–	–	21
	c	44	–	–	–	44

Source: Češka (2013)

a = number of VHJs; b = number of enterprises subordinated to the VHJs; c = number of workers (in thousands).

subordinated directly to branch ministries (with 51 thousand employees) and 21 organizations of local industry directly governed by County Committee (with 43 thousand employees) (Průcha 1988).

The sectors of the biggest companies (VHJ) at the beginning of the 1970s are depicted in Table 3.2.

The system of the VHJs was abandoned at the very end of the communist era. The government decided in 1988 to simplify the structure of the governing of companies to just two tiers – ministry and "state company" (státní podnik). Průcha (1988) mentions that the reasons were the negative aspects of the functioning of the VHJs – in the strengthening or creation of monopolies, in the growth of the administrative, in the application of bureaucratic management methods and creation of irrational extensive administrative structures in some companies. The individual companies obtained broader economic and financial autonomy after the application of the reforms. One of the significant changes was in establishing a socialist self-government in the form of a working collective. There was a possibility to elect the directors, who were responsible not only to the founder (ministry) but to the working collective as well. Most of the VHJ were transformed into "state companies" in 1988 and 1989. For the absolute majority of our researched period, the Ministries founded the VHJs or/and directorate-general that consequently governed the respective companies. Thus, we will not consider the formal changes that took place at the end of the 1980s in the empirical part of the book (Chapter 4). In fact, our respondents

Table 3.2 Sectoral structure of the 50 biggest Czechoslovak companies (VHJs) in 1971

Sector	*Number of companies*	*Number of employees*
Coal mining	2	118,435
Extraction of non-ferrous ores	1	31,765
Industry of stone and grounds	1	24,085
Food industry	3	54,303
Textile	7	277,052
Leather industry	2	63,932
Woodworking industry	3	85,529
Paper industry	1	29,600
Printing industry	1	18,420
Chemical industry	3	115,885
Rubber industry and plastics production	1	24,816
Glassmaking	2	43,463
Metallurgy	6	290,394
Mechanical engineering	11	421,226
Electrotechnical industry	1	58,998
Radio and telecommunication equipment	1	82,055
Automotive	1	137,240
Aviation industry	1	26,485
Electricity, gas, and steam production	1	40,228
Production of construction materials	1	18,977
Total	**50**	**2,331,886 [sic]**

Source: Teichová (1995)

mostly interchange the different VHJs' structures and due to this we use just the term "VHJ" for all these organization forms.

Socialist enterprise

The basic bottom units in the hierarchical structure were socialist enterprises – e.g., in industry socialist industrial enterprise. These units were in common/state ownership. Průcha (1988) writes that there were 867 industrial national enterprises with 2.7 million employees in 1985. They employed on average 3,145 personnel in an enterprise out of which 2,149 were workers. In addition, there existed industrial companies of local industry and manufacturing cooperatives. The local industry produced just around 2% of the goods and employed 3.8% of the industrial employees in the middle of the 1980s (Průcha 1988).

The highest inner-enterprise organization unit were production plants – especially in large enterprises. The enterprises combined detached production units as well. The lower tiers were operation, workshop, and workplace. The organization structure of the management of a typical socialist company is depicted in Diagram 3.4.

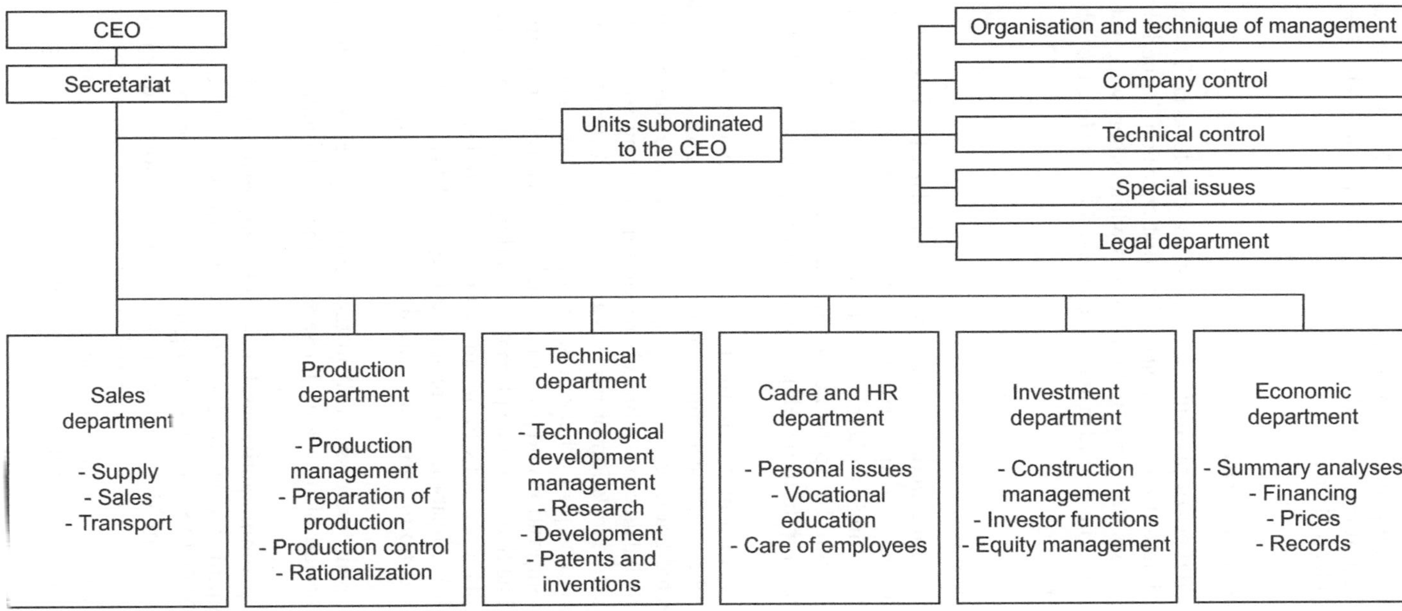

Diagram 3.4 The organization structure of the management of a typical socialist company

Source: Teichová (1995)

All of these levels of the production chains described were subordinated to all forms of the central planning. As respondent Bažant (Meopta) in Vaněk and Krátká said, the plan was delegated, to the very last detail, to each of the workshops (Vaněk and Krátká 2014).

3.3.3 Types of the central plan

There were several types of planning in socialist Czechoslovakia. The plans can be divided according to time and subject. The first criterion defined that some of the plans/prognoses were prepared for decades while others were just for one year or even shorter. The second criterion reflected different forms of plans (e.g., state or monetary).

Plans according to time

As far as time is concerned, the regime created plans for periods ranging from decades to one-year operative plans. The shorter plans were the more binding ones. The longest plans were ordered to be prepared by the 1970 law for periods from 10 up to 20 years. They were more like strategies. We can count among them developmental central program and state target program.

The medium-term planes were the five-year plans. They specified foremost the pace of growth, macroeconomic proportions, the goals of the development of the selected branches and social sphere. They were complex plans that were supposed to balance inter-branch relationships. They were expected to put emphasis on the revelation of reserves and improving the efficiency of the economic system. The plan otherwise set among others the main directions of the investment composition and growth of the living standard of the inhabitants (Průcha 1988). The five-year state plans were binding. They were imposed onto the enterprises sphere via tasks, limits, and set priorities and with the help of the tools of economic stimulation. The recipients (e.g., the VHJs) had to incorporate them into their economic goals and distribute them among the subordinated organizations.

The five-year plans were specified in the shorter/operative plans that were applied for the period of one year. These were the most binding plans in the system.

Besides these planning activities, long- and medium-term plans were supposed to be coordinated at the level of the Council of Mutual Economic Assistance (COMECON). It was an organization of the socialist economies, which was founded in 1949 and its task was to promote mutual trade and cooperation. Cooperation was expected in the areas of planning of individual branches, consultation, and development of the complex programs of science and technology. For a simplified scheme of the plans creating process, see Diagram 3.5.

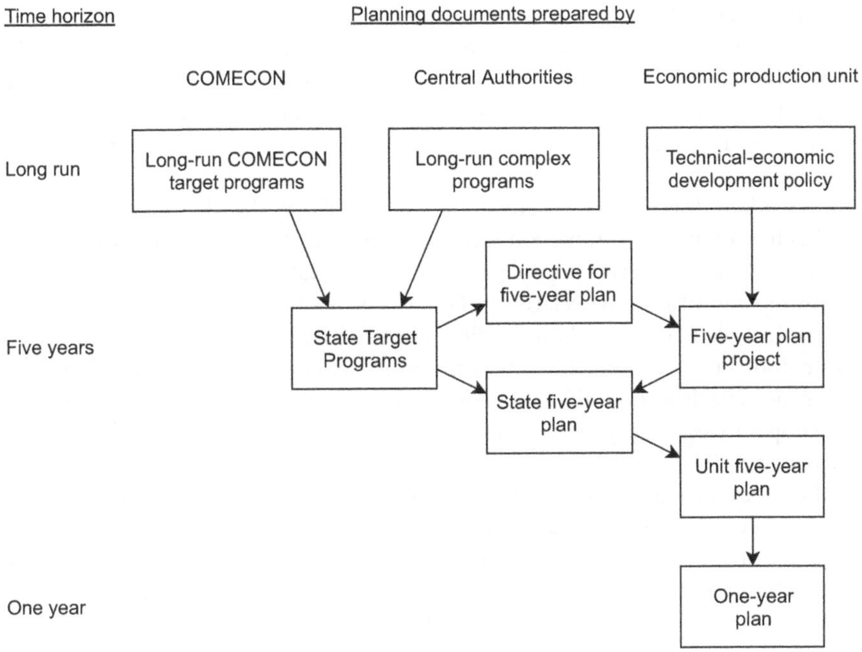

Diagram 3.5 Simplified planning scheme after 1980

Source: Stevens (1985)

Plans according to subject

The second attitude towards the planning process was according to subjects. The system of economic plans embraced the following plans:

1 State plan for the development of the national economy of the ČSSR, ČSR, and SSR (státní plán rozvoje národního hospodářství ČSSR, ČSR a SSR).
2 State budgets ČSSR, ČSR, SSR.
3 Monetary plan.
4 Economic plans:
   - central federal and national institutions
   - directorate-general/production economic units
   - socialist organizations (state, cooperatives, economic, budgetary, and state-funded institution)
   - national (county, district, and local) committees – for companies in their responsibility
5 Regional plans.

We discuss the individual parts of the planning system more deeply in the following paragraphs.

State plan for the development of the national economy – The state plan for the development of the national economy consisted of two parts. The first dealt with the summarizing indicators of the economy and indicators of economic efficiency. The other part embraced plans for the branches, sectional plans and special reports.

The plans for branches determined the goals of the development of the individual branches in the economy – e.g., in industry, the volume of production, plan of sales, structure of production, innovation programs, demand for consumption of raw materials etc. There were 16 branches in the system with individual plans: Industrial production, construction, agriculture, forest industry, water industry, transport, telecommunications, inner trade, tourism, foreign trade, education, healthcare, welfare system, services, local economies, and production of cooperatives. The plan for international trade embraced foreign exchange plan as well (Průcha 1988).

The sectional plans dealt with tasks that concerned more branches of the national economy – e.g., plan of development of science and technology, standardization, development of housing, protection of environment, wages, plan of price development, financial plan etc. The special compositions dealt foremost with tasks of socialist integration (meaning cooperation among the COMECON members).

The plans for branches and sectional plans had normative, table, and explanation parts. The normative part defined the main directions of development and binding and directed tasks that were expressed in natural or monetary indicators (e.g., tasks of sales of the industrial productions structured to exports, investment, inner trade, import limits, investment limits etc.). They were divided according to organizations in the Czech and the Slovak parts of the federation and captured expected development. They were allowed to lay out the plan up to individual organizations (managed by federal or republic institutions).

State budgets – The budgets that were the most important part of the financial plans consisted of a one-year budget and a five-year outlook. The incomes were mostly from the socialist economy (taxes, levies, etc.), from the citizens (taxes, fees, etc.), and from other incomes. The expenditures were directed to the national economy, cultural, and social measures, defence, safety, and administration. The fulfilment of the one-year budget was depicted in the state final account. The budget proposals and the final accounts were presented to the parliaments. For a typical budget, see Chapter 5.

Monetary plan – The monetary plan determined the development of the monetary system in Czechoslovakia and guided monetary relationships both inside and outside the country. It was created by the Czechoslovak State Bank (SBČS) and consisted of cash, credit, and foreign currency plans. The first determined the volume of incomes and expenditures of the issuing bank in cash and increase or decrease of money in circulation. The credit plan depicted volume, structure and use of free monetary funds and incomes of different sections. The foreign currency plan embraced payment and credit relationships with abroad and it was divided according to currencies.

Economic plans – The economic plans were assembled by the federal and central institutions, the middle chains in the planning hierarchy and the socialist organizations in the form of five-year and one-year plans. They specified the tasks given by the state plans and state budgets. They embraced similar information as the state plans for development and they ensured interconnections. The background materials were based on the past as well as expected development, and they laid out directives for the five-year plan. Consultations took place with superior institutions and on the horizontal levels with suppliers and customers. The fulfilling of the plan was ensured by short-run operative planning.

In the industrial VHJs and companies, the plans were divided to plans of industrial production, sales and foreign trade, energetics, protection of the environment, development of science and technology, reproduction of basic funds, materially technical supply, labour and wages, financial plan, plans of costs, plans of rationalization programs, etc. Special parts of the plans contained programs of economic efficiency (Průcha 1988).

Regional plans – These plans were prepared for economic-administrative regions – counties, districts, and municipalities – or they were divided purposefully – e.g., the High Tatras – with an intention to promote development of the region.

3.3.4 Creation of the central plan

The plans were based on directions that were drawn by a congress of the Communist Party (Kabele 2013). The congresses took place (under normal circumstances) in five-year periods. In practice, for example the 17th Congress of the Communist Party of Czechoslovakia in March 1986 approved a document "The main directions of the economic and social development of the ČSSR for years 1986–90 with outlook till 2000" (Hlavní směry hospodářského a sociálního rozvoje ČSSR na léta 1986–90 a výhledy do roku 2000). This document was issued in advance of the Congress and the final version of the document from March 1986 became the basis for the setting of the tasks for the eighth five-year plan for period 1986–1990. This approval was followed by negotiations and specifications of the plan – see the following paragraph. The final version of the plan was approved by the Federal Assembly (Federální shromáždění) in the form of law in December 1986 (at the end of the first year of the five-year plan). The five-year plan embraced all main aspects of the economy (e.g., plans of cadres, personnel, and social development) in very fine detail – in practice almost identically to one-year plans. The final version was binding for the whole planning hierarchy. The complexity of the process in described in Diagram 3.6.

The process between issuing the Congress document and the final approval of the plan was not straightforward. The planning process generally followed the Directive No. 55/1965 Coll. It was a detailed methodical guide for the SPK to proceed with the creation of the five-year plan. It was general and thus possible to stay in effect for 25 years. It instructed every entity that was a part of the

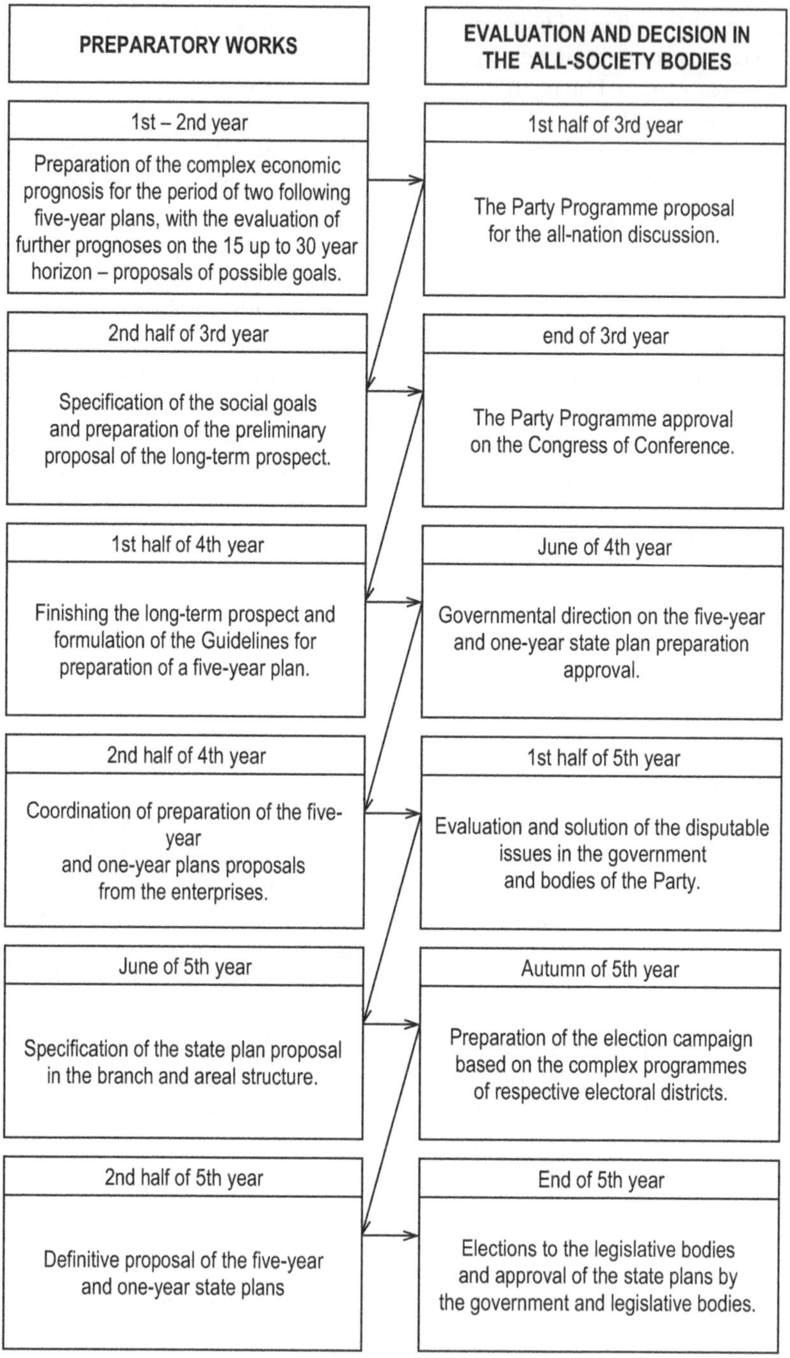

Diagram 3.6 Timeline of the creation of a central plan

Source: Rozsypal et al. (1981)

economy about what it was expected to do to contribute to the plan creation. Furthermore, it attempted to account for the efficiency of the overall system. The respective plans and analyses for which the directive provided methodology were as follows:

I Basic analysis of efficiency

Plans for production and other performances

II Industrial production, supplies, and their use
III Building industry
IV Agriculture and purchase of agricultural products
V Forestry
VI Water management
VII Transportation
VIII Communications
IX Geological survey
X Internal trade
XI Foreign trade and foreign currency plan
XII Education and culture
XIII Healthcare
XIV Social welfare
XV Local economy
XVI Production cooperatives

Conducting and cross-sectional plans

XVII Science and technology development
XVIII Investment construction
XIX Projects
XX Labour
XXI Finance, expenditures and gross income
XXII Prices
XXIII Regional development
XXIV National Committees

The directive was rather descriptive – it provided the definition of each and every part of the plan that was to be prepared. For example, the plan for agriculture was, according to the directive, supposed to provide foodstuff for the population and ingredients for the food industry. The basis for the plan was land available for the agriculture industry (Directive No. 55/1965 Coll.).

In the preparation of the respective five-year plan, it was necessary to specify the tasks for the participants. The SPK prepared "Guidelines for preparation of a five-year plan" (Rozsypal et al. 1981) – e.g., Guidelines for preparation of the 8th five-year plan (Směrnice pro sestavení návrhu 8. pětiletého plánu). These guidelines represented the first version of the plan – they defined relations between basic macroaggregates, especially the pace of the national product growth, its division into accumulation (investments) and consumption, etc. They also set tasks for all branches and prominent fields of the national economy (industry, agriculture, building industry, transport industry, internal and foreign trade, and the non-productive sphere). These tasks were partly defined in natural units (e.g., coal mining or steel production). In most cases, however, they were expressed in financial aggregates, either in absolute values (volume of production of an aggregated branch), or growth values (planned growth percentage). Centrally planned quantities included the planned development of employment, related wage funds, and numerous so-called quantitative indicators (growth of labour productivity, profit etc.). These central guidelines were itemized for individual branches (ministries) which further itemized them for production economic units (companies and corporate associations). Centrally formulated tasks had to be transformed into partial tasks that were clear and easy for companies to understand (e.g., gross value of production, or wage fund). The companies were then expected to prepare their own plans which specified the way how to meet the imposed plan. For illustration, the Guidelines set the task, for instance, that a plant production in agriculture would be intensified on the expenses of animal production and the whole of agriculture would increase by 3%. The enterprises were confronted with this vaguely specified task and had to prepare their own plans based on the Guidelines. Then the two plans were confronted, both sides typically found out that they differed (either in inputs or outputs), and negotiations began. All in all, it was a gigantic task. The negotiations had to lead to balancing the whole economy. The centre (SPK) used a balance method to achieve it (see Section 3.3.5) and the negotiations de facto accomplished it.

In the second stage, the production-economic units (VHJs) after consultation with the companies developed their proposals for the five-year plan based on itemized guidelines – these were summarized by respective branch ministries and submitted to the central planning authority. The second wave of balancing took place, which usually revealed that the proposals of companies differed from the centre's proposals. Generally, the centre expected too much and the companies proposed too little. Negotiations followed, usually resulting in the correction of the original plans. Corrections were mostly mutual but one-sided ones were not uncommon. Binding government tasks played a somewhat specific preferential role in the system – see for example Box Škoda Car in Chapter 5. They were highly prioritized but at the same time the government expected accurate meeting of the plan. All the previous steps eventually led to a specified, final version of the five-year plan. Its basic parameters were at the end of the process approved by the parliament as a law.

In the third stage, the planning centre, branch ministries and production-economic units worked on one-year implementation plans in the same way. They became laws as well – for an example of the law, see Box 3.3.

Box 3.3 Act No. 129/1985 Coll. The Act of the Czech National Council on the state plan for the development of the national economy of the Czech Socialist Republic for 1986

§ 1

The basic objective of the state plan for the development of the national economy of the Czechoslovak Socialist Republic for 1981 (hereinafter the "state plan") is to ensure a further smooth and proportional development of the national economy, above all by increasing the efficiency and quality of all work and thus improving the satisfaction of material and cultural needs of the citizens and consolidation of their social security.

§ 2

(1) The principle objectives of the state plan are

(a) to achieve a 2.8% rise in the national income and to cover its growth predominantly (about 93%) by growth in social labour productivity;
(b) ensure planned national income growth by adequate sectoral development; to increase industrial production by 2.7%, construction work by construction organizations by 2.8% and agricultural production by 2.6%;
(c) to ensure further strengthening of the role of science and research and promote concentration of the research and development sector on solving the key tasks of the development of the national economy and to increase the technological and economic level of production and product quality;
(d) to secure market supplies in order to gradually improve their assortment in response to public requirements;
(e) advance export growth over import; to continue in deeper socialist economic integration with the Member States of the Council for Mutual Economic Assistance;
(f) to ensure maximum efficiency in the consumption of raw materials, fuels, and energy and to maximize their efficiency in production and secure general conditions for reductions in energy and material demand in production;
(g) to create conditions for increasing the quality, technical level and operational reliability of the production and more consistent introduction of product innovations and introduction of new coveted products;
(h) to focus investments at the value of approx. CZK 150 billion on finalizing construction works and implementing new operational

capacities, to focus on modernization and reconstruction of selected basic resources and securing social priorities;
(i) be more consistent in rewarding based on labour productivity;

(2) To implement all the tasks of the national plan, it is necessary to use the measures adopted to improve the system of planned management of the national economy after 1980.

§ 3

The Government of the Czechoslovak Socialist Republic or, on the basis of its authorization, the Deputy Prime Minister of the Czechoslovak Socialist Republic and the Chairman of the State Planning Commission

(a) may, in the context of the preparation of the State Plan for the Development of the National Economy of the Czechoslovak Socialist Republic for the years 1981 to 1985, adjust the State Plan, even though it deviates from the indicators referred to in Article 2 (1) (a) and (b);
(b) ensure the specification of the value data of the State Plan at wholesale prices as of 1 January 1981.

§ 4

This Act shall enter into force as of 1 January 1981.

3.3.5 Balance method

Formally, the planned economy was absolutely balanced. To achieve this task, the centre (SPK) widely applied a balance method. It was constituted by a comparison of "resources" and "use," between income and expenditure, and among the development of the respective branches. The aggregate of all balances constituted an internally interlocked system (Rozsypal et al. 1981). At the end of the process everything had to fit together.

There were several different forms of balances, such as material (metals, coal, electrical energy) and value (money), for example a balance of citizens' incomes and expenditures, state budget, labour – it set the needs and use of labour force or land division. Types are provided in Diagram 3.7.

The process of the creation of the plan for the whole economy was described in the previous subsection. Balancing the entire economy was an enormous task. It was necessary to prepare a balance of the whole economy (see Table 3.2). Moreover, it had to fit with inter-branch and inter-disciplinary balances and balances of respective (selected) products.

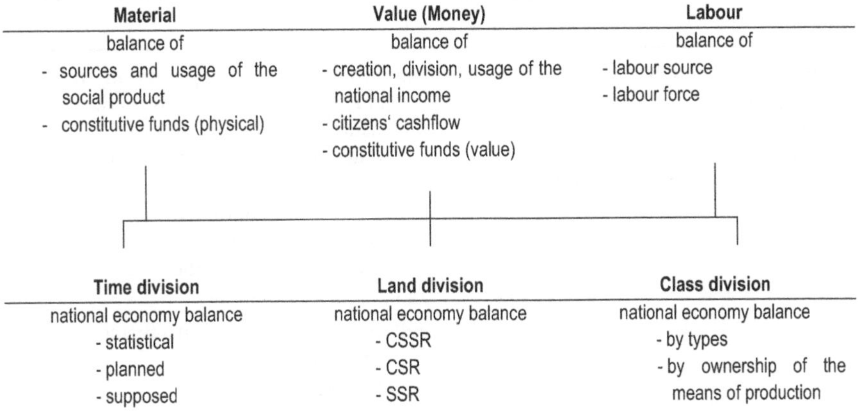

Diagram 3.7 Balance of the economy by the types of the reproduction process

Source: Rendl V. et al. (1988)

The complexity of the whole process is described by our respondent who worked as section chief in the SPK <ID040>, and who described the formal process in the following way:

> *The state plan always had some cross-sectors that just had to fit in. It surely started with the material aspect of production (pieces, tons, etc.), the balance sheet value point (index of, for example, gross production in industry, I believe later as of 1981, or 2) the so-called customized outputs, all in CZK, current prices reflecting their movement (and the basis of the state budget, and the currency and foreign exchange plan) and also in constant prices (and methodology), fixed at a certain date (1 January 1971, 1 January 1981, etc.) which eliminated changes in the prices, organizational structure, methodology, etc. and which enabled long-term comparability of data (coordination with statistics, re-pricing of wholesale prices, say once every five years). In addition, the plan had an organizational cross-section (vie the central managing authorities, i.e. the ministries, the VHJs, specialized enterprises, etc.) and finally, it had a regional cross-section (the Czech Republic/Slovakia). What is more, the five-year plan was further divided into one-year plans. These differed with every new five-year plan to reduce the volume of items in so-called binding nominal tasks of the state plan (production in the physical volume of strategic items – coal mining, steel production, cement, sulfuric acids, tires, etc., but of course not screws and nuts . . .) The key was always in the good balance among the individual elements.*

The crucial balance was the balance of resources and use of national product – see Table 3.3.

Table 3.3 Balance of resources and use of the social product

Resources	*Use*
a) Production of social (společenský) product (industry, agriculture, forestry, construction, haulage, telecommunication, trade, common catering and other branches)	a) Production consumption (industry, agriculture, forestry, construction, haulage, telecommunication, trade, common catering and other branches)
b) Imports	b) Final consumption (consumption in retail, on agricultural market, natural consumption, the others)
	c) Social consumption
	d) Accumulation (manufacturing and non-manufacturing funds)
	e) Reserves
	f) Exports

Source: Jelínek, J. (1984)

However, balances for several commodities were elaborated as well and the method was used in the very same way (see for an example Table 3.4 with balance for steel pipes). However, there was a limited number of these balances. The Minister of Finance – Mr. Lér said about the specific balances in the Parliament in December 1976 the following:

Table 3.4 Material balance for steel pipes (in tonnes) 1985

	1985
Production	1,554,553
Import total	148,374
a) centrally planned economies	13,472
b) market economies (all remaining countries)	134,902
other sources	5,538
Stocks of suppliers	
initial	66,309
final	76,668
Sources of supplies	1,698,086
for investment	–
for market funds	34,014
for export total	581,367
export to a)	493,165
export to b)	88,202
for other use	1,082,705
Supplies total	1,698,086

Source: Češka (2013)

> *The fifth five-year plan was constructed with the aid of some 110 or 115 material balances elaborated by the State Planning Commission and submitted to the government both as binding as well as indicative. In working on the sixth five-year plan, the material balances used reached 180. The number of balances thus increased substantially. When preparing a plan for this year, the number of material balances submitted by the Commission was around 160 and the plan for next year has about 190 of them. New balances have been added, for structural steel construction, for central heating boilers, for cables, for cast-iron pipes and for a number of other materials and products in order to synchronize the needs and production centrally and to create a smoother, more dynamic development among the sectors.*
>
> *(ČSSR, Federal Assembly of the Czechoslovak Socialist Republic 1976–1980)*

Rendl in the textbook on central planning admits that the method had its drawbacks. He writes that the balances expressed the final state and that they were static – set usually at 31 December. Thus, it could not incorporate changes that took place during the period, uneven development, etc. He adds that balance was not a guarantee of optimization. Due to higher level of aggregation there was possible shortage of specified types of good. The balance of labour market missed motivation, abilities, health of labour force, etc. (Rendl et al. 1988).

3.4 The specifics of the planning system

Several specific aspects of the ideological settings of the economic system were mentioned in the previous chapter. We follow the same pattern and deal with three topics – planning of labour market, non-monetary economy, and outer relationships. The last of the specific topics was the monopolization of the economy and elimination of competition. We have already described these settings in the previous text – we write that the global planning system de facto blocked competition and the organizational structures (including the VHJs) strongly limited numbers of companies in the economy.

3.4.1 Planning of labour market

The ideological framework expected the elimination of unemployment and full use of the labour force (see Chapter 2). But work was at the same time compulsory. Act No. 140/1961 Coll., Criminal Code set in §203: "Who permanently avoids honest work and obtains means of subsistence by prostitution, gambling or other dishonest ways, will be punished by imprisonment up to two years." Other acts set the punishment for "parasitism" by imprisonment up to one year or a financial penalty up to 5,000 CSK or forfeiting of property.

The centre designed the plan for an exact number of available labour force resources, as well as specific labour demand by companies. The planning was supposed to match the demand and supply – see Table 3.5. The statics of the balance method is well documented in the table because it did not count with (sudden) changes in population.

Table 3.5 Balance of labour force

Indicator	*1980*	*1985*	*1987*	*1988*
	Czechoslovak Socialist Republic			
A. Labour Force Resource (I. + II. + III. – IV. + V.)	**9,375,172**	**9,470,202**	**9,590,873**	**9,656,588**
I. Population in productive age	8,708,756	8,733,658	8,814,257	8,882,691
II. Working in post-productive age	652,732	699,311	745,197	741,433
III. Working commuters	x	x	x	x
IV. Workers leaving (Pracující vyjíždějíci)	–612	-1,040	-1,040	-936
V. Foreign nationals working in the Czechoslovak Socialist Republic	14,296	38,273	32,459	33,400
B. Division of labour resources (I. + II. + III. + IV. + V. + VI.)	**9,375,172**	**9,470,202**	**9,590,873**	**9,656,588**
I. Workers in the national economy with the only or full-time job	7,225,952	7,430,114	7,513,059	7,544,658
II. Women on maternity and other maternity leave	379,790	343,780	351,804	358,436
III. Pupils and students in productive age in schools	552,463	435,914	432,601	445,205
universities	143,954	138,555	135,254	136,005
colleges and vocational school (středních odborných a odborných)	219,691	171,872	163,738	168,836
high schools (gymnázium)	116,188	106,078	102,194	105,856
primary school	60,085	1,728	6,869	7,902
schools for young people requiring special care	12 545	17,681	24,546	26,606
IV. Pupils of secondary vocational schools in productive age	356,893	289,557	287,765	295,248
V. Population unable to work in productive age	274,229	266,473	266,360	267,003
VI. Other working age population including unplanned components	585,845	704,364	739,284	746,038

Source: Statistické ročenky Československé socialistické republiky (1966–1993)

The Directive 55/1965, Coll. named three streams of the labour plan – the number of workers and salary plan, the recruitment plan, and the cadre plan. The restriction for the number of workers plan was given by the size of population, and for the salary plan by the presumed production of the enterprise. The recruitment plan was based on the records of the population in different regions. The cadre plan was based on the graduates from the respective specializations.

3.4.2 Banking sector and non-monetary system

The other mentioned ideological task was a plan to abandon money in the economic system. The planning system in socialist Czechoslovakia did not achieve the total elimination of money, but it limited its functioning by fixing the prices. The partial reason was that stable prices were more convenient for planning. Even better for the planners was to deal with quantitative units instead of units displayed in prices.

There was a broad apparatus to deal with prices: The Federal Price Office (Federální cenový úřad), two republic price offices, and special price departments in all ministries.

There were four different types of prices in the socialist economy:

1 Wholesale prices – i.e., prices between socialist companies that reflected costs of production and profit of the producer.
2 Buying prices that were paid for purchasing of agricultural products from agricultural companies.
3 Retail prices – the prices for the final consumer. The difference between wholesale and retail price consisted of trade surcharge or trade spread, i.e. the retailers' costs, plus turnover tax. Retail prices for inhabitants were mostly fixed (see Chapter 5).
4 Prices in foreign trade.

(Hába et al. 1988)

The banking sector in Czechoslovakia was centralized already in 1950 and it was constituted as a one-tier/ monobank following the Soviet example. The Czechoslovak State Bank was subordinated to the government (Ministry of Finance) and its activity had to follow the central plan. There were individual banks inside the monobank which embraced specific roles in the overall system. The Česká and Slovenská Spořitelna were saving banks with a huge surplus of deposits above credits. Opposite to them was the Komerční Banka, which was the main institution to provide funding to companies. It had big surplus of credits above deposits. The planning process in this sector had forms of a currency plan, consisting of a loan, cash, and foreign exchange plans. All these plans were based on factual plans and itemized for individual banks (Brada et al. 1996). As a result, the central bank did not form monetary policy because it just followed the line set by the centre. Investments were controlled centrally as well. Companies were simply entitled by the centre (the plan) to be granted loans. The central bank functioned as a cashier providing credit or cross-subsidies to state companies.

3.4.3 Outer relationships

The ideologists of socialism generally supported the integration of the socialist economies into the world economy, but they planned for a trade monopoly (see Chapter 2). All outer relationships were organized and planned in the same way as any other aspect of the economy. However, of the outer relationships only international trade was of any importance. Trans-border investment was relatively limited as well as the movement of people. The socialist state had, in practice, a real monopoly over international economic relations, which gave the system exclusive rights to manage, organize, and supervise all economic relations with foreign entities.

The general trends in foreign trade policy were, as other features, determined by the Congress of the Communist Party. Plans of trade were created in order to meet the objectives set by the Congress. Operationally (see Diagram 3.8), planning and management of foreign trade at the highest level involved the country's central organs: The Federal Ministry of Foreign Trade, the State Planning Commission, the Czechoslovak State Bank of Czechoslovakia, sectoral as well as intersectoral ministries (e.g., engineering sectors, the Federal Ministry of Finance), etc. (Nykryn 1988).

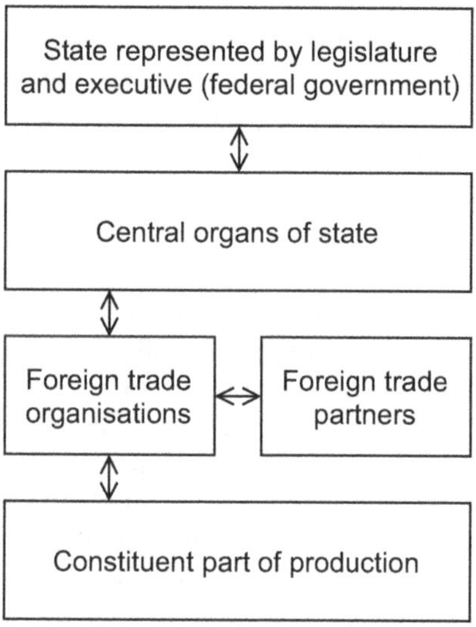

Diagram 3.8 Organizational structure of foreign trade in ČSSR

The basic function of the highest management was setting a plan which would regulate operations in foreign trade. The plan's fundamental part (material plan) determined the conditions for exports and imports and specified the volume of production which was to be a part of quantitative foreign exchange. Other parts of the plan, such as services and foreign currency plans[2] ensued the material plan. The material plan was divided according to sectors, respective products, regions, and time periods (Melicher and Procházka 1986). At the highest level, the material plan took the form of General Plan for Export and Import. Then, the general plan was elaborated in more detail at lower levels (see Nykryn 1988).

The Directive 55/1965 Coll. described the prices that were used for the creation of the plan. With respect to the socialist countries, it used the contractual prices. If these were not available, the average of the main world market prices was used. With respect to the capitalist countries, the prices that were achieved in the last foreign trade plan were used. For the one-year plan, the most recent prices were used.

In terms of regional division, the plan made clear distinctions in export and import decisions based on the respective partner country's position in the COMECON, with specific criteria applied for the SU. Likewise, the plan differentiated approaches towards advanced economies and developing economies. The plan was either for a period of five years or one year, in special cases, the plan could be set for shorter, quarterly or monthly, periods. All plans were set as balanced (planned imports were equal to planned exports).

The trade was not carried on by respective companies but by authorized enterprises, such as the Foreign Trade Companies (Podniky zahraničního obchodu) (PZO) (52 in total) (Dillon and Wykoff 2002). These concentrated on specific segments and their tasks were to (Nykryn 1988):

1 Purchase products from domestic, Czechoslovak manufacturers and export them to foreign buyers.
2 Import products from foreign manufacturers and suppliers and consequently sell these products to domestic, Czechoslovak companies.

The state-authorized foreign trade companies were not mere mediators or consultants. Their primary business activities were to carry out foreign trade in their own right and responsibility. These specific and monopolistic companies were in most cases solely responsible for all contacts with foreign business partners (Nykryn 1988). They thus represented yet another centralizing element in the organizational structure of Czechoslovak foreign trade. One such foreign trade organization was responsible for an entire sector's production. This monopolization lowered costs of centralized management on the one hand but separated respective companies from contacts with their foreign customers on the other.

The goal of this chapter was to provide description of the main features of the theoretical settings of the centrally planned economy in Czechoslovakia. It showed how the ideological basis summarized in the previous chapter materialized in the formal settings of the model. In most of the aspects, the theoretical setting followed the ideology – the overall system was based on the leading role of the Communist Party; the private ownership of the means of production was totally eliminated; and the organization system of the economy was transformed to central planning. We must notice that the planning system was rather complicated. Even though the entire economy was supposed to be balanced. These enormous and highly demanding tasks were entrusted to the SPK. The state and its officials were the substance of the economic system.

With the description provided in this chapter in mind, we can continue to day-to-day functioning of the Czechoslovak model of the centrally planned economy in the next chapter.

Notes

1 The official name of the central planning institution changed several times during the centrally planned period. However, we stick to the name of Státní plánovací komise which was the term used in the period under review.
2 Foreign currency planning included all foreign currency incomes and expenditures, namely those generated by export and payments for import (Melicher and Procházka 1986).

4 Practices of central planning in Czechoslovakia

This chapter summarizes our findings about the functioning of the centrally planned system in socialist Czechoslovakia. The chapter is tied to the previous one that analyzed the formal settings of the Czechoslovak system. This chapter, based on our interviews, on the contrary describes the everyday practice. The main intention is to show the relationships among the actors in the planned system. We firstly describe the key characteristics of the general environment (4.1). This description consequently provides a platform for an analysis of the role each constituent, i.e., the centre (4.2), the VHJs (4.3), and the companies (4.4).

4.1 General environment and settings of the system

The goal of this part of the text is to provide practical characteristics of the centrally planned environment in socialist Czechoslovakia. The system was founded on several pillars. The first of them was the common/state ownership of the means of production (4.1.1). The second one was the central plan on its own, with its inner rules and consequences (4.1.2). And the third was the influence of the Communist Party on the economic functioning (4.1.3). In these three sections we generally follow the links that already started in Chapter 2 when we considered the ideological aspects of the Marxist-Leninist thoughts with a direct influence on the economy. They were consequently analyzed from the view of the theoretical settings of the centrally planned model in Czechoslovakia in Chapter 3. In all of these sections we discussed the role of the party, nationalization, and the centrally planned system as the main characteristics of the system. These main environmental settings naturally directly impacted the behaviour of the economic centre – the VHJs and companies – which are dealt with in the following sections.

4.1.1 Ownership

The key characteristics of the centrally planned system was appropriation of the capitalist ownership. We elaborates this topic from the point of view of the Marxist-Leninist theory as well as from the point of view of the formal setting of the centrally planned system in Czechoslovakia in the previous two chapters.

The theoretical concept expected an all-society ownership that was supposed to be, in the first phase of the socialist development, represented by state ownership.

The first step in the direction towards nationalization in the Czechoslovak economy took place already in 1945. Large enterprises with the number of employees above the limit (several hundred, specified according to the respective sector) were nationalized immediately after the war. There were not only ideological reasons but economic ones as well because, after the withdrawal of previous German owners, managers, and employees, a number of companies were often in difficult economic conditions (Faltus and Průcha 1995). Nationalization was implemented by four presidential decrees and only later on approved by the parliament. In this wave, key and large industries, food industry, banks, and insurance companies were nationalized. As a consequence, 60% of industrial jobs were provided by nationalized industries already in 1945 (Havelková 2009b). This development was not uncommon after the war when nationalization took place also in other countries, e.g., the UK or France. The 1948 Constitution (following the communist coup) declared that ownership would be mainly national/common (see Chapter 3). All remaining bigger companies were nationalized, farmers were in three waves (sometimes violently) forced to join agricultural cooperatives and even small trade was not allowed to stay independent. Průcha states that already by the end of 1948 there were just several private companies with more than 20 employees even though the official legal boundary for nationalization was 50 employees (Průcha 2000). Vencovský (2003) adds that there were 409,815 holders of licensed trade in 1947, but their number declined to one fifth by 1953 and even the remainder quickly vanished. The whole process of collectivization in Czechoslovakia was completed in the late 1950s.

In the countryside, while the share of the socialist sector (consisting of agricultural cooperatives and state estates) in 1953 was 46.3% of the farmland, in 1960 it reached 92.5%. The level of nationalization in the Czechoslovak economy was extremely high even by the standards of socialist countries. The private sector played the smallest role in the economy and its level was comparable only with the Soviet Union (Půlpán 1993). Tošovský writes that 87% of national income in the 1980s was created by socialist enterprises, 10% by cooperatives, and 2% by the private sector (Tošovský 2000). He among others mentions that in 1949 there were 2 million private farmers, while by the end of the communist period, only 10,000 of them managed to retain their independence.

But what was the position and role of ownership like in everyday practice? Klaus concludes that companies did not have any direct owner (Klaus 2009). However, in everyday practice someone had to exercise the property rights. The then Prime Minister Štrougal writes in his memoirs: "In socialism, the state owned a dominant part of the national economy and thus we could make crucial decisions" (Štrougal 2009, p. 336). By which he means that the owner was de facto the government or the Party. Večerník writes about hidden ownership rights granted to the Party apparatchik, assistants of directors and directors (Večerník 1998). Kabele states that socialistic managers were endowed by quasi-ownership authority to handle with sources in the entrusted companies and social organizations (Kabele 2005). Baňouch comments that the management was, in fact, the real owner (Baňouch 2009). In Zieleniec's view, there were "secret owners" – meaning people who were "entrusted" with positions in the control hierarchy. The members of this hierarchy were interested foremost in gaining private benefits and revenues flowing from their administrative power. Their interest in the efficient functioning of the company or economic unit and their long-term economic prospects were, in practice, irrelevant to them (Zieleniec 1990).

The view that people in the hierarchy were the real owners became accepted even among the members of the Communist Party. Možný quotes Abalkin (the director of the Economic Institute of the Academy of Science of the Soviet Union) who said that socialist ownership seemed to be ownership by everybody at first sight and as ownership by no one at second sight. He also added that, in reality, and from the economic point of view, the ownership belonged to people with the right to disposal. This right to disposal was a basis for ownership even though it was illegitimate and unaccountable (Možný 1991).

Similarly, Mlčoch adds that "all-society" ownership was a typical example of introducing a term with a speculative meaning. Besides, he argues that someone (management) handled the property and the same person/persons made decisions. He thus points out that the ownership belonged to those who made decisions in the centrally planned model. He emphasizes that in practice all people along the decision-making hierarchy were de facto co-owners of the "all-society" property. Their share corresponded to their ability to make decisions about the property. It was partially concentrated in the centre, but a significant share of the decision-making power was passed to the companies. As a result, the managers were co-owners of the property. On the contrary, ordinary employees were in his view excluded from the decision-making process and thus they were not co-owners of the "all-society" property in practice. This view is supported by Kratochvíl, who worked as CEO in several companies. He writes about the impact of ambiguous ownership. He points out that companies were, in fact, run by the so-called power triangle comprising the KSČ organization, the ROH organization, and the management. This system, in his eyes, greatly complicated the management of the company (Kratochvíl 2011). Mlčoch believes that the loose coalition of owners created a new social class, which collectively owned the means of production and simultaneously the majority of the society was excluded from co-ownership of the "all-society" property. He even states that the wage was only a part of the nomenclature's income. The other parts were a share in the "internal profit" and participation in the monopolistic profit. The author concludes with a suggestion to rename the traditional model as "formally socialized economy." He adds that the highly complex and irrational division of the execution of ownership rights was a consequence of the all-society ownership and that the main culprit was the effort to concentrate property in the state hands. The state had appropriated the ownership rights to delegate them in practice consequently (even though not legally). He concludes that the all-society ownership was manifested as ownership of all and nobody (Mlčoch 1990).

The absence of real ownership resulted in the invitation of some people to "privatize" it. These crimes against common ownership were considered by the public as less harmful than crimes against private property. MP Řezáčová said:

> *Attacks against socialist property are morally regarded as less problematic than comparable attacks against private property and illegal benefits obtained at the expense of socialist property are considered almost as a matter of course. The culprits rely on the public's neglect of socialist property protection. These illegal activities are made possible not only by such ill moral stance but also by inadequate care for socialist property and a passive attitude towards these harms in organizations which are in charge of the socialist property. Among the most neglected areas here belong security of objects, warehouses and materials, existing defects in the inventory, inspection and acceptance of goods and materials, and also underrated importance of selection of workers responsible for the wellbeing of socialist property.*
>
> *(ČSSR. Czech National Council 1976–1980)*

Cases of such a kind were (very) common and some of them were investigated by the StB. It was, for example, informed about a senior worker in the Zbrojovka factory, who allegedly stole pieces of paperboard, cans with paint, and a chainsaw. He was reported to be "the biggest thief in the enterprise" (ABS, OB-957 OV).

Interestingly, our respondents did not mention the ownership topic at all. The probable reason was that the state/all-society ownership was self-evident, and they accepted these formal settings. The ownership issue was also not controversial at the time. Who, in fact, performed property rights was not discussed in the public and it was very rarely considered by (underground) academic economists – besides Mlčoch and Šulc. Therefore, we did not expect the respondents to talk about it. They could have possibly acquired this point of view only retrospectively.

To sum it up, the meaning of the term "all-society ownership" was unclear both formally and in everyday practice. Despite the fact that the companies had no direct owner, a quasi-ownership structures were formed, and the members of the decision-making hierarchy held the positions of the actual owners of the property. Regardless of this quasi-ownership, property without a clear and unambiguous owner is never superiorly efficient.

4.1.2 Central plan in practice

The second pillar of the centrally planned system was central planning on its own. The process of planning was formally described in the previous chapter. It seemed to be straightforward and hierarchical. However, the reality was different. The creation of the plan was in practice not a one-time act, but it was a sequence of several rounds when information was exchanged between the subordinated and the superior institutions in the planning hierarchy. This procedure was reported even by our respondent from the SPK <ID040>. All the tiers of the planning hierarchy had one eminent interest – meeting the plan. This was the genuine outright goal of the overall activity for everybody, starting from the companies via the VHJs up to the central institutions and even the communist organizations at different levels. Moreover, the StB reported those companies that did not meet the plan or cheated in meeting it (ABS, OB-957 OV, ABS OB-282 BN). All these institutions had to prove their abilities. Besides, the personal rewards (bonuses) of all participants depended on meeting the plan, and this was the main motivation. This fact fully appeared already during the creation of the plan, which turned out to be more flexible than one could expect from the formal settings of the system. On the other hand, all participants in the planning hierarchy also followed different individual goals and strategies during the process of the plan creation (see following subsections). In this subsection we concentrate on the overall characteristics of the environment and on two main topics – firstly the importance of markets in the planned system and secondly on achieving balance in the system.

Central plan or markets?

The goal and expectations of the theorists of the centrally planned system was the removing of markets. Pundits' opinions diverge about the ability or scope of the central planners to achieve this goal in practice. Some of them believe that this effort was successful. For example, Faltus writes that central planning resembled decision-making in the army and chain of command (Faltus 1995). However, most of the observers believe that the centrally planned economy was, in fact, a form of a highly inefficient and distorted market economy (for example Zieleniec 1990; Kabele 2005). In Kabeles' view, although nationalization enforced central planning, in reality the planning was only superficial because market forces were still effective. The practice of central planning did not have much in common with the original idea of a planned and harmonious satisfying of the objective needs of the society. In addition, the system was also impracticable in everyday reality (Kabele 2005). In his view the central plan was just a facade hiding the division of planning that was just pretending to be organized by the centre.

Šulc writes that even in the most rigid form of central planning market elements still existed. For example, negotiations between the centre and companies and between the companies took place as well as the existence of market with consumption goods (Šulc 1995). Other authors write explicitly that the centrally planned system was in practice based on market coordination and that market, though deformed, had never ceased to exist. Mlčoch mentions that the economy was coordinated by the institution of the market even though the markets were specific – monopolistic, compulsorily cartelized, with weak coordination, primitive, based on non-monetary relationships, protected, closed, and generally had low efficiency. He adds that these quasi markets sent the wrong signals, which did not allow real economic calculations, and that, in his view, the centre was one of the weakest players in the system. He agrees with Kabele that the whole machinery of the hierarchic system was in many aspects just a red herring and "a game" that was hiding motions which were anyway coerced by the markets (Mlčoch 1990).

Similarly, Komárek et al. write that the institution of the market is irrevocable and absolutely natural, and it asserts itself perpetually, regardless of circumstances. Nevertheless, if the economic policy is targeted not on cultivation but on suppressing of the markets, market principles appear in a deformed form (for example with prices separated from inner circumstances as well as from international markets). Market principles are projected into citizens' consumption patterns and their lifestyle, however, these deformations enormously burden the economy (Komárek et al. 1990).

The economists' point of view can be supplemented by sociologists: "In the social analysis optics, strictly speaking, there is no[thing] other than market-based society. Only societies that deny it are sometimes found" (Možný 1991, p. 34). Moreover, Šulc emphasizes another aspect of the system. He argues that the companies had a strong influence on the final state of the plan and he even uses a term "centrally-allocational" mechanism because the system was not one-way "top-down" (therefore it was not a directive system). As a result, the requirement that a company was given from above often expressed something that the companies, in fact, wanted (Šulc 1995; Eucken 1948).

The very existence of markets in the centrally planned economy was accepted even by that time by (socialist) authors who described the economic environment. The difference was that the term "market" could not be used due to political and ideological reasons. The authors were thus constrained to cloak it in "Newspeak" and talked instead about the "goods-money relationships" (e.g., Rendl 1988; Mlčoch 1990; Sitárová and Kliment 1981; Hába et al. 1988). This term was used for example when the reformers wanted to increase the significance of market in the planned economy. On the other hand, Hába in his textbook about central planning mentions that goods-money relationships were supposed to be dying out and the main reason for their persistence was the existence of the relative economic independence of the companies (Hába et al. 1988). Additionally, black markets in the system obviously existed (e.g., Stevens 1985; Šulc 2004; Teplý 1976) – an exemplary case was the black market with convertible currencies (e.g., Rychlík 2007). Additionally, the companies that were able to export to the developed countries came into contact with the markets indirectly via the PZOs. They did business directly on markets in western countries. However, the PZOs were the only organizations of the state economy that went directly into commercial relationship with market-based companies and experienced the mechanism of supply and demand first-hand.

Regardless of semantics, the central planners obviously at least tried to plan and organize the economy, which is the main focus of this subsection. But we should take into consideration that there were market forces and relations, however, hidden under the surface and influencing the behaviour of the decision-makers. Even though the economy as a whole obviously did not meet the definition of market economy (e.g., Jahan and Mahmud 2015) and the centre strived to abolish all the market relations.

Balance

The second general feature of the central planning was a continuous effort to achieve balance. At the level of the whole economy, the balance was supposed to be carefully planned and any undershooting or overshooting of the planned target should cause imbalance of the entire system (Šulc 2004). Our respondent from the SPK <ID040> agreed and told us that from his or her position the best was to simply meet the plan, even though it was prepared for 96–104% fulfilling. Not meeting the plan resulted in shortage because something (e.g., steel or sugar) was obviously missing in the economy. Over fulfilment, when achieved, could have consequences in overproduction, i.e., in producing goods that were not needed (idle goods). And the question is where the companies obtained material or semi-manufactured goods for their production if everything was planned? It was naturally possible to increase productivity, but the sources were necessary. On the contrary, the communist leaders were proud of overfulfilling the plan and they generally encouraged it. Either option had the potential to throw the plan out of balance and thus was highly undesirable. In everyday practice, the planners had to expect both options.

The plan was formally set as balanced. Our respondent, who worked as section chief in the SPK <ID040> believed that achieving of the balance was not difficult:

> *Making the plan was based on two things. Firstly, you could see, you know, there were several ways to approach it, the plan was multilevel. On the one hand, you could see how much you needed, I don't know, for instance, dental engines. You know these reclining, with all the appliances, blah blah blah. Well, they would have water, air, a motor to move the whole thing and electricity to make it work, some hydraulics and what have you. And the thing would cost some twenty-five thousand or so. And they found out that Chirana could manufacture 180 of these dental engines a year. And you knew, for you had info from the regional healthcare institutes, all the hospitals and faculties when their old dental engines and appliances would stop working and when it would be necessary to replace them. And it as when you would say, ok, Chirana can make 180 of these next year, and this manufacturer will supply such and such motors, and that manufacturer will make the steel construction for them, and other companies will also be contracted to participate. And a colleague in charge of the finance made a plan for the respective hospitals and the other supplicants for January, February, March, and so on. And it simply divided the 180 dental engines fifteen per month. And the supplicants were granted exactly the twenty-five thousand from the central plan budget to buy the thing. So, any overproduction was out of the question. Another thing was that, for instance in December, the guys were falling behind with the production and so they made only sixteen out of the eighteen planned for that month. This meant that their financial bonuses were cut. And they*

> *would deliver the engines like a little later in January. So, in the course of the 80s the degree of harmonization in these supplier-customer relations, as they were called then, was, thanks to the IT so balanced that the differences between what the centre planned and what really happened hardly exceeded some 3, 4, or 5%.*

The obvious question is what happened when the needs were higher than abilities of the production – if dentists needed 200 chairs or even more.

At company level, the aforementioned harmony of supply and demand was not felt. Partly because of the permanently changing environment and participant's needs. Change is an inherent quality of any economic system, market as well as centrally planned one. But admittedly the changes in the other were possibly less frequent due to its distinctive rigidity. The markets are generally self-regulating, whereas in the centrally planned system the planners had to try to adapt the economy to changes. It was not an easy task and it was even more complicated because, on the contrary to market economy, the prices were fixed (see Chapter 3). Therefore, it hindered the system from being balanced. Lack of price signals contributed to both kinds of imbalances – demand over supply, as well as supply over demand. The former case, which was the reflected shortage character of the economy, revealed numerous bottlenecks in the system (see the Section 4.4.2), whereas the latter was reflected in the production of idle goods (e.g., Šulc 2004).

Shortages were a ubiquitous feature of the system. We deal with this topic mainly in Section 4.4.2. Just one of many examples was a director of an engineering company <ID063> who described the shortage in the following way:

> *Well, it wasn't all that easy, but in all those years when I was in the business, when I really got into a tight spot was when I couldn't get a spare part for some machinery. This was a real mess. When the problem was in lack of material, well it wasn't such a problem as you could always use secondary materials, but when, for example, I needed a variator for a key appliance, I had to travel all over the country to find it.*

Shortage posed a serious problem to the smooth functioning of the economy. However, considering overall efficiency, idle goods (in "Newspeak" unsellable stocks) were equally serious. In a market economy, it is difficult to imagine a situation that companies permanently produce goods that no one is interested in. But in the centrally planned system, it was crucial to meet the plan regardless of profit or the satisfaction of the customers. It is difficult to estimate the volume of idle goods in the economy. However, we can observe the trend on the stockpile of goods and products that was nearly permanently growing. The same was true for the share of this stockpile on Czechoslovak national product. At the end of the 1980s, the share of stockpile of goods and products alone reached nearly 40% of the national income (see Figure 4.1). To compare, today's overall stockpiles in the economy reach some 30% of the GDP, with the goods and products accounting only for 14% of the GDP (CZSO, database of national account, balance sheets 2018).

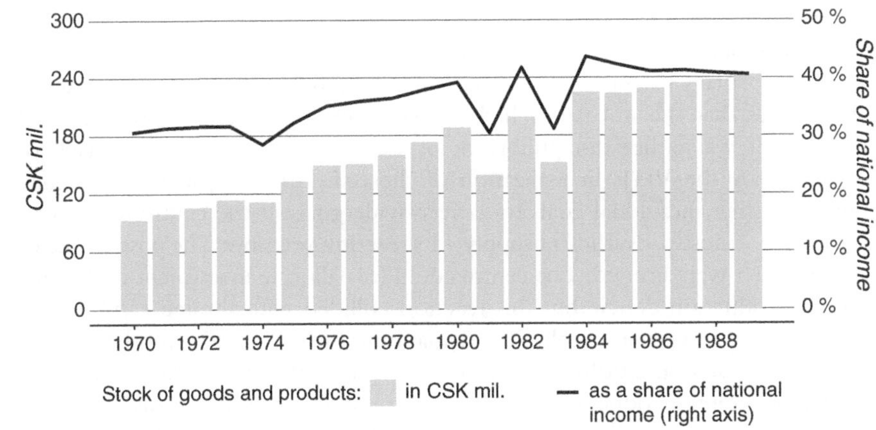

Figure 4.1 Stockpile of goods and products (in CSK mld.), and as a share of national income (in percent)

Source: Statistical yearbooks of CSSR (1971–1990)

Several of our respondents mentioned idle goods. For example, a planner and head of supplying in an engineering company <ID007> told us:

> *The company did not have any demand incentives. The way it worked was that the sales department reckoned that this much of the produce could be sold over here and that much of it over there, but, like I say, it was not based on any order or commission. It was only then, that these foreign trade companies were ordered to find customers somewhere, to sell the produce somewhere. For instance, the factory here, in Vsetín, I remember how a fence was built around it, it is still called the most expensive fence in the republic, there were some seven thousand containers, like seven thousand unsold machines.*

Possibly the same case as was described by the respondent was documented by the StB, too. Supposedly, "the machines could not be yet exported because they were not completed. They were however packed in the expedition cases and stored across from the firm's building, close to a brook over the bridge" (ABS, OB-957 OV).

The previous respondent's words were confirmed by an economic planner in an engineering company <ID008> who commented: I: "And, as for the stocks, well, how big a volume of yearly produce could end up in stocks?" R: "Huge. I think, there could have been some 30 or 40% of yearly produce." On top of that, what the planners could not calculate at all was the demand in the capitalist states. In 1978, the StB investigated long-term problems the TOS Kuřim company had with selling machine tools to capitalist markets. They wrote: "Because of the constant weak demand in the capitalist states, it was only able to sell

75 percent of the planned production. The fact is mirrored in the gradual overfilling of their warehouses" (ABS OB-282 BN).

The planners tried to react to imbalances in the economy. The whole economy was formally balanced – between "sources" and their "use" (see Chapter 3). Šulc writes that the imbalance had formally two reasons, apart from natural disasters. It was either disequilibrium of sources and use. Or it was lack of discipline by the VHJs in realization of the tasks, meaning in fact that they preferred their individual goals to society-wide goals. If the centre noticed an imbalance – mostly insufficient supply – its reaction was slow. The possibilities of how to react were limited. The centre could (re-)allocate investment in the area with a production deficit, but this reaction collided with limited capacities of the economy and it was highly time demanding (several years). Another option was an increase in the utilization of the capacities, but it was intricated, and the companies were uncooperative to reveal reserves in their productions. The third option was to import the missing items, but this solution further burdened the trade balance and foremost hard currency to pay for imports was severely limited. The last option were consumption restrictions (Šulc 2004).

The general conclusion is that although achieving balance was formally easy, the everyday practice was very different, partly due to the fact that prices did not play their informative role. But there were many more obstacles and the system suffered from omnipresent shortage that determined behaviour of all participants. But at the same time, it produced idle goods – production made only for stores that no one wanted to purchase and that only served to meet the planned objectives.

4.1.3 Influence of the Communist Party on the economy

Another key aspect that determined the overall economic environment was the policy of the Communist Party, which had a leading role in the entire politico-economic system. There were many different layers of the Communist Party organizations in the system and their role varied. From the formal settings, the Party local organizations were supposed to play a role of quasi supervisory board of the company. However, with a task to meet the plan and satisfy the employees but not maximize profit and thus dividends, like in the market system.

According to the Party materials, the Party institutions and organizations:

> *Unify the respective types of governing of the socialist economy and imprint them their official focus. [. . .] Even though the Communist Party is the decisive entity of the economic policy, it does not take over responsibility of direct governing of the national economy and intervention to the rights of executive. Party organizations respect the authority and responsibility of leading economic executives.*
>
> (*Pawera 1985*)

Votoček who worked as a technical deputy in Tesla Litovel pragmatically commented: "In fact, the leading role of the party was executed by appointing and electing their own party members into important posts, mostly. And they were obliged to do what the party said and if they had not, they were punished" (Vaněk and Urbášek 2005, p. 457).

We have already emphasized the importance of the Communist Party congresses because they made decisions about the economic priorities and the broad direction of the plan for the following period. An example of the Communist Party sequential activity from Congress to government decision is described in archive material – "Set of measures to secure the resolution of the Central Committee of the Communist Party of Czechoslovakia on the tasks and development in engineering, electrotechnical and metallurgical industries after the XVI Congress of the Communist Party," approved by the Government of the Czechoslovak Socialistic Republic on 30th August, 1984 (ČSSR. Vláda 1984). According to the material, first of all the Congress decided about modernization of the production technical base and acceleration of scientific and technological development, shortening of the innovation cycles and better integration of engineering into international division of labour among the COMECON countries. Consequently, a session of the ÚV KSČ took place on 17th and 18th April 1984. The session debated among others a report by the Presidium of ÚV "On tasks and development of engineering, electrotechnical and metallurgical industries after XVIth congress of KSČ" and proposed to "speed up progressivity" of the plan for 1984 (ČSSR. Předsednictvo ÚV KSČ 1984). The government then prepared a material called a "Set of measures," which embraced foremost references to practical questions of governing of the economy (ČSSR. Vláda 1984). It comprised of principles which the responsible authorities were supposed to consequently follow in the decisions-making processes (Handl 2018).

The highest everyday institution was the Presidium of the ÚV KSČ. Handl cites Kaplan who wrote that the Presidium's decisions were based on political goals and it did not take responsibility for these decisions. Responsibility was on the state institutions, mainly the government. Kaplan documented that the Presidium often decided without knowing the real situation because there was no genuine discussion among the members due to inner power competition. He concluded that the Presidium was not able to introduce neither innovations nor reforms because any changes could potentially jeopardize its position (Handl 2018). Mlynář, a former member of the ÚV KSČ and later dissident described the decision-making process at the Presidium: the members received the proposals that were to be discussed one or two days before the meeting. The proposals were prepared by rather anonymous "working groups." There was at least one kilogram of the materials – according to Mlynář, what was important was the volume and weight of the papers. The reason for the effort to propose such large volumes was simple – the more details that were to be approved by the Presidium, the less responsibility for the bodies who wanted them to be approved. Moreover, the members were not either able or willing to read through all of them. In cases when the Presidium needed to take immediate political stance on unexpected issues, Mlynář continues, there were no materials prepared. In such moments, two or three people from the Presidium, who were able to formulate the stances, were selected. The document was then presented to the Presidium, and the discussion which was usually not really to the point could begin. After hours of such debate, when the members were weary and exhausted, the stance was accepted more or less in the original reading (Mlynář 1990).

However, the everyday practice of the Communist Party at the level of companies varied and often was different from official directions. For example, one of our respondents (head of a production company in agriculture <ID010>), who was, during the period under review, a member of the KSČ, presented strongly negative commentaries about the influence of the party on the economy:

> *Well, it's not really true that there would be talks about it all being really, like dogmatic and directive, it always depended on communication between people. Who interfered, and I guess it was the worst about the situation, if I may say so, into the economic mechanisms was the party. Either the district or regional committees of the Communist Party, directly in charge of agriculture departments, industry departments and alike, and were headed by the respective secretaries. And these, whose primary task was the personnel cadre policy, that means placing politically aware people in respective posts (such was the then political mechanism) unfortunately interfered also into the production spheres, and if I may say, again, they did so in a rather insensitive way. They, of course, had political links leading to the district agricultural authorities, who were eventually the decision-making element. And the degree of this influence was very high. Like oftentimes politics topped the economy, which was very, very bad. Do often the people in the district agricultural bodies, who were actually the ones responsible for the sector, so they had to obey the decisions made by the district, or any other, political body. So, they had to obey and respect these, which, at times might have led to unfortunate consequences, maybe, because the decisions were made on the bases of political stance, not expert, economic viewpoint. So, this is the way the party influenced the economy. [. . .]*
>
> *Well the party had, and I exaggerate a bit here, such a politics-enforced role that, and politics was simply the dominant element, it could exercise influence everywhere. Or, I should say, anywhere it should desire. It it was because politics made decisions about cadres. There was nobody willing to put a head on the block to point it out, that the party. [. . .] These were really important and bad decisions that were made, but as long as they were approved by the party. [. . .] So, the party could do anything, but what I must stress is that the real tragedy was that the party interfered, it stuck its nose into the economy. Ok, if it only stuck its nose into issues like, to say, big strategic goals, like whether to focus on, and it is being discussed today a lot, nuclear of coal energy, or something of that kind, I could understand that. Well, the party was, I mean it appointed itself as the leading force in the country, it was constitutionally set, its leading role. But it gradually grew, in fact not even gradually, it all started back in the 50s, when there were party officials, and they were like, the more stupid one was, the more important one grew, which led to these deformations. [. . .] But it was a real mistake that the party stuck its nose into, like I said. The party approved the plans, it approved the cadres, approved everything and then, it was all down the drain.*

On the other hand, some of our respondents said that the Communist Party did not interfere in production process (e.g., chief designer in an engineering company <ID003>) and concentrated its activity on cadre policy. Several respondents told us that in the party structures there were reasonable people who did not try to directly influence the economic tasks (e.g., power plant director <ID014>, CEO in heavy engineering <ID021>, director in water construction <ID002>) or even helped with the superior institutions when the tasks were above the ability of the company (<ID043>, assistant to the director in engineering). This attitude is documented in other sources as well. Kratochvíl, who worked in several companies on managerial posts, wrote in his memoirs that political environment was highly conservative in some of the companies while it could be casual in others (Kratochvíl 2011).

We should note that a company director was, of course, at the same time a member of the KSČ and often a member of the party's County or District Committee of KSČ or even a member of the ÚV; for example, general director of Vítkovice – one of the biggest heavy industry producers (<ID025>, Chief Secretary of a District Committee). Our respondent <ID020> head of technical department in engineering described these relationships as dual because the director was at the same time senior to employee-members of the Communist Party. As a result, communication with the centre was dual as well because one link followed the economic hierarchy and the parallel one-party hierarchy.

In general, the party membership was in many cases not a result of ideological convictions. It was more about fulfilling the necessary conditions necessary for getting a leading position in the company (see Chapter 1). As was corroborated by the majority of our respondents, common workers were not obliged to enter the party. In the case of senior posts, however, party membership was mostly decisive. Either formally as a proof of loyalty but also for very practical reasons. Dealing with various party organizations was an essential part of any managerial job. Being both a party member and a top manager enabled him or her to enter communication with other party officials on equal terms. This would be mostly inconceivable for non-partisan managers. For example, a sectional construction manager in the building industry (<ID023>) said that:

> *In the expert posts, the influence of the Party was crucial, determining. I had a colleague, who worked as sectional road construction manager . . . he was efficient, smart, and even, you would say, ambitious, but as long as he was not in the Party, he did not have a chance to be promoted. He could easily work as a vice-chair or something. So, in the end, he just broke and although he was deeply religious and a really honest person, he did join the Party. And he came to me and said: "Vláďa, you know, I would get stuck otherwise, I know it is not something to be proud of, but I just had to do it." (laughter) Well the higher posts, it was all Party approved, I mean company directors, deputies, such posts – directly party decisions. And then lower posts, such as sectional and department heads – there was strong influence by the local corporate Party branch.*

However, in the case of highly qualified workers, which the firm necessarily needed, there was a possibility of an exception:

> *In those years, the Party had some million and eight hundred thousand members. My husband . . . worked as designer in an electrical engineering company and he said, yes, Party membership played a role . . . someone was needed to be put in charge of the department. And they had some, I don't know, twenty applicants . . . and about a third of them were not in the Party, the others were. And some were outed, for political reasons, for example, but out of the rest, they chose the best candidate. I mean, really, objectively the best, not politically most suitable, you know? . . . They chose the most suitable candidate, and he even had a daughter living abroad, but they just needed him, so, you know, it was possible sometimes.*
>
> *(Designer and leading worker in construction <ID031>)*

Such exception is confirmed by the StB files as well. The manager of the costs planning in the Zbrojovka Vsetín factory "was dismissed from the party because of his faulty political stances in the years 1968–69. However, [he] retained his position thanks to being an expert in his field, and he is highly evaluated when it comes to his work" (ABS, OB-957 OV).

Nevertheless, not everyone aspired to be promoted. On the one hand, some had moral principles and refused to enter the party, on the other, in reality leadership mostly meant only more responsibility and problems without higher wage valuation (Operating deputy in transport <ID009>).

The company committee was key in day-to-day business. It approved new members of management, controlled the People's Militia, etc. (a worker in large metallurgy company <ID027>). The company committee worked in cooperation with the all-company ROH and the management. They held meetings every Monday. They evaluated the previous week, set tasks for the following one and consulted meeting of the plan <ID027>. František Merta (in the 1970s and 1980s Secretary for Industry in Šumperk District KSČ Committee) provided evidence from the side of a party official. He said that they intervened in the functioning of the companies only indirectly via basic organizations in the companies. He complained that some of his colleagues wanted to govern the companies directly, but he opposed these tendencies because he felt that "four people (the team at Šumperk District Committee) could not replace the VHJ" (Vaněk and Urbášek 2005). He spoke about the role of the Regional Committee that dealt with the same troubles from the perspective of the whole region. Moreover, their meetings were adequately attended by ministries or their deputies (<ID025> Chief Secretary of the District Committee of the Communist Party).

Experience with party interventions in production varied but principally it had two official roles – supervision of the planning process and personal policy. From the top of the hierarchy, the highest supervision institution was the Central Control and Review Commission of the Central Committee of the Communist Party (Ústřední kontrolní a revizní Komise ÚV KSČ – ÚKRK).

It, for example, produced materials about situations in respective industries. For instance, between September 1987 and February 1988, the ÚKRK prepared a very complex material about metallurgy (ČSSR. Předsednictvo ÚV KSČ 1988). The global task in this production segment was to transition from extensive to intensive production of metallurgy, which was interconnected with investment, increase in productivity and quality, decline in inputs, etc. The report presented detailed key industrial data, often critical, from the branch. It, among others, evidenced a lagging behind the developed countries in this sector. The positive aspects of the economy were credited to hard work of communists. The material discussed meeting of the plan, investment or technical-organizational tasks of production in detail, and it pointed to particular members of the management who were, in the eyes of the report authors, responsible for irregularities. The report continued with analyzing the party life with an emphasis on increasing the quality of its members. The report concluded critically that some intentions of the plans had not been met and that the intensification process in the sector had been slow. Interestingly, in contrast, our respondent (<ID026>, MP and secretary of ObNV Ostrava) mentioned that the economic body always had the upper hand to the Communist Party hierarchy regarding examining because party inspectors did not have their own information channel and depended on the economic body. The only exception, possibly, were activities of the StB, which could obtain inner information about the functioning of the company (see Box 5.7).

The local/basic communist organizations had the right to supervise the company and they controlled personal policy as well. These two tasks were overlapping. Our respondent (<ID026>, MP and secretary of ObNV Ostrava) mentioned that in his or her company, the nomenclature controlled the personal policy tightly. But in case the basic organization supported a person (even non-member), the superior communist organizations did not replace him or her. On the other hand, the impact of the KSČ was double-edged, a respondent in Vaněk and Krátká described that her subordinates complained to the OV KSČ about her (Vaněk and Krátká 2014). Apart from that, the subordinates had plenty of opportunities to complain when the StB made a regular investigation in the enterprise. In the Zbrojovka factory, there were several reports on that. According to these, some of the seniors drank alcohol at the workplace, or they stole material from the enterprise (ABS, OB-957 OV).

The local communist party unit did not interfere in the everyday operation of the company when it worked well and met the plan. A respondent in heavy industry company (<ID035>, head of production in a rolling mill) added that if the plan was met the party did not initiate personal changes. But they quickly got activated when the plan was not fulfilled (e.g., MP and secretary of ObNV Ostrava <ID026>). Our respondent, a worker in one of the biggest metallurgy companies <ID027>, told us that weekly meetings included directors of plants, deputies of directors, deputies of the SPK, representatives of the party and the ROH. The party officials were mobilized in case there were problems connected with meeting the plan. If they decided that the trouble was in the person of the director, the OV KSČ could enforce a replacement through the party <ID026>. František Merta who worked in the Šumperk District KSČ Committee said that the directors were of various quality and that some of them needed to be replaced but that there was possibly no better candidate (Vaněk and Urbášek 2005).

The decision-making in companies was made more complicated by other parallel power centres – local townhalls (Národní výbory) – occupied by "elected" communists (see Diagram 3.1 in Chapter 3). Our respondent (MP and secretary of ObNV Ostrava <ID026>) told us that these institutions mostly supervised municipal companies and did not interfere in key regional companies. However, he added that the most powerful regional committees had strong connections to the SPK and ministries and due to it had even some (limited) chance to influence the plan. But another respondent (head of company in agriculture <ID048>) had a different experience. He said that the ONV interfered in the companies – mostly in a destructive way. In his view, the secretaries were "often incompetent and meddled in agriculture or anything else." He mentioned that these officials were in his experience irremovable and it was very difficult to influence them if they were on good terms with top-ranking party authorities. He gave an example of a distillery in Smiřice, which he was promoted to manage. He said that before his arrival, the technological equipment for the production of pectin had been purchased for 76 million schillings from Austria. "No one minded that this equipment had already been lying in cases for 3 years, even though according to the government decision foreign technologies had to be put into operation within 3 years. But it would have been necessary to build a factory for it at first". The respondent said that the managers of his company were not able to obtain a territorial decision from the local townhall because it was blocked by the head of the respective department. That man was a member of the ÚKRK and a good friend of Miloš Jakeš, who was at that time a member of the Presidium ÚV (later Secretary General). In the respondent's experience under such circumstances it was not possible to enforce a change of the decision even with the support of the ministers of the Federal Government nor to find another factory that would use the technology. The technology remained unused for the rest of the 1980s. It is not clear why the top-ranking official opposed construction of the factory, however, the situation illustrates the kind and ways of influence of the party.

In this first section we followed the links that were initiated in Chapter 2 and deepened in Chapter 3. We analyzed the practical aspects of the main characteristics of the system – nationalization and ownerships structures, global functioning of the central planning and the influence of the Communist Party on the running of the economy. Opinions varied about the practice of exercising property rights in the socialist economy. The insufficient definition of ownership rights probably influenced the behaviour of companies (see Section 4.4). We revealed that at least some market features were incorporated in the socialist economy through the behaviour of people and companies even though the system did not formally concede any markets. In the final subsection we discussed the party influence on the economy: From setting the strategic tasks by the party conferences and cadre policy to micromanaging individual companies. We may conclude that companies faced highly differentiated conditions including diverse ways in which the party exerted its command and control policy.

4.2 Behaviour of the economic centre in the CPE model

We start our analysis of the respective actors in the centrally planned system at the top – in the centre. The role of the centre was determined by the general settings of the economic and political system. The centre comprised of the government, the State Planning Commission (SPK) and ministries. This section deals first with forming and meeting of the plan. Then we analyze investment and wage policy, since these two specific topics were both in the hands of the centre. At the very end of the section, we answer a question: Who controlled the centre?

4.2.1 Forming and meeting of the plan

To begin with, we summarize the functioning of the centre with one of our respondents (General Director of company in knitting industry and later on Deputy Minister <ID073>), who told us:

I: *So how did the VHJ get the plan from above, or what kind of relationship was there?*

R: *Well, the whole system was controlled by means of meetings and plan. So, the General Director would officially get the plan from the Ministry of Industry. The ministry was structured so that each resort had its own assistant director and other, lower-ranking personnel. Then there was an economic unit, a planning unit, I mean, who got the plan from the State Planning Commission and set the detail and the figures to the respective VHJs, it was all . . . , a number of goods were balanced, that means you did not get just the financial figures, but also goods balance. So, you were ordered to manufacture this much (in thousands or millions) of infant goods, or hosiery, etc.*

I: *So, the ministry supplied all the detail.*

R: *Yes. It was the ministry and its balance. It it then interfaced with the trade and, understandably, the trade wanted more, so there were these negotiations, and so on and so forth. And it got to, in some resorts it got to such fine detail.*

The centre was obviously under a firm grip of the Communist Party. For example, of the 943 employees working in the SPK in 1986, 70% of them were members of the party. An important criterion was their social origin – 54.9% prided themselves on a working-class origin; 213 employees graduated from the VUML or another form of higher political education. Retirements cut into the ranks of the former communists sacked after the 1968 invasion, so the number of these politically inconvenient, but highly skilled people, decreased from 92 to 53 in the period. The number of employees with family members living in a capitalist country declined from 19 to 13, and none of them worked in a managerial post (ČSSR. Schůze předsednictva ÚV KSČ 1987). We should emphasize that some 950 people (probably including cleaners and secretaries) played a decisive role in the planning of the 14 million people economy.

Our respondent who worked as section chief in the SPK <ID040> described the SPK as a professional institution, relatively protected from political pressures. In his view, the trouble was that it behaved as a bureaucratic institution. That is, for example, it blocked the "natural" development of companies and sometimes forced them to focus on production based on political goals such as economic growth or exports into capitalist countries. However, the detailed technical realization of these goals was in the hand of the SPK's employees, he said. They were generally protected from influence of politics and concentrated on technical aspects of their work.

The central planning institutions wanted to show their competence and ability to achieve, in fact, political goals (the general goals of the planning were formally set by the Communist Party Congress – see Chapter 3). Our respondent from the SPK <ID040> however argued that his institution had the upper hand in dealing with politicians:

> *A totally general answer: an idea that politicians had a lot to say to our planning is just wrong. Politicians simply did what we wanted them to do, because, as they say, you can't squeeze blood out of a turnip, can you? That's an old rule.* But at the same time, he noted: *"You didn't need more than to hear on the phone. . . . 'This is Pavel Novák, from the Central Committee,' and you would wet your trousers, because they had enormous informal power, although they had no real one."*

Faltus concludes that what was socially needed and economically effective was decided by force by the centre (Faltus 1995). Šulc adds that the consequence of the "all-society" goals was that the motivation of the planners was non-economical. Additionally, the author points out that the planning system did not know the limits of the market economy and thus "the goals and preferences deemed by the governing group as socially desired could be implemented into the system easily" (Šulc 2004, p. 42). It means that the communists believed that there were no economic limits once the economy was "scientifically governed." Šulc further writes that:

> *Socialist, especially in the early stages of the movement, considered this characteristic to be the greatest advantage of the centrally planned economy. Marx considered it the key tool enabling people's liberation from the oppression of economy, a way to deal with labour-product alienation. Shorter working hours and changed character of labour, he believed, should make way for free development of an individual as a self-purpose for his self-realization. The real course of the development of these original socialist ideas, however, went in a different direction and Marx's followers soon forgot,*

or did not know, the original humanist motivation of focus on economics. The "limitations" of introducing "societal" preferences has so far been limited in countries based on the central allocation mechanisms to the delayed catching-up with lifestyle typical of Western consumerist societies.

(Šulc 2004, p. 42)

Our respondent who worked in the SPK <ID040>, mentioned that:

The plan was balanced with a rough estimate at 96–104%, which means it allowed for both not meeting as well as overfulfilling and thus consequent reserves or tolerances. [. . .] Of course, the process of the plan creation was a constant dialogue between the decision-makers and companies. [. . .] The final form of the plan was preceded by two or more earlier drafts, which considered ideas and expectations of all participants. The SKP had the upper hand not just because it was required by the law, but also that it had a top-quality apparatus and complex information, efficient comparative methods, etc. <ID040>.

Thus, he admitted that the process of the creation of the plan was negotiated, but he believed that the centre had the upper hand in this negotiation. But even though he believed that the process was de facto smooth, the economic planners had to face multiple difficulties. Foremost, they had to follow political orders that were unstable and potentially irrational (see Box 4.1). At the same time, even the members of the centre had their own interests in accomplishing of the plan of their subordinated units because they were evaluated accordingly (Malý and Herz 1988). Particular high-ranking communists were responsible for individual sectors of the economy. They were thus responsible for economic results of the subordinated companies, and their competitors in the political arena were always ready to point out their failure. The consequence was that they had to demonstrate the success of the subordinated units and the easiest way was to give them the easiest tasks or change the tasks to achieve success (Vraný 1995). As a result, each of the responsible communist leaders became a lobbyist for his or her (mostly his) subordinates. This attitude, in fact, weakened the plan under preparation.

Box 4.1 Setting of the plan in the SPK

The section chief in the SPK <ID040> told us about the setting of the general plan the following:

"Anyway, for the 1986 plan, we couldn't set the figure of the year-on-year growth any better than at some 1.8, 1.9 or 2%, I guess. An what happened was that the chairman of the SPK was called off to the party Politburo meeting, and it was not a short meeting. So he

came back at, I don't know, half past six, or seven in the evening, we were waiting for him with the SPK session proceedings. And he came, sat down with this kind of absent-minded look in his face and just sat and stared. And we all waited for him to say something. And he looked totally shocked. And finally one of the deputies couldn't wait any longer and asked: 'So what? What did the Politburo say?' And he answered: 'Well, generally, [. . .] generally fine, but we have to set it at 2.5.' And the whole plenary session went [. . .] and someone stood up and said: '2.5, that is ridiculous!' And the chairman said: 'I do not mean to discuss here whether it is ridiculous or not, I say we set the plan at 2.5% growth. So we just sat around uneasily and the man asked again: 'And Comrade Chairman, how do we set it for 87?' To which he replied: 'I say 2.5.' And the man says: 'No that was for 86.' And the chairman said: 'It is 2.5 for 87 too!' And the whole plenary session breathed in astonishment and went like, it could be managed, when you flip it, like the budget, you invoice January expenditures in December, because you need to play with the balance deficit. And then, when the plenary went quiet, someone asked: 'And for 88?' And the chairman, who obviously felt uncomfortable being examined like that said: 'Well, of course, it will be 2.5 as well.' At that moment, the whole plenary session turned from astonishment and shock to outright laughter, all the sixty people there. We just laughed our tears out. It was like when you watch a great silent comedy, like when someone falls off a railway engine. The whole situation was saved by one XY, a great friend of mine, dead now. He was about ten years older than me and stuttered a bit. And he went: 'We d-d-don't need to ask, 89 and 90 2.5 t-t-too, right?' And the chairman replied: 'Of course.' And this friend of mine finished it off with a fabulous line, and you may quote me here, he said: 'Comrade Minister, Comrade Chairman, and do you want the five-year plan in its new form by tonight or will you be kind enough to wait for it till tomorrow morning.' (laughter) We all knew very well that it was just monkey business. And the chairman replied: 'I can wait till lunchtime.' The thing is to re-do the five-year plan would take like three months and now, when he said till lunchtime, and it was late evening already, it was just clear that we would just draw a plan totally off any reality."

[. . .]

"Because there were people who knew how to make it happen. Because we had some 54 billion stashed away in reserves. And the difference was between the missing produce and bloated use. Because we knew that there was a risk that the Politburo would embargo the plan. That is why we had these reserves. So, it was like a cheat, a fake, dual accounting. One for the officials and one for

reality. Yes, that is the way it was in real. They didn't know, even Štrougal [the then Prime Minister] didn't know."

I: *"Wait, like the whole plenary planning session that set it up, they didn't, they managed to keep it secret?"*
R: *"Sure, no one betrayed it, ever."*
I: *"So you were given just one day from the Central Committee . . .?"*
R. *"We got one night."*
I: *". . . to like change the growth figure from 1.9 to 2.5?"*
R: *"Yes."*
I: *"And you made it by the morning."*
R: *"Well, by lunchtime."*
I: *"And you sent it back to the Politburo?"*
R: *"'Well done,' they said, 'see, where there is a will, there is a way.' It was real humbug. Of course."*
I: *"And what about the Central Committee?"*
R: *"They just bought it."*
I: *"There were like three people who knew. I mean, were there people who, using the common sense might . . .?"*
R: *"Well, we expected the idiocy. The politicians simply have no scruples. They demand something and then find out that it is a disaster. Well doesn't matter now. We knew that they had big ambitions to make decision without understanding the system and how it worked. It is always like that. The less you know, the easier it is for you to make decisions. [. . .] So, like cause we knew. Or not knew, but presumed, we had been ready expecting such development and knowing we would be under time pressure, so we had made a parallel version of the plan. It is simple."*

Regardless of political consequences, the other difficulty was with dispersed information in the economy as Hayek (see Chapter 2) argues. There is a general belief that the planners' knowledge about the companies' real abilities was highly limited (e.g., Landau and Průcha 1995, p. 52).[1] Hiding information by the companies has been well documented by our respondents. A typical example could be hoarding of raw materials (see 4.4.2). Respondent (<ID043>, assistant to the director in engineering) put it simply: "The people in Prague had no idea what the capacities of the company were." Associate professor and head of department in Prognostic Institution <ID071> confirmed: "Well, of course, each subject at the lower levels, down to company level had the most of information. And they would only release information they wanted to be known above." At the same time, the central party organizations were in further information disadvantage to economic hierarchy because they obtained information only from it (MP and secretary of ObNV Ostrava <ID026>).

Our respondent (planner in construction <ID058>) described another way of dealing with information:

> *They only report certain information, to certain people, often different people, so they only learn a bit. And often happened in long and detailed reports, knowing that hardly anyone will bother reading them and if anyone complains, you can go like, look, I did tell you here, on page 113! Sure I remember this, sure. I mean, who would read it, I surely wouldn't. There was this famous joke, once we are on this topic, I don't remember it exactly, I just heard it. A colleague of mine, higher ranking than myself, somewhere in his long report to the directorate general included page 150, which read his telephone number and a message: "Anyone who has read up to this page, call me and I owe you a bottle of wine." No one ever called (laughter). Indeed, they knew how it worked.*

Šulc writes about the centre's weak negotiating position based on the scarcity of information, and it was further limited by informal relationships, connections, corruption, etc. (Šulc 1995). Additionally, information was even further distorted because it had to pass several tiers of governing from the centre via the VHJs to companies (Mlčoch 1990). Malý and Herz mention that the centre was not able to objectively find out the local units' reserves and govern enormous number of details (Malýand Herz 1988). The centre, however, believed that it had enough information as confirmed by a respondent who worked in the central planning commission <ID040>. He even believes that the centre had an information advantage:

> *The need for the scientific approach to the planning process was felt namely at the level of the State Planning Commission, where we realized that we had huge competences and huge opportunities and, of course, huge responsibility. And in order to be ready to face the forces of both the middle management tier and the ministries, as we drew plans for all of them, in, I don't know, engineering or metallurgy, or what have you, coal mining, we had to have at least the same amount of information as they did. And on top of that, we had the connections, which is what they lacked. Connections between production, sales, prices, and so on. So, in this respect, the need for information superiority was conditioned by an enormous volume of information technology, automated data processing, for some time it was called automated management systems, and so on and so forth. And, of course, the advantage was that you could centralize all the information in one building.*

Šulc, on the contrary, asserts that the centre knew that companies were trying to hide their true capacities and it did not know the companies' production function (Šulc 2004). Even the ministries created reserves and the SPK knew about it, as our respondent <ID040> documented: "Obviously, each ministry kept some reserves to cover possible imbalances, because, there could be, I don't know, holidays and days off, or bad weather in agriculture, and so on." The result was that the centre (the SPK) permanently increased the planned production by application of a so-called index method. The practice was that the goals for the following year were increased by certain percentage every year to force the companies to use their reserves (Rendl et al. 1988). The growth achieved in the previous period was considered minimal for the following period regardless of real production abilities of the companies. Annual growth of planned target was applied even though it was not supported by additional investment (Landau and Průcha 1995). Application of the method resulted in perverse incentives for companies. One of our respondents, <ID007> a planner and head of supplying in an engineering company, documented the application of this method:

I: *On account of what did the plan for the company change over the years? According to how successful the company had been in the previous period, or what were the criteria?*

R: *Criteria? I don't really know. We were simply given some tasks and we had to meet them. What was behind the growth in the plan? I don't know. I just remember that we felt punished like we reached the best results and they punished us by increasing the plan and giving us more to do.*

I: *And how much did it grow? Like 2% or 3% a year?*

R: *No, what we got was . . . the record was, I think some 7.5% or 8%. And that was really big. And this was the overall, for the whole factory, while some of the departments got even as much as 13% or 14%*

Turek adds an example from the Jihotvar company in Veselí nad Lužnicí, which produced small concrete products. Its brownfield site was filled with scrap iron. The company offered to transport it to a scrap yard but only 50 tons out of, e.g., 500 tons. The reason was that otherwise the centre would have wanted the same amount to be delivered in the following years (Turek 1995).

The index method was for the centre generally the safest way to change production. Because globally any disproportional change in the plans was risky. Gregory and Stuart write that the planners wanted to make as few changes as possible in their plans (even though technology and tastes of consumers changed in the meantime) because of the second-round effect – they wanted to avoid major disruptions of the material balances (Gregory and Stuart 2014). The planning of material balances was extremely difficult because they embraced only about half of the production (Šulc 1995). The rest was covered by contracts between suppliers and buyers. On the other hand, the centre sometimes provided highly detailed orders that were more like political declarations. For example, Turek quotes: "The government is therefore obliging the Ministry of Agriculture, the Ministry of Food Industry, national enterprises and sugar factories to ensure better irrigation management securing even and quicker rise of sugar beet by working the field in the spring as soon as the ridges of furrow turn dry" (Turek 1995, p. 16).

Another method to force the companies to reveal their hidden reserves was a special tool called "friendly planning" (see Box 4.2).

Box 4.2 Friendly planning (vstřícné plánování)

The method was invented in the Soviet Union in 1930. The goal was to increase efficiency, mobilization of the inner reserves, progressive increasing of the state plan on the bases of the initiative, experience, and proposals of employees (Rendl et al. 1988). Mlčoch states that the companies had to prepare this friendly plan (Mlčoch 1990). Rendl et al. add that the friendly plans were used for declining on material and energetic demand, but it was sometimes applied only formally and even administratively for example by setting of the higher plan by the superior institution. The application supposed that if the company accepted in the course of the five-year plan period a more demanding (friendly) plan than expected, it was in a better position than if it should just surpass the original plan. Accepting of the friendly plan had a positive impact on wages. The authors, however, mention that this method was not successful. It resulted in companies' effort to minimize the goals of the five-year plan. Additionally, under the conditions of the permanently changing five-year plan they were not interested in increasing of the year plans especially because these achievements would be carried over to following years (Rendl et al. 1988).

The centre insisted on meeting the plan,[2] partially because it had its own eminent interest in meeting it. But it was complicated because the economy was permanently moving, among others due to changes in the world economy and in the needs of market participants. It resulted in difficulties in meeting the plan. But the formal reasons for not meeting the plans were just in insufficient discipline of the participants or in drawbacks in the plan creation (Šulc 2004). The general performance of the economy in meeting the planned goals is summarized in Chapter 5.

4.2.2 *Investment*

A specific area of the centre's activity was represented by investment. In practice, the centre drained the funds from companies (via sectoral corporate taxes) and households (via high saving rate due to low level of consumption) and reallocated them according to visions and preferences of the central planners. The five-year plans articulated the main investment ideas (Průcha 1988). The particular yearly investment plans were defined in financial quotas for respective branches in the economy. Šulc mentions that the direction of the investment followed the biggest deficits in the economy (Šulc 2004). Interestingly, in several attempted reforms ranging from the 1950s to the 1980s, the central planners usually decided to give the companies more freedom in using their investment funds. However, all these attempts ended with huge imbalances and a re-centralization of the investment decisions (see Chapter 5).

According to one of our respondents, head of a production company in agriculture <ID010>, it was extremely difficult to obtain an investment approval:

> *So, sometimes, the reasons for the company lagging behind were not objective, like that it failed to force its management decision or investment. Yes, there were these role-model companies, where political pushes led to pressure on the SPK, which then directed investments from the regional budget. And this meant that some of the companies were in a better position, while others were kept back, despite the fact that their efficiency was good. But they did not have the lobbying and political favour. So, you would take a crate of wine and went to visit the SPK in Prague.*

Approval of investment did not inevitably mean a victory because it was necessary to ensure the construction, and the capacities were highly oversubscribed. The consequence was a growing number of unfinished constructions. Šrein interestingly comments that, according to the official plan (and theory), unfinished constructions were not expected to appear in the system, because the compiled balance in construction compared with the claims of investors with the capacities of the construction industry. The centre approved the specific investment only if the construction companies obliged to keep deadlines (Šrein 1995). However, the everyday practice was different and the scope of unfinished constructions was increasing. According to one respondent (investment methodologist in construction <ID064>) there were cases when the investor was more or less helpless and unable to force the suppliers to meet their promised part in the deal, given the circumstances and the timing.

In practice, this situation got worse permanently each year and more and more constructions remained unfinished (Šrein 1995). Šulc observes that one third of constructions in 1980 was overdue (Šulc 2004). This situation was described by one of our respondents – a general director in the electrotechnical industry <ID047>:

> *Well, loans, loans, it didn't really work, as there was no such thing as unpaid debts. It was all controlled from the centre and the company never dealt with money, only on paper. You had to beg to be granted investment, you had to go to the planning commission and beg and beg. If not foreign currency, at least crowns. And even if you got some money, you couldn't buy anything, so you planned to build something, like a water cleaning facility, say. But then again, you might have been granted investment, but the construction capacities were all subject to the plan, so they had to meet their plan and couldn't build for you. Eventually, you often ended up unable to use the investment, as there was nowhere to invest. Of course, foreign [convertible] currencies, it was different, you always spent it all.*

The impossibility to finish a construction was often a consequence of the shortage character of the economy. For example, the interviewee who worked as an investment methodologist in construction <ID064> said that: "Our company ordered, I think seven or eight construction cranes, but the manufacturer could not produce more than one or two a year, so you had to wait for two years or so."

We have already mentioned that fixed prices limited the flow of information to the centre. The same is true for investment decisions. The allocation of the investment depended on the requirements of the companies and their abilities to convince the planners, not on interest rates. The companies (of course) struggled to maximize their investment funds and overstated their claims. They had an abundance of investment plans and tried to prove their necessity in the planned system; future profits were difficult to estimate as the head of trade department in investment engineering <ID050> described:

> *Of course, everything was planned, sales, exchange of goods, income and investments for respective companies as well. [. . .] And the SPK determined the volume of investment funds for the ministries and these then down to the VHJs and these then to the respective companies. [. . .] So we would bid our demands and send them up. [. . .] I think the greatest deficit of the planning system was that the investments were allocated, that the companies did not have to earn them. They were granted from above, so everyone asked for more than they really needed, knowing that they would not get as much as they asked for, so everyone exaggerated.*

Interest rates did not affect the allocation of the investment funds because investments were allocated by order. Šulc writes that they were set by the centre with the only purpose: to stimulate fulfilling of the plan. Interest rate was used as a deterrent – as punishment for failing to meet the plan or late repayment of the credit (Šulc 2004). However, Mlčoch remarks that the impact of the penalty interest rates on behaviour of the companies was very low in practice (Mlčoch 1990). On the whole, interest rates generally did not play a significant role as a regulation tool in the economy. Moreover, the amount of savings did not have an impact on the volume of investment either. Šulc concludes that financing of investment by savings was just a statistical not economic issue (Šulc 2004).

The then authors of textbooks on central planning declared that the centre carefully selected the best investment proposals. Rozsypal et al. write about technical-economic studies that evaluated the profitability and feasibility of every investment projects (Rozsypal et al. 1981). Rendl et al. mention evaluation methodology of the investment plans and obligations of each investor to prove efficiency of the planned investment. These proofs were supposed to be the main criteria for the incorporation of a particular investment project into the central plan (Rendl et al. 1988). Mlčoch opposes, claiming that the reality was different. He mentions that a decision about investments was a conclusion of a long-run labyrinthine process of preparation, discussion, and approval in an unclear jungle of institutions superior to the company. The companies had to struggle to be rewarded by an investment project (Mlčoch 1990). The investment approval formally depended on the promised future profits. However, Mlčoch writes about the non-existence of a relationship between the promised yields of the investment and responsibility of the managers. He mentions the "motivation euphoria" of the managers while promising the future profits of their investment activity (ibidem). They would use expected prices of costs and incomes in the future. Therefore, companies tended to underestimate the costs of investment and overestimate the technical-economic parameters of the future incomes from the finished investment. At the same time, they were interested in maximizing investment because their salaries, bonuses, and promotions depended on the growth of their company (as in the market economy) but contrary to markets they were not disciplined by stock exchange yields or by other limits (Nuti 1981). In addition, the company needed a confirmation from the supplier of the investment that it had free capacities for it. This confirmation was often obtained by means of connections, reciprocal service, or bribes. Consequently, there was permanent growth in costs and delays (Šulc 2004). Mlčoch adds that the construction suppliers were able to act from the position of power and the systems of technical-economic indicators (set by centre) could not prevent them from enforcing higher individual supplier's costs. Prices did not matter in his view because, among others, the success of investment was measured in the planned system by "invested volumes." Mlčoch estimates the growth of a hypothetic index of construction cost in period 1970–1980 to 250% and for machinery up to 800–1000% (Mlčoch 1990). These were horrendous numbers in comparison to the nearly stable official price level.

4.2.3 Wage policy

One of the other aspects that the centre de facto decided was demand for labour and wages. As referred to the demand side, in the socialist period, all economic activity depended on the decision of the centre, which decided on the planned output volume. This predetermined the labour force requested by the companies. Then negotiations followed relating to the number of resources allocated, as businesses typically required more resources than the central authorities assigned to them.

From the very beginning, labour recruitment was not governed by the law of supply and demand, but by regulations from the centre. According to Šulc, the planning authority was in practice involved in both, the formation of the labour supply, as well as the demand for it, and the centre also decided on the distribution of disposable manpower (Šulc 2004).

One of the typical features of the system was the obligation to employ graduates of universities, apprentices, and selected professionals. The companies were ordered concerning how many graduates they were supposed to employ over the plan because unemployment of the young was unacceptable (Kalinová 2012). Moreover, in a number of cases, the company had to accept unskilled workers just because the centre had decided for them to do so (Havelková 2009b).

In addition to decisions regarding the allocation of workforce, the centre also had a monopoly on determining the main part of the worker's wages. The ideology expected the appearance of a new socialist person (see Chapter 1).

Reform-minded Prime Minister Štrougal declared in his memoirs that some dogmatists in the 1980s still kept repeating that the main stimulus for work was supposed to be devotion to the country, company, and party (Štrougal 2009). This egalitarian character of the system was also reflected in wage policy. Šulc believes that the wages were set below their reproductive value (Šulc 2004). This was possible due to the fact that a large part of the personal income was provided in the form of transfers or public services financed from state budget (costs of education, social benefits, subsidized prices of goods, etc.) and was therefore included neither in wages, nor in enterprises' calculations. Because wages/income were relatively low, ordinary people used most of it and savings were generally not very high.

Wages in the socialist era consisted of three components. The principal one was the tariff wage. This was increased by supplementary charges (e.g., for overtime work or night shifts) and bonuses. This motivational component depended on the accomplishing the plan of the working team/company etc. (Havelková 2009b). According to a former director of an engineering company <ID006>, the tariff wages were limited, and their growth was also centrally set. Everything was subject to the so-called functional schemes in which every worker was categorized. It was precisely defined what each function's job description was and how it should be classified.

Similarly, most of the respondents complained that bonuses were set by the centre. These reflected sector-wide and enterprise results and the work of the collective. This strongly diminished the significance of an individual's performance and results. The collective results depended on the plan fulfilment, as it was one of the few possibilities of increasing earnings and ensuring employees' satisfaction: "It was clear that when the economic plan was met somehow . . . people got a pay" (Designer and leading worker in construction <ID031>). Our respondents told us that the higher the position the higher the bonuses. In some cases, the director and deputies had up to a 100% bonus to their wage (<ID003> chief designer in an engineering company). Another respondent said that if a director did not obtain a 100% bonus to his or her wage, he or she automatically cut the subordinates' bonuses as well (<ID028>, chief economist in agricultural company). He added that management often had bonuses only once a year but the lower positions monthly. And the technical director in construction (<ID041>) commented that the bonuses for a worker never reached 20 or 25% as in the case of a technician.

There were other possibilities regarding improving one's wage. One of them were improvement proposals. These were based on proposals made by employees with a view to saving material, improving performance, quality, etc. For example, in an engineering company, once approved and implemented, such proposals could result in a one-time reward at the amount of three times the wage and a subsequent percentage increase over several years (a planner and head of supplying in an engineering company <ID007>). Other possibilities consisted of a good collective performance in the Brigade of Socialist Work. The goal of socialist competition was, above all, to increase labour productivity and social efficiency in production. The Brigades were based on the competition of individual teams of workers, with the individual teams not competing against each other, but striving for the best possible fulfilment of their commitment. This was to make production more efficient and to improve the socialist morale and political awareness of workers. The individual teams were thus expected to contribute to increasing labour productivity and introducing new technology. Individual members were expected to increase their qualifications when needed and then share their experience with other workers in the company. The by-product was the consolidation of comradely relations within the working group (Kravarová 1983). The participants could get, for example, a travel permit to one of the affiliated countries. However, the reward of the Brigade did not always go to the most efficient team of workers. It was often awarded to another group that the centre wanted to motivate (Head of the technical department in an engineering company <ID020>).

Therefore, in general, employees were rewarded or punished nearly entirely for good or poor collective results, as meeting the plan depended on the work of the whole group, as well as the results of the competition in the Brigades of Socialist Work. In the words of our respondent, the performance rewards were mostly the same or very similar for all employees and were independent of whether they were a top worker or a low-performance worker (a planner and head of supplying in an engineering company <ID007>).

Indeed, our respondents told us that manual workers could earn the same or even higher wage than the management of the company (for distribution of average wages see Table 1.8 in Chapter 1). One of our respondents stated that, for example, in agriculture: "A good tractor driver often earned more money that the head of the cooperative" (head of a production company in agriculture <ID010>). The same was true for transport (Operating deputy in transport <ID009>), or engineering: "Differences in wages were relatively small. Well, it was not really the director who earned the biggest money. Usually, these were prominent workers. And service workers, who could travel abroad" (an economic planner in an engineering company <ID008>).

Another group of employees that received preferential wage treatment were the members of the Communist Party. Kohout and Kolář (1966) deal with vertical mobility, especially with the influence of potential job promotion on employees' productivity. They conclude that the aspirations of the party members were generally higher. Moreover, the possibility of promotion was often associated with party membership (see Section 4.1.3). Head of production in cold rolling mill <ID035> mentioned the negative influence of the party. He even considered party personal policy as "the grave of the whole system" because the party controlled the best paid positions and some of the foremen received very high wages – they were nicknamed as "workers aristocracy."

Vertical mobility discrimination had its specific manifestation also in gender discrimination. Men held almost all leading positions. Women did not even have access to them in the sectors where they dominated, even if they had sufficient qualifications (Jechová 2012).[3] Moreover, the regime officially declared equality between men and women. Nevertheless, the reality differed greatly from these declarations and despite the fact that the regime proclaimed equality between the sexes, this equality was far from achieved despite the liquidation of capitalist relations. In many cases, this inequality stemmed from the fact that men more often performed more physically demanding tasks. However, in some enterprises, for example Vagónka Studénka (an engineering company) women performed the same hard work as men, whose salary was, however, 1,000 crowns higher. It was a direct consequence of a belief that a man was the breadwinner of the family, and a woman's income was just a supplement to the family budget. According to the foreman from an engineering company: "They [women] were paid three to five crowns per hour and when they needed to use the bathroom, they had to ring a bell and ask a pardon . . . real hard labour it was, real. And they would work shifts, night shifts, too. You can't compare this, really" (<ID015>).

Thus, a system was created so that, on the one hand, it prevented wage differentials between professions, on the other, it tolerated unjustified differences in wages between men and women. The wage policy was generally not based on labour productivity.

4.2.4 Who controlled the centre?

The last question that remains is who held the reins. Who, if anyone, controlled the central planning institutions? The central planners obtained the instructions and tasks from the top Communist Party authorities and they were responsible to them. Meanwhile, they were under the permanent control of the secret police. For the investigations of the StB in the State Planning Commission during the last year of the socialist regime, see Box 4.3.

Box 4.3 Secret police in the State Planning Commission (SPK) during Perestroika

Our respondent in the SPK told us that relationships between the StB and the SPK were rather cooperative than supervisory: "As for the StB. You must realize that both institutions followed the same interest, that was, to protect the economic interests of the republic against foreign economic espionage. So, it was more of a collegial, rather than competitive of supervisory relationship. What is more, a 'top-secret' (in fact notoriously known) head of the department sat in the adjacent office 'disguised' as an ordinary clerk" <ID040>.

However, the StB's activity was not so easy-going. One of the regular reports by the StB from May to October 1989 (ABS, A34/1, inv.j. 1261) noticed growing uneasiness of the SPK's employees about the political development and fears for their personal positions and posts

(June 1989). Agents of the StB found out that the members of the commission were generally unenthusiastic about Perestroika. It is not surprising because Perestroika had many similar features to Czechoslovak reforms from 1968. The reformers were then replaced by conservative cadres. The members of the SPK compared Perestroika to these reforms. In their eyes, the process was not well prepared and caused chaos (May 1989). A majority of them believed it to be "destabilizing the economic centre." And they were convinced that the public did not understand the process for its lack of clarity of the basic concepts in relation to political system (June 1989). Members of the SPK believed that dismissed deputy chairmen of the SPK were laid off for their conservative views (September 1989). Otherwise, they refused the highly critical analysis of the state of the economy produced by the Prognostic Institute (more on the Prognostic institute in Chapter 5). The StB concluded that in fact "nobody was doing anything" (especially higher members of management) because they did not know what would happen to them personally, but they were at the same time not willing to express negative position because they did not know whom and when they would need (July 1989).

Additionally, the StB was informed about two subgroups among the SPK's employees. One of them consisted of ex-members of the Communist Party (dismissed after 1968) who expected moral rehabilitation and intended to influence young workers. The other consisted of young workers who invited the reforms and tried to gain political influence via membership in the Communist Party structures (May 1989). The StB were informed about contacts with illegal structures as well. And the reports noted that one member of the SPK cooperated with a group of professors at the University of Economics, Prague, who were contemplating an organization of inner trade based on market relationship. His superiors in the SPK assessed this approach in odds with Perestroika and semi-illegal (October 1989).

Generally, the reports show that the StB had realized that the centrally planned system had not been functioning. But the authors of the reports flatly refused the fall of the Communist Party. They instead followed the official Perestroika's policy. The reports from the SPK in fact informed mostly of non-cooperation and blocking of the reforms on the ground of institution. At the same time, they refused the idea of markets, but they were not able to distinguish the border between socialism and market. This chaos resulted in statements like: "We need marketing, but we do not want market economy." This schism generally reflected disputes among the high-ranking members of the KSČ in the given period. The clashes between reformers and conservatives are described for example in Handl (2018).

We started our analyses of the "actors" of central planning with the centre. We were foremost interested in the role of the centre in forming (and meeting) of the plan. It was complicated to keep the whole system balanced, especially when politicians intervened in the work of the SPK. On the other hand, our respondents brought various accounts of the centre lacking information. Investment and wage policies were under the control of the centre as well. The investment decisions were based foremost on the pressure of varying lobbying groups and not on the profitability of the projects. Wage policy was rigid and constrained functioning of the labour market. The companies were forced to find ways around to deal with labour force.

4.3 The role of the VHJs in the CPE system

The tasks created by the centre were passed to subordinate units. The VHJs played the position of the middle segment in the hierarchy below the centre.[4] The section follows the pattern of the previous one and it describes the plan-lifecycle process from the perspective of the VHJs. Special interest is paid to relationships inside the VHJs and their active role in meeting of the plan.

One of our respondents (General director of company in knitting industry and later on deputy Minister <ID073>) described the role of his VHJ the following way. I: "So the name of the VHJ was 'Knitting Industry?'" R: "Yes, it was 'VHJ Knitting Industry.' So we were the knitters, next to us you had the cotton VHJ, the linen VHJ, the wool VHJ and the clothes factory Prostějov. It was principally the entire textile segment, The VHJ of ours, I must try to remember hard now, comprised some 14 companies and two research institutes."

The VHJs' position in the system changed several times during the socialist period. But they were generally supposed to pass on and distribute the planning orders to subordinated companies, supervise and potentially punish them for failing to meet the plan (e.g., <ID005> analyst and mathematician in an engineering company). He described the process of dividing tasks the following way:

> *The SPK sent the plan down to the VHJ, where you had the five directors (general director and directors of respective companies) and then each company had its own five departments with specific responsibilities. The VHJ was in touch with the SPK. The centre created the plan, but the VHJs decided how it would be distributed down to company level.*

At the same time, the VHJs decided about investment, as an economic planner who worked in engineering <ID008> told us:

> *The volume of investment was balanced by the SPK, which handed out these "investment presents" to the VHJs on the basis of some macroeconomic indicators, I have no idea which ones. So this VHJ then had a bulk of investments to pass down to the subordinate company level, and they tried to do so in a*

> *reasonable way. This meant, in a way that would enable them to invest. The investment would come to their budget or plan, especially companies that had something to offer, to put it this way. Well, if there was a chance of a licence, licenced production, or if the company topped the others in the sector within the VHJ, well, then it would get bigger tasks and bigger rewards, for instants bigger investment funds.*

The unit as a whole, according to the technical director of the construction company <ID041>, had to accept the global indicators set by the plan:

I: *And, did you, as a company, had a chance to influence the setting of the plan?*
R: *Sure, sure, of course. It was because each company had . . . its capacities, its possibilities, it was aware of its material base, technological base, machinery, and a number of other things included. So the company would say: "Come on we cannot manage this." But the bulk was so big that it simply had to be distributed one way or another.*
I: *Now you mean among the companies?*
R: *Among the companies, of course.*

But the specific plan was a matter of negotiation among the different levels in the planning hierarchy as we have already showed. Two of our respondents (a power plant director <ID014>) told us the following. I: "So, how did you as a concern . . . how could you influence the plans that fell upon you, plans that you got from above?" R: "Well, it was interaction, you know, up and down . . . because between us and the centre, we had the concern, so the plan travelled up and down until it stuck somewhere."

At the same time, the VHJs' own evaluation (and bonuses) depended on their subordinated companies meeting the plan. The consequence was that the utmost goal of any VHJ was to negotiate the plans well within reach of its subordinated companies and thus maximize the chances that its own plan would be achieved as well. As a result, they understandably did not seek to appoint a demanding plan on the brink of companies' abilities, enforce them to cost cutting, or force them to reveal their hidden reserves (Mlčoch 1990). Our respondent (planner in construction <ID058>) affirmed:

> *It was all set so that we wouldn't get overworked, run into problems or panic. And like that. It was like, everyone knew how it was going to work, so we put it in the plan, you know. And it had to be coordinated through the company, the SPK and the ministries. At all levels, people wanted a plan that they could meet for their part, so that they could proudly confirm meeting the plan, so they helped to make it manageable.*

Additionally, informal personal relationships and contacts at ministry level were always valuable in a struggle to achieve a reasonable plan (Soulsby and Clark 1996). Another respondent who worked as a scientist in the Prognostic

Institute <ID034> summarized that the plan was decided at the level of the centre:

> *But when the plan proposal came out and the VHJ learnt (either formally or informally) what was coming, the CEO of the respective concern [. . .] went to meet the regional authorities or the ministry and started negotiating. And he would use his possibilities and methods, whichever they were, and said: "Come on, be sensible, if you draft such a plan, we won't meet it anyway and you will only have problems."*

Similarly, an economist and planner in agriculture <ID018> told us two possible variants when the cooperative asked a superior institution for a tractor:

> *"Look, Franta, there are 35 cooperatives and I can allocate four tractors for the next year . . . your tractor is ten years old and your neighbour's twenty, so I will give one of the four tractors to him this time." Or, he could have said: "Franta, you won't get anything, I go to pub with Pepa, he will get the tractor."*

A respondent (economic planner in an engineering company <ID008>) provided evidence that the struggle to achieve the overall plan for the whole VHJ resulted in relatively good relationships between the VHJ and its subordinate companies: "Ok, there were some dangers, discussion was on, but in the end, everyone tried to reach a compromise. The VHJ didn't try to be directive, they tried to be relatively open-minded. Definitely, a lot could be achieved through a discussion back in the 80s."

The main intention in meeting the plan was confirmed by another respondent (assistant to the director in engineering <ID043>) who mentioned:

> *Because it's from the top of the bottom, that's the system. Right. The CEO of . . . like the whole VHJ, of all companies, he had a plan prescribed by the ministry, by the State Planning Commission. The moment he says his twelve companies do not meet the plan, of course, it's his fault. So he did not have the slightest interest in that. He needed the directors to meet the plan, right? Actually, de facto, the interest was in keeping the unit, or . . . every CEO was from some engineering company. He knew well what it was about. Where the problem was, yeah. Everyone knew that the plan, as it was built, that it was unrealistic, that there were some 15% of . . . something that would not be made, that would simply be passed on. And now the thing was just to make sure it would not accumulate.*

Other respondents talk about very good cooperative relationship among the directors inside the VHJ – for example a Head of the Project Manager's Office in Metallurgy <ID066> said: "I still feel impressed by how the bosses of those companies, the directors of the individual companies, managed to co-operate and coordinate gradually at all levels below, that everything was interconnected within the concern. [. . .] And all the directors, as I regarded it, made up such a good, to use a regime term, 'collective.'"

The intention to meet the plan was of utmost priority for the VHJ because the bonuses depended on it, as director in engineering described <ID006>:

> *So, each company made an effort to overfulfill the plan, which meant to earn a bonus, but it was regulated by directives set by the company's directorate-general. And when the Directorate General met the plan, it was a part of the overall result of the general, the entire concern. So, these bonuses were conditioned by the whole concern meeting the plan, and if so, shares could be paid. So, to what degree the plan could be overfulfilled, it was decided by the General Directorate.*

Even if the VHJ had not been as cynical as the respondents stated and it had a good intention to increase efficiency it would have collided with the omnipresent information asymmetry. Important economic information was naturally spread among the subordinated enterprises but the VHJ had limited access to it. The same, to a larger extent, was true for the relationship between the centre and the VHJs (see Section 4.2.1).

We can conclude with Šulc who writes that the companies were the real masters of the planning process because all the superior authorities (the GŘ or the VHJs, via superior ministries up to the SPK) were dependent on the performance of the companies and their ability to reach the planed results (Šulc 2004). Our respondents told us about the role of the VHJs in the attempts to meet the plans for the whole unit:

> *Because, and that is something I may not have mentioned yet, with each director dismissed, the plan softened. This means that at the VHJ level you always . . . there it opened, and the decision reached said that the respective director was responsible for such a state, and that it had to be covered somehow, because we cannot, of course, send half of the factory management to prison, so the plan was softened. It was distributed to all those who fulfilled it up to 100.4%, so for each of these, the plan grew by half a percent, or a percent, the plan got softened, you know. And the new director started, say, with a drop of . . . I do not know . . . 50 million, like it was 10 million . . . so he started on a softer plan minus 5 and his task was to catch up. See?*
>
> *(assistant to the direction in an engineering company <ID043>)*

This was corroborated by a technical director in construction <ID041>, who confirmed that the objective was to redistribute the plan and provide mutual help so that all parts of the VHJ would meet its plan.

Mlčoch adds that the common goals of the VHJs and the subordinated companies on meeting the plan sometimes induced even "advisory activity" by the VHJs aimed at helping "less successful" companies with financial statements (Mlčoch 1990). In case of failure to meet the plan, the VHJs tried to concentrate the blame on one company and thus minimize the material consequences of non-fulfilling for the whole VHJ (Mlčoch 1990). None of the respondents, however, affirmed this particular practice. Consequences for the unfortunate company would probably be harsh and a laggard, meeting plan at, say, 80%, among all other 100% fulfillers would be most suspicious.

Even though some VHJs had possibly good intentions to increase the efficiency of their subordinated units, they always ran into barrier of their own appraisal and they were hardly willing to risk their own bonuses. At the same time, they became the disrupting element in the rigorous central planning system due to aggregating and dividing the plans or helping the subordinate companies with meeting their plan. It generally seems that they were more on the side of the companies than on the side of the centre, at minimum because they better understood the everyday problems the companies had to face.

4.4 Behaviour of companies

The centrally planned system was created with a theoretical idea that companies would be passive recipients of the centres' goals without any intentions or targets of their own and that they would simply make maximal effort to achieve these tasks (Ježek in Zieleniec et al. 1990). The everyday reality was different, and companies were obviously not just executive pieces in the perfectly administrated central plan, but they pursued their own goals and made their own decisions (e.g., Šulc 1995). Their behaviour reflected the incentives that they received from the socio-economic environment (see Section 4.1). And they behaved as rational agents – in an inevitable and understandable way.

In a market economy, the main motivation for companies is profit or sales. The centrally planned system liquidated this direct relationship. Success of the companies was not measured by their ability to make profit (because profit was in fact only a residual quantity) but by their ability to meet the plan and as such, it thus de facto depended on the behaviour of the centre (Šulc 1995). Možný even argues that the institution of profit was a taboo (Možný 1991) because it was considered as an extremely negative (immoral) aspect, typical of the capitalist economic system. Additionally, the common/state ownership of the companies resulted in a situation when they were generally uninterested in efficiency because it did not bring any reward to them. The ultimate theoretical reward – communism – was supposed to blossom in the distant future and it was not related to everyday economic problems. However, companies (as well as people) were supposed to work hard for it. In reality, the main motivation became meeting the central plan indicators because the earthbound material reward – the bonuses – were tightly connected to them. Dealing with planning indicators thus became decisive for the behaviour of the (rationally thinking) companies and de facto everybody because, as respondent Bažant (Meopta) in Vaněk and Krátká said, the plan was delegated, to the very last detail, to each of the workshops (Vaněk and Krátká 2014).

The companies generally tried to influence the plan already during its preparation period (4.4.1) with an effort to minimize their obligations, maximize their inputs, or increase their prices. The typical behaviour embraced piling up any form of hidden reserves because in the shortage economy the companies were never sure about the next delivery from their subcontractors. These conditions influenced their behaviour during the productions itself (4.4.2). And finally, the effort to accomplish the plan (4.4.3) led up to manipulation with the companies' results or even to illegal activities.

4.4.1 Plan formation

We have already documented that the creation of plan was not a one-way process – from the centre to the companies. The companies negotiated the plan with the centre and the VHJs. However, the reality was more complicated because companies had different bargaining powers. It seems that one of the aspects was the size or importance of the companies. For example, the director general of one of the biggest heavy engineering companies in Czechoslovakia <ID021> told us:

> *Well, in terms of autonomy, or the possibilities of your own decision-making, from the point of view of our company, basically when I consider it, the company was highly autonomous, yes, because its name and renown more or less predestined it to be in such a position. For example, negotiations with the Federal Ministry of Metallurgy and Heavy Engineering . . . we more or less always had our way. [. . .] We basically did not have problems with resources and materials. And I think we were respected not only by the Ministry, but by the government as well.*

On the other hand, the chairman of the local townhall (ONV) and director of a small-size company <ID048> spoke foremost about the necessity to be able to "have one's way" with the superior authorities (Handl 2018). Thus, verve of the management to improve the lot of the company was one of the key features.

Our respondent who worked as a scientist in the Prognostic Institute <ID034> attributed the managers with very specials skills:

> *They were not only bureaucrats wholly submerged in paperwork. No. They had to be able to find their way in the weird hybrid environment, otherwise they would not have fulfilled the plan, they would not have earned bonuses, they would not be directors because there was the power of the state to dismiss them. As a result, [. . .] all [. . .] somehow [. . .] participated in the decision-making, whether the objective to meet was to fulfill or trick the administrative directives, or whether the objective was to strive for economic quality. Primarily, of course, to trick, because the economic quality resulted from some administrative tasks.*

The general behaviour of the companies reflected their intentions and motivations in the system. Šulc writes that companies did not have responsibility for the setting of the goals, but the centre did. Therefore, the risks had to be taken, in principle, by the centre. The companies, in his eyes, wanted the centre to provide sources that the economy did not have. The centre did not have qualification for a serious evaluation of the companies' demand for inputs and thus it reacted pre-emptively with restrictive measures. Additionally, if a company did not achieve its goals, the loses went at the expense of the society. These general settings encouraged companies to irresponsible/inefficient behaviour already by forming of the goals (Šulc 1995).

The first strategy was naturally based on exercising influence on the planned tasks. The companies generally tried to minimize the planned output via bargaining with the centre (or via the VHJs) to secure bonuses obtained for its fulfilling (among other Zieleniec 1990; Šulc 2004; Malý and Herz 1988; Mlčoch 1990). This strategy was crucial especially due to the danger of application of the index method by the centre. The head of the department of mechanical engineering said <ID037> the following:

> *So, of course, the enterprise had some ideas that were expressed in various such . . . documents, short, longer . . . long-term, and so on. But when the plan came down to us, maybe, I do not know, there were requests for some, for some particular train cars. To some degree, . . . in some way it was usually that the plan was . . . sometimes . . . sometimes it was above the ability of the company, and therefore, in the first approach, the company tried hard to have the plan modified or moderated . . . and companies were able to fight back when the plan was not feasible, so it was just long negotiations for some changes to be implemented, and it was not just that they had no power to change the plan.*

Even the StB reported the dubious behaviour of the firms when it came to the setting of the plan. Their records speak about the TOS Kuřim company, which altered the actual capacity of its machinery in order to obtain a softer plan that was easier to fulfil. In 1989, the firm even refused the profit plan it was given inasmuch as it was in red, namely with regards to the foreign trade (ABS OB-282 BN). The effort to be given a softer plan was reported in the Zbrojovka Vsetín factory as well, when it "did not meet the plan in December 1987 in order to be given a softer plan for January" (ABS, OB-957 OV).

Having a good contact at the ministry or the VHJ was vital to securing a "better" plan for the company, as we already mentioned. Likewise, cooperation with suppliers or/and customers increased the bargain power (Soulsby and Clark 1996). Our respondent (an economist and planner in agriculture <ID018>) also noted that political connections were helpful:

> *As to how the co-operatives could influence it [the plan], well, they influenced it both by the conditions in which they were operating and, of course, the way the chairman was able to . . . well, of course it was that some of the chairmen were, you know. . . . The one from the village of Štěpánovice was a big fish in the District Committee of the party, so he definitely pushed for more than a cooperative chairman who was not so high in the party hierarchy.*

According to other respondents (e.g., an economic planner in an engineering company <ID008>), the possibility of influencing the plan increased in 1980s due to the gradual relaxing of environment during Perestroika. However, there was the lasting threat of ambitious influence of the local KSČ organization that did not take into consideration economic capacities of the company. A planner and head of supply in an engineering company told us:

> *So, we knew what to do, we did not admit the 400,000. We just put down 250 thousand, yeah. But then some of the, . . . those committees of the Communist Party, decided that some conclusions form a meeting of the Communist Party should be met, that so much and more must be produced – everything had to go through the party that authorized the final plan.*

However, another respondent who worked as Chief Secretary of a District Committee of the Communist Party <ID025> told us that companies' plans were checked by district, regional, and other Communist Party and ROH institutions but that they only consulted the plans: "The contours, and development of the whole industry in the region. [. . .] But we (neither the Communist Party nor ROH) did not directly interfere in the specific creation of the plan."

To sum it up, the role of the party varied highly, and it depended on the specific local conditions.

The second strategy consisted of maximizing planned/required inputs (raw materials, semi-manufactured goods or labour force). Our respondents generally admitted that they applied this strategy. A head of economic department in consumers electronics <ID044> summarized the strategy laconically: "The one who shouted more loudly was granted more." Others expressed the same ideas in a somewhat less expressive way: "Each planning entity created reserves because it was not sure how the plan would be drafted, who gets less, who gets more, so they had reserves to cover problems that inevitably occurred every year" (director textile industry, later deputy minister <ID057>). Even our respondent from the SPK <ID040> spoke about ways of applying for more sources. He pointed out:

> *Newcomers represented an interesting "inner" enemy, as they did not yet know the unwritten rules of the plan, like that they had to apply only for additional 5% of resources in order to get the 100% they actually wanted. If they asked for 115%, they got 110% and thus they were liable to overfulfilling the plan, which meant a balance error.*

Excessive demand for inputs embraced all sources. This strategy is illustrated by the interview with the operational deputy from the transport sector <ID009>:

I: *Regarding the plans, I assume that, of course, you considered some accounting criteria, or was there anything else? Like, what it was like the previous year and what the requirements were.*

R: *Sure. It was all part of the consideration and comparison, the real trick was to set it so that they would believe us although we all knew. [. . .]*

I: *Uhm. How did you do that, you know, the setting, like how much to exaggerate, on the basis of what?*

R: *According to experience, we knew how much we got ripped off last year, how much they reduced, in which products, maybe a few cables or something . . . that we knew the cables would take us a lot, so we had to exaggerate the cables, but we knew that no one . . . but us, so we could be quite exact there.*

Hoarding took place on the labour market as well, as described by a planner in construction <ID058>:

> *Under real socialism, there was the lack of manpower. That's part of that planning – we collect as many workers as we can get. Well, so we're planning a higher number, if possible, higher number of workforce. Not too much, so that it does not look like we are half understaffed and that there is something wrong with us. Well, if we miss 5%, what then? Even 10% can be explained in the construction industry.*

The third strategy was an attempt to change prices. Higher price was a way to achieve planned tasks, expressed in financial terms, more easily. The importance of prices was emphasized by our respondent – a head of economic department in consumers electronics <ID044>, who told us:

I: *Which indicators were followed in the plan?*

R: *The plan for the production of goods in financial value, but we need to specify a little bit now, because that would go into detail. What do you mean, what do call "the plan"?*

I: *I mean the production plan. I suppose that plan.*

R: *The production plan consists of a plan of production of individual coordination units, a plan for the production of individual products. Plan of production – week, month, year, and so on, that depends. But there was a demand that all points of view were included.*

I: *What units were used?*

R: *We were making electrical appliances, so the calculation started in pieces, but in cumulation it was converted to crowns.*

I: *Was the transfer ratio given by the price of that product? The price was determined by whom?*

R: *This was one of the important business activities that the company efficiency depended on when a new product was developed, and besides all that was associated with the new product, it ended with the price fixing. And now the price had to be set from two points of view, so that the product was saleable, which, I would say, was the crucial point of view and the other for it to be effective.*

I: *To be effective in the sense . . . ?*

R: *To make the difference between the price and the cost of producing positive, to make a profit.*

Ia: *Did the price of the product change during the course of its life?*

R: *Little.*

What was the price-establishing procedure when a new product was introduced, or an old product price changed? Mlčoch (1990) adduces the scheme depicted in Diagram 4.1.

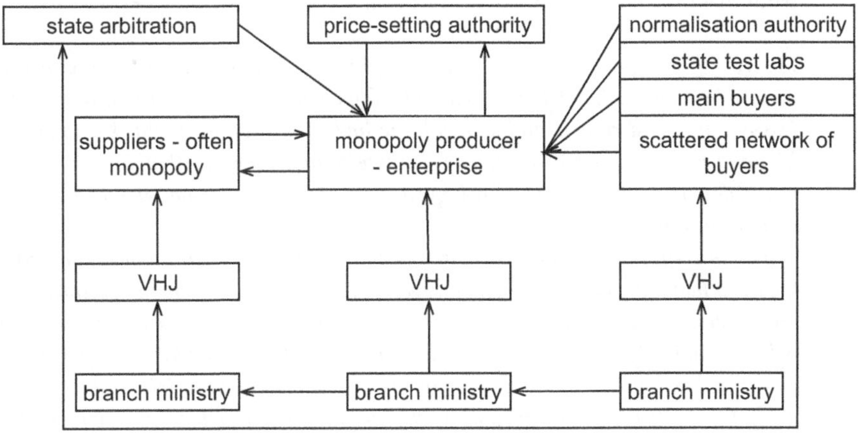

Diagram 4.1 Approving a new product and its price in a centrally planned economy
Source: Mlčoch (1990)

A monopoly producer introduces a new product trying to get a higher price. He prepares a price offer that must be approved by principal buyers (including technical specifications). In this phase, the producer should already have the prices of materials, semi-finished products and parts from his suppliers approved. Technical specifications and terms of delivery had to comply with technical standards and are assessed by state test laboratories. Buyers may resist the new, more expensive product, persistently, and this is where the verticals of the supplier and customers come to play in the mutual pressures. With the help of state arbitration, customers may enforce deliveries of old products, or the dead-end situation is solved as a "price dispute" throughout the price authorities.

Under normal circumstances, it was difficult or impossible to change the prices of the products. A general director in electrotechnics industry <ID047> told us: I: "Was it possible . . . was it possible to ask for a price change? Apart from the one-time complex price adjustment?" R: "That was not possible unless it was a brand-new product that had never been produced before, then . . . then the price was again approved at the planning board."

The price-setting authorities did not have any objective information about the costs. Companies, on the other hand, wanted to set the prices at their will to the greatest possible extent. Šulc writes that the price-setting authority sometimes tried to decrease prices by the index method (see Section 4.2.1). The companies reacted to this pressure by decreasing the prices of outdated or discontinued goods and increasing the prices of new products. The consequence was effective increase in prices (Šulc 2004). The only objective measures were the world prices, where they entered the economy, e.g., technologies bought in the western markets. However, Czechoslovakian wholesale prices and the world prices were mostly separated (see Chapter 5). Price changes had possibly led to tragic consequences as one of our respondents described (General director of company in knitting industry and later deputy Minister <ID073>):

> *He was such a purposeful guy and so frightened that the change in the assortment when he produced from polyamide, from polyester, where the price per kilo was one hundred crowns and suddenly he had to use cotton worth 35 crown per kilo and no one understood that the volume of production at that time went two thirds down. And the poor man begged and begged, but no one would listen, so he hanged himself.*
>
> *The price-fixing was built so that you had the base of the price of the material, then you had some margin, you had wages there, you had the company overhead and the wholesale price. And now imagine that you had a production volume made of polyester and polyamide, which polyester was over 100 crowns a kilo, that polyamide was probably, I do not know, 80 crowns or. . . . This is not essential. And now, suddenly, the market was on, I would say change, and these people stopped buying that stuff and start to love cotton. Well, then, the time is coming that you only need to make cotton and that cotton costs 36 or 38 crowns into the product. And now you have a production segment, it's like 20% or 25% in the business where you made the synthetics here, and now you have to switch to this cotton production, so you have a huge drop in the production volume, I do not know, that the material is worth 30 crowns and now you are saying that there is only 12 crowns in it, so simply the amount of money, it will cost like that.*
>
> *I: And the price of that product is expressed in those costs not in the sales price?*
>
> *R: Yes. So, then, at that wholesale price, the turnover tax and the retail price came on top of that. And for that, the store has made a margin for it and . . .*
>
> *I: And that means that those products were also cheaper when suddenly the material went like this to a third?*
>
> *R: Well, they were cheaper, but again the turnover tax was higher, so they were not so much cheaper, but they were cheaper in part.*

The same respondent shared his experience with the centre's decision about price reduction of their product:

> *So the dogma was that infant's goods were totally under-priced, so no one was able to do that, that population was big. And now, we would manufacture, as far as I remember, 32 types of baby clothes. It was a big export hit, everyone came to buy these, tourists and everybody would buy baby clothes. Or women's tights and women's stockings. Production costs of women's stockings were three crowns, stockings four fifty. They sold for 25, 30, 35 crowns on the market. Whoever came to Czechoslovakia*

from these countries well, . . . So when it was necessary to increase the price of, say, rolls or something, I do not know what, the centre decided would say, why don't we cut the price of the pantyhose and stockings? And the company CEO said quietly. . . . "We have earned a billion turn-over taxes on this merchandise. This unit only." And the price went down anyway, to 13, 15 or 20 crowns out of the 28 or 35. But it was still a huge turnover given the production price.

The companies generally tried to apply rational strategies during the preparation period that were supposed to enable them to meet the plan. It was necessary because the production phase was tricky for them.

4.4.2 Companies in the production phase

There were several interesting aspects of operating of companies in the production phase. Firstly, the main tasks during the production phase was for the companies to ensure subcontracts and inputs deliveries for the productions. The second interesting aspect was when they searched for new opportunities. Thirdly, the companies needed operation credit for their everyday functioning. And lastly, we evaluate the atmosphere in the working collectives.

Vicious cycle of shortage and hoarding

Socialist authors believed that, in socialism, the relationship of "comrade cooperation and mutual help" among the companies prevails (Hába et al. 1988). However, the main obstacle for the companies to fulfil the plan was not weak motivation or too ambitious settings of the plan but their own suppliers. The suppliers-buyers relationships were permanently tense. The troubles were admitted even by the then authors – e.g., Průcha (1988). The shortage economy appeared throughout the system and companies were both the main culprits as well as the main victims. The dominance of supplier over subscriber was enormous. Some of the authors even speak about blackmailing (Turek 1995). Almost all the respondents who participated in our research told us that the supply procurement and general lack of material were the most serious bottleneck, especially at the end of the socialist era. The consequence was that their economic performance in fact was not in their hands and depended on their subcontractors or partners. Foreman in an engineering company <ID015> described it in the following way:

Then it was, namely, the last six years. It was mainly about finding screws. Well, it was a problem to get anything. Whatever was necessary to be manufactured a manufacturer could not be found. We wanted to build something, no construction company was available. It was a huge problem to find anything. . . . That was the hardest time then. It was frustrating, one piece, spare part was missing and the whole production line with workers ready could not run.

An StB's report from the Zbrojovka factory confirms that as well. It was concerned with the fact that the workers were constantly either short of raw materials to work with or avalanched with new deliveries (ABS, OB-957 OV).

The general shortage economy appeared in all aspect of the functioning, including inputs (for example of labour market see Box 4.4).

Box 4.4 Shortage in the labour market

Companies had to face permanent shortage on the labour market as on any other market. Shortage was expressed by slogans like "people not available." The socialist companies reacted to the requirements of the centre, which demanded production increase by their own demands for higher numbers of employees. (We deal with the problem from the macroeconomic point of view in Section 5.3. In this box we just show the reaction of the companies).

On the other hand, the fact that the wage rates were set by the centre and the enterprises had an exact budget of wage funds, the egalitarian ideology and the scarcity of the economy at that time forced the companies to compete for labour force. As has been already mentioned, wages did not reflect the cost of labour and thus did not fulfil their function typical for the market economy. One illegal way was the use of black funds for wages. These crimes were embraced in Law No. 140/1961 Coll. Criminal Code. In specific, § 127 dealt with "Breaking of obligations when managing financial and material resources." However, some other crimes were possibly connected with labour shortage. The Supreme Court dealt with a case of a manager from the Severomravské cihelny brickworks in Nový Jičín. He gave instructions to his subordinate staff to report higher than actual production of earthenware. The consequence was overestimation of annual production by 1,327,612 CSK, which resulted in undue payment of 122,590 CSK in bonuses. The motivation of the crime was in preventing workers' outflow by paying higher bonuses (Coufalová, Lipovská, and Žídek 2017).

Our respondents spoke about finding other ways how to attract the workforce – for example head of a production company in agriculture <ID010>:

> *That means, they would haggle about someone, like, I don't know, agronomists or livestock specialist at a regional level. A free company flat was offered, for example, better conditions, better pay. . . . So he would leave one firm to join another and the director of the firm he was dumping would go to complain to the local Communist Party branch about me using unfair employment policy, as he could not offer the man a free company flat and that I was thus using unfair personnel policy.*

This quotation also illustrates another typical way – related by our respondents – how to attract skilled labour, which lay in housing policy, as there was a general shortage of flats and very long waiting times. The vast majority of our respondents replied that their companies offered accommodation facilities to potential workers. For example, an interviewee from an engineering company (chief designer in an engineering company <ID003>) stated that the company proposed to specific workers the possibility to live in corporate flats. These were flats that the city had allocated to the company. Housing policy was in fact very widespread (e.g., a general director in the electrotechnical industry <ID047>; chief designer in an engineering company <ID003>; or head of a production company in agriculture <ID010>).

Last but not least, according to one of the interviewees (Head of the technical department from an engineering company <ID020>) in selected cases, there existed a possibility for wage motivation, for example, promoting to a higher wage category if possible. However, due to the central management of wage rates, the room for attracting labour force by means of offers of higher salaries was very small. This respondent also stated that the recruitment of new employees took place mainly through personal ties:

> *They came to my house and simply lobbied. Indeed, it was a common practice, then, to lobby and persuade people on a personal level . . . come on, join us, you will be given more money, better work conditions, it is also closer to where you live, we have many amenities, catering and what have you, just better than they give you here.*

Kalinová writes that, since the 1970s, workers were sometimes deployed in a kind of informal economy. This led to an increase in their working hours, as well as to an increase in their income. This was particularly true for construction workers and those working in communal services, not so much for workers in other industries (Kalinová 2012).

Another policy was employment of apprentices. Some workers signed apprenticeship agreements during their training. Based on this, the apprentices were provided with a job after finishing the training, during which they received pocket money from the company. Their commitment to the company was for at least ten years. Otherwise, they had to pay a contractual penalty (production controller in optical engineering <ID053>). Alternatively, companies selected college students. A respondent from the building industry company (Sectional construction manager <ID023>) worked regularly with a university which sent the most skilful students to him for a trial period. Also, the Vagónka Studénka company, whose representatives in the late 1970s and 1980s frequently visited universities, offered a number of scholarships in order to attract qualified labour force (chief designer in an engineering company <ID003>).

The managers were in situation when they could not rely on deliveries (see, e.g., Box 5.7 – Škoda car). Director in textile industry, later minister deputy (<ID057>), told us: "The system was such that you either had a surplus or lack, you never had enough." The buyers had to go beg their supplies to secure deliveries. For example, deputy in transport industry <ID009>: I: "So how did you deal with it when you needed a supply of material?" R: "It was hard. Eventually it had to be done, but anyway, well. [. . .] you had to go to the suppliers and beg."

Scrounge was a very common method of assuring supplies. Another option was to utilize political connections. A planner and head of supplying in an engineering company <ID007> told us the following. R: "And I remember, even foreign exchanges were solved this way once. We went . . . to the Treasury to ask . . . with the Director, . . . and he said, 'You know, just to make sure, we will take the Chairman of the local Communist Party with us . . . ' (laughs) . . . what if . . . " I: "Did it help?" R: "It did, there was a reasonable person, anyway, there it helped, yeah."

The natural reaction of the management was that they were trying to assure the inputs that they needed because without them they would not be able to meet the plan. In order to ensure meeting of the plan, the managers hoarded materials and components on the stock. This behaviour was formally illegal and it inevitably led to the creation of unduly reserves. Šulc writes that average stuck-up time in engineering companies was, in 1979, 252 days for screws, 147 days for cables, 215 days for electrical insulating materials, 195 days for armatures, and 158 days for rolling bearings etc. (Šulc 2004). This behaviour was very often documented in our interviews as well – for example a planner and head of supplying in an engineering company <ID007> said: "The plan allowed us to have, I reckon, some 250 million in stock, but we had some 270 or 280 all the time, or so."

Similarly, an economic planner in an engineering company <ID008> confirmed that situation, stating that the astronomical volumes of stock and the way they were managed were one of the greatest ills of the time. Some companies just purchased what was in supply regardless of urgency of their needs. At the same time, creating reserves became the most common economic crime. However, findings of the 1982 Supreme Court mentioned that the companies' primary task was to ensure steady plan fulfilment. The authors of the report quoted an example of a manager of the Prior department store who was prosecuted for retaining daily revenues of up to 183,693 CSK and using these funds to replenish (lower) revenues in the following months (Coufalová, Lipovská, and Žídek 2017).

The overall situation worsened due to the (frequent) monopolistic position of the suppliers or buyers. Our respondent, a planner in agriculture <ID045>, even told us: "By the way, and I know it, sometimes there were these trends, like some idiot would come up with an idea that the whole country could do with just one flour mill. Why should we have more of them? (laughter) . . . Well, yes, stupidities like this really happened." On the other hand, shortages of supply of raw materials or semi-manufactured goods was one of the reasons for vertical monopolization because the companies needed to gain control of their suppliers and thus minimize uncertainty. A respondent who worked in a price department in engineering (<ID059>) described it in the following way: "There came a time when you could not get a good quality lumber. Yeah, there was some kind of calamity or faulty planning, and we had a huge problem getting a good quality wood because the wood had to be dried in a natural way, which was a problem, so we got ourselves, as a company, our own wood drying facilities." A planner in construction <ID058> mentioned another reason for mergers:

> *Occasionally, some company, or mainly the Directorate-General, got a boss who was very ambitious and wanted to become a minister. And in order to become a minister he needed to demonstrate how, under his leadership, the company grew. These companies usually grew by simply swallowing someone else.*

Regardless of reasons, the monopolistic suppliers maximized their strength and behaved accordingly (Šulc 1995). They among others did not need to adapt to the needs of the buyers, decline cost or increase quality of their production (Rendl et al. 1988).

The general delivery times were long. Our respondent who worked in research department of engineering company <ID036> described the situation in the following way:

> *In socialism, preparation of technical documentation lasted from one to two years. Designs, yeah. And then the thing was being produced for about two years, right? That means we produced the documentation, and the supply person had a year to get the engine somewhere and bring it here. It was only after two years that it was assembled here. And while we were assembling, meanwhile, we might have made more . . . designs, yeah. So we were always like . . . the cycle from the beginning to the end was essentially two to three times longer than it is today. This is essentially shorter now. Like today, like telling someone to wait for three years for the delivery, it's like I'm sorry.*

Šulc mentions that delivery times of common industrial products (profile steel, tubing, electrical engines, etc.) lasted up to a week or at worse up to a month in developed countries. The same products were delivered between 3 to 20 months in Czechoslovakia and the period kept prolonging (Šulc 2004). Due to this, companies had to place their orders a long time before they knew their own binding plans (in accordance with the proposals of their plans). As a result, the suppliers had to order raw materials, prepare the production, or even start production of supplies or intermediate products. However, consequently, the subscribers sometimes needed to change their orders after the final settings of the plan. Their suppliers were already producing the order and had to follow their own final plan. It resulted in a further prolonging of delivery time. The centre could issue a list of priorities. In reaction, the bottlenecks could widen for some companies (ibidem). All in all, any change in priorities caused involuntary substitution and deepened chaos in the whole system because of chain reaction in the supplier-buyer relationships. It was difficult for all of them because all companies tried to meet the plan.

The conditions got even more complicated if the delivery was in convertible currencies. For example, famous Czech cardiologist Jan Pirk recalled applications for purchases in convertible currencies in healthcare:

> *[The bids] were collected throughout the whole year. At the end of the year the representatives of the cardio centres were brought together and they were told: 'We have registered bids worth 20 million, and we have 5 million to cover these bids. That means that each of you can realize one quarter of the proposal. It was the end of the year and they kept waiting the whole year and then it was up to the Healthcare Supply Division, which of the bids would be granted funding. That meant sometimes a two-year-long waiting for what you ordered."*
>
> *(Soldát 2015, p. 126)*

That the management had to safeguard their inputs by any means – including grafts to suppliers or other criminal activities seems strange, with hindsight, from the perspective of the market economy. According to our respondents, paying bribes was a common practice. For example, director in textile industry and consequently minister deputy <ID057> stated that:

> *So, it was famous these bottles that were offered (laughs) because there was little to give, you know. The plan looked nice, but in fact everyone, even the subcontractors had a tight plan. So now it was, somehow, at the expense of someone else to get it, so there were the famous bottles to be given away.*
>
> *T: A tight plan, you mean, if one of your suppliers who supplied not only to you, but to someone else, . . .*
>
> *A: Yes, he faced the problem of preference. . . . So, on the one hand, he was deciding on a model. Like who can least harm him (laughs), so he did not give it to the other side, so we knew where the weak spots were, so we tried to be somehow in good relations with those people.*

Even the Supreme Court dealt with cases of bribery to obtain material. They presented an example from the District Court in Dolní Kubín where the manager was tried because he offered bribes to ensure material supply. He testified that offering bribes to ensure material supply was common in that time in the planned economy. In a different case, the accused explained that without bribes, the concerned would have only 32% of spare parts that it needed for production (Lipovská, Coufalová, and Žídek 2018).

Contrary to common logic, the buying firm had to fill the needs of the suppliers. Mlčoch writes that the deliveries were sometimes conditioned by helping their suppliers to obtain material (even by using subscribers' limits for convertible currencies) or even by "voluntary" assistance in suppliers' factory. But Mlčoch finds these conditions "fair" because the companies were in both positions (supplier and subscriber), so while they were blackmailing as suppliers they were blackmailed as subscribers. This dismal state was even reflected in the communist parliament – e.g., vice-chairman of the Federal government Ladislav Gerle stated in the Federal Parliament session on 20th of October 1987: "All buyers feel to be in their successful activity harmed by their suppliers, at the same time they as suppliers harms its buyers but they do not speak about it" (ČSSR. Federal Assembly of the Czechoslovak Socialist Republic 1986–1990).

The described patterns reflect a vicious circle of shortage that resulted in hoarding, which even worsened the shortage. From a managerial point of view, this behaviour contradicted modern methods such as the just-in-time system that intends to minimize companies' stockpiles. The consequence was that, on the contrary to capitalist companies, their Czechoslovak counterparts had to try to maximize their stocks of raw materials, semi-manufactured goods, or even labour force. The omnipresent shortage was worsened by chain relationships in the monopolized economy, because, for example, a lack of iron ore impacted production of metal and other links of the value chain. Furthermore, the companies could not turn to other suppliers because of the monopolistic character and isolation of the socialist economy. Not surprisingly, these troubles resulted in problems with meeting of the plan that are described in the following subsection.

Search for opportunities

The general environment of the central planning was not in favour of initiative and searching for business opportunities. The centre was supposed to be omniscient.

Korbel provides a semi-anecdotical evidence about initiative which collided with the KSČ interfering in the book by Vaněk and Krátká. Working as a director he wanted to build a network of shops selling 99 frozen products. (It was a rare example of initiative.) He planned to name the shops Severka 99 (North Star 99). But due to the limited offer, he had to decline the range of products to 77. He supposed to change the name accordingly to Severka 77. He described the following events this way:

> *It didn't last long and I had a phone call from the highest party officials, possibly the UV KSČ, and they asked me: "Listen, what is the Charter to you?" And I knew I was in trouble, that they somehow linked it with Charter 77. And they figured out that it was somehow encoded in the name. And I had to call the printing facility that was already printing packaging and advertisement material and asked them to change the name to Severka 70 and later, for safety reasons, just Severka.*
>
> *(Vaněk and Krátká 2014, p. 200)*

Our respondents told us that the opportunities that appeared in the so-called associated production were also enlarged in the period under review. These were centres (usually in agriculture) where products other than those usually manufactured by the company were fabricated, and whose business was not official and therefore not included in the central plan. This way of production offered the company, and hence its employees, an opportunity to benefit financially. The share of workers in associated production was significant – e.g., in 1986, it was 10% of employees of all agricultural companies (Hába et al. 1988).

For example, an economist and planner in agriculture <ID018> told us:

> *What is worth mentioning is the associated production that stood practically outside the plan. In addition, it was a way for cooperatives to make good money: And if the cooperative caught up with some of the associated production, meaning non-agricultural, then the co-operatives did not even have to steal and they were well off (laughter).*

Such a production may have comprised, for example prefabricated wooden roof frames made by an agricultural cooperative (JZD) that somehow found their foreign customers (an economist and planner in agriculture <ID018>). A true cultural phenomenon aroused in the 1980s in the JZD Slušovice cooperative, which proved to be highly efficient. It enormously diversified its productions and among others assembled and sold personal computers (see Box 5.2: JZD Slušovice).

Credit

Companies needed operating credits for day-to-day functioning as well as companies in the market economy did. The situation with providing operating credit was similar to investment. The conditions for providing operating credit were formally tough as well (Mlčoch 1990). However, the everyday practice was again different because there were many gaps in the interpretations of rules and in control of the documents provided by the companies. As a result, the credit policy on the side of banks was relatively relaxed. For example, our respondent who worked in economic planning in engineering <ID008> told us: "Back then, payment was merely a technical act. . . . When there was no money, the bank would grant a loan and . . . payment could be carried out." One of our respondents described a (very rare) credit in convertible currency that was provided to his company – director in textile industry and later deputy minister <ID057> this way: "My predecessor obtained a huge loan in convertible currencies, so we modernized a lot and the loan was being paid back from export revenues . . . thanks to this loan we exported a lot to the West, to be able to pay it back."

Mlčoch comments that it was hardly possible to be strict in a situation when a company for example did not have funds for paying wages because such a situation would have had social and political consequences. He believes in creation of informal both inner and outer "stakeholders" coalition that struggled to achieve their goals. The members of the coalition were in his eyes among others people from the banking sector and their role was to help to obtain funds and operating credits for the company (Mlčoch 1990). But the view about easy access to money was partly disputed by our respondent who worked as a chief economist in agricultural company <ID028> who told us that once the SBČS lent him money gotten under permanent control and that the SBČS guarded its money closely. He added that if the company received subsidy on, for example, the purchase of combine harvester and it did not use it – it had to return not only the original funds but pay a fine as well.

Cooperative, non-competitive environment

Not all aspects of socialist society, however, were negative, especially concerning workplace relationships. It seems that this point is the only one that was, in practice, achieved in accordance with the ideology and which was corroborated by our respondents.

Our respondents told us about cooperating among the companies at the VHJ level (e.g., technical director in construction <ID041>). He mentioned that they unified to meet the global plan for the VHJ and put this recollection in contrast with the contemporary economy.

A great part of the respondents spontaneously[5] positively evaluated interpersonal relationships at the workplace. These resulted from collective labour valuation and wage levelling, which largely prevented envy among workers, or the Brigades of Socialist Work. The cause of the positive effect of these Brigades was that they strengthened the collective. It was not about competing individuals, but about competing groups, which forced its participants to pull together. The trade unions also had positive influence in this respect. Their influence was particularly important in taking care of the non-professional activities of the workers. They organized recreational stays in which all the employees, regardless of their position, took part as well as summer camps for their children. All of these activities were assessed positively by the respondents:

> *What was important and interesting for me . . . were the relationships among people. That people really pulled together within their level, for instance department level. And there were these Brigades, where people kind of shared their lives and belonged, all the way up to the highest spheres. No problem, I, for instance, experienced several times a visit by Minister Saul, or his Deputy, Tibor Kurta, who would come, discuss a few things, what goes, what does not and then there was a kind of party and these informal settings helped to make a lot of things possible. A head of waterworks came to congratulate our director on his birthday and he says: "Boy you do have a nice new company car, how did you come to it? A part of central planning?" And he replies, out of fun: "I got it as a gift." Anyway, these interpersonal relationships really impressed me back then . . . the atmosphere was a kind of egalitarian, well not really, but we all knew . . . we all had families to feed, the conditions are such and such, we know how to have fun, we have ways to have fun, it was all sort of collegial. All the way up to the top management. They could have sharp elbows, they did. Like: "I need this*

> *and that from you . . . " I witnessed a few pretty sharp discussions, but they would finally shake hands, maybe out of the protocol, but they did. Let's fix it and go play cards. And you would have four directors of four big companies sitting in the meeting room and playing cards for small coins and drinking wine.*
>
> *(Head of the Project Manager's Office in Metallurgy <ID066>)*

Therefore, in this sense, socialism seemed successful. It was, however, rather a consequence of wage levelling than the success of ideology. Nevertheless, even with regard to workplace relationships, the system was not perfect. The influence of the Communist Party and the possibility of career advancement for cooperation with the party acted in the opposite direction, for example by motivating individuals to report colleagues or acquaintances for activities not approved by the communist ideology (the Assistant to the Director in engineering <ID0043>). The overall atmosphere was damaged by the presence and activities of the secret police as well (Vilímek 2012).

4.4.3 Meeting the plan

Most of our respondents told us that (in their experience) their companies always at minimum formally met the plans (e.g., analyst and mathematician in an engineering company <ID005>; CEO in heavy engineering <ID021>; Head of the Project Manager's Office in Metallurgy <ID066>). The reasons were obviously economic incentives – foremost bonuses and share of "profit." Almost all of our respondents said that these incentives were the most powerful motivation for their companies to meet the goals defined in the plan. Ivan Kratochvíl (several different CEO positions) writes in his memoirs about the importance of bonuses. He recalls regular working meetings with directors of the company at the end of November and for fears of not meeting the plan another one at the end of year. His colleague emphasized the importance of bonuses that were tied to the meeting of the plan. Consequently, he described the other working meetings at the end of the year and "many liquid presents" (often homemade) that he received for meeting the plan and as new year gifts (Kratochvíl 2011).

However, bonuses were rarely intended only for managers – in most cases, they were distributed among all employees. The centre generally appreciated the outcome of the sector (VHJ), the enterprise and the collective. Individual performance was therefore of little value (Havelková 2009b).

Companies tried to maximize their rewards in tune with incentives provided by the system – foremost meeting the plan. They, nonetheless, had to respond to several questions about fulfilling of their plans that reflected their overall strategies, reality of the environment and their relative freedoms. These questions could be surprising because the companies' strategies were far from straightforward. The first question was "What exactly to produce?" – how exactly fulfil the general plan because the plan was often expressed only in global values or numbers. The second questions was "How to achieve this plan?" – what steps to take to reach the desirable plan? The third question was "What is the best result for the company?" – what figures were the best to achieve in relation to the plan at the end of the year. And the fourth one was "What to do in case of failure?" The following paragraphs discuss these dilemmas more deeply but do not refer to the individual strategies.

What exactly to meet/to produce?

The first question was what exactly the company should produce. The crucial setting of the overall system was that the company's revenues did not depend on sales of the production but on meeting the plan. In some cases, the plan was specified in number of pieces. However, in most of the cases the plans were only general, and the companies had various possible production combinations that satisfied their plans. They decided on their own specific production mixture that met the global volume of their plans the easiest way. As a result, the companies did not need to produce anything that their customers needed (Rendl et al. 1988). The choices were expressed by our respondents a director in an engineering company <ID006>:

> *So, these prices, they were quite an important element and the economic plan was one thing and the business plan stemmed from it, as it was meant to give us the economic indicators. Of course, it was possible say, when we failed to meet the plan in terms of sale of machinery but exceeded it in terms of sale of spare parts, so the economic indicators overall were met at company level and everything was ok.*

Motivation was generally perverse. Once glass production was planned in tonnes, companies were motivated to produce heavy production. If the criterion of production was changed to square metres, then the produced glass was light and fragile. This was well documented on the examples of the Soviet economy – for example Grossman writes that if the production of paper was planned in tonnes so the companies tried to produce heavy paper and avoid production of light one (Grossman 1963).

Similarly, Šulc argues that the companies tried to find such variants of their products that enabled them to meet the plan with the least effort. He writes that the company changed the production or combination of inputs according to this goal. If the income depends on fulfilling the volume of the plan in a type of "gross production" the company points to material-intensive production because then the volume of their production was quickly increasing (Šulc 2004). Rendl comments that the planned indicator of gross production supported inefficiency in cooperation between the companies because subcontracting from a different company became profitable – it was for example higher for transportation costs etc. against production in the own company. Similarly, the StB's investigation in the Zbrojovka factory from 1979 found out that the firm "focused on production of goods that were more advantageous with regard to fulfilling the value of the plan. Such behaviour threatened fulfilment of the entire plan as assigned" (ABS, OB-957 OV).

Another procedure was accounting manipulation of the material inside the company or generally application of other uneconomical behaviour by the companies (Rendl et al. 1988). If the goal was specified as net production, then it tried to avoid production of goods with low profit in price and oriented on production of goods with high "rentability" (Šulc 1995). Turek gives an example of a quarry – it had produced 3 different kinds of stones in the interwar period – ashlar, smaller final products – kerbs and crushed stone for construction of roads. During socialism, the planners decided to increase the use of the stone breaker because it had previously been used only for 1% of time. The consequence was abandoning of the production of the middle size final products for good because they were "spoiling efficiency." In the production program stayed the ashlars that were planned and balanced at the centre (Turek 1995). Šulc adds that majority of planned indicators did not have any direct impact on the company's income but all of them had indirect influence. The company met firstly the indicators with possibly the highest penalties – meaning that it fulfilled firstly the indicators that were crucial for basic wages, then the indicators important for additional incomes (bonuses, rewards, developing fund and other collective needs of the company) and only then the other indicators (Šulc 1995). Rendl comments that the centre tried to react to this behaviour by increasing the numbers of binding production indicators. But he concludes that this strategy did not bring significant relief because the needs of the customers were ever changing, and the centre was unable to recognize them (Rendl et al. 1988). The companies sometimes even reported investments for production, as the StB informs us in the report on Zbrojovka. The firm counted the value of the investment to the planned value of the production, so that the plan was met. In another year, they even counted a production that was not yet made (ABS, OB-957 OV).

We can conclude with Mlčoch, who writes that an inevitable consequence of the companies struggling to achieve the planned goals was that economic logic or efficiency was never the top priority of the companies and they stood at best in the shadow of the main tasks (Mlčoch 1990).

How to achieve the global plan for the company?

The second question was how to meet their plan in situation of huge predominance of suppliers above customers. The views of our respondents greatly varied. Some of them described that their obligations to meet the plan were very strict but a great part of them told us that there was a chance to "circumvent" the plan. Certain plan flexibility is not surprising in the system of insecure deliveries as evidenced by our respondents.

An economic deputy in the Sigma company quoted by Vaněk and Krátká provided an example of the first attitude:

> *The economic deputy had a volume of money specified by the plan that the company had to generate, that is that the factory had to produce 250 million a month and he had to fill the sum with machinery, equipment, like pumps. And that it was no easy*

task. And by the end of month he had to have a document approved by the production quality inspection department that the produce worth 250 million actually had been manufactured checked and could be dispatched. And it did not happen there was a lot of fuss, shouting, a problem, questions. It was really tough.

(Vaněk and Krátká 2014)

However, the conditions in the companies varied as head of economic department in consumption electronic <ID044> recalled:

Like my favourite director-general, with whom I worked on daily basis, he knew that if he wanted to stay in power, he had to meet the plan, for the superior institutions, the party, etc. So, it was a speciality of his to check how the plan was being met on daily basis. He had this strange management tool, a daily meeting, which would always start with the plan fulfilment check. [. . .] So, he implemented this method not to have to worry about meeting the plan at the end of the respective period.

Similarly, our respondent in construction <ID064> told us that they were checked every month which forced them to meet the plan. However, other respondents had different experiences and described a more relaxed environment in their companies. One of them said that in some cases even under fulfilment was not trouble:

I: *Was it possible to amend the plans? Like you said that you knew, you were getting short of the plan, could you ask for changes to be made in the plan?*

R: *For what I know, yes, changes were made. You know that plans were uniform, like they said that we should make, I don't know, ten thousand pieces of magnifiers, so it was planned without actually knowing whether there was demand for them. So, when we did not meet the plan and it was discovered that there was actually no demand for them, nothing happened.*

(production controller in optical engineering <ID053>)

There was even a possibility to alternate the plan. A planner in agricultural company <ID045> told us: "Well, it was normal, in autumn, changes were made to the plan so that the plan would be met. I mean, you had to assess the plan, didn't you? And that the plan was met was a joint interest of everyone involved. Even the OV KSČ (laughter) as it indicated their job done well as well. So no one objected to changes in the plan."

Other respondents – director in textile industry and later on deputy minister <ID057> (and similarly, e.g., operative in foreign trade <ID030>) described the reality in the following way:

R: *[The plan] was set and negotiated, you simply got it in a form that did not allow space for discussion, as the plan was a law. But as time went by, it was like, opportunities emerged allowing possibilities to discuss the plan. So the figures changed in the course of the year.*

I: *And why was that?*

R: *That soon it was clear that the plan was faulty, that it did not work (laughter), there were all kinds of disproportions, which could lead to serious problems. So, these disproportions had to be dealt with.*

One of our respondents in construction sector (planner in construction <ID058 >) described the specific situation in the sector and troubles with deliveries:

> *Sometimes, we would find out that the company in the town of Košice had a problem. So, the plan was changed downwards. No prefabricated blocks? We can't build, the plan won't be met. But it wasn't our problem . . . so, you would apply Commander Helmut von Moltke senior's principle: each plan needs changing after its first contact with reality. Contact with reality – no prefab blocks – need to change the plan. And, in fact, everyone was happy, no big deal. Actually, it was sort of expected. Things like that had happened before and would happen again. But you couldn't put that in the plan. It will change, when there is a reason.*

Other respondents mentioned the influence of the KSČ on meeting the plan. A head of department in an engineering company <ID037> commented:

> *The other approach was that it was approved, but then, in the course of the year, changes were made and in these the party apparatus played an important role, as all the economic deputies were members of the OV KSČ economic commission and some of them were big fish. So, when changes to the plan were being negotiated, the influence of the Communist Party was always very efficient.*

Similarly, another respondent from the Communist Party apparatus <ID025> told us that in case of troubles with meeting of the plan the party line was one of the channels to influence the centre – for instance by explaining that the existing plan was unrealistic. He gave an example when ministers came to criticize the directors for weak work and the regional secretary explained to them the difficult situation in the companies. Similar comments were provided also by other respondents (MP and secretary of ObNV Ostrava <ID026>).

> *But I can say that it was interesting sometimes, see this example from the mid-80s. There was this company director of ours, who was also a member of the OV KSČ. And he constantly failed the plan, it called for dismissal, but he would transfer the majority of the capacity to Prague and always changed his plan at the end of the year, so in fact, for eleven months he was whipped and liable to dismissal and in December, they changed his plan, so that he would meet it.*

A respondent from catering <ID052> told us about softening the plan in the course of the year thanks to his connections at the Regional Office. On the other hand, another respondent – planner and head of supplying in engineering <ID007> – mentioned the role of the Communist Party in tightening of the plans: "Sometimes, there were even things like that the ÚV KSČ decided in their plenary that the plan was to be met a month in advance."

Similarly, a worker in a large metallurgy company in North Moravia <ID027> told us that the KV KSČ for North Moravia region decided abruptly to increase production in the fourth quarter of the year with the goal to prepare for the following year. This measure was however applied only for this region. The long-term head of the regional committee among others enforced "voluntary" working Saturday – they were named after him as "Mamulas' Saturdays."

An associate professor at university and head of section in Prognostic institute <ID071> even told us that it was possible to change the plan after the end of the planned year:

> *Now, the basic principle was that the rudiments are in meeting the plan. And the objective being to meet the plan, even if it should fail, required that the plan be changed ex-post after the end of the year, and again in order to secure bonuses. And indeed, the plans were changed in retrospect.*

These findings are in accordance with Mlčoch (1990).

Companies took advantage of whichever procedure in order to meet the plan. Vaněk and Krátká write that personal relationships, corruption or possibly barter were used to achieve the planned results (Vaněk and Krátká 2014). The other possibilities were "creative accounting" or cheating, see Box 4.5. Nuti agrees with this view and writes that the directors were hiding reserves, exaggerated demand, took what was possible and used informal ways for that purpose. The bureaucracy knew it and discounted everything. It also tried to make their life harder and punish success by increasing the requirements above the achieved level (Nuti 1981).

Box 4.5 Cheating

Most of our respondents talked openly about manipulations with the results at the level of companies, some of them even said that these were common. For example, head of technical department in engineering <ID020> told us: "When numbers did not fit, they just got adjusted. An in-depth inspection? There was none of the economic mathematics. [. . .] It may sound stupid to say it like this, but, when I was short of some savings, I would just make them up." Similarly, head of a production company in agriculture <ID010> mentioned: "'This 'do the best you can' was sometimes done by cheating the books, like, there were more cattle than there actually were, you cannot count 30,000. So, there were, say, 200 more and it got written as reproduction growth, and so on. Yes, you might say it was cheating of a kind, but everyone did that."

The other frequently used way of manipulating the results was based on the accounting category called "work in progress." A sectional construction manager in the building industry <ID023> described it: "These things happened, for instance an investor would allow them to bill things that were not finished yet. This was called forwarded billing."

Manipulation with economic outcomes was proved by our research in the archives – Moravský Zemský Archiv (Regional State Archive in Brno) as well. We analyzed aggregate data from archived files about meeting of the plans in several dozen companies. In practice we applied a set of statistical tests of conformity of outcomes reported with the so-called Benford law. The results of statistical tests suggest probable widespread occurrence of real outcomes manipulation (Coufalová, Mikula, and Žídek 2017).

Moreover, manipulation is as well observed for example by Mlčoch who thoroughly analyzes the entrepreneur's environment. He concludes that cheating was not a marginal phenomenon of economic crime. In his view, it was a totally common practice. And only a case that deviated from "common" cheating was considered as a "real economic crime." Even in obvious cases superior authorities defended the frauds appraising them as worthy employees. The courts consequently tended to perceive such crimes leniently, recognizing the good will of the responsible executives (Coufalová, Lipovská, and Žídek 2017). Mlčoch adds that the system allowed multiple manipulations that were on the brink of legality – it was foremost manipulation with cost timing, scheduling, and reporting of arbitrage items of all-company overheads and consequent influencing of economic results of internal departments and final calculations, controversial cases of accounting for the costs of technical development repairs and reconstructions and a number of others (Mlčoch 1990). Šulc adds that companies highly valued the work of the economists who had good knowledge about "procedures" enabling them to meet the plan (Šulc 2004). The procedures were arguably of various kinds. A planner in construction <ID058> for example told us: "Well, yes, they could be either in disagreement or they waited too long or, sometimes there were these details that they did not follow but can see later, like growth in expenses, which, . . . at the end of the year, the revenues were higher than the plan had set, which meant a problem as the figure could be used as the basis for the next year plan. This had to be prevented from happening. But it could be solved at the lower levels, like by adding two zeros into the figure."

Mlčoch mentions that companies' counterfeiting methods were well known to the centre (Mlčoch 1990). We can add that the centre not only knew about the methods, but that it was cheating on its own, the SPK kept double accounting books (see Box 4.1).

What was the "optimal" fulfilment of the global plan?

Companies wanted to look the best in their superior's eyes. But at the same time, they had to avoid astounding results. Due to this, the answer to the question was as not trivial as it might seem to be.

The under fulfilling was "not an option" and the companies obviously did their best to meet the plan. This also emerged from interviews conducted in our research. Most respondents, from all sectors of the economy, told us that meeting the plan objectives was strictly monitored and exceeding the plan (even by a small percentage) was remunerated. For example, the respondent from the mechanical engineering company said: "Well this exceeding, yes, it happened, because, like, you did more than the plan said and you got some money from the SPK . . . yes, some benefit" (chief designer in an engineering company <ID003>, or similarly the head of human resources <ID024> from a textile machinery industry). This evidence is in contracts with our respondent from the SPK <ID040> who said that he or she preferred meeting the plan due to efforts to keep an overall balance.

On the other hand, overfulfilling was, for the company, extremely undesirable because it resulted in revealing the company's potential and it was "punished" by increasing the plan for the following period. Even our respondent from the SPK <ID040> admitted that "standing out too much meant trouble – you had to be careful to avoid tougher plan for the next year." The conclusion was that the company's task was at best to hit the target as precisely as possible. One of our respondents (<ID058> planner in construction) told us: "We can always explain why we failed to meet the plan . . . but to try to explain why we had done better than planned, that was quite risky, something you wanted to avoid."

Similarly, assistant to the director in engineering (ID043) – described the dilemma in the following way:

> *No, no, no. I don't remember anyone ever being arrested, or even the economic crime people coming to investigate. [. . .] We had these inspections from the People's Inspection Committee, which would proceed according to part regulations that state that problems are to be dealt with internally, not externally. So, once it even led to cuts in the plan as the Directorate-General had the authority to move the plan among individual companies. So, a clever director would not significantly overfulfill the plan, because the moment that happened and you showed that you had reserves and could overdo the plan, the moment you get a more demanding plan.*

Interestingly, this was true even for agriculture, which is a highly climate-dependent sector. A production assistant director in agriculture <ID011> answered that in years when the weather and the harvest were good, the centre authorities always called for a rise in objectives for the next period.

Mlčoch comes to a similar general conclusion. In his view, a good-looking number for the meeting of the plan was for example 101.2%. On the other hand a 100.1% felt like a "scam" (Mlčoch 1990). Our research in archives reached similar conclusions. The histogram of plan fulfilling showed the mode of relative deviance from the plan being slightly higher than 1. It means that typical reported outcomes slightly exceeded the planned value. Such results put a company into a favourable position with minimum risk of plan increase for the next year (Coufalová, Mikula, and Žídek 2017). Rendl et al., however, add that the "autonomy of some business processes" sometimes resulted in situation when the company was not able to achieve its own goals and the situation ended against its own interests – and it was "not able to avoid over fulfilment of its plans" (Rendl et al. 1988, p. 160).

Failure to complete the plan

The fulfilment of the plan was the utmost goal of the companies but sometimes the companies were simply not able to achieve it. There is evidence that missing the targeted plan was not uncommon and the authorities were well aware of it. For example, Ladislav Gerle (Vice-Chairman of the Federal Government) admitted in the Federal Parliament on the 20th of October 1987: "The highest number of companies that did not fulfil the plan were in the sector of general engineering where 88 companies were not able to deal with the plan. The main problems appeared in the car industry and ZVS Brno" (ČSSR. Federal Assembly of the Czechoslovak Socialist Republic 1986–1990). Similarly, for example according to Interparty information number 25 for the members and Presidium candidates, and members of the Secretariat of the ÚV KSČ mentioned many dozens of companies that were not meeting the plan (ČSSR. Sekretariát ÚV KSČ 1987).

Our respondents mostly told us that the plan had to be met. It is well documented by a planner in construction <ID058> who told us: I: "Did it ever happen that your bonuses were cut?" R: "No, never. The whole system had only one goal and it was to win the bonus, not to meet the plan. It was just a technical means and it was manipulated with and cheated and revised, simply so that the bonus conditions were met." On the other hand, the positions of our respondents in the hierarchy often did not allow them to see the backstage of the dealing with the superior authority. However, they often mentioned a possibility to fulfil the plan in another way: "It didn't happen oftentimes. We must say that mostly, the plan was met in the global number . . . and if the specific range of goods fulfilment failed, it was another thing. But when it failed in the global perspective, you had to deal with the authorities" (a worker in metallurgic company <ID027>).

An instance of not-meeting the plan was a source of worries because the punishment was mostly in cutting down or even eliminating of bonuses. On the other hand, Vilímek writes that the AZNP (Škoda Car) was able sometimes to pay bonuses even though the company did not fulfil the plan. However, losing bonuses was the main worry of the ordinary workers (Vilímek 2012). But there were potentially stronger punishments. Nearly half of our respondents told us about the potential threat of dismissing an unsuccessful company director. It was not uncommon, that this threat was put into practice. However, Votoček claims that in case of not meeting the plan the director was firstly given a warning, then a party penalty, consequently he did not obtain the bonuses. Additionally, he was, for example, allowed to lay off deputies and if it did not help he was eventually dismissed (Vaněk and Urbášek 2005). For instance, a report by the ÚKRK from 1987 mentions complex evaluation of employees (based on their work, social-political engagement, character, and moral qualities). This practice was applied in accordance with a resolution of the Presidium of the ÚV KSČ. Based on this review 32 managers were relieved in 1987 in the VSŽ Košice company for not managing their tasks and 95 managers at various levels were discharged from cadre reserves (ČSSR. Předsednictvo ÚV KSČ 1988).

However, discharging managers was the highest level of punishment in the system because anything even vaguely resembling bankruptcy was entirely impossible (there was not even a law dealing with such situation), as our respondents corroborate:

> *And that was not the case, so companies did badly, mainly on account of lack of direct competition and contact with the customers, as well as on a number of regulations preventing the companies from removing inefficient production and competing for a better position on the market. Everything was screened and hidden in the central plan, so in fact, there was no risk of bankruptcy for individual companies, as the whole economy was orchestrated in a different way.*
>
> *(Production leader in the chemical industry <ID029>)*

Companies as well as the centre wanted the plan to be met and inefficient companies always obtained funds to avoid production failure or a termination of production. The means of support were credit, subsidy from the state budget, rationing from a superior authority, or adjusting prices to the detriment of the purchaser. Fritzová mentions that companies spent much more energy on finding arguments for obtaining subsidies than on efforts to decline the costs (Fritzová 1995). Circumstances when credit is easily accessible for companies are sometimes defined as soft budget constraint (Kornai 1980). Because credits were allocated by the plan, the bank officials were not interested in the companies' ability to reimburse loans or in the credibility of the debtors.

Additionally, companies introduced several strategies to avoid the threat of not meeting the plan. Mlčoch writes about "games" on "objective troubles-poor relative." Also, a company that was not able to meet its plan behaved on the principle "whatever it takes." The reached economic results were possibly deeply under the company's potential because the company management was preparing ground for a "new initial" level for the next period of the plan. Typically, companies tried to fail the plan in the fourth quarter of the year in order to keep bonuses in the three previous ones (Mlčoch 1990).

We showed with our interviews that the direct hierarchical vertical structure often did not work in practice. In some of the cases, the companies significantly influenced the plan. Additionally, the KSČ intervened into the functioning of the system. The overall behaviour of the companies can be regarded at least as strange and incomprehensible from the perspective of market economy (among others, a lot of time had to be spent on the administrative). But in fact, it was very rational and natural from the perspective of the company in the CPE system. The companies just followed the intentions of the system. The main intentions were in the form of the plans and in struggle to deal with the omnipresent shortage. The result was a situation Mlčoch defines as "upturned minimax" when the company tried to maximize its inputs and minimize its outputs (Mlčoch 1990). This behaviour is in fact quite the opposite to the behaviour of companies in a market economy, which try to minimize inputs and maximize outputs. Even though it was entirely rational from the point of view of the companies, in aggregate it resulted in fatal and inefficient behaviour of the economic system as a whole.

Notes

1 We do not have any estimation about the size of information spread for the Czechoslovak economy, but Rutland (1985) mentions a study about the Soviet Union. The study mentions approximately 120 to 170 billion data circulating in the economy in the 1980s. However, the centre had access to only 3 billion of these. Similarly, Šulc quotes a Soviet author Fedorenko and writes: "If we make our task easier and conclude that our economy generates about two million products (in reality, the figure is much higher) and uses about a million products more (in reality, the figure is again much higher) and that it uses about a million starting products and semi-finished products, in order to prepare a plan for production for all the companies there are in the economy, the centre would have to carry out 10^{18} arithmetic operations. If these operations are carried out on the BESM-6 electronic computing machine able to perform one million operations per second, it will take 30 thousand years for the machine to carry out all the operations or 30 thousand machines to be done with the task in one year. This is, obviously, unreal" (Šulc 2004).

2 Aleksìjevìč provides an extreme case of insisting on the plan from the Soviet practice. She writes about the Chernobyl disaster. She mentions that some parts of the affected Belarus territory were really totally abandoned. But next to them people lived and worked in large areas with extreme radioactivity and the collective farms had to fulfil the plans. It resulted in the delivery of contaminated products – flour, milk, meat, etc. – to the processing industry. The manufactures consequently used these deliveries in foodstuff for people or at minimum for animals (Aleksìjevìč 2017). The plan had to be met.

3 This was one of the reasons why there were only 2 women among our 80 respondents.

4 Our respondents often use terms VHJ, conglomerate/group, and GŘ interchangeably. The role of these middle units in the planning hierarchy was similar (see the schemes in Chapter 3) and they changed during time. Due to it we will not distinguish them either and we use general term VHJ on the following pages.

5 Respondents were given room for the free appreciation of the positives and negatives of that time. Among the former, the very good interpersonal relationships in the workplace completely prevailed.

5 Macroeconomic results

The previous chapter provided evidence about the day-to-day functioning of the centrally planned system in socialist Czechoslovakia in different layers from the centre at the top down to the companies. This chapter demonstrates the (macroeconomic) results that were achieved by the system in the last two decades of the socialist rule. Meeting the plan was the ultimate operational objective of the central planning economic system and it is dealt with in the first section (5.1). Then we analyze the development of the main economic indicators – GDP and economic growth (5.2), functioning of the labour market (5.3), price stability and inflation (5.4) and international relations (5.5). These partial analyses provide an overall view of the economy.

5.1 Meeting the global plan

Meeting the plan was the main criterion for the evaluation of companies, the VHJs, and the whole system. The communists presented meeting the plan as the main operational objective and a measure of success. There are several subtopics connected with plan fulfilment. The first of them is the time criterion. The five-year plans were strategic in nature and certainly less binding than the operative one-year plans. Faltus and Průcha remark that the fifth five-year plan (for the period after 1970) was the only period when the majority of constituent plans was met. However, even in that period, the system was not able to achieve all its plans targeted at growth of efficiency and scientific and technical development (Faltus and Průcha 1995). One of our respondents, a planner in agriculture <ID45>, described one previous experience with plan fulfilment:

> *Now, I am trying to remember what year it was, 57, I reckon. Simply, what happened was that a five-year plan was not met. So, what do you do about it? Five-year plans must be met, right? So, a revaluation of the basic resources was made. At the beginning of the planning period, old prices were applied but at the end of the period new prices were introduced, and thus by this increase in prices, an increase in yield was achieved.*

Similar manipulation with the plan securing positive results was admitted by our respondent from the SPK <ID040>, who described a scheme through which the planners dealt with unexpected threat of a drop in national income. This drop would be a result of a shortage of crude oil supplies from the Soviet Union. Unable to accept a potential drop of 2–2.5% (which would devour the entire growth planned for the next year), the planners did not hesitate to redefine the standing net national income into gross national income.

Table 5.1 depicts an example of the interconnection between five-year plans and one-year plans for the AZNP Mladá Boleslav company (Škoda car). The plans changed from the original five-year plan after 1977 because of the inability of the company to achieve the ambitious goals of the original five-year plan. However, even though the company was not able to meet its original plan, it was able to slightly overcome the modified numbers.

Table 5.1 The plans and reality in production of cars in Automobilové závody národní podnik (AZNP) Mladá Boleslav – Škoda car (in pieces)

	1976	*1977*	*1978*	*1979*	*1980*	*Sum for sixth five-year plan*
A) Original plan for sixth five-year plan	175,170	176,500	180,500	187,000	198,500	917,670
B) Executive one-year plan for AZNP	175,170	156,730	170,400	174,250	176,850	853,400
C) Reality	175,595	154,896	170,967	176,049	177,819	855,326
Difference A-C	425	–21,604	–9,533	–10,951	–20,681	–62,344
Difference B-C	425	–1,834	567	1,799	969	1,926

Source: Vilímek (2012)

The general fulfilling of the plan could be seen in Appendix 1. The tables there show all the main indicators on the year-to-year basis. Compilation of these tables was extremely complicated as can be seen on the number of used sources below the table. The regime was highly secretive, which was evident, among others, by the insufficient information flow on the plan's fulfilment. Additionally, we can doubt the reliability of the statistical data – for example, the defence expenditures were, at that time, just estimated (see Chapter 1). Moreover, meeting the basic plan did not fully reflect the overall situation of the economy.

Other doubts appeared at the micro level. Our respondents documented that meeting the plan was often only formal, and that cheating was not uncommon. Another point was in the production of idle goods that were included in the overall production even though no one wanted to purchase them and they stayed in storage, so they formally inflated the figures.

5.2 Economic growth

This chapter discusses economic growth and other akin measures. We use comparison of the GDP per capita, a short note about grey economy, analysis of productivity, structure of the economy, and the share of investment and consumption in the product, in order to assess the economic results of the centrally planned economy in Czechoslovakia.

The most common measurement of production is GDP. The socialist countries used a similar indicator called net material product.[1] The Czechoslovak economy, with its 15 million inhabitants, was relatively small. Economic growth – GDP estimates – and its trend can be seen in Figure 5.1. The economy was able to achieve high economic growth in the first decade following the communist coup – in the 1950s – when the economy was still recovering from WWII. But the ability to grow was declining in following decades and, by the 1980s, the growth nearly stalled.

The socialist indicator – net material product – shows similar outcomes (see Figure 5.2). Interestingly, contrary to the expectations of socialist economists,

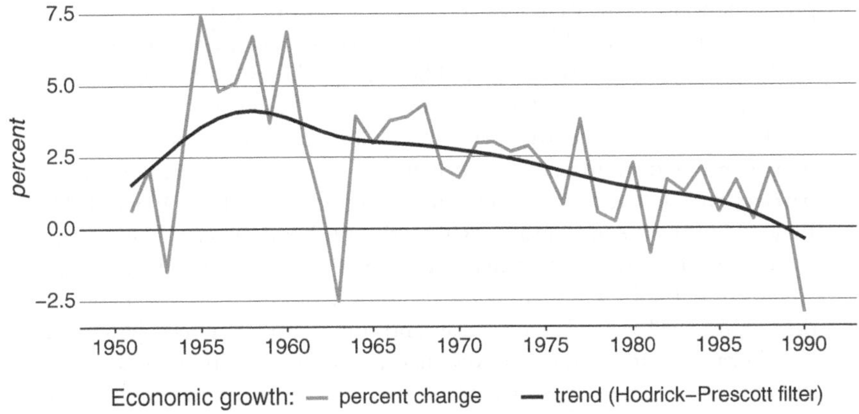

Figure 5.1 Estimation of GDP in Czechoslovakia 1950–1990, and its trendline

Source: The Maddison-Project (2013)

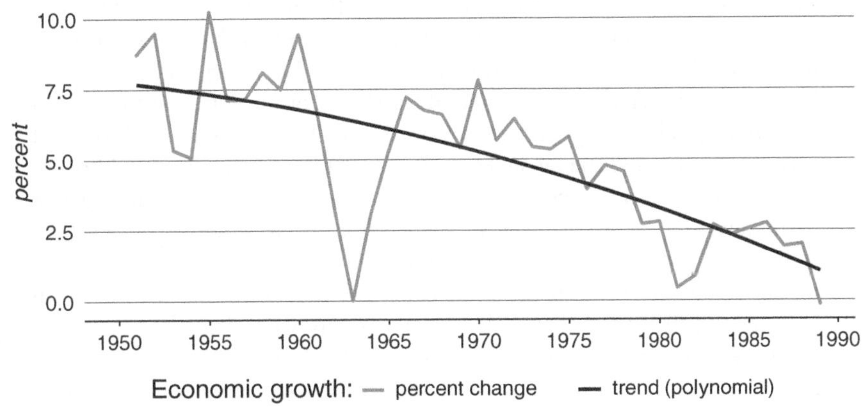

Figure 5.2 Net material product and its trendline 1951–1989

Source: Statistical yearbooks of CSSR (1971–1990)

the socialist economy was not free from business cycle (see Box 5.1). Apparently, the gradual decrease in growth potential of the socialist economy was evident even in its own metrics.

Box 5.1 Investment business cycle

Initially, socialist economists believed that the centrally planned economies would grow permanently and completely avoid the business cycle, an undesirable feature of capitalist economies (see Chapter 2). The early years of central planning seemed to prove these expectations. However, later on, the centrally planned economies suffered from cyclical fluctuations as well as market economies. Socialist theorists tried to explain this phenomenon. There were two interpretations of the matter.

Goldmann presented his theory of "socialist quasi-cycle" in the 1960s (Goldmann and Kouba 1969). The theory blamed the sub-optimal growth rate of the plan. The negative parts of the cycle appeared when the aspiration of the centre overcame the abilities/capacities of the economy. It resulted in an erecting of material, and energetic and/or import barriers that led to a slowdown in economic growth (Mlčoch 1990). Bauer is more specific and adds that the problem appeared due to the poor coordination of investment between the first level (raw materials) and second level (manufacturing) of production. The investment into the second level was relatively easier and thus natural material (raw material) became scarce. Šulc believes that, at the bottom part of the cycle, the creation of the national income was slower than consumption (use of national income), and so an ever bigger part was stuck in unfinished production construction and other stocks (Šulc 2004). Rendl comments that this situation led to a slowdown in economic dynamism because the economy had to "wait" for completion of the unfinished capacities at the first level – in energy and material sectors (Rendl et al. 1988). He adds that this cycle had two accelerators. One of them was that the companies reacted to the first hints of a lack of raw material or energies by increased hoarding and increasing the demand for these commodities and the overall deficit quickly deepened. Šulc, contrary to Rendl, does not think that hoarding magnified the cycle. He believes that the companies used hoarding as a safeguard to secure material for meeting the plan and against extremely long delivery times in the economy. Movement of stock thus in his view did not have anything in common with the cycle. The stocks in the economy were, in the long run, growing more than the national income and thus the situation was permanently worsening (Šulc 2004).

The second accelerator of the cycle, Rendl continues, was in an area of foreign relations. The lack of some inputs led to an increase of imports. This development tapped the country's scarce hard currency reserves and resulted in the necessity to increase exports of domestic production. That then led to pressure on the domestic production and over optimal use of the domestic capacities and thus to an increase of domestic costs (though official inflation was concealed due to fixed prices). This development broadened the shortage on the domestic market. The consequence was decline or stagnation of economic growth, which enabled a reduction of the imbalances, a finishing of constructions, and a decline in demand for material and imports. Companies ceased hoarding and due to this the overall shortage declined. And the whole cycle could start again with the setting of maximal growth target (Rendl et al. 1988).

The second possible explanation of the cycle was in Bauer's view that the centre was biased to design a plan with excessive economic growth. When the planners realized it, they applied restrictions. For political and social reasons, the cuts fell disproportionately on investment rather than on consumption. The consequence was the rise of unfinished projects (Bauer 2005). Šulc states that in practice the centre was really highly sensitive to political aspects of economic imbalance and applied restrictions in several years – 1964, 1970, and 1980–1982. The restrictions took many forms – restraints of investment, curbing the imports, or shifting the funds from manufacturing to consumption goods. These restrictions were in his view highly effective for quick restoration of macroeconomic balance (Šulc 2004).

Some of the communist leaders were aware of the negative trends in economic growth (as well as microeconomic imbalances and inefficient behaviour of the companies) and they tried to introduce reforms that were expected to deal with these deficiencies. The first reform – Rozsypal's – was applied already in the second half of the 1950s. The next reform took place in the 1960s. It was associated with the name of an economist Ota Šik. This reform attempt was terminated by the suppression of the Prague Spring in 1968. The third attempt at reforms took place at the beginning of the 1980s and the fourth round of reforms was reluctantly introduced after 1985 in the Perestroika period. For the studied period the last two reforms are relevant. Štrougal (that time Federal Prime Minister) writes that the energy crisis of 1979 commenced discussion about a reform of the system. The federal government was in favour of reforms because of the enormous energetic requirements of the Czechoslovak economy, which the companies were reluctant to tackle by energy savings. The government wanted to implement reforms to increase companies' involvement and their independence. Nevertheless,

> *as already many times, the majority of leaders of the party decided that we do not need reforms, but more discipline. [. . .] It was proceeded in the 'time-proven way': the troubles are not in the system but in the supervising of people. We will check even more, write reports and set commitments to overcome the deficiencies.*
>
> *(Štrougal 2009, p. 252)*

It resulted in only a mild reform program introduced in 1980. Rendl even writes that the reforms led to more detailed plans, further individualized plans, and the geometric growth of directive planning (Rendl et al. 1988).

The reforms in the Perestroika period were more ambitious, but the support of the top-ranking communists was lukewarm at the best. The reforms embraced among others an Act on State Company from 1988 (Zákon č. 88/1988Sb., o státním podniku) that expected for example the election of directors of the companies by newly established assemblies. At the same time, the system of the VHJs was abandoned and replaced by new state companies with higher economic independence. The directing system was thus transformed from four to three tiers – the SPK – the ministries – the companies. The system allowed experiments with companies' autonomy – the most famous case was the Slušovice cooperative (see Box 5.2). However, our respondents viewed Perestroika reforms variously, from documenting of relaxing environment (economic planner in engineering <ID008>) to zero progress (head of agricultural company <ID048>). Nevertheless, what really happened was an 18.6% decline in the number of companies in the economy from 17,676 to 14,391 between 1987 and 1 January 1990. Other drops were registered in transport (70%), construction (61%), industry (35%), and in agriculture (2.7%) (Janeček and Knobloch 1991). Thus, the consequence of the reforms was higher monopolization.

Meanwhile, special institutions were established with ambitions to prepare reforms that would result in improving the state of the economy. The most famous were the Prognostic Institute of the Czech Academy of Science (Prognostický ústav ČSAV), and the Economic Institute of the Czech Academy of Science (Ekonomický ústav ČSAV). At the practical level, the regime allowed and in fact supported business trips or even education of some people in the developed countries. The Prognostic Institute was founded in the 1980s, and it analyzed processes, interconnections, and trends in the economy and society (Masarykův ústav a Archiv AV ČR, v.v.i. 2015). It was a specialized institution in the Czechoslovak Academy of Science. The institute published a confidential, relatively critical analysis of the state of the Czechoslovak economy. The most famous was Prognóza a program that was officially published only after the fall of the regime (Komárek et al. 1990). The Economic Institute was formally supposed to focus on economic laws from the Marxist point of view. It was therefore supposed to improve the efficiency of the planned economy, as well as to analyze selected problems of the capitalist countries (Masarykův ústav a Archiv AV ČR, v.v.i. 2015). Some of the Economic Institute employees later became leaders of the economic transformation – they were aware of the errors of socialism since they were allowed to travel or read books by Hayek or Friedman. These were, for example, Václav Klaus (later the Prime Minister), Dušan Tříska (the co-author of the voucher privatization) (Klaus 2002), and Tomáš Ježek (later Minister of Privatization) (Husák 1997). A respondent who worked as a scientist in the Prognostic Institute <ID034> said that the level of freedom was high for that time, and that the Institute employed for example even people who had not passed the party checks after 1968 or even those with ties to dissent. They were supposed to bring knowledge to improve the efficiency of the system. The employees of the Economic Institute had the same task – e.g., Tomáš Ježek consequently stated that the regime paid them to come up with a miraculous formula how to save socialism (Husák 1997). However, other research teams were supposed to prepare reform programs to improve the functioning of the economy as documented by our respondent (researcher <ID061>).

All the reforms during the socialist period were intended to increase the activity of companies by granting them more freedom of decision and increasing their "material interest" – which meant more direct connection between performance and reward at the level of companies. None of the reforms' attempts was able to change the trends and compensate for microeconomic imbalances. In all the cases, it collided with ideological inability to consider changes in ownership and clashes between reform and conservative cliques in the Party. The proponents of the reform wing in the regime still believe today that reforms (similar to Šik's reforms of the 1960s) would have been able to save the socialistic system in Czechoslovakia, if they had been given the time to be carried out (Štrougal 2009). Similarly, a researcher from the Prognostic Institute <ID034> considered the "enormous inertia" on the side of the main client – the leaders of the Communist Party – to be the main reason why the bureaucratic planning was not overcome. Štrougal concludes that the conservatives were led by both "ideological blindness and low professional erudition in the main parts of power structures in the centre as well as in regions." These people kept on repeating that everything was all right and that total majority of people was satisfied even though, in his words, just a superficial glance around evidenced the opposite (Štrougal 2009). At the end of the 1980s a critical analysis of the state of the economy was even published not only in professional journals but in a freely accessible magazine as well (Zeman 1989).

Regardless of this, the Czechoslovak system kept a high overall level of restriction until the end. Politicians in most of the other centrally planned countries at least partially liberalized their economies in the last decades of the socialist era. For example, in Hungary liberating reforms started already in 1968. These reforms, generally, deepened in the period of Perestroika. The essence of the reforms was in a lower degree of involvement by the government – by partial price and trade liberalizations, by increasing the role of the private sector, by allowing foreign investment in the country, etc. However, Czechoslovakia was a laggard and the local communists applied significant reforms neither in the political nor in the economic sphere. The economy, as well as society, stayed nearly fully bounded until the collapse of the regime. The liberalization index depicted in Table 5.2 illustrates this.

Handl concludes that the party was aware of the situation but was not able to solve it. Its formal and factual position as the leading entity of the state did not allow reforms. In his view the interest in stability of power monopoly was superior to interests in economic modernization and prosperity (Handl 2018).

Table 5.2 Liberalization Index 1989 and 1997

Country	*1989*	*1997*
Bulgaria	0.13	0.79
Czech Republic	0.00	0.93
Hungary	0.34	0.93
Poland	0.24	0.89
Romania	0.00	0.75
Slovak Republic	0.00	0.86
Slovenia	0.41	0.89

Source: Hare (2001)

Liberalization Index – a weighted average of three components: domestic market liberalization (weight 0.3), foreign trade liberalization (weight 0.3), enterprise privatization and banking reform (weight 0.4). For each component, the average is reported in the table, scored in the range [0, 1].

Box 5.2 JZD Slušovice

In the late socialist period, Agrokombinát Slušovice, an agricultural cooperative (JZD), excelled. It became a truly massive and highly productive socialist large-scale enterprise in the 1970s and 1980s. Slušovice can be considered as an experiment where the agricultural company obtained more freedoms for its economic activities.

Despite the fact that the cooperative was operating under worse production conditions (tenth zone of natural conditions according to the classification of the Federal Ministry of Agriculture and Nutrition), it achieved exceptional results at that time. The average output in the field of crop farming production led to a specialization in the cultivation of spring barley and forage maize, which allowed the rationalization of production and its mechanization (Vácha 1988). Their production of livestock was especially successful, in which the Slušovice cooperative ranked extensively above the Czechoslovak average. They were supposed to be on a par or even better than western producers (see the Table 5.3). Regardless of possible manipulation with numbers for propagandist goals, Slušovice achieved outstanding success in breeding dairy cows, embryo transplantation to increase milk production, and in growing corn (Čuba 2012).

Agrokombinát Slušovice rose through a series of mergers and in the end, it was comprised of 21 cooperatives. Nevertheless, like a number of other cooperatives, they expanded to other sectors unrelated to agriculture. The cooperative (at the national level) excelled, for example, in computer science and industry-leading production for agriculture. The role of agriculture was declining and it accounted for only 6% of its total gross production in 1986 (Vácha 1988).

Table 5.3 Productivity of Slušovice in comparison with other countries

	Yield of cereals in 1986 (tonnes per hectare)	*Average annual milk yield in 1985 (kg/year)*
Slušovice	6.21 (1985)	5,922
Israel	n.a.	8,125
United Kingdom	6.21	4,909
Japan	5.68	5,046
France	5.29	n.a.
West Germany	5.27	4,710
USA	4.68	5,844
Denmark	4.65	5,346
Czechoslovakia	4.50	n.a.
Hungary	4.37	n.a.
Yugoslavia	4.26	n.a.
Bulgaria	4.17	n.a.
Canada	n.a.	4,762
Switzerland	n.a.	4,379

Source: Vácha (1988)

The field of activity of the Agrokombinát was really wide. Slušovice had their own bank, racing track and was breeding English full-blood horses. Renault and Audi tested their cars on Slušovice runway. They also founded an airline (Air Moravia) and a retail network that among others offered consumer goods imported from capitalist countries. The cooperative gained the foreign exchange to obtain imported goods mainly because of its activities in the Soviet Union, Austria, Egypt, Vietnam, and its cooperation with companies from Canada and Switzerland (Čuba 2012).

Slušovice succeeded in business management. After the initial alternation of the team presidents, František Čuba took the position in 1963. Slušovice reached a turnover of CSK 130 thousand that year. It increased to CZK 7 billion by the late 1980s. The key was primarily the ability to motivate employees, whose reward was directly linked to the results of their work. It was not tied to the results of the cooperative as a whole but directly to the results of the workplace. In the background was above all an effort to make each worker an active co-owner and co-creator of the team's results, which emphasized the entrepreneurial participation of each worker in the cooperative business (Vácha 1988). For example, workers were often personally responsible for the machines they worked with and had their own business account, deciding what amount of money they would use to repair the machines, and how much they would pay themselves in rewards (Čuba 2012). The leaders were not appointed from the top but selected by other team members. The promotion was based mainly on their qualification and working results, rather than on their membership in the Communist Party (Vácha 1988).

Management was considerably decentralized, and the managers were evaluated every three months. If they did not get the required number of points, they were moved to a lower post and were automatically replaced by someone who had an excellent score. In the next quarter, the situation could be reversed. Leading workers had to travel to advanced capitalist countries to learn directly about modern production processes and staff management (Čuba 2012). Within the cooperative, the Science and Technological Development Department also worked, which collected information from around the world. Based on this, the latest scientific and technical knowledge was put into practice.

Under the system, Slušovice functioned on the so-called principle of passive tolerance, which in fact meant that the state did not provide the cooperative with any means but allowed it to be very entrepreneurial (Vácha 1988). Čuba himself regards Slušovice as an example of true socialism (Čuba 2012). Nevertheless, the way in which the enterprise was managed, based on the motivation of employees who were encouraging an initiative and independent approach to work, seems closer to capitalism. What was socialist, however, was the care that the enterprise provided to its employees. Care for former, retired workers, single mothers, fully paid rehabilitation in spa centres or recreation in Italian, German, and Austrian resorts was only a fraction of the care the company provided to its employees:

> *That system of care for the people was top. When a co-worker's cottage burned down, the next day, we built a new cottage for it from mobile blocks, and he moved in the very next day. He had a kitchen there, a living room, a bedroom one, and a bedroom two. He also had tables, chairs, plates, mugs and cutlery, everything and about 5 thousand crowns in wages. [. . .] He just did not have to worry about what could happen because he knew that this company would always take care of him.*
>
> *(Čuba 2012)*

According to Vácha (1988), this further encouraged employees to pursue the profit of the whole cooperative alongside their personal one.

The respondents in a project by Vaněk and Krátká admitted that the cooperatives or in fact their chairmen had to have contacts to "top brass" who help them (e.g., "friends" at the Ministry of Agriculture) (Vaněk and Krátká 2014). We can speculate whether it was the case of Slušovice as well. However, the long-term chairman Mr. Čuba said that their success was just a matter of their persistence in obtaining the official stamps (permissions) that allowed them various activities (Vaněk and Krátká 2014).

Interestingly, the communist authorities allowed this whole experiment, but its success consequently caused disputes between "reformers" and "conservatives" inside the party. Rudolf Hegenbart (Secretary of Zlín OV KSČ) said that he obtained unofficial instruction to "eliminate Slušovice, dispose of Mr. Čuba [its chairman] and prevent contra-revolutionary trends in the Slušovice system." Hegenbart was offered promotion in exchange. When he became familiar with the situation in the company, he did not classify it as contra-revolution and on the contrary believed that it was a model that fully fit into the socialist economic and political system. Despite the instructions, he enforced Mr. Čuba to the OV KSČ in Zlín (Vaněk and Urbášek 2005). In Handl's view this case demonstrated not only a schism inside the KSČ but a limited ability to keep one's own views inside the Communist Party hierarchy as well (Handl 2018). The cooperative went bankrupt after the fall of the socialist regime.

5.2.1 *Character of economic growth*

In general, economic growth comprises extensive or intensive factors. The former means increasing inputs, the latter, in short, means increasing efficiency in usage of the existed sources. In practice, growth is always a combination of both. But in socialist countries, extensive factors were always prevailing and thus expanding production always stimulated demand for inputs. (e.g., Adam 1995). On the contrary, in the market economies the intensive component is more important. Table 5.4 shows the results of the findings provided by Žídek and

Table 5.4 Planned and real growth of selected indicators and the shares of extensive and intensive economic growth

Growth rates (%)	*1971–1975*	*1976–1980*	*1981–1985*	*1986–1990*	*All periods average*
GDP	4.94	2.81	0.93	1.91	2.65
GDP plan	5	5	1.5–2.1	3.2	
Labour	0.48	0.74	0.52	–0.21	0.39
Labour productivity	4.44	2.06	0.40	2.13	2.26
Labour prod. plan	4.75	4.55	1.4–2	2.9	
Capital	9.69	1.98	–3.02	1.81	2.61
TFP	–0.41	1.41	2.55	1.33	1.22
Shares (%)*					
Extensity	65.96	58.89	51.18	47.63	56.44
Intensity	34.04	41.11	48.82	52.37	43.56

Source: Žídek and Soukup (publication in process)

* the overall shares are computed from absolute values.

Soukup (publication in process), who show the key planned indicators, their real values, and shares of extensive and intensive components of economic growth. The table demonstrates that plan indicators always reached substantially higher values than the real ones. From the point of view of the individual components of economic growth, it is clear that an extensive component prevailed over the whole period. Only in the last phase of socialism did the component of the intensity predominate, which might indicate, among other things, exhaustion of the possibilities of extensive economic growth.

The extensive character of growth is generally not surprising considering the fact that the goal of the companies was meeting the plan regardless of efficiency. If the companies functioned on the reverse minimax paradigm, as our respondents evidenced, they were just supporting this character of growth because they tried to obtain a maximum of inputs and to minimize outputs. One of our respondents – who worked in a research department in engineering <ID036> shared his experience:

> *The colleagues of mine who worked in civil engineering used to say. "You know, civil engineering is the basis. What you drown in the foundations, well, that is what remains there. And what no one can check, right?" Because when they dug a hole . . . you know, the builders were evaluated according to how much concrete they poured in there. Well, once they managed to pour in 20 concrete mixers, it was, like, 20 mixers were needed then. Or, as I spoke of these tensioners, like, . . . the tensioner is probably this tall, it's four and a half tons, yeah. So, when we supplied it, we supplied it and added the money and the tons on top.*

The extensive character of economic growth had multiple reasons, as well as negative impacts. Firstly, it expressed low general level of productivity. This contributed to extremely high energy- and material-intensive production. It can be seen for example in Table 5.5.

Table 5.5 Energetic and material burden for creating USD 1,000 of GDP in ČSSR and comparable developed countries (Austria, Switzerland, Belgium, the Netherlands, Finland, and Denmark) in the 1980s

	ČSSR	*Average developed countries*
Consumption of primary energy (GJ)	20	13.3
Consumption of row steel (kg)	77.1	27
Consumption of cement (kg)	72	36.3
Volume of train transport (hrtkm)	998	160.2

Source: Půlpán (1993)

A problem connected with extensive growth were growing stockpiles in the economy. They were a consequence of the natural behaviour (hoarding) of the

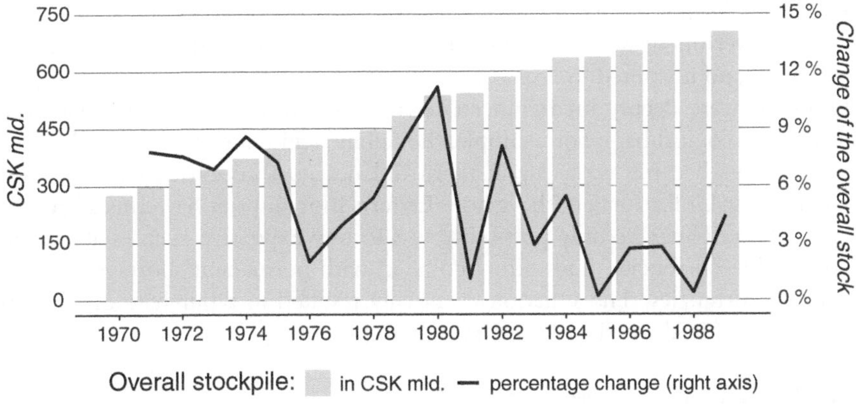

Figure 5.3 Stockpiles in Czechoslovak economy (in CSK mld.) and year-to-year change (in percent)

Source: Statistical yearbooks of CSSR (1971–1990)

companies analyzed in the previous chapter. For overall figures for goods and products, see Figure 4.1 (in Chapter 4); for the total stockpiles value and year-to-year changes, see Figure 5.3. Moreover, the percentage growth of stockpiles was significantly higher compared to the percentage growth of net material product.

The main consequence of the extensive character of growth was in the economy's declining ability to grow. It became more and more difficult to acquire new inputs which would sustain growth because they were more and more scarce (for example labour force). The views of pundits vary as to when exactly the sources for extensive growth were already exhausted, but a lack of the sources was certainly limiting growth already in the 1980s (for example Adam 1995). The socialist economists and even politicians were well aware of this problem and were unanimously calling for improvement and change in the character of growth to an intensive one (e.g. Pawera et al. 1985; Rendl et al. 1988; Průcha 1988; Hrnčíř 1987). However, the problem with the character of growth was deeply rooted in the general characteristics of the central planning and it was impossible to overcome it without a radical change in the functioning of the economic system. The reforms were at best only half-hearted and the opinions of political leaders were divided.

The negative side effect of the extensive economic growth and enormous energetical demand of production was a disastrous ecological situation. Especially mining and power producing regions (Northern Bohemia) were strongly affected by air pollution. Water pollution was high as well. Zieleniec writes that at the end of the communist rule, 54% of the land was threatened by erosion, and 80% by acids; 65–70% of sewage water was not cleaned in water-cleaning facilities, and around one half of all drinking water did not meet the official standards; 2/3 of Czech forests were damaged. In Slovakia, the respective number was 1/3 (Zieleniec 1990).

The government was aware of the horrifying ecological situation (e.g., Štrougal 2009) and it wanted to deal with it, but there were obstacles. The ecological problems were deeply interconnected with economic situation and with the low technological base. For example, the falling acid rains were caused by coal powerplants because waste air in them did not go through desulphurization technology. Unfortunately, the whole Eastern Bloc did not have this advanced technology. Thus, the only possibility was to buy expensive licenses abroad in convertible currencies. This effort collided with permanent shortage of convertible currencies. The situation eventually resulted in a purchase of western technologies in the early 1990s (Kratochvíl 2011).

GDP per capita and real wages

Hába in his textbook about central planning points out that: "under socialism, the aim of social production is to satisfy, as fully as possible, the growing material and spiritual needs of society and to create prerequisites for the all-round development of personality on the basis of constant development and improvement of social production" (Hába et al. 1988, p. 12). He adds that socialism was successful in this effort and that the "dynamic economic development of the socialist countries resulted in equalizing of average economic level in both of the systems [socialism and capitalism] and in achieving of the same production per capita" (ibidem). However, the reality was different and the weak economic performance in the socialist period was reflected in the declining relative position of the Czechoslovak economy in comparison to developed countries. Figure 5.4 shows the post-war development of GDP per capita in relation to

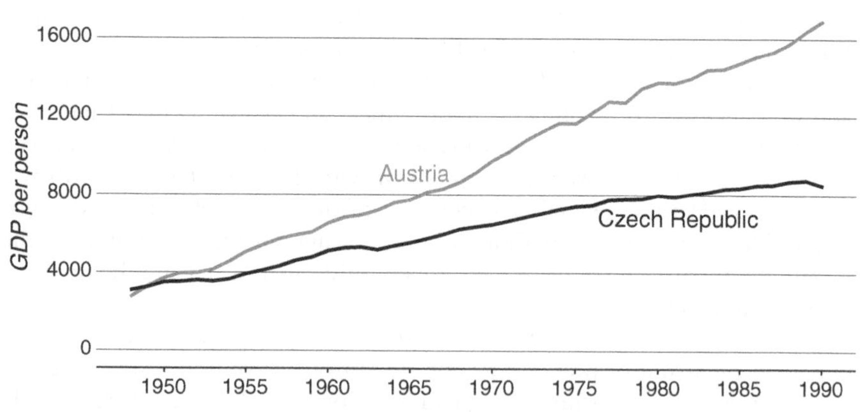

Figure 5.4 GDP per person in Austria and Czechoslovakia 1950–1989 (converted at Geary Khamis PPPs)

Source: The Maddison-Project (2013)

Austria. We can see that the living standard at the beginning of the 1950s was roughly the same, but in the following years, the figure in Czechoslovakia relatively declined. At the end of the socialist period, GDP per capita reached approximately one half of GDP per capita in Austria. We can find slightly different results in other authors (for example Dillon and Wykoff 2002 write that Czechoslovak GDP per capita was at just one fifth of the Austrian one in 1990; for other estimations, see Vintrová 2006) but regardless of these discrepancies, all estimates show a lasting trend of the Czechoslovak economy lagging behind the developed capitalist countries. At the same time, Czechoslovakia still ranked, together with East Germany, as the most developed country of the Eastern Bloc.

Interestingly, the proponents of the regime still believe that the socialist economy was not in a bad state. The then Prime Minister Štrougal writes that "socialist economy and common ownership was – despite all the errors [. . .] – successful and socially beneficial." Štrougal admits that there were problems on the inner market but that the west would happily provide a few million credit for the "missing" bananas, personal cars, new facades, roofs etc. And that the credit was not even necessary if the reformers in the party had been able to enforce several affordable and rational measures, but the conservative majority did not allow it. Besides malevolent conservatives, he mentions two reasons why the economy was not as efficient as the western one – because the economy did not have significant financial funds and investment in afterwar development as other western countries – the Marshall Plan – and that the strictly enforced embargo acted against them (Štrougal 2009).[2] This statement and alike show flagrantly the extent of the communist elite missing the point. Even though they knew that something with the economy went wrong, they were not able to grasp the situation and its implications. Or, at least, they did not admit it, not even with hindsight, as Jaroslav Jeník (Chief Secretary of the OV KSČ in Pardubice in the 1970s and 1980s) said: "The society was rich. Yes, it is true that everyone was as poor as a church mouse, but the state was rich, it had no debts" (Vaněk and Urbášek 2005, p. 317).

The theorists of the regime believed that, in socialism, the "living standard of all employees is permanently growing, because planned production is permanently growing" (Pavlát and Vojtíšek 1959, p. 30). However, in practice, real wages trends expressed an ailing economy as well. Their growth average between 1970 and 1989 was approximately 1.4% per year but in the 1980s only, the average reached only 0.5% per year – see Figure 5.5. Moreover, it should be mentioned that the development inside Czechoslovakia diverged, with economic growth in Slovakia significantly higher than in the Czech part, this, to some degree, was due to lasting fiscal transfers to the eastern part of the federation (Slovakia) (for example Vintrová 2006). During the entire course of the socialist period, the economy in Slovakia was catching up with its Czech counterpart. The Slovak national income per person grew from 60% of the Czech one in 1948 to 88% in 1989 (Vintrová 2008).

The rigid structure of the society and tough restrictive measures everywhere were reflected in a relatively low level of grey activities in the economic system. One of the estimations of the size of the non-official economy is depicted in Table 5.6. The level of black market with goods was relatively modest but moonlighting of service jobs (for example plumbers) was quite common. The craftsmen frequently used equipment and material from their company and provided the service in their official working time without any guarantee (Průcha 2000). Moonlighting often included services that were supposed to be provided for free by the public sector (by state, municipal, or cooperative firms) but that were in practice available only after an enormously long waiting period and/or in poor quality. It is not surprising, when we consider the low employment in this sector. Císař writes that 566 thousand people worked in craftsman jobs (out of them only 2.5% in the administrative) in 1948 in the Czech part of the country. The number declined to 287 thousand in 1988, out of which 33% worked in the administration (Císař 1995). As a result, there were generally few craftsmen who were topped-up by massive bureaucracy. Kalinová even comments that the regime tolerated development of grey economy because it realized that the needs of the inhabitants were impossible to be satisfied by legal means (Kalinová 2012).

Table 5.6 Estimation of share of non-official economy in 1989 in %

Countries	*1989*
Bulgaria	22.8
Czechoslovakia	6.0
Hungary	27.0
Poland	15.7
Romania	22.3
Soviet Union	12.0

Source: Åslund, Boone, and Johnson (2001)

Productivity

The previous chapter thoroughly described the behaviour of the centre and foremost the companies. There was a political order to increase productivity and the economic centre intended to meet it. The regime realized that the productivity was a key factor of growth and development. (Lenin had predicted that growth in productivity would be crucial in competing with capitalist countries, see Chapter 2.) But the overall environment and nudges led the companies the opposite way. We must remember that the incentives were not positive in respect to productivity – for instance, the struggle to minimize the plan, hoarding (including labour), weak motivation, shortages hindering smooth production, etc. At the same time, there was no competition which would have forced the companies to be efficient, and bankruptcies did not exist as well – in other words, the system made no effort to remove the weakest participants in the economy. In this situation both pull and push factors provided limited (if any) motivation for improving efficiency. The everyday reality documented our respondents. One of them for example told us: "For instance, emphasis on productivity and dismissal of employees were things impossible to negotiate . . . there was a political need not to lower employment figures, or, in fact, employment cuts were not included in the plan, nor was lowering of fixed expenses by doing away with inefficient companies" (Production leader in the chemical industry <ID029>).

Additionally, companies in the centrally planned economy were characterized by a "lack of interest in technical progress, efforts to fabricate production as long as possible, efforts to reduce the number of R&D workers who appear to be unproductive in the face of plan indicators, efforts to replace the increasing labour productivity of other raw materials, materials and artificial cooperation, etc." (Šulc 2004). As has been previously stated, the price of labour was lower than its reproductive value, and acted, therefore, as an anti-motivating factor against technical developments. It also contributed to excessive labour demand, which contributed to its shortage (Šulc 2004). Moreover, as the StB reported, the workers sometimes even feared the company's purchase of a new machinery. They were worried that these would replace their work, which, according to the StB, might have led to intended damages (ABS, OB-957 OV).

Šulc also points out that there was a planned productivity indicator. However, labour productivity was defined simply as gross production divided by the number of workers. Its real value could have been influenced, for example, by changes in prices. As for companies, they wanted prices to be as high as possible (see Section 4.4.1). This also meant a larger source of additional corporate income and, above all, higher production and labour productivity and easier fulfilment of the planned indicators relevant to wage and salary formation. This system, therefore, did not motivate companies to introduce more effective techniques of production.

The consequence was a very low labour productivity, as was corroborated by our respondent from the Prognostic Institute of the Czech Republic <ID034>: "Those structural imperfections were there, for sure, and they went hand in hand with, on the one hand, quantitative and extensive indicators that showed we were beating the advanced economies, but on the other hand, we lagged behind in labour productivity." For estimation of the lagging behind the developed economies in productivity indicators see Table 5.7. The most efficient Czechoslovak industry – vehicle manufacture – achieved just 45% productivity of similar-sized small western countries. The least efficient industry reached just 5% and the average was at a feeble 25%.

Table 5.7 Estimation of labour productivity (value added method, US $) in industry in ČSSR and selected developed capitalist countries in 1985, in USD thousands and ČSSR level to respective countries

Branch (ISIC classification)	*ČSSR (USD thousands)*	*ČSSR level (respective countries = 1)*				
		Small countries (a)		*Large countries (b)*		
			Of which		*Of which*	
			Austria		*FRG*	*USA*
Food industry	10.3	0.22	0.2	0.24	0.14	0.24
Textile industry	7.3	0.28	0.33	0.32	0.17	0.27
Clothing manufacture	3.9	0.23	0.28	0.23	0.17	0.18
Leather manufacture	4.8	0.18	0.24	0.2	0.18	0.16
Shoe manufacture	6.0	0.3	0.4	0.34	0.27	0.27
Wood products manufacture	8.9	0.25	0.37	0.33	0.28	0.24
Furniture production	4.8	0.15	0.15	0.19	0.14	0.16
Paper production	12.6	0.27	0.32	0.3	0.32	0.22
Printing industry	7.0	0.19	0.22	0.19	0.18	0.17
Light industry	7.6	0.21	0.24	0.24	0.17	0.19
Chemical and rubber industry	17.9	0.35	0.5	0.31	0.34	0.22
Metallurgy	14.2	0.37	0.53	0.3	0.27	0.25
Non-metal materials procession (c)	10.1	0.3	0.29	0.28	0.27	0.2
Metalworking industry	7.3	0.23	0.25	0.23	0.3	0.18
Mechanical engineering	10.6	0.28	0.38	0.25	0.28	0.19
Vehicle manufacture	14.4	0.45	0.34	0.37	0.32	0.27
Electric machinery manufacture	10.1	0.29	0.33	0.24	0.24	0.22
Machine production	9.3	0.26	0.42	0.23	0.2	0.29
Heavy industry	12.0	0.32	0.38	0.28	0.28	0.22
Manufacturing industry	10.5	0.28	0.33	0.27	0.25	0.21
Energy industry	25.3	0.22	0.31	0.52	0.26	0.48
Mining	10.3	0.05	0.3	0.11	0.3	0.11
Sum	10.9	0.25	0.31	0.26	0.25	0.21

a) Belgium, Denmark, Finland, Norway, Austria, Sweden
b) France, Italy, Japan, FRG, USA, Great Britain
c) Glass, porcelain, and ceramic production

Source: Zeman (1990)

Structure of the economy

The structure of the socialist economy was clearly biased towards industry. The reason was foremost ideological because industry was the most favoured sector. It was heavy industry which won particular attention and support since the very beginning of the socialist period. This emphasis was generally based on the assumption that workers are the key people (and ideological allies) for the regime. In addition, heavy industry was crucial for armament production. This preference appeared despite the fact that, historically, Czechoslovakia was a traditional producer of light industries and lacked raw materials and experience for heavy industry production.

Nevertheless, thanks to a better initial position and its relative development, Czechoslovakia was considered as a "great engineering power" of the Eastern Bloc (Kaplan 1995) and Czechoslovak companies were expected and forced to produce a wide range of various engineering products with limited chance for specialization. The service sector was generally considered as non-productive and thus was not supported. This industrial bias can be documented for example in the employment structure. The shares of the sectors in 1980 were corresponding – industry at 63%, services at 30%, and agriculture at 7% (Lašek 1998). Půlpán writes that the share of industry in Czechoslovak GNP at the end of the 1980s was around 43%, while in comparable developed countries adequate numbers were between 24–32%, the share of coal mining was 3.5% vs. 0–0.9%, engineering was 16% vs. 6.7–7.8%, metallurgy was 3.6% vs. 0.6–2%, textiles was 2.5 vs. 0.5–1.4% etc. On the contrary, Czechoslovakia recorded lower shares in advanced chemistry, electrical engineering, printing, paper production, and food processing (Půlpán 1993).

The government applied industrial policy in the form of Principal Development Programs in the 1970s – there were more than 100 of them and more than 100 companies participated. Later, in the 1980s, more complex State Target Programs were introduced. These programs intended to support specific segments in the Czechoslovak economy – e.g., the State Target Programs supported fuel-energy sector, electronics, car and tractor industries, engineering, chemical, and consumption industries, agriculture, and transport (Průcha 1988). At the same time, regional policy was applied as well. One of the examples were fiscal transfers from the Czech to the Slovak part of the federation. Other attempts at helping underdeveloped or negatively affected regions also occurred – e.g., North Bohemian Coal Basin (Průcha 1988).

Considering the size of the companies, available data document bias towards large industries and monopolization. The industries (both heavy and light) were highly concentrated with a few large companies – see Table 5.8. Moreover, there was often one dominant producer – for example in the shoe industry (Box 5.3).

Table 5.8 Industrial organizations according to the number of employees in Czechoslovakia to end of 1989

Branches	*Total number of organizations*	*Number of employees*										
		up to 100	*101–200*	*201–500*	*501–1,000*	*1,001–2,500*	*2,501–5,000*	*5,001–10,000*	*10,001–20,000*	*20,001–30,000*	*30,001–50,000*	*more than 50,000*
Industry total	*1133*	*31*	*42*	*273*	*257*	*267*	*151*	*66*	*22*	*9*	*11*	*4*
Out of it												
Fuel industry	11	1	–	2	–	–	1	1	4	–	1	1
Energy industry	3	–	–	1	–	–	–	–	–	1	–	1
Iron Metallurgy	20	2	1	1	–	3	4	4	2	2	1	–
Metallurgy of non-ferrous metals	19	2	–	2	4	6	3	2	–	–	–	–
Chemical and rubber industry	65	2	2	17	17	11	6	6	2	–	2	–
Engineering	194	6	6	35	34	47	31	18	8	4	3	2
Electrotechnical and metalworking industry	61	2	–	6	17	16	14	4	–	–	2	–
Industry of construction materials	53	2	4	6	2	34	1	4	–	–	–	–
Wood processing industry	114	1	13	48	24	8	17	3	–	–	–	–
Metalworking industry	162	1	2	48	63	35	10	2	–	–	1	–
Pulp and paper industry	22	1	–	1	3	10	6	1	–	–	–	–
Glass, porcelain, and ceramic industry	15	–	1	3	1	2	3	1	3	1	–	–
Textile industry	82	3	–	15	8	19	27	10	–	–	–	–
Clothes industry	86	–	6	32	31	8	4	5	–	–	–	–
Leather industry	50	–	3	18	14	8	4	1	1	–	1	–
Polygraphic industry	6	1	–	1	–	2	1	–	1	–	–	–
Food industry	96	1	1	11	11	49	18	3	1	1	–	–
Manufacture of frozen, natural spring and tobacco products	10	1	–	5	–	3	1	–	–	–	–	–
Other industrial production	66	5	3	21	28	6	2	1	–	–	–	–

Source: Federální statistický úřad (1990)

Box 5.3 Bata (in Czech Baťa) – shoe company

The Communist takeover meant a considerable turn in the trend in the Czechoslovak shoe industry. Before 1939, thanks to the introduction of modern production and sales methods, it was able to compete in the developed western markets (including countries such as the USA, the United Kingdom, or France). The dominant company at that time was Bata. After 1948, the situation reversed. The nationalization of the industry (Bata 1945) and the subsequent subordination of production and sales to the needs of the Communist government of the country and the Soviet Union led to the interruption of almost all contacts with the world markets, with the exception of the COMECON countries. Exports to the west were considerably limited, very often subsidized, and served primarily as a source of convertible currencies (Bata 1991).

Like other industries, the footwear industry was also monopolized: 90% of the footwear production in 1989 was produced by the SVIT company, which replaced the nationalized Bata plant at the beginning of 1949. Cooperatives and small businesses accounted only for the remaining 10% of the production, with SVIT employing a total of 94% of the workforce in the sector. In the last year of the socialist era, 54% of SVIT's output was sold on the domestic market, 37% in the Soviet Union, and only 9% on the developed western markets (ibidem).

According to Bata (1991), in comparison with the west, the Czech shoemaking industry lagged behind in a number of aspects. Just as businesses in other sectors, also shoemakers suffered from the lack of material. Labour productivity was low due to inefficient work organization. The working conditions of the employees were difficult and, in general, well below the standards of job security in the developed countries. The production base was obsolete, often from the period before the Communist coup and the sector also lagged behind in marketing and distribution. The only purpose of the marketing departments consisted in moving the goods from the production plants to the distribution system. The latter fully reflected the negative consequences of the high stock production. While, on the western markets, only 30% of the production was in the stock and the rest was available to the customer, in the Czech part of the Federation the ratio was 50–50. While the supply chain in the Czech Republic lasted for 24–31 days, in Western Europe, the final product arrived at the shop in one to eight days. The average time for the development of a new collection, its production, and the expedition of finished shoes to stores in the Czech lands was 360 days, which was shockingly more than the 60 days that this process lasted in Western European countries (ibidem).

Another shortcoming identified by the author was the lack of emphasis on consumer needs. While the principal consumers in the developed markets were women (50% of total sales), the Czech shoe industry did not provide sufficient supply of women's shoes. Their sales accounted only for 31% of the total. In contrast, children's shoes accounted for 42% of total sales (compared to 20% in the west), mainly due to state's subsidies. For the same reason, a considerable part of the Czech shoe industry production often ended in the hands of foreign tourists. The subsidies together with the lack of interest in production costs (ibidem) led to considerable price distortions, common to the whole system.

The share of investment

The privileged position of (heavy) industry led to other distortions. There was a bias towards investment and against consumption at the macroeconomic level. The share of investment in GDP was high, compared to consumption share, which reached only 44–48% against the 60% in the western countries in the 1980s (Komárek et al. 1990).

However, investment in socialist Czechoslovakia was in a highly paradoxical situation. On the one hand, the nominal figures were very high, but regardless of it, the machinery park and other constructions and equipment were significantly obsolete. The share of investment in the economy was "extremely high" – one third of GDP – it was high even by the Eastern Bloc standards (Vintrová 2006). Officially, growth in investment in the 1970s was higher than economic growth. But the reality was possibly different if we consider hidden inflation – see the following estimation in Table 5.9. Moreover, the situation changed in the 1980s.

Table 5.9 Czechoslovaks' basic economic indicators and estimation of results after discounting hidden inflation (average year-to-year change)

Indicators (stable prices)	*1970–1980*	*1980–1990*
GDP (approximate)	4.77	1.5
Net national income	4.66	1.31
Private consumption	3.22	1.69
Gross fixed investment	5.77	0.89
CPI	1.14	2.17
Average real wages	1.99	–0.09
Indicators corrected for hidden inflation		
GDP (approximate)	2.7	–0.7
Net national income	2.1	–1.5
Private consumption	1.5	0.4
Gross fixed investment	3.1	–5.1
CPI	2.8	3.5
Average real wages	0.3	–1.4

Source: Šujan and Šujanová (1997)

Our respondents described the investment assigning process in the previous chapter. It is not surprising that the efficiency of many investment projects was at least questionable. Political interfering only made things worse. Šrein gives an example of a decision to construct a broad-gauge rail track from the Soviet Union (Ukraine) to the Slovak town of Košice, which was made by president Novotný during his stay in the Soviet Union in the 1960s. Šrein remarks that even top-ranking senior members of the SPK learned about this approval only from the newspapers (Šrein 1995). Another example of highly criticized inefficient investment was the foundation of Bratislavské automobilové závody – car producer (see Box 5.7). Both of these cases could be examples of politically motivated investment in the Slovak part of Czechoslovakia. Bálek mentiones that investment per person in Slovakia was 22.6% higher than in the Czech part of the republic (Bálek 1995). However, in our view, these cases were rather examples of generally inefficient investment allocation in socialist Czechoslovakia. Moreover, the investment often headed to (heavy) industries at the expense of other sectors in the economy. Teichová comments that the planners' basic mistake was an idea that massive growth of investment and industrial production would lead to growth in the productivity of the whole economy. She remarks that this idea proved to be wrong already at the end of the first five-year plan (Teichová 1995).

At the micro level, the banking sector funded the investment, but banks worked only as accounting headquarters. Their role was not to evaluate the project, and they were not authorized to refuse it, but just to direct the funds to the selected company. The already mentioned "soft budget constraint" expressed that it was generally not difficult to obtain funding. Šrein sees a direct connection between the unfinished constructions and absence of budget limits as well (Šrein 1995). Our respondents, on the other hand, spoke about difficulties to obtain investment and struggle to convince the superior authorities. The centre decided about investment, at least partly, according to the pressure from the side of companies (the VHJs). Landau and Průcha comment that over-investment was balanced by a shortage of capital for some perspective companies (Landau and Průcha 1995). A hint on the value of a loan was provided in a report by StB, which informed readers about a head of an investment planning department who, when drunk, boasted about the Zbrojovka Vsetín factory being given a loan from the COMECON bank. The value was 600 mil. convertible crowns (meaning a possibility to purchase convertible currencies). The StB was concerned about the issue because it happened at an international trade fair in front of representatives of western companies.

In straight contrast to high nominal level of investment was the state of the houses, machinery, and equipment which were tremendously obsolete, and the economy as a whole was hugely underinvested. For example, our respondent from the automotive industry said that: "There were these . . . these long-term contracts. And they all had to be met. But the capacity was inadequate, well, because to extend the capacities, you needed investments. And the investments just were none" (director in automotive industry <ID049>).

The overall numbers were frightening. Machines in operation were, in the 1980s, often decades old and already written off (Půlpán 1993; Zeman 1990). Zieleniec for example points out that machinery and equipment of fuel-energy complex were written off by 40%, in light industry often more than 70% at the end of the 1980s (Zieleniec et al. 1990). Zeman mentions, among other examples, rolling mills. There were 70 rolling tracks in Czechoslovakia – more than 40% were older than 60 years, 15% between 30–50 years and 40% younger than 30 years – these numbers were incomparable not only with the western producers but even within the COMECON (Zeman 1990). The insufficient investment could be found everywhere in the economy – for example the Prague water system was leaking one-third of its volume of water (ibidem). The so-called inner debt (meaning funds needed to improve the situation to normal) was estimated, for the Prague house fund, at 100 billion crowns (ibidem). Underinvestment into maintenance of housing was one of few negative aspects that even the socialist prominents were willing to admit (e.g., Štrougal 2009). The regime was so desperate that it forced the inhabitants to build (self-help) civic amenities, which the state was unable to construct on its own (see Box 5.4).

Box 5.4 Akce Z

The general level of underinvestment was so high that the regime was often not able to build civic amenities. A common situation was that, for example, a newly built housing estate lacked a shop, a school, or a kindergarten. The solution was found in a self-help initiative called "Akce Z," where the letter Z stood for improvement (in Czech "zvelebování"). This initiative originated as organized mass cleaning activities of housing estates or similar events. Participation of inhabitants was not paid and formally voluntary, but in practice there was a pressure on people to take part in the projects and their absence likely appeared in their cadre materials. The state delivered the building material and the inhabitants themselves were forced to build facilities on behalf of the state and its responsible authorities. This way, houses, cultural centres, cinemas, sewerage systems, and even a tram track in Prague were built. Consequently, Akce Z grew into an integral part of the central planning with a guideline from the SPK. Moreover, Akce Z became an important part of the local budgets – for example in the town of Velké Meziříčí, Akce Z events were conducted in the total value of 4.7 million CSK in 1983. The overall budget of the town was 17 million. All these municipal projects built within Akce Z took 450 thousand working hours, out of that, 390 thousand non-paid (Municipal Council of Velké Meziříčí 1983–1987).

The underinvestment and dubious directing of the investment contributed to general technological backwardness of the economy. Head of trade department in investment engineering <ID050> told us:

> *What was really planned was the amount of money for technical development, like what would be available, how much for us. These were the limitations. Like, yes, nowadays it's limiting too, but today you can earn to pay for it. Back then, you got the money allocated.*

According to Soulsby and Clark, the low level of technology in the Eastern Bloc countries in this period was even referred to as "Czechoslovak illness" and it was, not surprisingly, supposed to be a consequence of underinvestment (Soulsby and Clark 1996).

The share of (personal) consumption

We documented the overall scarcity in the economic system in the previous chapter. The orientation on investment contributed to a relatively low share of consumption in the economy and thus to scarcity of consumption goods. There were periods of shortage of even staple goods (like sugar and toilet paper) but the system was mostly able to deliver these very basic goods. However, deliveries and distribution were inefficient too, and queues in shops were common.

Prices of basic goods were often subsidized, which contributed to their shortage. Kočárník writes that subsidies to retail prices increased by 931.2% in period 1970–1988, and that subsidy reached 50 billion crowns in 1989 – 11% of overall budget. He gives an example of 1 kilogram of beef that cost CSK 46 with a subsidy of CSK 49.9, or butter that cost CSK 40 but its subsidy was CSK 35.31 (Kočárník 1990). Rents and energy services were heavily subsidized as well. Komárek adds that many sophisticated products had to be looked for from shop to shop and from week to week and consumers had to ask, beg, and bribe in order to obtain them (Komárek et al. 1990). The regime was aware of this shortage and tried to deal with it because it was rightly worried that shortages contributed to its declining popularity (especially when people watched western TV broadcasting with abundance of consumption products in shops). In a 1978 StB report from the Zbrojovka Vsetín factory, the workers even complained that the standards of living were stagnant. It read: "As a proof of the phenomenon, they provide and compare the significant rise in the standards of living in Hungary. According to the staff, there is a sufficient supply of goods in Hungary and the shops are full of products just like in Austria" (ABS, OB-957 OV).

A report – "Regular regional information for the UV members" – dealt mostly with two topics: meeting of the plan and scarcity in the respective regions. For instance, a report in July 1987 stated that in the South Moravia region:

> *There is dissatisfaction with scarcity of supply of pork meat and mineral waters in the inner market. However, the consumers are critical foremost of shortage of industrial*

> *goods. . . . Citizens above all point out a lack of portable and table TV sets, freezers and bicycles. They express dissatisfaction with high prices and low quality of shoes for men and women. Additionally, the range of women's and girl's year-round shoes is limited. There is a lack of both ceramic and concrete rooftiles, bricks, windows and stairs for construction.*
>
> *(ČSSR. Sekretariát ÚV KSČ 1987)*

Similarly, for example a brave archivist of a small town of Doubravice in 1982 wrote the following:

> *We have not only a lot of good things but also shortcomings, especially in supply. It is, for example, a constant shortage of porcelain goods such as plates, mugs or tin ware, bicycles, sewing machines, various textile goods, i.e. daily necessities. But also consumption, this year there was a temporary shortage of lard, cheese, spice, juices and all we do is that we just look for this so-called goods in short supply. And eventually, all we get is a repetitive answer from the bored and frustrated shop assistants to come back tomorrow or after Sunday. However, being present at the delivery of such high-coveted goods means the same stroke of luck as winning the state lottery.*
>
> *(Municipal Council of Doubravice nad Svitavou 1982)*

The Vice-chairman of the ČNR Zbyněk Žalman explained that the shortage of foodstuff or industrial products was often caused by problems in distribution or delivery or in the late order of the goods by the shops. Moreover, he added that the shortage was deepened by the citizens who were "groundlessly" making reserves at home (ČSSR 1981–1986). The solution of scarcity was in exchange. A respondent from restaurant services described the situation in Vaněk and Krátká:

> *Well, as for the supply, it was like that because there was nothing, the goods were not to be had. When the supplier arrived, he said: "You will get a ration." I do not know, for instance, we were short of bottled Pilsner beer, so he said: "Okay, you'll get twenty cartons at Christmas." So, we would take one carton of Pilsner, took it to the sales department in a food store and said that we needed Cinzano and canned fruit. So, we got the Cinzano and canned fruit. And we would take two bottles of Cinzano and went to the meat processing factory, where we traded it for Hungarian salami. This we traded for cigarettes (laughs), so we just did all we could so that the assortment was good.*
>
> *(Vaněk and Krátká 2014, p. 369)*

Interestingly, the overall scarcity can be demonstrated also on foreign travel because shopping trips abroad were common – for example 55% of all trips to East Germany in 1986 were one-day (realistically nearly no transit to West Germany). East Germany responded to these foreign buy-ups by export bans on meat, sugar, spices, almonds, raisins, coconut, footwear, towels, dishcloths, infant, and child garments, stocking, curtains, etc. The shop assistants often refused to sell these commodities to foreigners (Petrov 2013). Vice versa, trips from neighbouring countries to Czechoslovakia had a similar pattern. Czechoslovak authorities likewise forbade exports of sleeping bags, tents, etc. (ibidem). Though equally plagued by scarcity, each country lacked different goods so the exchange in petty shopping trips was advantageous. The result was that 70% of East Germans, 89% of Poles 74% of Hungarians made just one-day trips (including transit) to Czechoslovakia in this year (Statistická ročenka Československé socialistické republiky 1987).

Demand generally exceeded supply to such an extent that the retailers had the upper hand over the consumers who did not have the market power that they would have under normal conditions in a market economy. The consumers were consequently forced to increase savings or to consume substitutes – something else than they wanted (Brada et al. 1996).

The system's other practice of draining excess money was via high prices of "luxury" goods like cars or electronics. These were relatively costly in comparison to the western markets (see, e.g., Box 5.7). The same strategy was, however, not followed in housing because houses and flats were often owned by the state or municipality and were considered elementary service. There was a chronic shortage of them. The same was true for family houses, 98% of them were built by self-help during the socialist period (Císař 1995). Additionally, personal loans of any kind were rarely provided and for approved purposes only, such as houses and household appliances. All these aspects along with subsidized prices led to different consumption structure in comparison with developed countries, as can be seen in Table 5.10.

Table 5.10 The shares of Czechoslovak inhabitants' expenditures in comparison to developed capitalist countries

	Czechoslovakia	*Developed capitalist countries*
Foodstuff, beverages, tobacco	35.5	24.8
Footwear, textiles	11	6.8
Rents, fuel, energies	7.2	20.9
Household operations	14	7.6
Transport and communications	10.5	14.6
Healthcare	0.9	5.9
Culture, educations, recreations	4	8.3
The rest till 100%	16.9	11.1

Source: Půlpán (1993)

The consequence of limited consumption possibilities was that basic household equipment was at a much lower level, compared to western standards (see Table 5.11). In addition, limited offer and high prices led people to self-production, for example 44% of households produced their own furniture and 25% households made their own clothes (Zeman 1990).

Table 5.11 Household possession of long-term consumption goods (in percent)

	Czechoslovakia		*Germany (FDR)*	
	1976	*1985*	*1976*	*1985*
Colour TV	0.8	24.5	42.2	87.6
Automatic washing machine	16.8	45.5	63.2	74.7
Freezer	1.3	14.5	57.8	66.4
Telephone	–	26.5	57.3	91.7
Dish washer	0.5	0.2	13.0	34.1
Kitchenaid	15.0	22.6	28.2	38.5
Hi-fi system	–	2.8	26.7	45.5
Video recorder	–	0.8	–	14.7
Car	37.1	47.0	76.2	90.2

Source: Zeman (1990)

5.3 Unemployment and functioning of the labour market

The situation on the labour market was highly specific. We consider first of all the rule of the right and obligation to work and its consequences. Then we look at the reasons and impact of permanent imbalance on this market and on the functioning of the economy. And finally, we discuss the attempts of the centre to increase labour supply in order to tackle the imbalance.

As has been previously stated, ideological regulations of the communist system dictated zero unemployment. There was even a constitutional right to work. Therefore, there were no unemployed people. However, people had, at the same time, a legal obligation to work for the common good (Act No. 100/1960 Coll., Constitution of the Czechoslovak Socialist Republic). Those who did not work were considered "parasites" (see Chapter 1) and could be imprisoned (Havelková 2009b).

For this reason, repeated absenteeism was reported to the police, as our interviews reveal: "When suddenly someone stopped going to work, then, like three months later he was listed and fired. And the police were informed about that. The personnel office and everything, it was so interconnected. You know, going to work was, in fact, compulsory" (Leader of Associated Brigades in an enterprise in the metallurgical industry <ID027>). In principle, a job dismissal could only come as a result of a gross violation of labour discipline:

> *Well, when someone caused trouble, maybe had drinking issues or something, or didn't go to work, it could lead to giving them a sack, but that was just in very rare cases. Mostly, they would be just demoted to a lesser, less important post. Right, posts that were more exposed and important, you wouldn't find such people in. When someone was, excuse the term, a drunkard, then, he was fired."*
>
> (Head of production in heavy industry *<ID035>*)

Indeed, according to our respondents, the most common problem at that time was alcohol in the workplace (e.g., Operating deputy in transport <ID009>; Production leader in the chemical industry <ID029>; or Head of production in heavy industry <ID035>). The vast majority of them, however, said that an employee dismissal occurred only rarely. A more frequent way to punish employees was to shift him or her to another job or to take away a personal benefit. A typical solution to such a situation is illustrated in the following extract from an interview with a production leader in chemical industry <ID029>:

> *If a shift foreman had a suspicion, a person had to take an alcohol-detection test and when positive, he was forced to leave the work site. As punishment, there were some sanctions, money cut and when it repeated, he was fired. But making someone redundant was, by the then laws a difficult thing to do. That's because everyone was legally entitled to have a job or, if I remember correctly, the law said everyone had to be employed.*

The potentiality to lay off an employee was seriously considered even by the StB. In a report from the Zbrojovka Vsetín factory, the secret police investigated a deputy for cadre and human resources, who did not conduct his work properly. Allegedly, he accepted bribes when he was in charge of company flats assignment, and he consumed "larger doses" of alcoholic beverages at the working place. The conclusion was a "consideration to lay him off" (ABS, OB-957 OV).

As has been previously stated, there was also a problem with absenteeism. In this sense, child benefits played a positive role as the threat of their removal was a way of forcing workers to come to work every day: "all that was necessary was just one-day absenteeism and the child benefit was cut. And believe me, the benefit was more than the person actually earned." (Director in water construction <ID002>).

The emphasis on job stability was characteristic for the whole period of socialism. Kalinová stated that due to the frequent confusion of the right to work with the right to a particular job, fluctuation was generally considered undesirable. However, for example, as a result of the events of 1968 and the massive support of reforms by the working class, companies, and schools were allowed to lay off workers and students for political reasons (Kalinová 2012). Nevertheless, in general, it was extremely difficult to dismiss workers:

> *I fired just this one and only man (laughter) . . . it was possible to fire a person that committed a crime, I mean an intentional crime. And this man, he was rascal, an outcast and he did break the law on purpose. And still I had a lot of difficulty wanting to fire him. All the explanations and reports, as to how many disciplinary meetings took place, and such. It was really tough.*
>
> *(A planner and head of supplying in an engineering company <ID007>)*

Our respondents told us that these conditions forced corporate executives to employ even very problematic workers whose intention was not to work. A head of the technical department in an engineering company <ID020> pointed out that in the market economy these workers would probably not belong among the economically active population.

Even when a person was sentenced to imprisonment, the company was obliged to accept him or her back once released. According to a planner and head of supplying in an engineering company <ID007>, this related mainly to the unskilled labour force:

> *A number of people were employed there, you know, such characters . . . in spring and summer, he would more or less go to work, sometimes failed to do so. And in autumn he would do something so that he could spend the winter in jail. It was a kind of routine. But I knew a hundred percent he would be back like February 15 or March 30 or so. They always did. And we got so used to it to the point that . . . we almost did not mind it. Twenty-eight Romani people . . . and they would even cause trouble, didn't they (laughter) . . . we just had to employ them, it was unthinkable that someone would be without a job.*

Employment policy was used for political goals as well. A new act of 1968 allowed a dismissal of employees if "they by their activities disrupt the socialist social order and due to it do not have the trust needed to hold their current office or occupation." Meaning that the labour law was used as a tool against political opponents of the regime and dissidents (Havelková 2009b). Many people, who were forced to quit their, often good, jobs during purges in early 1970s, experienced a downward spiral of job interviews. Asking for less and less qualified jobs and refused due to prohibitive political record, many managers, academics, or artists ended up in boiler rooms or as a night-shift watchpersons.

From the aforementioned characteristics of labour supply and demand, as well as from the general characteristics of the centrally planned economy, serious consequences emerged for the Czechoslovak labour market. Although everything was carefully formally planned and balanced, in practice, it turned out that equilibrium was not the same as balance. The most serious imbalance was one associated, on the one hand, with the excess of demand for labour over supply, and on the other hand, with the overemployment of the labour force.

Achieving balance was influenced by two contradictory, though mutually interrelated aspects, based on the reality of the centrally planned character of the economy. The lack of the labour force was primarily the result of extensive growth and the planned nature of the economy. This type of economic growth, of course, also significantly influenced the labour market. It was, as well as the rest of the economy, characterized by pervasive scarcity that was the result of the central planning (see Chapter 4, Box 4.4 Shortage in the labour market).

Kalinová notes that the lack of manpower was evident since the early 1950s when, as a result of the so-called steel concept, massive movements of male labour, from light to heavy industry and between regions occurred (Kalinová 2012). It was just one of the manifestations of the shortage economy, which resulted from the incongruence between the planned demand and supply and their actual counterparts. The fact that the centre decisions were the main determinants of the distribution of the disposable manpower, together with the planning of the investment in the long run, led to a faster job creation than an increase in the available workforce. Šulc writes that the number of unused jobs increased by 150–200 thousand during each five-year period. In the fifth five-year period, investment activity created 62% more new vacancies than it did in the labour force increment Šulc (2004). MP Tichý mentions that 735 thousand working positions in the industry (28% of the total) stayed vacant in 1987 (ČSSR 1986–1990). However, the excessive demand for labour was not (and could not be) reflected in their corresponding wage increases (see later). Contrary, it caused efficiency decline. It was thought that labour shortage could be overcome by growth in investment activity. This was, however, a fallacy. It resulted in even faster job creation and further boosted the growth of excess of demand for labour over its supply (ibidem).

The increase in planned objectives resulted in a higher demand for labour. The companies were not interested in revealing their real production capacities. Hoarding and creating reserves of any kind (which was supposed to assure smooth plan fulfilment) concerned labour as well. The consequence was labour market imbalance. Our respondents documented the lack of the workforce. One of them said: "Look, personnel policy (laughter) . . . was that employment was compulsory, right, someone, everyone had to have this employment stamp in their papers, so, in a way, the labour market had no vacant labour force (laughter)" (head of trade department in investment engineering <ID050>).

The suppression of market mechanisms, together with the ideological unsuitability of unemployment, had serious consequences for the labour market balance. There was a general uncertainty of companies concerning both available jobs offered as well as the requirements of the centre. The accumulation of workforce led to further deepening of the excess demand for labour and the so-called overemployment. This term refers to the situation when companies hoarded labour force without (urgent) need. There was no real use for this manpower and if it had been laid off, no negative impact on production would have happened. Our respondent – head of cold rolling mill <ID035> – for example talked about significant overemployment "in supporting workplaces, mainly maintenance and administration already at the company level." Vaněk and Krátká mentions a bizarre experience, described by a shop assistant working a shop in a district town:

> *Even when we worked in that shop called Orient and I was here alone or my colleague, Květa, was here alone we would normally sit in the back office and read. The shop was empty, like, two times an hour someone came in, it was all and the day seemed endless, especially when I was alone, and it was really from eight to six, half an hour or an hour at noon. So, normally I had a book in the office desk and I would read or knit children's sweaters. And it was like that everywhere. I remember when I started work in the Klenoty jewellers, there was a shop in Pacov, like no customers*

> *at all, and there was this shop assistant and she had a knitting machine bought for her from the ROH budget, so that she wouldn't have to just sit there doing nothing.*
> *(Vaněk and Krátká 2014, p. 399)*

These stories show the perversity of the system, where companies on the one hand did not have enough workforce but at the same time they did not dismiss workers that they did not need. This as done to prevent problems with their possible future shortage. The problem was serious, for example, estimates say that overemployment in Czechoslovakia reached up to half a million people (Pellešová 2002) or up to 20% of the labour force (Komárek et al. 1990).

In a market-based economy, the imbalance on the market (excessive demand) would be solved by adapting wage rates. However, this was not possible, as they were set centrally and there was a general effort to level them (see Chapter 4). The respondents told us about a typical effort the companies made to attract the workforce from other enterprises, for example by offering accommodation possibilities, which, as well as the workforce, were scarce (see Chapter 4) and other non-monetary bonuses.

The centre was well aware of these imbalances in the labour market. For example, on 28 March 1979, the federal government's Prime Minister, Lubomír Štrougal, declared: "There is a shortage of labour . . . and the structure of labour is not optimally deployed" (ČSSR. Federal Assembly of the Czechoslovak Socialist Republic 1976–1980). The centre strove to solve the permanent shortage of labour force by maximizing job offer.

This took place in a situation when average real working hours were significantly higher in comparison to developed countries – the people in Czechoslovakia worked on average 43.5 hours per week, the Austrians 34, the Swedes 35.6, the Finns 40.4, the Norwegians 31, and the (West) Germans 41.6 (Zeman 1990). Likewise, length of holiday was shorter in the Czechoslovak Socialist Republic (15–20 days) even in comparison with other countries of the Eastern Bloc (GDR 18–24 days, Hungary 15–24 days) (ibidem). Another typically difference was also a high proportion of working retirees. According to Štrougal (ČSSR. Federal Assembly of the Czechoslovak Socialist Republic 1976–1980), they amounted to more than 800 thousand in 1979 and Pilátová claims they accounted for more than 10% of the working population (ibidem).

Another area that was high was women participation in the labour market. For example, in the Czech part of the country, the share of women in the economically active population rose from 19% to 46.7% between 1950 and 1980. The most significant tendency in this area was employment of women with young children. While in 1952, 52% of women in an economically active age were in the household, in 1970 it was only 15.6% (Jechová 2012). It was generally very uncommon to stay at home as a housewife – it was considered as bourgeois behaviour and, what is more, most of the families could not afford it. Women were forced back to work soon after giving birth by a relatively short maternity leave and by the government policy that provided very early day-nursery (for already one-year-old babies) to convince mothers to return to work as soon as possible. According to Průcha (1988), in Czechoslovakia, women participation reached 71.5% (which contrasts with the 47.3% for West Germany, 41.2% for Belgium, 27.6% for the Netherlands and 52.3% for France), and after 1970, women represented about 45–46% of the total labour force (ibidem). However, the possibilities of part-time jobs lagged behind the demand (Jechová 2012). The final consequence was a high level of employment and labour force participation in comparison to other economies. Adam writes that the participation rate was at 83.2% already in 1975 (Adam 1995).

The government even tried to increase labour force by implementing natality subsidies in the 1970s. Since 1971, the Communist Party increased children benefits for families, prolonged maternity leave up to two years, and decreased interest rate from mortgages for young families. This policy indeed led to a temporary population boom, which peaked in 1974 when 194 215 children were born (Statistické ročenky Československé socialistické republiky 1966–1993). However, the policy did not have a lasting impact on the birth rate and ended as a one-off example of social engineering. Consequently, the educational system (from kindergarten up to universities) and later on labour market had to adapt to a several-year long wave of children, students, and young people on the market. This demographic phenomenon and the strong generation it produced is still visible in today's population figures, and it was nicknamed Husák's Children, after the then communist leader Gustáv Husák.

Wage levelling created by the centrally planned economy wiped out differences between excellent and under-performing workers. It was based on political and social influences at the expense of economic ones. Wages were not determined on the basis of differences in qualifications, complexity, and job responsibilities, nor on labour factor productivity (Šulc 2004). Večerník even claims that remuneration in socialism was at best explained by Marx theory of exploitation than prophesy of communist society because the system did not reward workers according to their productivity but according to "reproduction costs," which covered only the basic needs of the employees (Večerník 1998). An a scientist of the Prognostic Institute of the Czech Republic <ID034> told us about wages the following:

> *It was all interconnected. Another principle that failed to come to practice was Lenin's slogan – catch up and overtake, meaning in productivity. And yet another was that in socialism, wage level was to depend on labour efficiency. That is a principle that was in fact never met, as the wages were assigned based on categories and tables. And it was the white-collars who decided which table was the right one to use and which one wasn't. All this depended on the pressure from interest groups, production units, etc. For instance, miners and steelworkers whined and whined until they got wages higher than in other industries. But in a way, it was a white-collar decision, technocratic and not something the economy would have generated naturally.*

Večerník (1992) states that the 1959–1988 period was characterized by remarkable wage stability. In a sociological survey focusing on a period between 1970 and 1988, however, he concludes that, despite the stability, the gap between wages in services and in sectors such as industry, construction, and transport increased. It reflected the surviving interest of the regime to keep workers contented and its general bias to (heavy) industries. The managers had a limited chance to influence the amount of these wages. Therefore, their manoeuvring space was limited to the payment of bonuses from the reward fund (Operating deputy in transport <ID009>).

This system was therefore totally inflexible and the labour market was full of distortions and, according to Šulc:

> *A society governed for a long time by principles of central planning and allocation creates gradually a demoralizing atmosphere of escape from productive, efficient work to demand for "secure places," where you work little and get a lot of money. The ideal of a "successful person" measured by accumulation of material possessions, originally created by the bourgeois society, in socialism got a new dimension.*
>
> (*Šulc 2004, p. 128*)

To sum it up, the socialist planners and managers had to deal with several contradictions and imbalances in the labour market that were foremost caused by equal wages and a high degree of levelling. The first contradiction was between excessive demand over supply. The "market solution" in the form of wage increase was not, for political reasons, possible. Indeed, the vast majority of our respondents, regardless of the sector in which they had worked, said that one of their major problems was a permanent lack of workers.

5.4 Price stability and inflation

Another important economic indicator is inflation. We deal first with various prices in the centrally planned economy and then with aggregate inflation results.

The most important part of the planning process took place in physical units and prices were just a technical means to allow balancing (Šulc 1995). However, prices, of course, played a role (see Section 4.4.2) and the companies had to deal with them and their changes. One of our respondents (chief designer in an engineering company <ID003>) for example told us:

I: And you automatically raised it by the price of the, . . . the inflation, right?

R: Well . . . with the customer, with the customer, yes. But sometimes simply, the customer said, "no guys, no inflation included, understand?" But it had to be in the contract, a commercial contract which did not mention any inflation. Then couldn't include it.

I: That is clear.

R: But once it was included, this inflation clause in the commercial contract it was not a problem, yeah.

Prices were strictly controlled and there existed several different layers of prices in the economy (retail, wholesale, buying prices for agricultural goods and prices in foreign trade – see Section 3.4.2). These price layers were mostly mutually independent and disconnected. The fixed prices did not respond to the situation on the market and thus lost their information function and were of no use as coordination mechanism. Šulc even writes that they were a source of "mystification and disinformation" (Šulc 1995). The loss of information function of the prices was evident at both microeconomic as well as macroeconomic level. That is, the disconnections between different price layers were needed to be balanced with taxes and subsidies, and the overall price setting then mirrored in the inflation rate. Both perspectives are considered bellow.

Under normal circumstances, the different price layers (e.g., wholesale and retail prices) are interconnected in the economy. However, in the centrally planned economy the system of disconnected price layers caused enormous practical distortions. Firstly, the wholesale prices were derived from the costs of production. They were supposed to reflect "socially necessary" costs. These, however, were very difficult to define, let alone estimate (e.g., Hába et al. 1988), and thus in practice they reflected individual company's costs. Mlčoch writes that under the high level of monopolization of the economy, the difference between individual and "social" costs disappeared (Mlčoch 1990). Companies had, at the same time, different motivation than the centre. Their natural strategy was trying to overvalue and maximize wholesale prices if it was possible (Komárek et al. 1990).

Politics played a significant role as well. The socialist government tried to maintain low prices as one of its achievements. Komárek writes that costs of black coal production were about one half higher than the wholesale price level – the differences varied according to production sites. In case of coal production from Ostrava, the difference was 35–45%, but in case of Kladno, production was 260–270% in 1985. He adds that the general costs of energy production in 1985 were by 100 CSK/MWh higher than price at that time. Had desulphurization been included, they would have been higher by 750 CSK/MWh. Further estimations of the differences between costs and wholesale prices are depicted in Table 5.12.

The disproportions sometime excessed a tolerable size and the regime decided for one time "price adjustment" – mostly upwards (Brada et al. 1996). These "adjustments" were sometimes "complex" (e.g., that of 1 January 1977) or partial for selected branches (e.g., in 1972). The complex adjustment took place generally once in 10 or 15 years. These changes had a dubious impact on the overall system and they generally did not increase pressure on the companies to boost efficiency. Profits changed just nominally, but the reserves in the system stayed untouched (Mlčoch 1990). One of our respondents

Table 5.12 Wholesale prices and costs of selected energies in the 1980s

	Overall social costs	*Average wholesale prices*
Energy coal (CSK/ton)	275	97
Coke (CSK/ton)	973	598
Heavy fuel oil (CSK/ton)	3,760	1,020–1,090
Light fuel oil (CSK/ton)	3,880	1,100–1,160
Natural gas (CSK/m3)	1,900	830
Electric energy (CSK/MWh)		
– very high voltage	863	254
– high voltage	943	360
– low voltage	1,115	458

Source: Šulc (2004)

(associate professor at university, department head at the Prognostic Institute <ID071>) described the process and intentions of the centre during the complex adjustment.

> *Its principle was that for several hundred sectors, indexes were calculated, based on the intersectoral relationships, their balance, which reflects the prices. Simply, you know that this particular sector makes use of products made by five other sectors, so, you can do the calculation and you can, at the national economy level, recalculate wholesale prices in a day if you want. Another thing is how it was being done, but in principle, it is possible. And so it was done. And the policy favoured low wholesale surcharge so that companies with ineffective management would be quickly identified. Because they would quickly fall into red numbers. So the surcharge in wholesale prices was really small.*

The second disconnection was between retail and wholesale prices because the latter were supposed to originate from costs and the former were a consequence of political decisions. The difference consisted mostly of the turnover tax. It was often negative on foodstuff or other staple goods, which was in fact a subsidy. Komárek writes that the tax schedule contained 1,443 items in 1989 (Komárek 1990). For the spread of the tax rates see Table 5.13. For the whole economy the lowest rate was minus 291% and the highest 88 %.

There were broadly two types of retail prices, let us call them necessities and luxuries. Mlčoch writes about commodities that were supposed to demonstrate retail prices stability. The reasons were political. The regime wanted to express social sensitivity (Mlčoch 1990). Low prices of necessities are up till today a source of pride for the advocates of the regime (Štrougal 2009). Necessities consisted mostly of basic commodities – staple goods, rents, energy services, and public transportation costs (Mlčoch 1990). But the wholesale prices were increasing during the time and due to it companies had to receive higher

Table 5.13 Turnover taxes in various branches in percent

Branch code	*Branch*	*Lowest rate %*	*Highest rate %*
0	agriculture, forestry	–240	66
I	fuels, coal, oil	–189	76
II	heat, electricity	–181	0
III	iron and steel	–33	25
IV	non-ferrous metals	–27	33
V	chemicals, rubber, asbestos	–216	71
VI	engineering and hardware products	–291	83
VII	construction material	–171	20
VIII	wooden products	–75	46
IX	paper	–80	52
X	glass, china, ceramics	–69	69
XI	textile	–137	70
XII	clothes	–44	79
XIII	leather, shoes	–222	52
XIV	printing industry and culture	–111	76
XV	food	–224	88
XVI	other industrial products	–100	62
XVII	construction industry	0	0
	combined	**–291**	**88**

Source: Heady, Rajah, and Smith (1994)

subsidies in the form of negative turnover tax. Kočárník states that subsidies to retail prices increased by factor of 10.5 between 1970 and 1989 by 1555% and they reached CSK 50 billion at the end of the period (Kočárník 1990). Šulc mentions that a CSK 100 foodstuff basket needed CSK 40 subsidies already in 1981 (Šulc 1995). For the overall development of the negative turnover tax, see Table 5.14. The amount of this kind of subsidy was growing fast in the 1970s

Table 5.14 Negative turnover tax in Czechoslovakia 1970–1989 in millions of crowns

	1970	*1975*	*1980*	*1985*	*1986*	*1987*	*1988*	*1989*
Sum of negative turnover tax	3,228	4,184	7,287	26,637	28,625	29,764	29,806	49,057
Foodstuff	1,371	2,032	4,806	17,957	18,727	19,426	19,404	36,122
Out of it: meat products	421	835	1,838	4,280	4,390	4,529	4,446	11,919
Out of it: milk products	246	257	469	8,923	9,132	9,584	9,419	13,020
Industrial goods	**1,857**	**2,152**	**2,481**	**8,680**	**9,898**	**10,338**	**10,402**	**12,935**
Out of it: solid fuels	1,478	1,589	1,034	3,540	3,872	4,019	4,210	5,070

Source: Federální statistický úřad (1990)

and 1980s. Low prices obviously contributed to waste and increased pressure on the trade balance because some subsidized commodities were imported. On the other hand, Šulc mentions that the centre reacted to piling up stocks of some products by a decline of the subsidy in the form of negative turnover tax (Šulc 1995).

The second group of retail goods consisted of "luxury" commodities. Their prices were generally high and were liable to increase. The intent was to siphon off excess money from circulation. The examples could be fashion goods, luxuries, or technologically progressive goods – in the 1980s, e.g., colour TV sets or cars. For example, a new model of the Škoda car – Favorit – cost CSK 90,000 in 1988 – approximately 30 average monthly salaries but the demand anyway exceeded the supply and it was necessary to register for a long waiting list (Drda, Mlejnek, and Škoda 2010). Vilímek adds that the prices of Škoda cars were always set to drain money out of consumers. But he mentions that, sometimes, the planners set the price too high. Thus, the demand for the cars declined during 1970s and Škodas became idle goods. He mentions that, at the end of 1972, 65% of idle goods were from the Škoda car factory. The following temporary decline in prices resulted in decline in stocks (Vilímek 2012). The fact, that Škoda cars were used for elimination of money from the system was supported by one of our respondents, who worked as a director in automotive industry <ID049>. He said:

R: And at that time, there were reasons for car production. Before the revolution. There, the cars had three of them . . . three reasons. One reason . . . priority, maybe, or priority . . . all were priority. . . . One reason was to drain money out of people. Because in socialism, there was no unemployment no homeless people, they were no people that could not pay the rent, all these costs were covered and the money stayed with the people. [. . .]
And people, like, wanted VCRs and I do not know what all, but it was necessary to get the money from the people and get it to the market. So there was a certain number of cars that had to get to the domestic market to draw money from people.

I: And that . . . and that priority was defined by . . . ?

R: The government.

The third disconnection layer was between prices on inner and foreign markets. The domestic prices were detached from the world prices and companies were, as a result, isolated from information on both sides – inputs as well as outputs (Zeman 1990).

The centre reacted to changes in the world prices with a huge delay, if ever. For example, in case of oil, the input price from the Soviet Union was counted as a five-year moving average of world prices due to an agreement with the Soviet Union. Companies tried to take advantage of the system as much as possible. Mlčoch writes about variants of identical goods with negligible practical differences but with formally different type label and foremost with highly different wholesale prices for domestic market and for exports. He adds that there were sometimes even three prices of the same goods – the highest for domestic market, for exports to socialist countries with lower prices, and with the lowest prices for exports to non-socialist countries (Mlčoch 1990).

A conversion between the domestic and foreign economies is carried out by exchange rate. They were fixed as well, and their settings in the CPE system were, again, highly irrational from an economic point of. For example, Rychlík presents values and calculations that were binding for 1 September 1987. The official exchange rate was CSK 5.35 per dollar and it was formally applicable for business transactions. In practice, however, there were many exchange rates and for business transactions the exchange rate was de facto individual. For non-organized incoming tourism, the exchange rate was CSK 9.36 per dollar and for organized there was an additional 14.17% non-organized rate. If a Czechoslovak citizen was allowed to purchase dollars (after being granted a formal permission to buy foreign currency), the exchange rate was CSK 22.24 per dollar, almost three times the official rate. However, black market prices were even higher. The dollar was purchased for CSK 25–30 and sold for CSK 30–35, with a mark-up of CSK 5–10 (Rychlík 2007). The system of multiple exchange rates created a favourable environment for illegal money vendors who were able to take advantage of this situation.

The exchange rate system was even more complicated for business transactions. For companies, it worked via the system of de facto individual exchange rates, and the so-called internal reproductive price compensation (VRCV) that was added to the official exchange rate. The VRCV coefficients were calculated from mean replacement costs for the foreign currency acquirement – which was a kind of average converted price. The calculation was based on the average wholesale price and the average retail price in USD. If the resulting ratio was for example CSK 21.60 per USD and the official exchange rate was set at CSK 7.2 per USD,[3] the coefficient would be 3 (Jirges and Plchová 1996). The head of the economic department in producers of consumer electronics (<ID044>) told us: "talking about exports, the price changed with each order, and for each customer there was a specific treatment and always the biggest quarrels and disputes were about the setting of the price."

The government provided subsidies to cover the differences between wholesale prices and foreign prices especially with export to the western countries because it desperately needed convertible currencies. A director in a textile company and later deputy minister <ID057> stated:

R: Of course, the productivity here was lower than in the west and basically, the differences in productivity were levelled by price setting . . . the companies that exported to the west were compensated for the difference between the export price and the local wholesale price . . . The way it worked was that you would sell it at some price in dollars or German marks and this price was recalculated by the official exchange rate set by the bank and the difference between this price and the wholesale price, we are talking about, basically production costs, so, the difference was covered by the state.

I: Yeah. And the export price was usually lower than the production costs?

R: Not usually, but it could be said often, often it was lower.

I: So, we are talking about, basically, a significant subsidy.

R: It was a significant subsidy.

The StB concluded similarly:

> *In 1986, machines from the Zbrojovka Vsetín factory that were to be sold in capitalist countries were priced at 800 thousand CSK each. However, the production costs of one machine amounted to 2,800 thousand CSK each (that is, the firm lost 2 mil. Kčs on each machine it sold to the capitalist country). The loss is to be paid either from the state or the firm budget.*
>
> (*ABS, OB-957 OV*)

The ultimate goal for the regime was, in practice, to obtain hard currency for nearly any price. Jirges and Plchová write that the reproduction costs for obtaining one USD ranged from CSK 2.35 up to CSK 144.21 in 1988, and the average wholesale prices reached CSK 18.11 per USD (Jirges and Plchová 1996). The situation was not much better even in trade with COMECON markets. Šulc writes that, in the middle of the 1970s, the reproduction costs in engineering products were between CSK 8 to 28 per rouble (the official exchange rate was CSK 10 per rouble) (Šulc 1995).

Even the then economists wrote openly about the irrationality of multiple exchange rates and argued that the separation between domestic and world prices caused distortions in the socialist economy (for example Hrnčíř 1987; Svěrák 1983).

One of our respondents summarized the complex attitude towards prices and their separation (associate professor, department head at the Prognostic Institute <ID071>) following way:

> *The principle of setting the price was such that the wholesale prices and the retail prices were set independently. These wholesale prices basically reflected the production cost of domestic producers. Regardless of whether they used domestic or imported materials, . . . the basic principle was the production cost price. And, of course, they tried to include as much as they could, but the principle was the production costs. Complete production costs it was called and then the derived wholesale price and now the retail price set independently. Of course, most of the products did not go to*

retail, of course, they sort of rotated in wholesale or between the companies. Simply, a private person does not buy steel, does he? Or wheat, and so on. Well, now, the retail prices were set independently, because political priorities were the factor. The authorities were afraid, so they preferred to keep the prices as they were, and only occasionally, when there was a real mess somewhere, or when there was something urgent or a new product was being introduced, they would apply a different strategy. I don't know, some of these players and recorders, they cost some twenty thousand, and it was a lot, you know. And the price, it possibly reflected the import price times the ridiculous exchange rate and surcharge. So now, when you have a retail price of milk set at two crowns and its wholesale price set at five crowns, you have to level it with three crowns per litre, which is what really happened. The explanations spoke of social needs, and what else, but the core of the problem was in what I said.

The changes of prices at the microeconomic level resulted in inflation. As far as practical economic policy is concerned, communist leaders in Czechoslovakia were generally conservative and the planners kept basic macroeconomic indicators relatively stable (especially in comparison with other CPEs). This statement is true foremost for official inflation that was on average kept at mere 1.3% a year in the 1970–1989 period (Statistické ročenky Československé socialistické republiky 1966–1993). The development of inflation can be seen in Figure 5.5.

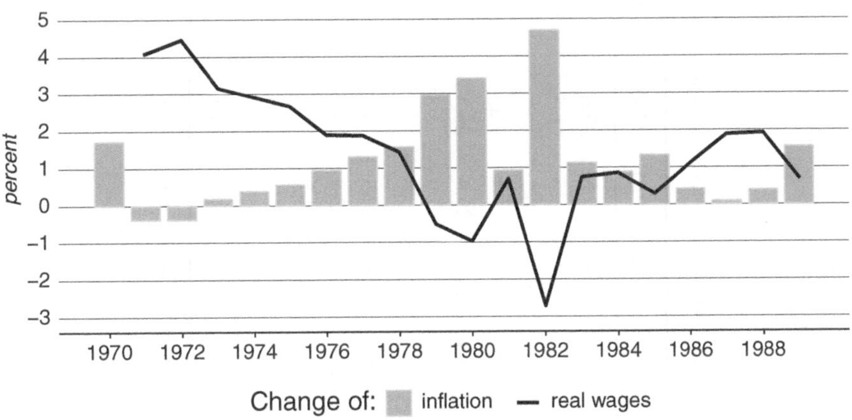

Figure 5.5 Year-to-year official inflation and the development of real wages 1970–1989 (in percent)

Source: Statistical yearbooks of CSSR (1971–1990)

Low retail inflation reflected rigid price policy resulting in fixed prices – see Table 5.15 – accompanied by subsidies in the form of negative turnover tax. However, at the same time, fiscal policy was sound and the government allowed only low level, if any, of the deficits' monetization (see Box 5.5). Such reasonable macroeconomic policy was not common among the CPEs at that time.

Table 5.15 Retail prices in CSK of selected goods and services in Czechoslovakia 1953–1988

Type of good	*Unit*	*1953*	*1960*	*1963*	*1965*	*1968*	*1970*	*1973*	*1975*	*1978*	*1980*	*1982*	*1984*	*1987*	*1988*
Bread	kg	2.8	2.6	2.6	2.6	2.6	2.6	2.6	4.4	4.4	4.4	4.4	4.4	4.4	4.4
Rice	kg	28	5	5	5	5	5	5	5	5	5	10	10	10	10
Potatoes	kg	0.6	0.6	0.7	0.7	0.7	0.7	0.7	0.8	1.4	1.6	1.6	1.6	1.6	1.6
Butter	kg	44	38	38	38	40	40	40	40	40	40	40	40	40	40
Oil	kg	34	25.4	25.4	25.4	25.4	25.4	25.4	25.4	25.4	25.4	25.4	25.4	25.4	25.4
Cube sugar	kg	14	9	9	9	8	8	8	8	8	8	8	8	8	8
White wine	l	26	19	19	17	17	17	17	17	17	24	28	24	28	28
Rum (40%)	l	68	80	80	65	65	65	65	65	65	83	100	100	100	100
Pit coal	100 kg	22.4	22.4	22.4	22.4	26.2	26.3	26.2	18.6	25.9	25.9	25.9	25.9	25.9	25.9
Man's socks	pair	8.8	4.5	4.5	4.5	4.7	7	6.8	6.7	11.7	12.8	13.7	14.4	14	14
Rent (two rooms)	month	75	75	75	106	106	106	106	106	121	121	121	121	121	121
Electricity	kWh	0.8	0.7	0.7	0.7	0.7	0.7	0.7	0.7	0.7	1.1	1.1	1.1	1.1	1.1
Haircut	service	2	2	2	2.5	3.1	5.1	5	5	5	5	5	7	7	7

Source: Statistické ročenky Československé socialistické republiky (1966–1993)

Box 5.5 Fiscal policy

The government's fiscal policy was sound. The federal budget was planned in surplus until 1979 and balanced in the following years until the fall of the regime. The year-to-year fiscal practice was, at least formally, in harmony with these plans. The budget was balanced for the whole period, as we can see in Figure 5.6.

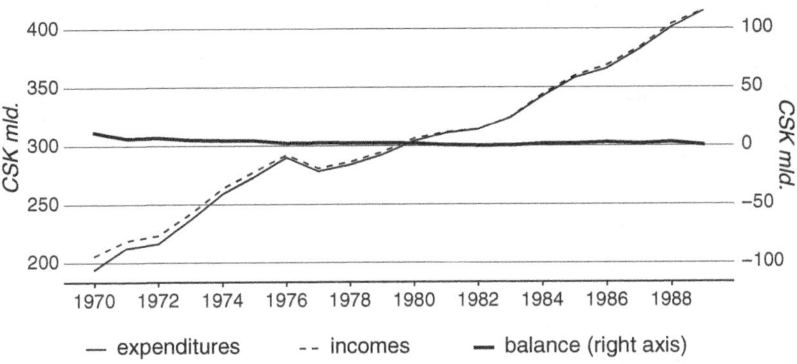

Figure 5.6 Incomes, expenditures and balance of governments' budgets and budgets of National Committees (local city halls), in CSK mld.

Source: Statistical yearbooks of CSSR (1971–1990)

The budgets were prepared for the federal level, for individual republics, and for national committees. A typical budget can be found in Table 5.16.

The income side of the budget was rather unclear. The taxes and fees imposed on the citizens accounted for just 14% of the budget's revenues in 1982. The taxes collected from companies accounted for 85% of the revenues (Hába et al. 1988). Three quarters of the revenues were comprised by turnover tax (at the rate of 32%) and other levies by economic organizations (Šulc 1995). The tax rates were in practice individual – individual companies were imposed considerably different tax rates. Higher requirements were planned for companies with good economic results because there was a higher probability that they would meet them. Worse companies faced lower tasks. Profits of the better-off companies covered losses of the unsuccessful ones (Hába et al. 1988).

The budget expenditures were used for redistributive goals – among others for subsidies. They accounted for a significant part of government expenditures. One of the estimations is depicted in Table 5.17. The share of subsidies to GDP was in Czechoslovakia high and growing during the 1980s.

Table 5.16 Federal budget and regional budgets net earnings for 1987 (in CSK million)

	ČSSR	*County committees*	*ČSSR + CC*
REVENUES	**314.630**	**69.102**	**383.732**
turnover tax	74.169		74.169
economic units levies	172.042	12.487	184.529
public-benefit, financial and insurance organizations levies	19.931	390	20.321
budget organizations revenues	4.212	6.479	10.691
financial revenues	35.122		35.122
social security levies	672	4.651	5.323
other revenues	8.482	14.496	22.978
local tax charges and fees		30.599	30.599
EXPENDITURES	**245.191**	**136.960**	**382.151**
investment building	7.527	22.414	29.941
material costs	8.145	45.647	53.792
services and non-production costs	71.620	6.688	78.308
business trips costs and other natural persons refunds	1.055	536	1.591
salaries	7.741	30.295	38.036
social security benefits	84.211	4.235	88.446
public-benefit and similar organizations benefits	17.933	8.917	26.850
economic units benefits	46.959	18.228	65.187
county committees subsidies and subventions	69.439	−69.439	0
BALANCE (excl. CC subsidies and subventions)	**69.439**	**−67.858**	**1.581**

Source: Statistická ročenka Československé socialistické republiky (1988)

Table 5.17 Total amount of budget subsidies as percent of GPD

	1982	*1985*	*1986*	*1987*	*1988*	*1989*
Czechoslovakia	10	11.9	12.3	12.5	13	16.1
Bulgaria	13.3	12.8	15.4	17.2	17.6	15.6
Hungary	18.7	17.1	16.6	16.2	13.8	13.3
Poland	20.7	16.5	16.3	15.9	16	14.1
Soviet Union	–	–	–	–	15	13.5

Source: Jonáš (1997)

Inflation in the socialist period was formally low. But even from this macroeconomic point of view, the situation was not as optimistic as the official statistics presented it. Besides open inflation, two specific forms of inflation appeared in the socialist environment. The first was suppressed inflation. It occurs when the grounds for inflation exist, but the price hike is formally blocked by the government decision to fix prices. Artificial barriers preventing price growth contributed to the market imbalance. Suppressed inflation caused, at the same time, money overhang that consequently contributed to forced savings because people had limited possibilities to spend their money. The size of suppressed inflation revealed itself during price liberalization in early 1990s. Then, prices jumped by nearly 60% just in 1991. This surge, however, was relatively small in comparison to other centrally planned economies (for example Žídek 2017). Price stability was clearly an important consideration for Czechoslovak economists (and politicians) during the centrally planned period.

The other form of inflation is hidden inflation (see Table 5.9). This kind evades official record thanks to particular configuration of the consumer basket. It reflected for example price increase related to so-called innovations. Brada et al. write about pseudo-innovations when the same product was "innovated" by minor changes. Different colour or cover allowed its sale for a higher price even though there was no cost increase. Likewise, wide price adjustment was scheduled some years ahead could stand behind a price growth (Brada et al. 1996). True inflation in the 1980s was estimated to be around two or even three percentage points a year higher than the official figure (Dyba and Kouba 1989; Půlpán 1993, respectively). This hidden growth of prices was illustrated by one of our respondents (associate professor, department head at the Prognostic Institute <ID071>) too, whose conclusions about hidden inflation were similar to Dyba and Kouba.

I: *I do not understand how the hidden price growth was recognized.*
R: *Well, I compared GDP, I had the people to do it, too. We compared it with the West Germany and we had the data from the mid-1960s. . . . And now we had the same thing in the second half of the 1980s and the growth rates in general and prices. And now we compared it, and even if the statistical office did not fake anything, I do not know, we never discovered such a thing, anyway, the result was elsewhere. And the only sensible explanation was that prices had risen. So, this is the deduction. When you just convert it to a single denominator and when one has dynamics like this and the other one like that, it must be the prices. The prices were set independently, regardless of economics, to a great degree. We knew that.*
I: *So, it means that . . . on the other hand, the prices were nominally the same.*
R: *A 1.5% increase a year on average.*
I: *And that meant in fact?*
R: *In fact, a 4% increase.*

If these estimations of hidden inflation are correct, then average economic growth in the 1980s was negative.

We can conclude that the prices clearly did not carry the information needed to get system into balance. Additionally, different prices at different layers of the system created distortions. The governments formally did not allow high inflation, which was good, but the true state was actually hidden behind fixed prices and negative turnover tax subsidies.

5.5 Foreign (economic) relationships

The Czechoslovak outer relationships were limited mostly to foreign trade (5.5.1). Even though trade openness (exports to GDP) was limited, our respondents had relatively rich personal experience with foreign trade. On the contrary, joint ventures or any other forms of foreign inward or outward investment were rare (5.5.2). Only one respondent mentioned attending a meeting in a bank for COMECON countries (Head of department in engineering <ID037>). The third aspect of across-the-border contacts: movement of labour force (5.5.3), was limited as well but some of our respondents had experience with foreign workers in the Czechoslovak economy. They also made occasional short business trips and some of them even longer study stays (e.g., respondent <ID49> automotive). Czechoslovak professionals were also sent abroad on investment, or in fact aid, projects or as advisors.

5.5.1 Foreign trade

International trade reflected the state and efficiency of the overall economy. Considering the outer relationship, the general level of openness was low if we take into account the small size of the Czechoslovak economy – exports to GDP amounted to roughly 20% (Jonáš 1997). We can speak about the inclination to autarky. Orientation of trade was nearly totally towards the CPEs markets – see Table 5.18. The Council of Mutual Economic Assistance (COMECON) that was founded in 1949 promoted trade among socialist CPEs. The goal was not to create a typical common market, rather, the organization was a place for bilateral agreements among the participating countries. The organization otherwise for example set standards for products that were produced in the COMECON countries. Votoček complains that these standards were very low to satisfy the needs of the weaker members of the organization (Vaněk and Urbášek 2005). Trade was realized in the so-called convertible rouble.[4] In the second half of the 1980s, approximately 15% of exports were directed towards markets in developed countries.

Table 5.18 Territorial orientation of Czechoslovak trade between 1948 and 1989 (percent of turnover)

	1948	*1953*	*1960*	*1970*	*1980*	*1985*
Socialist countries	39.7	78.5	71.8	70.0	69.9	78.8
Out of which:						
Soviet Union	16.2	35.5	34.4	32.5	35.8	44.8
Other COMECON countries	-	36.4	29.4	32.8	29.7	29.3
Other socialist countries	-	6.6	8.0	4.9	4.4	4.7
Non-socialistic countries	60.3	21.5	28.2	30.0	30.1	21.1
Out of which:						
Developed capitalist countries	45.5	14.9	17.8	22.4	23.0	15.5
Developing countries	14.8	6.6	10.4	7.6	7.1	5.7

Source: Průcha (1988)

The foreign trade was planned and organized (as other parts of the socialist economy) – via foreign trade companies (PZO), which were specific official monopolistic organizations in charge of foreign trade. The producers could reach foreign markets and contact their customers only indirectly through the PZOs.

Apart from several exceptions, the system of Czechoslovak foreign trade severed domestic producers from their foreign suppliers and customers, which inevitably led to increasing coordination costs and deepening information asymmetry. Therefore, respective companies lacked expertise in the functioning of foreign trade, marketing, legal provisions, etc. The sales departments in the companies were degraded to carrying out mere standardized administrative tasks and they were small especially in comparison to supply departments.

Assistant to the director in a major engineering company <ID043> described their role this way:

> *Individual companies are not involved in foreign trade. Not directly. It was, in fact, not even in local trade. It was all planned in advance. [. . .] Well, the marketing department more or less just contacted a prescribed partner company, which was all part of the central planning. Therefore, we actually did not sell anything on our own. As for foreign trade, our products were sold via the Strojimport company [a foreign trade company].*

The same respondent stressed the mechanical nature of the marketing department's work, which was limited to strictly standardized tasks:

> *Simply standardized contracts, and in January, we would get a list specifying in which month which piece of machinery would be delivered. And the people in the marketing department simply finalized the specifics of the contract. Details, such as what was to be delivered with the machinery, spare parts, etc.*

The centre generally sought balance of international trade. The balances suffered from growing deficit in the 1970s due to the increase in prices of oil and raw materials. It was achieved only after applying serious restrictions on imports from developed countries at the beginning of the 1980s. Trade was tightened, and imports limited by the central plan. The consequence was a relative stability in trade balance in the 1980s – for eastern and western markets, see Figure 5.7.

The struggle to achieve balance was omnipresent even at the level of companies as our respondent described (a power plant director <ID014>):

> *This, moreover, brought worries about the rouble balance. There were terrible things happening in the convertible ruble regime, as there were technical solutions, ideas, patents, and so on as parts of the exchange. And it always had to come out so that . . . what we bought from [East] Germany had to be for the same convertible rouble as what we sold to [East] Germany. That's how they changed . . . inventions and the upgrading proposals were converted to money, and then it was a hard task to convert it back in order for it to be the same price, so that we would not owe anything.*

The effort to keep foreign trade in balance simultaneously resulted in limited borrowing on the international markets, as can be seen in Figure 5.8. Several other CPEs (including Poland and Hungary) had serious problems with one or both of these indicators having high inflation or even hyperinflation and huge deficits of the current account and a high level of indebtedness abroad. Czechoslovakia avoided these imbalances. In 1989, the average debt per person in Czechoslovakia was $757, contrary to $2,843 in Poland and $4,261 in Hungary (Swain 1998).

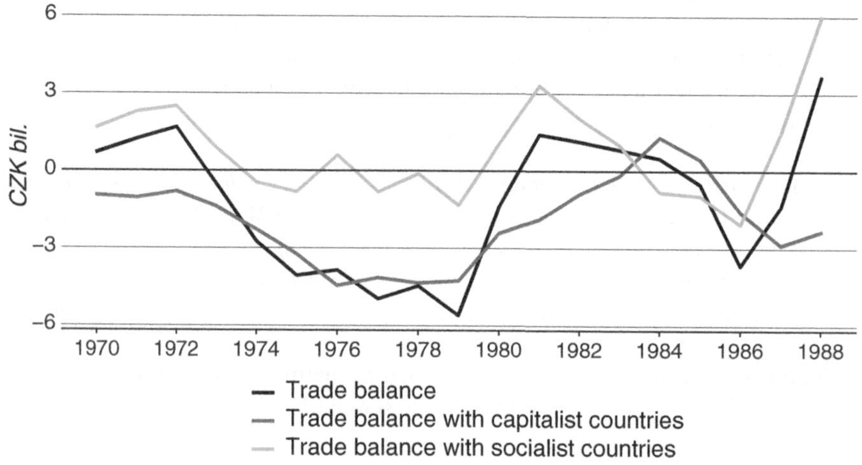

Figure 5.7 Czechoslovak trade balance 1970–1988 (in CZK bil.)
Source: Statistical yearbooks of CSSR (1971–1990)

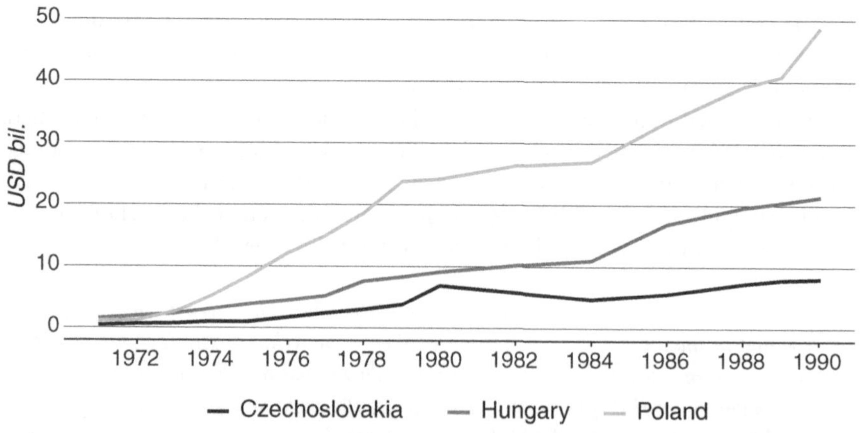

Figure 5.8 Gross governments' debts to the west in billion dollars 1971–1990
Source: Swain (1998)

The commodity structure of Czechoslovak exports was different for each of the territorial directions. Exports towards the COMECON markets consisted mostly of machinery, vehicles, and generally goods with a higher added value. On the contrary, exports to demanding western markets was constituted mostly of goods with a lower added value – raw materials and semi-manufactured goods – for example sulphuric acid or steel. Exports of goods with a higher added value (like cars) were rare and their quality considered inferior at western markets. The Czechoslovak representatives were well aware of this state. The StB provided an anecdote on a situation when an Austrian firm wanted to buy machinery from the Zbrojovka Vsetín factory. The negotiations went on in a PZO office, and Zbrojovka representation attended as well. The PZO Strojimport representative advised the customer: "Do not buy the looms from Zbrojovka, these are not good." Allegedly, based on this note, the customer was not interested in signing a contract anymore (ABS, OB-957 OV). There were just a few world-class Czechoslovak products – mostly piece production, e.g., the Kaplan turbines (Zeman 1990).

The structure of Czechoslovak imports was just the opposite – the economy imported from the western markets machinery, vehicles, and goods that were needed for adding value to Czechoslovak exports. The economy suffered from lasting shortage of hard/convertible currencies, which highly limited import possibilities. On the contrary, imports from the other CPE countries mostly consisted of raw materials and semi-manufactured goods. There were exceptions from these patterns. Trade with developing countries was mostly realized with friendly regimes (with "socialistic orientation") – including countries like Iraq, Syria, and Libya and Czechoslovakia exported industrial products or weapons. These countries often did not pay for the delivered goods, and foreign trade was just a different form of political support.

Additionally, trade with services was generally low – the share of services on tangible Czechoslovak exports was only 10% in the 1980s compared to 24% in Hungary, 34% in Switzerland, and more than 40% in Austria (Zeman 1990). At the same time, other incomes, such as tourism, were just a fraction of those in other states, one tenth of a million USD vs. 6 to 7 million USD per year in Austria (Komárek 1990).

The relative competitiveness of Czechoslovak goods on the world markets declined in a long run. The evidence is, among others, in the development of terms of trade, which were worsening for all destinations – see Table 5.19.

Table 5.19 Czechoslovak terms of trade (1977 = 100)

	1948	*1967*	*1975*	*1980*	*1985*	*1987*
With centrally planned economies	132	123	104.6	94.3	77	79.5
With the Soviet Union		129	102.4	88.6	57.8	62
With developed and developing countries	172	118.2	112.6	99.6	96.2	94.7

Source: Michal (1994)

Czechoslovak crown (CSK) was not convertible in the common meaning of the word. The system of multiple (fixed) exchange rates was applied. The trade transactions were further distorted by aforementioned system of subtractions, surcharges and VRCV. One of our respondents described it in the following way:

> *Which, for example, on the basis of difference in the VRCV I found out how to reduce foreign air transportation, because, and it is necessary to say that the Czechoslovak Commercial Bank stood above all this, especially its foreign exchange supervision Mr. Kubiznak who simply made everyone wonder at how much understood (though he, in fact, did not). . . . Consider that back then, we flew to Paris three times a week, and alternate routing existed only via Helsinki, when Mr. Kubiznak decided that it was a better option because the Finns gave us some rebates. Yeah and stuff like this. Well, we and colleagues came to realize that when we bring it to East Berlin and sell it to our colleagues from the Interflug, we take the VRCV coefficient from 2.25 to 1.4, and the shipping is much cheaper and what is more, we do not spend convertible foreign exchange. You know, such kinds of things were done, . . . and moreover it had the advantage that they liked us because one of the main indicators was not a profit, . . . but it was a share of expenditures in convertible currencies and convertible rouble. The convertible rouble, it was another miracle that one.*
>
> *(operative in the PZO <ID030>)*

The subsequent text follows the common distinction of Czechoslovak trade on territorial and commodity structures. Considering a spatial dimension, the trade breaks into three distinct areas: COMECON/socialist, developing, and developed countries. Among commodities, we emphasize engineering products which were considered the flagship of the Czechoslovak economy.

Socialist countries

The most important trading partners were the COMECON countries and foremost the Soviet Union. There were several aspects of trade with these destinations. Some authors see COMECON mainly as a tool for achieving Soviet strategic goals (e.g., Landau and Průcha 1995). The Soviets used direct and indirect subsidies supply to exert leverage on its satellites (see Table 5.20). Voráček mentions that the Soviet Union provided objective-directed transactions helping Czechoslovakia especially at the beginning of the 1970s (immediately after the Soviet-led occupation) with an intention to support political stability in Czechoslovakia (Voráček 1995). They maintained favourable rates of raw materials, fuels, and machinery deliveries and opened Soviet markets to Czechoslovak companies.

The key commodity subsidized by the Soviets was oil. Some of the socialist countries including Czechoslovakia were even allowed to re-export it. Komárek mentions that around 2/3 of Czechoslovak exports in convertible currencies at the end of the 1980s resulted from the production of oil and petrochemical products that were based on inexpensive oil imports from the Soviet Union (Komárek 1990).

Table 5.20 Estimation of the Soviet support to countries in the Eastern Bloc 1971–1978

	Billion USD	*USD per capita*
Bulgaria	3.5	390
Czechoslovakia	2.6	170
East Germany	4.8	290
Hungary	1.0	100
Poland	2.1	60
Romania	−0.1	−0.5

Source: Voráček (1995)

Regardless of the soviet strategies, Czechoslovak exports (as well as imports) targeted nearly absolutely the COMECON markets with the primacy of the Soviet market (see Table 5.18).

Some of our respondents said that their companies exported only to the allied countries markets. For example, our respondent from an engineering company said the following:

R: *. . . And as far as I know, I mean as long as I was there, that is, from seventy-one to nineteen eighty-nine, Strojexport was exporting cars to Hungary, to the Soviet Union, and outside . . .*
I: *. . . outside the COMECON?*
R: *No, it was always COMECON markets.* (chief designer in an engineering company *lead engineer <ID003>).*

The organization of trade among the CPEs was based on bilateral inter-governmental agreements negotiated in COMECON. Obviously, common market could not be established because the economies of individual members were based on the concept of central planning. Our respondent explicitly stated that the trade was done by means of "handle an item after an item" meaning de facto barter (section chief in SPK <ID040>). The financial transactions were arranged via bilateral clearings. Attempts at creating multilateral clearings were unsuccessful (Fojtíková 2009).

For decades, the COMECON markets represented reliable and non-demanding customers of Czechoslovak production. And for several companies it was even the main market, as our respondent from a company that produced electronic equipment mentioned:

> *Let's admit that around twenty percent of the EJF company production was left on the Czech market. Approximately sixty percent could be placed in the affiliated COMECON countries and twenty percent were sent especially to the Middle East. Again, let's not be naive we were not successful on advanced western markets at that time. Or, at least, the EJF company was not at that time.*
>
> (an economic planner in an engineering company *<ID008>*)

The quality of Czechoslovak's exports was often even worse than the quality of goods for the domestic market (Mlčoch 1990). In spite of this, Czechoslovak goods had usually very good reputation among the consumers in the COMECON markets. "Of course, if there was a switch that had a hallmark of, say, almost European or Western quality, it was very desirable and could be placed in the whole COMECON" (an economic planner in an engineering company <ID008>). Made-in-Czechoslovakia brand was so strong that some of the producers could even "abuse" their position: "It was quite a problem because Russia did not pay, it was a big volume. But we didn't bother . . . when talking about quality, not that we would have . . . , that is, in many cases . . . as the quality of the VHJ in general was good. But it was known that everything would be sold in Russia" (analyst in textile industry <ID055>).

On the other hand, one respondent (a head of human resources in textile industry <ID024>) mentioned that even the position of Czechoslovak goods on Eastern markets was artificial:

> *The evidence is that when we used to manufacture these small-diameter knitting machines, they were sold to the Soviet Union, but elsewhere as well. But after the revolution, their demand for these ceased significantly, at least it was not what it had been before. And the reason was that just like we were obliged to export, they were obliged to import, it was just that they didn't need them, so they would lie in their warehouses.*

The exporters to these markets had secured incomes based on bilateral agreements and thus did not need to care about the quality of their production or marketing (Borensztein and Masson 1995). But there were drawbacks of the participation in the COMECON structures as well. It was supposed to facilitate a division of labour among its members to increase overall efficiency. According to the founding agreements, the member states were supposed to mutually pass their production knowledge, technical solutions, provide training for new foreign producers free of charge, etc. (Hába et al. 1988). Czechoslovakia suffered from being one of the most developed parts of the Eastern Bloc. The feeling was often that the domestic producers had to pass their know-how to foreigners who consequently started to produce the same goods and competed with the original Czechoslovak producers (Teplý 1976). Hába (author of a socialist textbook about central planning) agrees that the whole concept of COMECON was foremost supposed to help the less developed countries, but he states that the Czechoslovak economy gained from the agreements rights to keep and develop several important productions as well (Hába et al. 1988).

All in all, the decisions about production were often dubious. One of the problematic results of the artificial division of labour inside COMECON was the broad scale of Czechoslovak engineering production. Komárek mentions another drawback stating that Czechoslovakia was supposed to produce iron and steel industry products. But the country neither mined for the ore needed for the production, nor produced the needed semi-finished batches. The result was that the worst quality ferrous batches were imported from the Soviet Union and, what is more, at permanently increasing prices (Komárek 1990). Similarly, Drda comments that East Germany was able to produce a better car than Trabant, but the socialist division of labour situtated this production to the Soviet Union (Drda, Mlejnek, and Škoda 2010). Yet another argument is that deliveries from the COMECON partners were not always reliable. MP Říman for example complained:

> *In the current maize harvesting period, the need for repairs of all kinds of cutters, including the most common type SPZ 35 – Toron, the product of Agrozet Prostějov, is logically increased. Some parts and spare parts are imported from the Polish People's Republic. We needed at least one piece of a new drum on the farm as a spare part. Agrozet Olomouc told us that the drums had not been delivered, and nobody knew when and how many of them would be, because their Polish partner did not meet the negotiated agreements for the 1st quarter of the year.*
>
> *(ČSSR. Federal Assembly of the Czechoslovak Socialist Republic 1986–1990)*

The socialist countries realized the technical inferiority of their production vis-à-vis western economies even at the highest COMECON level. The 41st session of the organization in December 1985 approved an ambitious program of scientific and technological progress. The goal was to catch up with developed industrial countries by 2000 (Levcik and Stankovsky 1988). The practical impact was, however, negligible.

Developing countries

Developing countries were common target markets for both Czechoslovak production and for large industrial projects such as a refinery for Iraq, Iran, or Syria; cement factory for Cuba; or sugar factories and breweries for other destinations. The quality of the production can be described by the experience of the Czechoslovak salespersons abroad. Vaněk and Krátká collected interviews with representatives of the authorized foreign trade companies (PZO) (Vaněk and Krátká 2014). Their respondents exemplify that export was oriented towards developing countries:

> *[The respondent talks about Bolivia] the Jawa motorcycle, because again, it was not the last model, no big show-off for the boy who bought the bike. But it was simple, robust, inexpensive, easy to fix, in other words, in the developing world our backward Czechoslovak goods were relatively interesting. [. . .] The territories where these products or industrial projects could be exported were either a friendly socialist country or a third world one. They could not be exported to advanced countries because the technical level was already somewhere else, which again had the advantage that such demands on cadre requirements were not imposed on those people who headed to the third world countries. So, I managed to avoid having to enter the party in my foreign trade business experience, while, for example, those who travelled to the*

exclusive Western countries or the United States, and so on, either had to meet the cadre requirements or otherwise they couldn't go to those countries.

Otherwise, Czechoslovakia was the second largest armament producer in the Warsaw Pact – just behind the Soviet Union. Three quarters of the weapon production were exported, mostly to allies and to developing countries with "socialistic orientation" – in specific to countries like Libya, Iraq, and Iran (Kaiser 1995). These countries were often unable to pay and the business would probably have never taken place without the political context. This was why Czechoslovakia had huge trade surpluses with these developing countries. The trades were financed only in a very long-term perspective, and, in practice, the Czechoslovak government ultimately covered the costs (Nykryn 1988).

Both weapons and industrial projects were mostly financed by export loans with long-term maturity. Vencovský points out that, at the end of 1988, the sum of Czechoslovak foreign claims reached 20% of the national income (Vencovský 2003). And our respondent from the SPK <ID040> told us that "in 1989, the volume of unpaid debts amounted to USD 7 billion (including armament industry contracts)."

Developed countries

Exports to the capitalist countries were much more demanding. Mlčoch comments that Czechoslovak companies were spoilt by the easy-going situation at the domestic market with negligible, if any at all, competition. The situation was totally different in the world markets where the domestically omnipotent Czechoslovak monopolies were outsiders. Additionally, Czechoslovak companies were not very enthusiastic about exporting to the west. In most cases, they were ordered to do so (Mlčoch 1990) and they could not retain the earned hard (convertible) currency although a company successfully exporting to the west was more likely to obtain hard currency allocation for importing investment goods (see later).

Czechoslovak exports to the west consisted of the best quality goods. However, the exports were mostly based on low-value-added production (Coufalová, Mikula, and Žídek 2019). The ability to export high-value-added production was limited and even diminished overtime. Despite the ability to offer production at lower prices, the technological gap made the production gradually uncompetitive. It can be demonstrated in Table 5.21, which compares prices for one kilogram of industrial production. This kind of measure was highly popular among the researchers in socialist Czechoslovakia in the 1980s, probably because of the unreliability of exchange rates as a measure. For example, Komárek writes that one kilogram of electronic components made in the European Economic Community (EEC) was sold for USD 20. It was, however, sold for USD 2.3 when made in COMECON and for just USD 1.8 when made in Czechoslovakia (Komárek 1990). This worsening trend in the measure appeared in other productions like textile, glass, or porcelain as well (Zeman 1990). This is despite the fact that the latter two were considered Czech family silver.

Table 5.21 Average kilogram prices of industrial products exported into the EEC markets (USD/kg)

	1970	*1980*	*1986*
Czechoslovakia	1.15	2.70	2.34
Hungary	1.81	3.98	3.47
Rumania	1.00	3.17	2.84
Austria	1.96	7.84	9.33
Switzerland	4.94	17.56	19.39
Japan	3.68	8.04	11.38
USA	8.65	21.13	37.62

Source: Zeman (1990)

Declining exports to the west, which were the primary source of convertible currency, put the regime under increasing pressure and resulted in a maximized effort to export to these destinations. Regardless of this effort, the economy suffered from an outer dollar imbalance at the end of the 1970s, which was connected with increasing oil prices on the world markets and ever-sharpening competition. This furthermore curtailed the imports. There was not only lack of modern western machinery and technologies but even some essential raw materials because the Czechoslovak government applied a strategy of non-borrowing. Obtaining convertible currencies became the utmost goal. One of our respondents (university lecturer, Member of Parliament <ID075>) described a situation that illustrates the overall level of desperation. A general director of a company that produced toilet paper and sanitary napkins managed (thanks to personal contacts) to sell these products to the western markets. He managed to obtain convertible currency and was even praised by the ÚV KSČ. However, the consequence was the limited delivery of these products to the domestic market and a persistent shortage. The women workers in the Škoda Plzeň factory even threatened with a strike and the Parliament received outraged mails from the citizens. The Communist Party looked for a culprit and he was found in the very same general director. He was even threatened with imprisonment. The situation was calmed only by the PM, who ordered the press not to refer to the situation, explaining that it would be ridiculous for one and the same person to be praised by the state one month and punished for the same deed the next one.

The inability to export was omnipresent and the regime was willing to pay any price for inflow of convertible currencies as was described earlier. In practice, the support for exports resulted in individual exchange rates for individual transactions. The inefficiencies can be illustrated in an example from a transportation vehicles production:

> *Well, in fact, when we exported, we recorded loss, but the system of surcharges and reductions balanced it out. On the other hand, when we imported thick sheet metal from the Soviet Union, the import prices were so low that we brought tens of millions into the national budget as price difference. So, when we exported, we were on the losing side, while when we imported, we actually made profit for the government.*
>
> (*Head of department in an engineering company <ID037>*)

Nykryn mentions quarrels between the PZOs and the VHJs because the PZO required the producers to work harder and, for example, increase the quality of their production (Nykryn 1983). As a consequence, in the PZOs' view, Czechoslovak production could either compete by means of lower prices, or try to import advanced technologies, or both. On the other hand, interestingly, the StB detected dissatisfaction on the side of the VHJs with the PZOs activities. According to their analysis, the VHJs criticized low success rate of finding trade partners or undervalued sales (ABS, A34/1, inv.j. 1261).

Our respondents declared that the ability to offer the production at a lower price was a key to export. According to the head of the economic department of a consumer electronics industry <ID044>, the chance to export to the western markets was dominantly because of the low price: "What gave away a socialist economy product was a low price [reason to buy a product] . . . and it was not to be rumoured as a faulty product that breaks down immediately." Despite the ability to offer cheap products, export to the west was declining. The key problem was the technological gap which could not be fully compensated by lower prices. To overcome this unfavourable development, enterprises needed to acquire western technologies, capital equipment, or intermediate products. The foreign firms were aware of it, and the StB's investigation provides us with an interesting case of buying machinery from abroad. The investigated person was a high-ranking manager in the Škoda Plzeň factory who was able to influence the company's decision on buying new machinery from abroad. In September 1983, the manager allegedly took a bribe from an Italian businessman who wanted to push the firm into contracting his company. Later, the manager was investigated further due to a business trip to Italy, from which he brought back goods worth more than what the StB counted he could have spent. The report concluded that the manager was not eligible for any contact with foreigners, that he questioned the morals of the StB's work, and that his thoughts were different from what they were expected to be given the fact he was a member of the Communist Party (ABS, OBŽ-17366 PL).

In Zemans' thorough analysis, practically all competitive sectors used machinery imported from the west (Zeman 1990). His view finds support in our interviews. The respondents described introduction of western technologies as a necessary condition to supplement Czechoslovak products and often the only way to make Czechoslovak higher-added-value products competitive. One of our respondents said:

> *Good quality, precision, very good low-end reliability and . . . was agreed that it would use Western operational systems. . . . Simply everything responsible for the machinery operations had to be imported from non-socialist economies. . . . Automatic production lines, they all worked with our [i.e., made in Czechoslovakia] operational systems, which were impossible to sell on Western markets.*
>
> *(Director's assistant in an engineering company <ID043>)*

The inability to produce native modern technologies is confirmed by a respondent from an authorized foreign trade company (PZO), who said "well, there were a number of things we could not manufacture, namely electronics, so we got it from Siemens or other firms from West Germany or England" (Vaněk and Krátká 2014, p. 252).

Enterprises attempted to keep up with western companies by participation in trade fairs held in advanced countries. A CEO from an engineering company <ID022> described his experience from the west Germany trade show:

> *Of course, we tried to keep in touch with the best producers in Europe, in a special way, by means of going to various trade fairs. [. . .] It was that products and manufacturers that seemed exotic to us all of a sudden had real people representing them, and we would go to these trade fairs and tried to collect all kinds of brochures and advertisement material for the machinery they made and all the information about them we could get so that we could somehow progress.*

Enterprises could gain access to supplies from the west via obtaining binding government tasks. By assigning these procurements, the state often gave companies priority access to foreign technology and could thus prioritize firms that were able to export to the West. I: "And does that mean that when you managed to bargain for these government procurements, it opened a lot of doors for the company?" R: "Yes, because it allowed me to buy some machinery or technology for the foreign currency" (Director in automotive industry <ID049>).

However, the acquisitions of Western technologies were complicated by a western embargo on some COMECON imports and activities of The Coordinating Committee for Multilateral Export Controls – COCOM (Bálek 1998). A section chief of the planning bureau in our interview also acknowledged problems caused by the embargo:

> *After the 1968 occupation . . . we got into this kind of a tougher embargo zone of countries. [. . .] Simply, we were not allowed to import modern machinery, technologies, qualified chemistry, such kinds of things. So nowadays, nobody knows about it. But Czechoslovakia cannot be a developed economy without international*

cooperation with the West. And when this is made difficult, the country gets badly beaten. And we could not import Western products with higher added value, for instance chemistry, information technologies. . . . This embargo had a devastating effect on the economy <ID040>.

The authors from the socialist period and advocates of the regime often complained about the western embargo/COCOM (e.g., Nykryn 1988; Zeman 1990; Štrougal 2009) that was effective during the Cold War period on selected western exports to the socialist countries. It targeted mainly advanced technologies with potential use in the military. However, in the view of the communist propaganda, the socialist economies were vanguards and world technological leaders and as such they did not need western technologies at all. Another aspect is that it was possible to bypass the embargo by secret transactions that, nevertheless, increased the costs (Landau and Průcha 1995). Yet another option was industrial espionage (see Box 5.6).

Box 5.6 Espionage

The Czechoslovak espionage and contra-espionage historically followed mostly political tasks but it included a special unit that concentrated on science and technologies (Vědecko-technická rozvědka – VTR). The main task of the VTR was to obtain western technologies and scientific information that were impossible to gain a legal way and that were of use for the Czechoslovak economy. Sobek – ex-Deputy Chief of the VTR – writes that the main directing of the VTR activities followed the plan of development of the economy! This shows that even activities of an espionage unit were, de facto, planned. The unit was active already in the 1960s, but at the end of the following decade this activity became priority for the secret service (Pacner 2002). The goal was to increase competitiveness of Czechoslovak products, obtain foreign currencies by exports and save money for research and development.

Coverage of the VTR agents was provided mostly by the PZOs or the SPK (Sobek 2011). However, some of them were for example sent abroad as university students. They got established in western institutions and gradually penetrated into higher positions in the academia, scientific institutions, or industrial companies. Pacner states that motivation of these agents was mostly patriotic and not ideological. Sobek writes that the agents acquired, for example, technologies for automatic production of TV screens, semiconductors, and equipment for night vision or high-resolution cameras. For the chemical industry, they obtained technologies for the production of ammonia, paraxylene, tyres, titanium-white for automotive, silicones, or cheaper production of vitamin C (Sobek 2011).

However, Pacner adds that the obtained information was sometimes so advanced that even the top Czech or Russian scientists did not understand it – for example in case of artificial intelligence (Pacner 2002).

Ex major of Czechoslovak VTR confessed to Pacner that it was possible to overcome the embargo (COCOM), however at high costs (included huge risk bonuses). He said that the market offered everything with the exception of nuclear, rocket, and space weapons technologies. He adds that, for example in the 1980s, the VTR was tasked to obtain technology for burning coal at high temperatures in order to decline pollution. They purchased it via an informer (Pacner 2002). An ex-lieutenant colonel adds that there was even a special department that dealt just with the embargo equipment and that the rule was that the companies had to deliver the equipment onto Czechoslovakia's territory. He comments that, for example, the latest computer was imported hidden in the back side of a wardrobe. Another time they obtained software for operating of a modern company, but it was so complicated that Czechoslovakia was not able to use it and it was passed to the Soviets.

All together the VTR acquired 9,310 materials between 1970 and 1989. Seven percent was of the highest quality. One-third of the materials was transferred to companies, one fifth to military research and production and the rest to food processing industry, education or basic research. The Czechoslovak companies preferred information in the form of technical documentation – it constituted 11.8% of the materials and was valuated up to 615 million crowns. According to estimations, the VTR saved the national economy around 900 million crowns during the last two decades of the regime's existence (ibidem). However, all these estimations are obviously questionable. Regardless of it, without the VTR, the technological gap would be even deeper.

Another legal possibility how to overcome or moderate the technological gap was the acquisition of western licenses or technologies. Interestingly, Czechoslovakia purchased license for several products of the Coca-Cola Company. Purchase of licences, however, collided with shortage of hard currency:

> *all the technology was from Western Europe. There was nothing manufactured for this technology in the Eastern Bloc. . . . But getting it was very difficult, because you had to . . . [record company] had the demands and there they had to go to the planning committee . . . and try something there, just how to get it, so it was . . . it was . . . that, the system was stupid, no matter how much of the hard currency we were producing . . . or not, so we submit everything to the last mark. And then we had to beg on our knees somewhere to be given some of it.*
>
> *(A general director in the electrotechnical industry ID047)*

The acquisitions were generally highly limited. Zeman writes that for example in 1982 Czechoslovakia purchased licenses for USD 17.2 million, Austria for 137 million, Norway for 107 million, Finland for 90 million, France for 1 billion, Italy for 1.6 billion and Japan for 2 billion. At the same time, Czechoslovakia was able to sell licenses only for USD 4.4 million, Norway for 87 million and Italy for 1 billion USD (Zeman 1990). It just contributed to a vicious circle, resulting in a gradually increasing technological gap between Czechoslovak and advanced economies.

Moreover, some companies tried to abuse the situation. Vilímek writes about machinations. A license for producing a part of production was purchased abroad so that the part could be produced in Czechoslovakia. However, the very part was imported anyway because higher-priced imports increased the overall value of the production (planning in gross production values) – e.g., a ton of domestic production cost CSK 10,000 and a ton of imported production cost CSK 45,000 (Vilímek 2012).

The general shortage of convertible currencies was worsened by the fact that enterprises were not allowed to retain convertible currencies that they had obtained from exports and were forced to hand them in to the centre.[5] Consequently, they had to request foreign currencies from the centre back again in order to buy western supplies or technology (a power plant director <ID014>). As a result, while the economy badly needed convertible currency, the individual enterprises were not systematically motivated to generate them. Furthermore, the StB even reported a case where the Zbrojovka Vsetín factory was discouraged by the PZO Investa from its intention to export more than it was tasked by the plan. In 1979, Zbrojovka intended to export more than had been planned to be able to import technologies, but this intention collided with the PZO interests. The PZO refused Zbrojovka's plan to earn foreign currencies via exports and made Zbrojovka import the technologies directly, using irretrievable credit from the SBČS (ABS, OB-957 OV). The central authorities were not the only redistributor of the convertible currencies stock. The PZOs and concerns redistributed it as well: "the redistribution of excess foreign currencies was done by the general manager, based on requirements by the Strojimport company. Once he said that such and such machinery was to be sold to the west with such and such operational systems, the foreign currency to buy these systems was granted" (assistant to the director in an engineering company <ID043>).

Redistribution of convertible currencies weakened motivation to export to the west even further as successful companies had no guarantee of preferential access to it. This changed only before the fall of the regime. Under the valid foreign currency regulations, companies were allowed to retain a certain (usually small and individually set) part of foreign exchange in order to reinvest it at will:

> *The money was used to buy first computers in the company, and such, that is what the foreign currency regulation made possible, you know. It was 1986, 87 or so and really, first computers started to appear, and they came thanks to this. Like I say, the foreign*

> *currency regulation enabled the purchases of these computers, because the company was allowed some of the foreign currency to spend. We are talking about a percent of each exported piece of machinery. Exported to the West, I mean. And still, it was just a negligible one percent that the state bank gave the company to buy some technology to use.*
> (*assistant to the director in an engineering company <ID043>*)

However, the late introduction of relaxation of the foreign currency regulations could not have a significant effect on the performance of the economy under the central planning.

Commodity structure

Considering commodity structure of Czechoslovak exports, the biggest share and the flagship of the Czechoslovak production was supposed to be mechanical engineering. Czechoslovak enterprises produced the widest portfolio of engineering production in the entire Eastern Bloc and possibly in the world (Kaplan 1995). Nykryn writes that there were around 600,000 basic types of engineering products listed worldwide. Producers in the USA manufactured around 50% of the range of items, Germany 20%, Japan 17%, and Czechoslovakia around two-thirds and possibly more (Nykryn 1983). However, the international position of Czechoslovak engineering exports did not reflect the alleged superior position. The reality was rather worse than hoped. The share of Czechoslovak mechanical engineering exports in the world imports declined from 2.1% in 1970 to 1.59% in 1985. The decline in the share of developed countries' imports was even worse – from 0.32% to 0.15% (Zahraniční obchod 1988).[6]

The general share of machinery in Czechoslovak exports achieved similar results. Tíkal claims that the share of machinery and equipment in total exports was, at the end of the 1980s, 58%, but 91.5% of it went to other socialist countries, 5% to developing countries, and only 3.5% to the developed ones (Tíkal 1990).

According to the UN Comtrade data, the drop in the share of advanced countries (current OECD members with exclusion of the then COMECON countries) in machinery exports in the 1980s was even deeper. In the 1982–1988 period, advanced economies bought on average only 2.1% of the machinery and transport equipment exports. Kolanda and Kubišta claim that there were 813 companies in the manufacturing industry in the 1980s: 713 of them were exporters, but only 72 (9%) were able to export more than 20% of their production to the western markets (Kolanda and Kubišta 1991). And although they were able to export, their position on the western markets was highly dubious – see the case of the Škoda car company in Box 5.7. The quality of export was generally questionable. For example, the StB reported problems with machinery already exported. In the case of the Zbrojovka Vsetín factory, the StB dealt with issues concerning machinery exported to England in 1983. The products were malfunctioning, which resulted in a need of maintenance, as well as lower demand. The same situation emerged in 1986, when Spanish customers complained about the machinery (ABS, OB-957 OV).

Box 5.7 Škoda car

The Škoda car company (officially Automobilové závody národní podnik – AZNP – Mladá Boleslav) was one of the pivotal companies in socialist Czechoslovakia. And it was one of the sources of badly needed convertible currency as well. The company was able to sell cars to the western markets even though they were considered there as technically obsolete, cheap, and possibly even not safe. Their price in comparison with western cars was relatively low. As a result, many jokes about Škoda cars circulated in Great Britain (one of the main export markets). One of them said: How to double the price of a Škoda car? – Fill the tank with petrol. The share of the Škoda car company on the British market was only 0.62% in 1983 (Nykryn 1988).

However, at the same time, Škoda cars were supposed to be the showcase of socialism partly because passenger car production was from a long tradition in Czechoslovakia. Vilímek describes in his profound research the situation and development in the company during normalization. He mentions that the rejection rate of some parts (e.g., cylinder heads) reached up to 50% at the end of the 1970s. The reasons were foremost bad technical conditions of the production machines and low quality of the used semi-finished products. The company had around 200 subcontractors and many of them were not able to deliver their parts in reasonable quality and on time. Škoda's dissatisfaction with them was permanent and enormous. For example, in some periods in the 1970s, the company's aerotaxi had to fly five times a day to Škoda subsidiary in Bratislava for door hinges to avoid an interruption of the assembly line (Vilímek 2012). Another problem was the permanent struggle with shortage of labour force. Škoda employed students, trainees, foreign workers (Polish, Vietnamese, Cubans), prisoners, and even Soviet soldiers! The amount of overtime work was extremely high – 9.5% of working hours (Vilímek 2012). Not surprisingly, the quality of the produced cars was appalling in some years – e.g., the company exported nearly 50 thousand cars in 1977 but 73% of them were complained about. The director of the company was removed at the end of the decade and investigated by the police mainly because of clientelism and overcharged demands for inputs. However, Vilímek comments that his behaviour was in accord with other managers at that time who tried to secure delivery of subcontracting parts or materials for their companies (Vilímek 2012). The company was under the permanent influence of high politics as well. It was, for example, forced to prepare for several years a cooperation on construction of a new car with a producer from East Germany. But these attempts at cooperation ended in 1979. A similar situation happened with the Bratislavské automobilové závody car factory (BAZ). The party centre tried to initiate car production located in Slovakia because of political pressure by high-ranking Slovak party members. When the BAZ was finally established, no one knew what the Bratislava-based company should produce. Consequently, the BAZ was subordinated to the AZNP in 1976 and became a highly unreliable subsidiary that was permanently struggling with overcapacity and lack of labour force (Šrein 1995).

At the beginning of the 1980s, the Communist Party made a decision about preparing a brand-new model of car – Favorit. The project classified among the binding government tasks. This status gave the car priority in construction and production and access to convertible currencies on the one hand. But on the other hand, it defined binding parameters of the car – for example fuel consumption, production price and stand-by weight. These became consequently obstacles – for example its designers wanted to make the car 15 centimetres longer, which, however, made it heavier, or they planned a bigger tank (Králík and Hrdlička 2016). But these were relatively minor issues because the construction had to undergo a fundamental technological change – the engine was shifted from the back to the front of the car (cars with a back engine were already a thing of the past). This technological change would have been difficult under any circumstances, but the regime insisted on extremely quick development. The chief engineer became Petr Hrdlička. The design of the new car was entrusted to an Italian company – Bertone. But the designers' ideas clashed with socialist reality. The designers, for example, proposed smaller/modern headlights, but these were impossible to produce in socialist Czechoslovakia and thus Favorit had to be content with unfashionable old large headlights. The technological change coerced purchases of machinery from the developed countries (ibidem). However, the contracted construction company did not build the assembly halls in the Škoda factory in time and thus these expensive machines were located on the courtyards and went rusty. Consequently, there were permanent attempts at sparing convertible currencies and installing, for example, Czech brakes instead of foreigner ones. But the quality of Czech products was low and specifically in the case of the brakes it was 75% lower in comparison to the western ones (Vilímek 2012). With the same intention, the company terminated purchasing West German carburetors at the end of 1988. Their delivery was instead contracted with a Czech company – Motor. But the company delivered only 300 carburettors by April 1989 – a supply that covered only one day of production. The consequence was that the workers parked the finished cars in the company's parking places, took away the carburetors, and re-installed them into the cars on the assembly line to avoid its interruption (ibidem).

Interestingly, Vilímek describes the practice of the StB in the company production and among others their extreme interest in the person of chief engineer Hrdlička. He was blamed for purchasing expensive western machines and licenses instead of using Czechoslovak subcontractors. But the secret police investigation concluded that these purchases were the only option and that his steps did not harm the socialist economy (Vilímek 2012).

Regardless of the frenetic effort, the start of the serial Favorit production had to be delayed mainly due to subcontractors, who were unprepared for the change. On the other hand, Králík writes about positive aspects, as some of the subcontractors were able to improve their attitude and production thanks to the experience with western markets (Králík and Hrdlička 2016). The car was in the end a relative success and without doubt a significant improvement when compared to the previous models.

At the end of the centrally planned period, Czechoslovakia was losing its position with engineering products even among the centrally planned consumers because they started to purchase engineering products from developed countries and Czechoslovak products became outdated (Komárek 1990).

5.5.2 Foreign investment

The economy was rather closed considering the cross-border investment as well as trade. Půlpán mentions that only 50 companies with foreign share operated in Czechoslovakia in the 1980s, compared to 500 companies in Hungary and Poland (Půlpán 1990). Even the common investment activity among COMECON members was generally rare. The author adds that, according to rules, the joined constructions stayed in ownership of the country where the construction was realized. The foreign participants thus did not have any ownership rights to the constructions – it can be considered as a kind of brotherhood help. Czechoslovakia contributed, for example, to the construction of oil pipeline Družba. Nykryn states that the Czechoslovaks participated only in nine multilateral projects of this kind and in several bilateral ones with the Soviet Union (Nykryn 1988). Voráček comments that the Soviet Union benefited from the common projects that were built on its territory with joined financing because the participants de facto provided credit to the Soviets (Voráček 1995).

One of the well-known common projects was the oil pipeline Družba (Friedship). It was presented as a huge victory of socialism. In practice, the construction needed import of many parts from the west. Up to 40% of the 100-centimetre steel pipes were purchased in Sweden, Italy, and later in West Germany even though NATO did not recommend these transactions (Vassiliou 2009).

Other forms of across-the-border investment were scarce too. Hába writes about providing credits to the COMECON member countries. He mentions that the credits charged an interest rate which was supposed to support prudent behaviour. On the other hand, rates were low because the banks did not seek profit, they simply followed the plan (Hába et al. 1988).

To support mutual investment, the International Investment Bank was founded in 1970. The intention was to support middle- and long-term loans for the COMECON member countries. Loans were granted for the implementation of joint investment projects, development programs, and constructions facilities provision. The Bank financed, for example, the construction of oil pipelines or Czech nuclear power plant Dukovany.

However, its activity was questionable as well. One of our respondents told us about experience from the launch of the bank. He said that the Czechoslovak representative for the first bank meeting in Moscow asked before his departure for a document/project that he could possibly present there. And he obtained a huge development project proposal of the Czech lorry producer Tatra Kopřivnice. Our respondent said:

> *And now imagine the bank official launch session in Moscow, so . . . when they signed and drank and everything, now somebody said: "Now the official part has ended and we should start working. And . . . who, then, who comes with a request?" There were no bids, but our man had the developmental plan of the Tatra Kopřivnice company, so they solemnly accepted the developmental plan, but it had been prepared in haste and was not really finished. . . . So, when the people in Kopřivnice learnt that their plan had been approved, they got shocked. [. . .] The plan comprised a lot of facilities, the city hall office, new administrative buildings and I do not know what . . . it included new railway stations and . . . (laughter) Well, but it was just because then, then people started thinking all day long what else they would include and so on.*
>
> *(head of department, engineering <ID037>)*

In the final stage of the communist rule, economists started to realize that the gap between the local economy and developed countries was unbeatable and it was not realistic to hope in catching up using merely the inner sources in the economy. One of the ways to bridge the gap was in cooperation with western manufactures and creating joint ventures. One of our respondents (director in textile industry, later deputy minister <ID057>) commented on the situation in the following way:

> *Well we could not use any financial indicators because the convertible currency did not have prices, it was nothing but the parameters of the machines, the parameters of*

the products that was what we compared with the world. And, of course, the parameters in the world were different from ours, so we followed the product line from the world manufacturer until we found a product that was more or less comparable and we looked at when the product had been manufactured and it was like 10–15 years such was the gap. So, thanks to that we did not have any great illusions about our competitiveness, and there was also a strong pressure in the Ministry of Industry to look for strategic partners for our key businesses that somehow formed the backbone of the economy.

I: *Who took this initiative?*

R: *It can't be said that it was one place, but it was a few places that demanded that without cooperation with foreign countries we could not get anywhere. And one of these places was, except for our ministry, the Ministry of Industry and Electrical Engineering. . . . And each meeting or most of these negotiations ended with "we have to buy it abroad." . . . so the idea was that as a part of the perestroika effort, we could open up to the west, we were not bold enough to sell it whole or even a majority.*

I: *And did this come into effect before the revolution?*

R: *It came into force before the Revolution.*

I: *But there was no case.*

R: *I only know one case and it was a shop, it was a textile shop. And I know the one who started it was an immigrant.*

I: *As a retailer? Retail?*

R: *It was wholesale. So, I know, this was the only case.*

I: *And what was the idea of the ministry with these companies, because, after all, the strategic partners, I suppose it was only for those big companies.*

R: *Well, the idea was that it would go to those big companies and companies that made the final product. And if we have these final producers at an appropriate level, they will just make sure the subcontractors are to their image. So, we looked at it like some kind of multiplier effect, in the direction of the economy.*

5.5.3 Business trips and foreign workers in Czechoslovakia

Our respondents mostly mentioned only temporary business trips abroad. Some of them stayed even in capitalist countries. Longer stays were rare, partly because the foreign posts were mostly occupied by employees of the PZOs. One of our responds told us: "Over time I managed to enter a group of people who were considered for a foreign stay, and finally, with my wife, we enjoyed three happy years in Syria" (operative in foreign trade <ID030>). Another one talked about foreign stays of his or her technicians abroad. And in the relaxed 1960s some were exceptionally allowed for longer stays in developed countries (for example one of the respondents spent two years in Switzerland). Generally, contacts with foreigners were highly limited and considered suspicious and the StB scrutinized all interactions (see Box 5.8).

Box 5.8 Contacts with foreigners in Zbrojovka Vsetín

Concerning the workers' contacts with foreigners, the state was almost paranoid. We register a number of reports from the StB investigation in the Zbrojovka Vsetín factory. The secret police investigated every worker that came back from abroad, namely from the capitalist states. The workers were asked how they evaluated the behaviour of the partner firms' representatives, and what they had seen in the foreign country. Some workers reported insufficient life conditions in the countries, such as one who was satisfied with the negotiations, but described the development in Yugoslavia in 1978 as declining, explaining the discourse with Tito's "dissent" policy due to his old age. More interestingly, a worker who arrived from the USA confirmed correct treatment from the partner. At the same time, he criticized the unqualified foreign staff who "borrow the tools from their customers since they do not possess their own." These reports felt rather fawning, inasmuch as they were to give impression of bad workers' conditions in foreign states, namely the capitalistic ones.

The StB was also watching closely emigrants, as well as their families who visited them. A CFO's deputy, whose son emigrated to Western Germany, and who went to visit him several times, was interviewed, investigated, and continuously watched. The same was true for other workers, such as a brother-in-law of an emigrant to Canada. Or an ex-wife of an emigrant to the USA, who unsuccessfully attempted to come back to the ČSSR in 1986, which was not permitted due to his "former adventurous nature and negative attitude towards socialism. He would also be provided with the US pensions, which would negatively influence the thoughts of the Czechoslovak people."

Moreover, the StB prevented the staff from any contacts with foreigners visiting the plant; only selected people could do so, and these were instructed in advance via the so-called "defensive talk proposal." It also screened the workers, and eventually prevented some from going abroad on behalf of the firm, because they might want to emigrate.

Lastly, the StB was watching closely workers with access to photocopiers, and it investigated the workers' stance on political issues as well, namely their stance on "issues in 1968–1969" (ABS, OB-957 OV).

However, workers travelled in the opposite direction and several of our respondents talked about experience with foreign workers in Czechoslovak companies. They came mostly from developing countries with socialistic orientation. Their stays were supposed to be partly expressing "international solidarity" with less developed countries, but it was foremost a way to moderate the permanent shortage of employees in the socialist Czechoslovak economy. Experience with foreign workers was evaluated by our respondents as generally very positive. Their jobs were mostly relatively easy – semi-automatic tasks. For example, assistant to the director in engineering <ID043> told us:

I: *Were any foreign workers employed in your company?*
R: *There, of course, the Vietnamese worked there. My first calculator is also from the workshop where the Vietnamese worked. I did not encounter any complications that would have been connected with these foreign workers, no really. They were accommodated in hostels. The big advantage was that they had mastered their work on those simple machine tools. They had a basic knowledge of Czech, so we could communicate with them. And they were willing to work six days a week, 12 hours a day [. . .] Then there was a kind of migration of the Slovaks. In Slovakia, perhaps, the professional opportunities were a bit smaller, so some Slovaks came to work here. But otherwise I do not remember other foreigners. [. . .] They did not do the assembly. These people did not do any final work, they did not work servicemen. They did simple, automated work which did not require much. You simply needed a labour force, as there were no automatic machines yet, that could do the work.*

A planner and head of supplying in an engineering company <ID007> shared his good experience with foreigner workers:

> *Vietnam sent here, sent workers, welders, and they learnt here, yeah, they worked for two years here, and it is possible to say that the company was very satisfied with them. I mean really satisfied. Because, firstly, they were really hardworking they did not talk back but what was the main thing, yeah, they had a firm hand and their muscles were really perfect. Yeah, they were just really happy with them, they just learnt it beautifully.*

And an operative in the SPK <ID019> continued:

> *Well . . . Vietnam, Mongolia, Laos and Cuba these cases were not exchange of labour, it was about education opportunities, we gave people from these countries the opportunity to learn a profession. Of course, you are talking about Mongolia, so I know there were a lot of people who were learning leather processing, but there were also people who were supposed to learn here, in our apprentice programmes, how to operate machines for the leather processing and the like.*

Some of our respondents had even semi-anecdotical experience with people working in Czechoslovakia. A power plant director <ID014> pointed out:

> *We had a lot of Cubans, blacks from Angola, but it was with the supply companies. Repair companies. They worked for someone else who worked for us. Yes, foreigners lived here, but they were not our employees . . . painters here, diggers there. . . . Servicemen, diggers, and so on. . . . There are villages where, there are . . . today the*

children are already adult, where simply there is a lady, she has three children and each of them is different shade. (laughter)."

A head of the technical department in an engineering company <ID020> spoke about business talent of foreigner workers:

At that time, relief workers came from Vietnam, Cuba, Algeria. I remember a constant inflow of various foreign workers who worked for us.

I: And how did they get here?
R: Through the PZO and the ministry . . . through our headquarters in some way and the people there were a lot of them. At that time, we had two hundred and eighty employees as a company, and twenty . . . sometimes even more, were foreigners. In particular, the Vietnamese were here and . . . they were the big traders already at the time, with all possible (laughs). When digital watches came out . . .
I: Screwdrivers (laughs).
R: . . . the digital watches, they had pockets full of these and all the employees bought them.

We can summarize the macroeconomic results. In general, economic growth was declining in a long-run horizon and the Czechoslovak economy was de facto stagnant in the 1980s. If we consider hidden inflation, the results were even worse. On the other hand, the economy was still able to deliver most of the staple goods on a regular basis and living standards were slowly improving. The planners did not allow huge macroeconomic imbalances. There were many distortions in the functioning of the system, and the declining export ability to the world markets demonstrated diminishing world competitiveness of Czechoslovak products. The economy was closed from other respects as well. It was nearly totally oriented towards the COMECON markets. International investment inflows and outflows were generally negligible. There were only very few joint companies – mostly with other CPEs countries. Both labour immigration and emigration rates were, with a few exceptions, low too. Generally, the economy was (similarly to the whole society) to a large extent isolated.

Notes

1 Socialist economies officially used a Net Material Product (Social Product) indicator. The main difference in comparison to the GDP was that it counted nearly solely material productions and excluded most of the services.
2 Czechoslovakia originally wanted to participate in the Marshall Plan, but refused it after pressure by the Soviet Union. Regardless of it, the impact of the 40-year-old event is marginal and such argumentation dubious.
3 Note that this book uses direct quotation of the exchange rate – it means that the exchange rate is expressed in the amount of crowns needed for a single unit of a foreign currency; for example, 21 crowns per one USD. Indirect quotation is used, for example, in the United States. It would mean that one crown corresponds to 1/21 of USD.

4 The word "convertible" in the name did not have any practical meaning.
5 At the end of the 1980s, companies could retain a small part of the gained convertible curries. However, this share was just 5% from the price of exported machinery and 3% in the case of consumption goods.
6 For example, Nykryn writes that Czechoslovak exports to Austria (one of the biggest western partners) consisted of 75% of coke, coal, raw materials, raw wood, and semi-manufactured wooden products; machinery accounted for only 6% of exports and the rest were consumption goods (Nykryn 1988).

6 Results and conclusions

In the previous chapters, we walked the journey from the description of the functioning of the society in socialist Czechoslovakia, via the Marxist-Leninist ideology, the application of this ideology into the formal settings of the Czechoslovak model, the everyday functioning of the economy, and up to the economic outcomes. The transformation between the respective tiers created problems of its own and sowed the seeds of the economic outcomes. This chapter presents the general conclusions of our analysis.

One of the conclusions is that the everyday practice was much more colourful than could be expected from the formal settings of the model. Our respondents provided us with their experiences from the functioning of the model and their personal evidence often varied and sometimes was even opposite. They described the regime as both strict as well as relaxed. At times the communist interventions were commented on as being totally destructive and other times as being helpful. Some of the then managers took the initiative while others were absolutely passive, etc. Together, it provides a plastic picture of the everyday economic life in the socialist country.

There were some aspects of the functioning of the socialist model that could be interpreted in a positive way, at least from the macroeconomic point of view. The most positive one was that the planners in charge of the everyday functioning did not allow huge macroeconomic imbalances and the consequent falling apart of the economic system. For example, Poland and Yugoslavia suffered from hyperinflation, which brought huge economic costs. The Czechoslovak planners were able to avoid such discrepancies – they managed to keep inflation within reasonable margins, and maintained negligible public and foreign debts as well as trade balance. The regime considered the elimination of unemployment as one of its biggest achievements. From an economist's point of view, zero unemployment results in the malfunctioning of the labour market regardless of the fact that such a state obviously provided security for the labour force, which most of the employees appreciated. Moreover, differences in income among people were very low, which most people acknowledge as well. There were other aspects at a micro level that, at minimum in the short run, were possible to be interpreted as being positive – the cutthroat market competition was replaced by cooperation among companies. The overall environment was generally softer – government always provided help to companies. And the proponents of the socialist system often mentioned stability (against the chaotic markets) as one of the great achievements. The regime boasted about its alleged achievements up until its very end. For example, Hába in 1988 wrote: "Imperialism cannot recover the lost historical initiative and reverse the development of the contemporary world. The main path of development is determined by the world socialist system, the international working class, all the revolutionary forces" (Hába et al. 1988, p. 61).

What is more, the advocates of the system still try to convince readers, quoting long lines of numbers that should demonstrate the huge success in growth of living standard, production of steel, or nearly any other commodity during the communist rule after 1948 (see for example Štrougal 2009). It is, of course, true that the economy was growing and living standards were improving. And indeed, the experiment was viable for several decades and the economy did not collapse. However, growth appeared in the given period in all normal economies and consequently living standards were improving as well. Thus, the true state of the economy under the planned system reveals itself only in international comparison, which is something that its advocates regularly omit to carry out. The only comparison they provided on a regular basis was the current state of the economy compared with the state before the communist coup. That means right after the disastrous WWII. The actual condition of the system appeared at both macro as well as micro levels. The real outcome was that, in the long run, the socialist economic system did not have any chance to compete with the market economies – see Figure 5.4 (GDP per capita comparison with Austria). The trend in economic growth was declining together with depletion sources for extensive economic growth. At a micro level, the strongest evidence of lagging behind was provided by the inability to saturate the insatiable hunger for convertible currencies. Even though the system tried its best to obtain dollars or German marks, the economy was not able to generate goods that would be sellable on demanding western markets. And if there were any exports, they were mostly goods with low added value, such as wood or sulphuric acid. Additionally, these exportable goods often obtained subsidies from the government, had to be produced on western machineries, or needed to add western components to be sellable. Total majority of the socialist products could not be offered on the western markets because of low quality or their technological retardation.

The general conclusion is that Czechoslovakia was lagging behind the developed countries. There is one topic that runs like a thread throughout our whole analysis – efficiency/productivity. Its low level was the cause behind the appalling economic outcomes and it stood in straight contrast to capitalist obsession of profit and effectivity. Lenin expected that superior productivity would be the engine of the socialist/communist system dominance above capitalism, which "will be utterly vanquished" (e.g. Lenin 1972c). Moreover, some even believed that such changes in the Soviet Union were really happening: "The growth of the socialist system is conditioned by constantly growing labour productivity, in the Soviet Union, unbelievable changes happen. And even in our economy, we are witnessing this. We are going through the greatest breakthrough in our history. We are building socialist produce" (Oliva 1952, p. 22). The reality was in fact opposite and productivity was the weakest aspect of the socialist economic system. The question is why efficiency was so weak. We are going to summarize the answers dealt with in the previous chapters. We consider the topic of productivity from the points of view of the main discussed topics. We generally follow the previous themes – ideology (including the consequences of nationalization and wage levelling), the central planning on its own – behaviour of the centre and behaviour of companies with emphasis on absence of competition, rigidity of the system and technological retardation. The last subtopic deals with the role of the communist party in the socialist economic system.

6.1 Ideology

We started our argumentation about the centrally planned system with a description of the Marxist-Leninist philosophy (Chapter 2). From the economic point of view, the problem was that, in Marx's concept, philosophical aspects dominated over economic ones. The ideology was based on several presumptions and goals. The economy was supposed to be a tool helping to achieve these high goals, but Marxism on its own offered highly limited hints about practically accomplishing these ambitious ideas. The result was that only the later ideologists and foremost the everyday practice were supposed to put these ideas into practice. The very core of the economic problems lay in the transfer of the grand ideas into day-to-day practice. The practical implementation of the ideas became more complicated than the ideologists probably had expected. Their expectations that new scientific attitudes or technological development would generate a totally different sort of economy became just a dream. These earthbound problems turned out to be the stumbling blocks to efforts trying to bring the grandiose ideas into practice. We need to add that economics is a pragmatic science and provides some understanding of the functioning of the economic systems. It was hubris on the side of the communist ideologists (who mostly were not economists) to believe that they were able to create an entirely new economic system based on their new "laws." We might remember Stalin's first law – "the securing of the maximum satisfaction of the constantly rising material and cultural requirements of the whole of society through the continuous expansion and perfection of socialist production on the basis of higher techniques" – which is nothing more than a dream or political manipulation. From an economic point of view, there is nothing in the statement that would justify the term "law" and the economy never followed it either. The statement does not have anything in common with understanding of the economic systems. The consequence was that the system was based, from economists' point of view, on nonsenses with many side effects that the ideologists (probably) did not realize. It may remind readers of the ideas behind Bastiat's famous "That Which Is Seen, and That Which Is Not Seen" (Bastiat 1995). People often do not understand the problem in its entirety, because there is a difference between experience and foresight. And since only experience is that which is seen, the system's advocates easily forget to realize the consequences and lost opportunities that might be and certainly often are not as positive as the initial results are. People who do not understand the problem offer "easy" solutions that have strongly negative side effects which the advocates do not realize because they do not understand the roots of the problem or real functioning of the system.

There were several economic goals from an ideological perspective that were supposed to be achieved by the introduction of the system. We argued that the main ideological condition for development of socialism was in elimination of private ownership, which was considered responsible for the evils of the capitalist system and the cause for exploitation of workers (Chapter 2). Nationalization, introduced by the fathers of socialism, became the natural reaction to this injustice. Consequently, nationalization in practice led to central planning because the nationalized companies had to be somehow governed. The ideologists were supposed to create a new form of society/economy, in which workers would willingly take the initiative because they would not be exploited by capitalists anymore. At the same time, totally "new socialist men" would arise that would work hard without material rewards just for the better future of all beings. To eliminate any injustice, it was supposed that all the labour would be rewarded equally in general. The ideologists likewise believed that the mix of these highly motivated people and scientifically planned economy would result in achieving great economic results and beating the chaotic markets with exploited, demotivated, and suffering labour force. These grand and utopian ideas inevitably ran into problems in the course of their transformation to day-to-day practice and crushed against economic reality. They possibly achieved some of their goals. However, the unintended or ill-conceived aspects of the system thwarted these achievements. We pay attention to respective steps in this ideological construct and their deficiencies. Even though the consequences of the settings were naturally interwoven. We generally assume that companies (and even the centre) behaved as rational agents although the economic system was distorted. All the participants reacted to the nudges (or their absence) provided by the general environment. At the same time there were, without doubts, natural exceptions that worked in a different way (more efficient, more active, or a more initiative way) but these were just exceptions.

To sum it up – the grand utopian visions that expected change in human behaviour collided with human nature. Some people surely followed these ideas, especially immediately after the war, but the numbers of idealists shrunk to just a small fraction by the 1980s. The distant dream of reaching "the ultimate goal" (communism) was not as attractive as the ideologists had hoped.

6.1.1 Consequences of (nearly) entire nationalization and income levelling in the society

The first step in eliminating exploitation in the society was nationalization. The Czechoslovak economy was nearly entirely nationalized in the first years after the establishment of the communist regime. The elimination of private property of production means was at the same time supposed to safeguard very similar rewards for everybody. The system really achieved near-entire elimination of income differences among the people, as we documented. The natural and unsurprising side effect was in negative motivation of both employees as well as managers. Interestingly, neither representatives of the regime (Štrougal) nor its supporters (e.g., Bottomore, who in 1990 still believed that socialistic economies were functioning "very well") mention any problems with motivation (Štrougal 2009; Bottomore 1990). They probably do not realize or do not want to realize it. At the beginning of the socialist rule some people truly believed in a better future and were willing to work hard for it, this attitude evaporated during the time even among these few. The naïve/idealistic/stupid views could be documented for example by Oliva who wrote:

> *The bourgeois economists prophesied that the removal of private property would do away with all initiative, but what we are witnessing is not just initiative, but mass initiative, something impossible to achieve in capitalism. In one of our most successful cooperatives, the February 25 Cooperative [name glorifying the communist coup] in Václavice, prizes were given to the best work teams, for example an annual trophy banner, various utilities, such as radio receivers, etc. Team compete against one another and desire to be the next banner holding team. They go after the banner, not the material possessions, which are, naturally, coveted. Work becomes a matter of honour and glory.*
>
> (Oliva 1952, p. 21)

These sentences would sound ridiculous and ironical already in the 1980s.

Other step was the levelling of income. It eliminated the source inequality (or envy), but at the same time eliminated motivation because nonmaterial rewards (in the form of a hoped-for better future or honours and medals) were not functional incentives for the absolute majority of population. We well documented that during our study period monetory incentives stayed by far the most important stimulus for work.

Motivation was even more distorted by labour shortage and near impossibility to lay off employees. Another aspect to be considered is the emphasis on wage levelling as it also led to the suppression of employees' motivation. Besides the fact that wages did not serve as positive motivation, they neither served as a deterrent for low-performing workers.

Almost all respondents said that they had little opportunity to motivate their subordinates and that the whole system was not motivating. Moreover, the paternalistic features of the system were easy to abuse. A former communist and later dissident Karel Bartošek summarized it just one month before the invasion of the Warsaw Pact forces into Czechoslovakia in 1968: "Bureaucratic system had its support even among 'ordinary people.' It allowed dishonesty in labour process [. . .] freedom of not doing something useful and being paid, 'freedom of stealing' (not just materialized, but also 'time stealing' for oneself) was significant. One of the sad mottos of that time was: who doesn't steal, steals from his family. [. . .] Corruption was spreading especially on the field of services – people said 'You can get everything if you have connections'" (Bartošek 1968, p. 3).

The regime was aware of the insufficient level of motivation and consequent lower productivity. The hardliners believed in the application of honours and medals. However, these were not motivation factors for majority of people. Some employees or managers tried hard without adequate material rewards just because they wanted to do their best. But the majority was ill motivated. On a more practical level the regime applied various systems, such as khozraschyot, which in practice expressed resignation to the nonmaterial motivation of people. But the method generally failed to improve motivation in an environment marked by a high level of wage levelling and common ownership. The regime knew it. For example, the authors of inner information for members of the Central Committee of the Communist Party from 1987 wrote:

> *In some of the companies, for example in Adast Adamov, ideas spread among the workers and technicians that obligation movement would not be necessary, if they had a modern machinery park, sufficient amount of quality raw materials and equipment.* (*ČSSR. Sekretariát ÚV KSČ 1987, p. 12*)

State ownership broke the motivation of owners who under normal circumstances seek opportunities and generally work hard to increase efficiency of using their property. Moreover, the state ownership of production means had other side effects. It, in fact, had to create the "casual" environment (including soft budget constraint). Since companies were state owned and the state was fully responsible for them, it is not surprising that it was, for example, not willing to let them go bankrupt. There were obviously ideological reasons connected with employment safeguards, but in practice the system could never allow its own property to fail. Something like Schumpeter's creative destruction was thus entirely impossible, and it contributed to a static business environment and low efficiency. At the same time, the centre was not able to force or convince companies to be efficient (partly because it was not much intended – the goal was merely to meet the plan), and in fact the centre had to provide subsidies to keep many inefficient companies afloat (or for example negative turnover tax). It also could not allow companies to "earn" too much money and it had to drain "excess" money from the system. If a company was successful, the centre applied the index method and it wanted even higher production in the following year and/or simply taxed the company. These steps sent pervasive signals and were demotivating for the behaviour of the companies as well. If they tried they were "punished" by higher tasks next year which threatened the bonuses, and if they were not successful they received subsidies in some form.

Proponents of the regime gave examples of successful new products or new technologies. And it could be even true. We documented several examples of progressive directors (Severka, Gramozávody, or Slušovice). However, these cases were exceptions in the overall static economic environment. In most of the cases the managers did not intend to seek new opportunities, did not want to take risks, or generally did not struggle to be efficient. There were no reasons for such active behaviour because the task was not to be efficient but to meet the plan. Exceptions never form the system (in any type of an economy), and therefore the exceptions of progressive management could not improve the overall level of efficiency because ordinary (average) companies are important and the average level of efficiency in socialism was low.

6.2 Impact of central planning

The next step in our analysis was central planning that resulted from nationalization. We followed the previous structure and considered behaviour of the centre, companies, and the role of the Communist Party in overall efficiency of the system.

6.2.1 Behaviour of the centre

Economic systems are very complex. The whole idea of organizing and governing the economy, even though with "only" 15 million inhabitants, hundreds of thousands of products and thousands of companies, is presumptuous. We can compare it with the famous case of the production of a pencil (Read 1999). The case shows the difficulty of production of such a very simple product as a pencil. The complexity is not even imaginable by the majority of people. The whole process of producing pencils has to start with planting of a tree. Someone then, after many years, has to cut the tree trunk with a chainsaw that someone had to invent, assemble, and deliver. If you imagine the production of a chainsaw, it is again a very intricate process. The trunk has to be transported to a sawmill on a lorry that someone had to design and produce. The sawmill and the lorry were again very difficult to produce with a complexity of their own. Meanwhile, somewhere on the other side of the world someone else had to mine graphite, another one produce lacquer, gum, etc. To sum it up, there were millions of people working all around the world without knowing each other and most of them without knowledge of the final product – the pencil. It works on its own without organizing it and it is very difficult to imagine that anyone could really dare to organize the whole process. Consider that the central planners wanted to organize not only such (on its own) a difficult production of pencils but everything in the economy. We do not know the number of products in the socialist economy and it was definitely less than Amazon.com sells today (2018) – 353 million products – but it was anyway a very high number. Moreover, the ideologists believed themselves to be more efficient than markets. It somehow worked only because the planned system continued after the market system and the planners knew at the beginning among others the productions hierarchies or demand for pencils etc. Because without past data we do not know how many pencils are consumed, and we are sure no one does. Starting from the scratch, any attempt at a scientific calculation would equal a mere look out of the window. Is the demanded number of pencils 20 thousand, 1 million, 3 million, or 20 million?

Under these circumstances, the system would immediately collapse because it would never be able to balance any of these infinite imbalances.

Additionally, there was no safeguard that the system would tend to equilibrium especially when prices, which carry information to participants in the market economies, were fixed and, at the level of retail prices, often irrationally low. This socialist achievement contributed to wasting. On the other hand, the fixed prices were a necessity because they would be impossible to plan or calculate in real time according to changes in demand and supply, as it happens in markets economies. This only added to the static character of the system. Regardless of it, the equilibrium was very difficult to achieve, and it expected to avoid any huge (external) shock to the system. As our respondent from SPK told us the general plan expected a range between 96% to 104%. The consequence was not only shortage, but the appearance of idle goods as well. It was generally difficult to achieve satisfaction of the real needs of the participants. They were not known in the first place even if the centre genuinely tried to satisfy them.

The economic centre behaved, in our view, rationally and reacted to nudges as any other participant in the system. It reacted foremost to political assignments – presumably meeting the plan. We documented that even the economic part of the centre (the SPK) lied to the political part and concealed reserves (Box 4.1) from politicians in case of abrupt political requirement. It is not astonishing because the planners were evaluated based on the achieved plan by people (politically in power) who did not understand economics and could be generally rather simple and often uneducated. The centre at the same time tried to squeeze companies and force them to efficiency (for example by the index method) but meeting the plan was for everybody the predominant task. The centre was further restricted by its limited knowledge of information in the society and economy. Nevertheless, it believed in an omnipotent state that knows everything and is able to make the best decisions.

Another aspect with negative influence on efficiency was a generally complicated structure of directing companies. The orders went through three of four different layers and had to get through ossified bureaucracy at all these levels.

6.2.2 Behaviour of companies in the system

The companies were naturally the main actors of the efficiency of the economic system. There were several aspects that tied the efficiency up. The first of them was the general directing system, but we should consider the economic environment without competition, the rigidity of the system, and technological retardation as well. Interestingly, Faltus writes that the official slogan was that rentability at the company level had to yield to the needs of the society and to efficiency from the point of view of the whole economy (Faltus 1995). The question is how the whole system was supposed to achieve efficiency once its units were inefficient.

The companies as well as the centre behaved as rational agents. They reacted to the assignments from the superior institutions – meaning foremost meeting the plan. All their activities were subordinated to this goal regardless of efficiency or productivity. We documented that the managers were able and willing to do nearly anything to meet the plan (including falsification of economic results).

But at a less dramatic level they had to foremost create reserves. This hoarding, which appeared at all levels of the planning hierarchy (from the SPK, via the ministries and the VHJs up to the individual companies), was inevitable in an environment marked by omnipresent scarcity. Naturally, a reasonable level of reserves is necessary in any economic activity, but the size of the reserves in central planning (including raw materials, semi-manufactured goods, or labour force) were highly exceeding any rational level. It led, for example, to perverse situations when companies were on the one hand in need of a labour force while, at the same time, they over-employed huge numbers of people who did not do anything valuable. This is just one of the examples of the enormous wasting of resources – consider for example the weight of the machineries that was partially caused by the planned incentives (plan in gross value), partially by obsolete technologies, and partially by missing incentives to produce anything lighter and therefore cut the costs. Thus, the economic system led to an absurd situation of pervasive shortage accompanied by a giant wasting of sources. Moreover, piling up reserves was meanwhile a cause of deepening shortage and thus it became one of the vicious circles that was pulling overall efficiency down.

The second determinant of companies' efficiency was in attempts at negotiating a "reasonable" plan. The companies' natural tendency was in reducing the plan to ensure its meeting. It was again inevitable natural behaviour. The centre possibly wanted to force the companies to reveal their true abilities, but this effort led to information asymmetry and the strong will of the companies. The consequence was that the companies generally intended to maximize their inputs and minimize their planned outcomes or at minimum the incentives went in this direction. Hardly any other behaviour could be less efficient. These trends were deepened by limited competition.

The competitive pressures among companies pressures: are the main engine of progress in market economies. This competition is based on profit (and as such unacceptable for socialist ideologists). It can be limited, for example, by monopolies but nevertheless it is the crucial aspect of market economies. The CPE model substituted competition by organizing the entire production from the centre. We argued that the economic structures were in the end much more monopolistic than in the market economy. The overall environment forced companies to further cooperation as our respondents told us. That was partly aligned with the view of the regime ideologists, who believed in the substitution of competitive pressures from other companies by "socialist competition." The companies were supposed to work hard to be efficient without the competitive pressure that was considered as wasting of their energies. The ideologists possibly believed that companies (or their managers) would voluntarily improve their efficiency just because they thus contributed to the creation of the great new world order. Or because the scientifically organized economy would force/convince them towards efficiency. And possibly they really expected that the companies would be just following the orders of the superior institutions. These assumptions underestimated the rational behaviour of the companies that just reacted to nudges from the system and they followed their own goals. It generally seems that the ideologists did not understand (or underestimated) the role that competition plays in the economic systems, nor the incentives they themselves were creating. Competition is an unpleasant aspect that companies generally dislike, but it is the force behind improvement at the same time. It is only presumable that socialist companies that were not under pressure of their (neither domestic nor foreign) competitors were not forced to be efficient and to permanently improve quality of their production.

We mentioned that the proponents of the regime believed that one of the key advantages was stability. However, stability is in practice very close to rigidity. The world is changing every second and thus one could expect that the planning system with five-year or one-year plans was under these circumstances very static and necessarily insufficiently flexible. This characteristic was fully incorporated in the lack of fashion goods that the economic system was not able to deliver at all. However, it foremost appeared in the omnipresent scarcity as well. One of our respondents (general director in knitting industry, later deputy minister <IDO73>) even considered inflexibility as the crucial drawback of the system. He summarized it in the following way:

I: *Well, you said that when all the general managers of all these VHJs met, you actually agreed on the rather unpleasant state of the economy, right? So if you were to summarize and say, would you identified it as the key problem? Was it the rigidity? That the plan, as if it tied the companies and prevented them from any attempt to respond to trends or anything? So, what was the state of the economy in the second half of the 80s anyway?*

R: *That's exactly what we discussed in that meeting more than anything. And we put things down to paper and drew plans looking for what change was to be introduced, you see? Cause, the more a white collar dwells on detail and elaborates on detail, the worse this rigidity gets and makes it virtually impossible to react to changes. And as it is all based on these timelines that are artificially created, what happens is that the dogma gets as it gets. And what happens is that the plan is not met and that the producer negotiates some change, even at the expense of lower production, capacity, this escapes the planners totally and they just keep the same year in and year out. It's because they don't have contact with the bottom, with the production level.*

The technological gap, which contributed to low efficiency, was the reason as well as the consequence of the malfunctioning economic model. Companies were not under the pressure of competition and they took advantage of the low cost of the labour force. They were isolated from the world markets and thus they were generally not motivated to improve their technologies. Šulc even writes:

> *Companies in the centrally planned system are characterized by a typical neglect of technological advancement, an effort to maintain established production as long as possible, efforts to minimize the number of people involved in research and development, who are considered by the plan as unproductive, an effort to replace growing production demands by more extensive material consumption, artificial cooperation, etc.*
> *(Šulc 2004, p. 115)*

The truth is that the technological lagging behind was intensified by an embargo that the western countries applied against the socialist economies, which was something the advocates of the regime have always complained about (e.g., Štrougal 2009). Nevertheless, the embargo was foremost targeted at blocking military technologies. In addition, and above all, the regime permanently proclaimed its technological superiority, which had no need of technologies from the rotting capitalism. Especially as long as it could make use of the "indefinite resources" of the whole "camp of peace under the leadership of the Soviet Union." Moreover, most of the western technologies were perfectly accessible, but their potential purchase collided with an absolute shortage of convertible currencies for imports. The consequence was that the Czechoslovak production was obsolete because it was produced by means of old technologies (the machinery was old; sometimes even from the interwar period). As a result, it was uncompetitive on the world market and it could not generate convertible currencies that were needed for the import of technologies which could have been used to manufacture more competitive products. To put it in other words, the consequence was another vicious circle that kept the efficiency low. However, the troubles sprang from problems in the domestic economy.

The economy was inefficient, therefore it did not generate enough funds (among others) for investment and thus for the replacement of machinery. This state was worsened by an inefficient directing of investment by orders of the centre, which responded to the pressure of the respective companies. It resulted in a huge investment gap and obsolete machinery park. The situation is aptly summarized in a question asked by MP Flídr: "What can be expected of the machinery base of the Agrozet Prostějov company, whose average age is 23 years?" This state resulted in a situation when the workers were not able to produce competitive goods so the production generated less and less funds for investment including technologies (which applies to consumption as well) and this further worsened efficiency and contributed to the lagging behind the developed countries. It can be added that the regime was so desperate that it regarded the stealing of technologies by espionage as perfectly fair.

6.2.3 The Communist Party

The efficiency of the economic system was even more distorted by the activity of the Communist Party. The party was fully responsible for the economy because of its leading, constitutionally anchored, role. At a personal level, the degree of influence of the Communist Party was manifested by the way it selected people not according to their abilities or knowledge but according to their loyalty to the regime. The best talents did not have a chance of promotion if they were unwilling at minimum to pretend acceptance of the ideology. This biased selection, without doubts, in a long run negatively resonated in the efficiency of the whole economic system.

The direct role of the party at a macroeconomic level started with Party Congresses that defined the tasks for the following five-year plan. However, it spread throughout the whole economic system up to interferences in basic organizations at a micro level. It generally expressed the view that the party knew what was best for the whole society. The interventions were often disruptive and lacked economic rationality.

Nevertheless, the party was not undivided, and its attitudes towards the economy oscillated. These oscillations are visible on the reform attempts that in practice meant to give the companies more freedom with hope that they would become more efficient and that economic growth would become more intensive, which expresses the same idea at a macroeconomic level. But all the reform attempts ultimately failed. It was partly because the regime was never able to overcome the main barrier to efficiency, which was in general low motivation connected with state ownership. But the struggle had another obstacle in lasting fights between conservatives and reformers. The former, who were often in the position of decision-makers, were often overwhelmed by their own illusions and possibly their own propaganda. They keep their views of superiority of the socialist system up until today (see, for example, interviews in Vaněk and Urbášek 2005). Moreover, they, of course, wanted to stay in power and were (rightfully) worried about reforms or changes.

But the communist reformers were blinded by their own illusions as well (Štrougal 2009). They believed in a switch to intensive economic growth. They were unable to understand that the extensive character of their economic system (read inefficiency) was inherently, unavoidably and unsurpassably rooted in the system. It was the very essence of the planned economies (in all the socialist countries regardless of the variant or the reforms).

Another important aspect was, in our view, the isolation of the whole society, denial of critical thinking, and general disapproval of nearly any criticism as capitalist propaganda. Reluctance to reforms among the high-ranking communists lasted until the fall of the communist regime. Using archive materials, Handl writes about disputes in this group in 1989. He documents opinion controversies between conservative and progressive powers in the Presidium of Central Committee. The Prime Minister presented a critical analysis of the state of the economy. One conservative MP even reacted that he could not understand the critical attitude of the analysis and called it "the Wailing Wall." The Secretary General of the Communist Party called for unity and expressed his worries regarding the beginning of the "Hungarian development" (Handl 2018). Such advocates of the regime even today still blame Perestroika for the fall of the regime (for example respondents in Vaněk and Urbášek 2005). It means that they were not willing to realize the true state of the economy or that they trivialized it and in contrast idealized the achievements of the system.

The macroeconomic outcomes had obviously their roots at the microeconomic level, foremost in low efficiency. We argued that all participants, in fact, worked against efficiency. And at the same time, the ideologists of socialism believed in "scientific" governing of the economy. They believed in the new economic rules that would be materialized with the centrally planned economic system. In practice, they did not understand the common rules of the functioning of economic systems and often lacked even common sense. The communist ideologists and economists believed that they "shall transform the whole world, and shall command the wind and rain." As young pioneers would sing:

> *Boys and girls, forward, we are building a new world, one – it has little power, so all hands to the work, we are building a new world, boys and girls, forward! We shall light up the sun of luck, for everyone it will shine, we shall command the wind, the rain when it should blow and when it should rain. We shall turn the whole country into a flood of red blossoms, we can do it all united from the east to the west!*

And it was the economy that betrayed them in the end. The reason why the economy betrayed them was that the proponents made several mistakes in their assumptions about the economy and behaviour of ordinary people as well as companies, which eventually resulted in the unfortunate economic results. There were probably multiple overlapping reasons that contributed to the fall of the socialist regime but material/consumption lagging behind the geographically nearby capitalist countries was definitely one of them.

The economy was obviously only one of the deficiencies of the socialist system and not the worst one, in our view. The worst was the absence of freedoms in all aspects of life and fear to express one's own opinions and views. This lack of freedom and pervasive fears de facto influenced the economic outcomes of the regime as well, because without freedoms there is no creativity and thus no dynamics in economic sphere. Capitalism is efficient among others because it allows market participants to be highly creative. What socialist ideologists considered to be chaos is, in fact, a fertile ground for economic vitality.

References

ABS, A34/1, inv.j. 1261. Archiv bezpečnostních složek, KR ochrana průmyslu a zemědělství – svodné informace 5. odboru II. S. Sign. A34/1, inventární jednotka 1261.
ABS OB-282 BN. Archiv bezpečnostních složek, sbírka Objektové svazky, reg. č. OB-282 BN, krycí název "Průmyslovák" (reg. č. 14996 BN).
ABS, OB-957 OV. Archiv bezpečnostních složek, sbírka Objektové svazky, arch. č. OB-957 OV, krycí název "Obrana" (reg. č. 5550 Vsetín).
ABS, OBŽ-17366 PL. Archiv bezpečnostních složek, sbírka Objektové svazky, arch. č. OBŽ-17366 PL, krycí název "Škoda").
Academy of Sciences of the U.S.S.R. (1957). *Political Economy*. London: Lawrence & Wishart.
Act No. 114/1948 Coll., on the nationalization of some further industrial and other enterprises and factories, and on adjustments of some relations of the nationalized and national enterprises.
Act No. 115/1948 Coll., on the nationalization of some further industrial and production enterprises and factories in the food industry, and on adjustments of some relations of the nationalized and national enterprises in this branch.
Act No. 150/1948 Coll., Constitution of the Czechoslovak Republic.
Act No. 41/1959 Coll., on the State Planning Comission.
Act No. 100/1960 Coll., Constitution of the Czechoslovak Socialist Republic.
Act No. 140/1961 Coll., Criminal code.
Act No. 36/1964 Coll., on the organization structure of Courts and election.
Act No. 44/1971 Coll., on the election to the Federal assembly.
Act No. 121/1975 Coll., on the social security.
Act No. 69/1976 Coll., on the state plan of the development of the national economy of the Czechoslovak Socialist Republic for 1976–1980 (on the sixth five-year plan).
Act No. 129/1985 Coll., by the Czech National Council, on the state plan of the development of the national economy of the Czech Socialist Republic for 1986.
Act No. 88/1988 Coll., on the state enterprise.
Adam, J. (1995). *Why Did the Socialist System Collapse in Central and Eastern Europe?* Houndhills: MacMillan Press.
Adamec, L. (1989). Zpráva předsedy vlády ČSSR o vývoji národního hospodářství a současných úkolech. *Federální shromáždění*, 20th June.
Aleksijevič, S. A. (2017). *Modlitba za Černobyl: Kronika budoucnosti*. Příbram: Pistorius & Olšanská.
Arltová, M., Langhamrová, J., & Langhamrová, J. (2013). Development of Life Expectancy in the Czech Republic in Years 1920–2010 with an Outlook to 2050. *Prague Economic Papers*, 22(1), pp. 125–143.

Åslund, A., Boone, P., & Johnson, S. (2001). Escaping the Under-Reform Trap. *IMF Staff Papers*, 48, Special Issue 2001.

Bálek, A. (1995). Přesun zdrojů z České republiky do Slovenské republiky a stabilita Československa. In: Váňa, D., *Systém centrálně plánovaných ekonomik v zemích střední a jihovýchodní Evropy a příčiny jeho rozpadu: Praha, 24.–26. března 1994*. Praha: Vysoká škola ekonomická.

Bálek, A. (1998). Vývoj výkonnosti československé a české ekonomiky v 70. letech. *Acta Oeconomica Pragensia*, 5(5), p. 101.

Bálek, A. (2007). Československá ekonomika v osmdesátých letech 20. století. *Acta Oeconomica Pragensia*, 15(7).

Baňouch, H. (2009). Hospodářské právo. In: Bobek, M., & Molek, P., *Šimíček: Komunistické právo v Československu: Kapitoly z dějin bezpráví*. Brno: Mezinárodní politologický ústav, Masarykova univerzita.

Bartošek, K. (1968). Revoluce proti byrokratismu? *Rudé právo*, 48(197), 18th July.

Bastiat, F. (1995). *Selected Essays on Political Economy*. Irvington-on-Hudson: Foundation for Economic Education.

Bata. (1991). *Významný krok do budoucnosti: Úvahy o českém a slovenském obuvnickém průmyslu*.

Bauer, M. (2005). Karel Kouba a jeho místo v českém ekonomickém myšlení. *Politická ekonomie*, 53(4), pp. 527–543.

Bieliková, J. (1984). *Dějiny Komunistické strany Československa v datech*. Praha: Svoboda.

Boenisch, P., & Schneider, L. (2013). The Social Capital Legacy of Communism-Results from the Berlin Wall Experiment. *European Journal of Political Economy, Elsevier*, 32(C), pp. 391–411.

Borensztein, E., & Masson, P. R. (1995). Devizové režimy v dříve centrálně plánovaných ekonomikách. IMF Occassional Paper 102, IMF, 1993. In: Bulíř, A., & Jonáš, J., *Ekonomie reformy*. Praha: Management Press.

Bottomore, T. (1990). *The Socialist Economy: Theory & Practice*. New York: Harvester Wheatsheaf.

Brada, J., Dvořák, P., Kodera, J., Mandel, M., Musílek, P., & Revenda, Z. (1996). *Peněžní ekonomie a bankovnictví*. 1st ed. Praha: Management Press.

Bukharin, N., & Preobrazhensky, E. (1969). *The ABC of Communism*. London: Penguin Books.

Čapka, F., & Lunerová, J. (2012). *1948: Vítězný únor: cesta k převratu*. Brno: CPress.

Carr, E. H. (1966). *The Bolshevik Revolution 1917–23*. London: Penguin Books.

Černý, P. (2008). *Právní ochrana před extremismem*. Beckova edice právní instituty. Praha: C.H. Beck.

Češka, J. (2013). *Československo: Česká a Slovenská federativní republika: Přehled oficiální statistiky v letech 1980–1992*. Praha: Futura.

Císař, J. (1995). Střední stav v Československu v období administrativně direktivního modelu. In: Váňa, D., *Systém centrálně plánovaných ekonomik v zemích střední a jihovýchodní Evropy a příčiny jeho rozpadu: Praha, 24.–26. března 1994*. Praha: Vysoká škola ekonomická.

Clarke, S. (1994). *Marx's Theory of Crisis*. Basingstoke: Palgrave Macmillan.

Coase, R. (1991). The Institutional Structure of Production. *Price Lecture to the Memory of Alfred Nobel*, Stockholm, 9th December.

Coufalová, L., Lipovská, H., & Žídek, L. (2017). Economic Crimes in the Shortage Economy. *Proceedings of the Law & Political Science Conference*, Vienna, pp. 29–51.

Coufalová, L., Mikula, S., & Žídek, L. (2017). Misreporting in Financial Statements in a Centrally Planned Economy: A Case of Czechoslovak Companies in Late Socialism. *European Historical Economics Society Conference*, Tübingen.

Coufalová, L., Mikula, Š., & Žídek, L. (2019). Competitiveness of Czechoslovak exports under socialism and its impact on industries output growth after 1989. *Economics of Transition* (in press).

ČSSR. Chamber of Deputies 1971–1986. Parliament of the Czech Republic, Members and Chamber Bodies.

ČSSR. Czech National Council 1971–1976. Stenoprotokoly. 13. schůze, 17 & 18. října 1974. URL: www.psp.cz/eknih/1971cnr/stenprot/index.htm

ČSSR. Czech National Council 1976–1981. Stenoprotokoly. 5. schůze. 27. & 28. října 1977. URL: www.psp.cz/eknih/1976cnr/stenprot/index.htm

ČSSR. Czech National Council 1981–1986. Stenoprotokoly. 2. schůze. 6. & 7. července 1981. URL: www.psp.cz/eknih/1981cnr/stenprot/index.htm

ČSSR. Federal Assembly of the Czechoslovak Socialist Republic 1976–1980. Společné schůze Sněmovny lidu a Sněmovny národů. Stenoprotokoly. 2. schůze, 14. & 15. prosince 1976. URL: www.psp.cz/eknih/1976fs/slsn/stenprot/index.htm

ČSSR. Federal Assembly of the Czechoslovak Socialist Republic 1986–1990. Sněmovna lidu. Stenoprotokoly. 2. schůze, 20. října 1987. URL: www.psp.cz/eknih/1986fs/sl/stenprot/index.htm

ČSSR. Joint Czech and Slovak Digital Parliamentary Library 1971–1989. URL: http://public.psp.cz/en/sqw/hp.sqw?k=82

ČSSR. Předsednictvo ÚV KSČ. (1984). Důvodová zpráva. In: *Předsednictvo ÚV KSČ, zasedání 3. 9. 1984, zápis č. P 116/84, sv. 1.* Zápis 3, č. 7175/23, k bodu: Soubor opatření k zabezpečení usnesení ÚV KSČ k úkolům a rozvoji strojírenství, elektrotechnického a hutního průmyslu po XVI. sjezdu KSČ, zápis č. P 116/84, sv. 1, zápis 3, č. 7175/23, příloha III.

ČSSR. Předsednictvo ÚV KSČ. (1988). Výsledky kontroly, jak komunisté – vedoucí pracovníci a stranické organizace na ministerstvu hutnictví a těžkého strojírenství ČSSR a na vybraných podřízených organizacích plní závěry XVII. sjezdu KSČ, zejména z hlediska intenzifikace a efektivnosti hutní výroby. Zápis č. P 67/88, sv. 2, zápis 8, č.j. P 4734/24 (n.d., an appendix dated on 17. 3. 1988).

ČSSR. Schůze předsednictva ÚV KSČ. (1987). Usnesení 25. schůze předsednictva ÚV KSČ ze dne 21. 1. 1987 k bodu 2: Výsledky následné kontroly plnění opatření přijatých k dalšímu zdokonalování činnosti stranických organizací a zvyšování kvality práce Státní, České a Slovenské plánovacích komisí. Zápis č. P 25/87, zápis 2, č. 1804, č.j. P 1804.

ČSSR. Sekretariát ÚV KSČ. (1987). Vnitrostranická informace č. 25. Pro členy a kandidáty předsednictva, členy sekretariátu ÚV KSČ. 10. července 1987. Č.j.: inf./03224/25.

ČSSR. Vláda. (1984). Usnesení vlády Československé socialistické republiky ze dne 30. srpna 1984, č. 235 o opatřeních k úkolům rozvoje strojírenského, elektrotechnického a hutního průmyslu po XVI. sjezdu KSČ. In: *Předsednictvo ÚV KSČ, zasedání 3. 9. 1984, zápis č. P 116/84, sv. 1.* Zápis 3, č. 7175/23, k bodu: Soubor opatření k zabezpečení usnesení ÚV KSČ k úkolům a rozvoji strojírenství, elektrotechnického a hutního průmyslu po XVI. sjezdu KSČ, příloha IV.

ČSSS. Czech National Council. (1990). Stenoprotokoly. 27. Schůze, 18. května 1990. URL: www.psp.cz/eknih/1986cnr/stenprot/index.htm

Čuba, F. (2012). Projekt "Česká společnost v období tzv. normalnizace a transformace: životopisná vyprávění." The Oral History Center at the Institute of Contemporary History, Academy of Sciences, Czech Republic. Interviewer: Lukáš Valeš. URL: www.coh.usd.cas.cz/projekt/csnt/

CZSO (Czech Statistical Office). (2018). *Database of National Account, Balance Sheets* [online]. URL: http://apl.czso.cz/pll/rocenka/rocenkavyber.makroek_rozvaha_en

Dahrendorf, R. (1990). *Reflections on the Revolution in Europe: In a Letter Intended to Have Been Sent to a Gentleman in Warsaw.* 1st ed. New York: Times Books.

Dillon, P., & Wykoff, F. C. (2002). *Creating Capitalism.* Cheltenham, UK: Edward Edgar.

Directive No. 55/1965 Coll., methodological directive of the state planning commission for the preparation of the state plan of the national economy development.

Dolejší, V. (2015). Autor privatizačních zákonů: Dneska bych to udělal jinak. *Hospodářské noviny*, 31st March.

Doležalová, A. (2009). Co dělat? Místo marxismu-leninismu v hospodářském vývoji komunistického Československa. *Acta Oeconomica Pragensia*, 17(4), pp. 62–83.

Drda, A., Mlejnek, J., & Škoda, S. (2010). *Mýty o socialistických časech: Jeden svět na školách: Příběhy bezpráví*. Praha: Člověk v tísni.

Dyba, K., & Kouba, K. (1989). Czechoslovak Attempts at Systemic Changes: 1958, 1968, 1988. *Communist Economies*, 1(3), pp. 313–325.

Engels, F. (1967). *Anti-Dühring. Herr Eugen Dühring's Revolution in Science.Part II: Political economy*. Beijing: Foreign Language Press.

Engels, F. (1975). *Socialism: Utopian and Scientific*. Beijing: Foreign Language Press.

Eucken, W. (1948). On the Theory of the Centrally Administered Economy: An Analysis of the German Experiment. *Economica*, 15(58), pp. 79–100, 15(59), pp. 173–193.

Faltus, J. (1995). Slovenské hospodárstvo v podmienkach systému centrálne plánovaného hospodárstva. In: Váňa, D., *Systém centrálně plánovaných ekonomik v zemích střední a jihovýchodní Evropy a příčiny jeho rozpadu: Praha, 24.–26. března 1994*. Praha: Vysoká škola ekonomická.

Faltus, J., & Průcha, V. (1995). *Hospodářské dějiny*. Praha: VŠE.

Fassmann, M. (2007). *Stínová ekonomika a práce na černo*. Praha: Sondy.

Federální statistický úřad. (1990). *Statistické údaje, které jsme nesměli znát*. Praha: SNTL.

Fojtíková, L. (2009). *Zahraničně obchodní politika ČR: historie a současnost (1945–2008)*. Praha: C.H. Beck.

Friedman, M. (1981). *Market Mechanisms and Central Economic Planning*. Washington, DC: American Enterprise Institute.

Fritzová, M. (1995). Míra únosnosti dotací do zemědělství. In: Váňa, D., *Systém centrálně plánovaných ekonomik v zemích střední a jihovýchodní Evropy a příčiny jeho rozpadu: Praha, 24.–26. března 1994*. Praha: Vysoká škola ekonomická.

Fučík, J. (1951). *V zemi milované*. 3rd ed. Praha: Svoboda.

Gendell, M. (1998). Trends in Retirement Age in Four Countries, 1965–95. *Monthly Labor Review*, August, US Bureau of Labor Statistics.

Goldmann, J., & Kouba, K. (1969). *Economic Growth in Czechoslovakia*. Praha: Academia.

Gregory, P. R., & Stuart, R. C. (2014). *The Global Economy and Its Economic Systems*. Boston: Cengage Learning.

Gros, D., & Steinherr, A. (2004). *Economic Transition in Central and Eastern Europe*. Cambridge: Cambridge University Press.

Grossman, G. (1963). Notes for a theory of the command economy. *Soviet Studies*, 15(2), pp. 101–123.

Hába, Z., Čermák, M., Čmelinský, B., Herman, P., Chyba, A., Ivánek, L., . . . Zlý B. (1988). *Politická ekonomie: stručný základ*. 1st ed. Praha: Státní pedagogické nakladatelství.

Handl, V. (2018). KSČ a řízení centrálně plánované ekonomiky: mezi mocenským imperativem a ekonomickou racionalitou. *Acta Universitatis Carolinae – Studia Territorialia*, 18(1), pp. 13–56.

Hare, P. G. (2001). Institutional Change and Economic Performance in the Transition Economies. *Külgazdaság*, 16(10), pp. 4–34.

Havel, V. (1975). Dopis Václava Havla Gustavu Husákovi ze dne 8. dubna 1975. In *Perzekuce Václava Havla: dopisy a dokumenty z let 1968-1989*. (2015). Praha: Knihovna Václava Havla.

Havel, V. (1985). *The Power of the Powerless: Citizens against the State in Central-Eastern Europe*. London & New York: M. E. Sharpe.

Havelková, B. (2009a). Genderová rovnost v období socialismu. In: Bobek, M., & Molek, P., *Šimíček: Komunistické právo v Československu: Kapitoly z dějin bezpráví.* Brno: Mezinárodní politologický ústav, Masarykova univerzita.

Havelková, B. (2009b). Pracovní právo. In: Bobek, M., & Molek, P., *Šimíček: Komunistické právo v Československu: Kapitoly z dějin bezpráví.* Brno: Mezinárodní politologický ústav, Masarykova univerzita.

Hayek, F. A. (1948). Socialist Calculation II: The State of the Debate. In: Hayek, F. A., *Individualism and Economic Order.* London: Routledge.

Hayek, F. A. (1982). *Law, Legislation and Liberty: A New Statement of the Liberal Principles of Justice and Political Economy.* London: Routledge.

Hayek, F. A. (1988). *The Fatal Conceit: The Errors of Socialism.* Edited W. W. Bartley, The Collected Works of F. A. Hayek, Volume 1. London: Routledge.

Hayek, F. A. (2001). *The Road to Serfdom.* London and New York: Routledge.

Heady, Ch., Rajah, N., & Smith, S. (1994). Tax Reform and Economic Transition in the Czech Republic. *Fiscal Studies,* 15(1), pp. 64–80.

Heywood, A. (2012). *Political Ideologies: An Introduction.* 5th ed. Basingstoke: Palgrave Macmillan.

Hiršl, M. (1992). *Analýza struktury chudého obyvatelstva v Československu v roce 1988.* Bratislava: Výzkumný ústav práce a sociálních věcí.

Hoppe, H. (2010). *A Theory of Socialism and Capitalism.* Auburn, Alabama: Ludwig Von Mises Institute.

House of Commons Information Office. (2010). *Women in the House of Commons.* Factsheet M4 Members Series, June, FS No.M4 Ed 3.9.

Hradecká, V., & Koudelka, F. (1998). *Kádrová politika a nomenklatura KSČ: 1969–1974.* Praha: ÚSD.

Hrnčíř, M. (1987). *Vnější ekonomické vztahy a hospodářský mechanismus.* Praha: Academia.

Husák, P. (1997). *Budování kapitalismu v Čechách: rozhovory s Tomášem Ježkem.* Praha: Volvox Globator.

IPPKID. (2015). Institut pro péči o kulturní a intelektuální dědictví: Dialog o transformaci s Janem Vrbou. *Fenomén transformace.* Interview 2015–10–18. URL: http://ippkid.cz/author/jan-vrba/

Jahan, S., & Mahmud, A. S. (2015). What Is Capitalism? *Finance and Development,* June.

Janeček, V., & Knobloch, V. (1991). *Liberalizace cen v praxi.* Ostrava: KORT.

Jánošíková, P., Knoll, V., & Rundová, A. (2010). *Mezníky českých právních dějin.* 3rd ed. Plzeň: Vydavatelství a nakladatelství Aleš Čeněk.

Jechová, K. (2012). Postavení žen v Československu v období normalizace. In: Tůma, O., & Vilímek, T. (eds.). *Česká společnost v 70. a 80. letech: sociální a ekonomické aspekty.* Česká společnost po roce 1945, sv. 11, p. 288. Praha: Ústav pro soudobé dějiny AV ČR.

Jelínek, J. (1984). *Ekonomická encyklopedie.* 2nd ed. Praha: Svoboda.

Jirges, T., & Plchová, B. (1996). *Zahraniční obchod a národní ekonomika: teoretické přístupy a implikace pro českou ekonomiku.* Praha: Vysoká škola ekonomická.

Jonáš, J. (1997). *Ekonomická transformace v České republice: makroekonomický vývoj a hospodářské politika.* 1st ed. Praha: Management Press.

Jones, R. J. (2001). *Routledge Encyclopedia of International Political Economy.* London: Routledge.

Kabele, J. (2005). *Z kapitalismu do socialismu a zpět: Teoretické vyšetřování přerodů Československa a České republiky.* 1st ed. Praha: Karolinum.

Kaiser, P. J. (1995). The Czech Republic: An Assessment of the Transition. In: Hardt, J. P., Kaufman, R. F., & Sharpe, M. E. (eds.). *Transition.* New York: Armonk.

Kalinová, L. (2012). Dělníci v normalizaci: Dělnictvo a sociální stát v Československu. Sociální postavení a posoje dělnictva v 70. a 80. letech. In: Tůma, O., & Vilímek, T. (eds.).

Česká společnost v 70. a 80. letech: sociální a ekonomické aspekty. Česká společnost po roce 1945, sv. 11, p. 288. Praha: Ústav pro soudobé dějiny AV ČR.

Kaplan, K. (1995). *Československo v RVHP 1949–1956.* Praha: Ústav pro soudobé dějiny AV ČR.

Kirzner, I. M. (1997). *How Markets Work: Disequilibrium, Entrepreneurship and Discovery.* London: Institute of Economic Affairs.

Klaus, V. (2002). *Ekonomický ústav, česká ekonomika a česká ekonomie.* Článek do jubilejního čísla k 50ti letům existence časopisu Politická ekonomie. URL: www.klaus.cz/clanky/848

Klaus, V. (2009). *Kde začíná zítřek.* 1st ed. Praha: Knižní klub.

Kočárník, I. (1990). Státní rozpočet v roce 1990. *Finance a úvěr,* 40(4).

Kohout, J., & Kolář, J. (1966). Komplexní sociologický průzkum v Tesle Pardubice. *Sociologický časopis/Czech Sociological Review,* 2(4), pp. 546–557.

Kolanda, M., & Kubišta, V. (1991). Czechoslovak Processing Industry Enterpirses in the World Markets during the 1980s. *Czechoslovak Economic Digest,* 2, pp. 10–15.

Komárek, V., et al. (1990). *Prognóza a program.* Praha: Academia.

Kornai, J. (1980). *Economics of Shortage.* Amsterdam: North-Holland Publishing Company.

Kornai, J. (1992). *The Socialist System.* Oxford: Oxford University Press.

Kouba, K. (1968). Plán a trh. In: Kouba, K., *Úvahy o socialistické ekonomice.* Praha: Svoboda.

Králík, J., & Hrdlička, P. (2016). *V soukolí okřídleného šípu: Zákulisí automobilky Škoda pohledem tří generací rodiny Hrdličků.* Praha: Grada Publishing.

Kratochvíl, I. (2011). *Život není jen náhoda.* Praha: Academia.

Kraus, J. (1961). Naše beseda: Dorozumění s časem. *Rudé právo,* 17th September.

Kravarová, N. (1983). Hlavní rysy vývoje hnutí brigád socialistické práce v Československu. *Sociologický časopis,* 19(4), pp. 132–136.

Krč, M. (2000). *Vojenské výdaje v letech studené války a po jejím skončení.* Praha: Ústav mezinárodních vztahů.

Kvasil, B. (1986). *Malá československá encyklopedie.* Volume 3, I-L. Praha: Academia.

Landau, Z., & Průcha, V. (1995). Systém centrálně plánovaných ekonomik v zemích střední, východní a jihovýchodní Evropy a příčiny jeho rozpadu. In: Váňa, D., *Systém centrálně plánovaných ekonomik v zemích střední a jihovýchodní Evropy a příčiny jeho rozpadu: Praha, 24.–26. března 1994.* Praha: Vysoká škola ekonomická.

Lange, O. (1936). On the Economic Theory of Socialism. *Review of Economic Studies,* 4(1), pp. 53–71.

Lašek, J. (1998). Strukturální aspekty transformace ekonomiky ČR. *Politická ekonomie,* 46(1).

Lenin, V. I. (1961). What Is to Be Done? Burning Questions of Our Movement. In: Lenin, V. I., *Collected Works,* Volume 5. Moscow: Foreign Languages Publishing House.

Lenin, V. I. (1964). State and Revolution. In: Lenin, V. I., *Collected Works,* Volume 25, pp. 381–492. Moscow: Progress Publishers.

Lenin, V. I. (1965a). Eight All-Russia Congress of Soviets. In: Lenin, V. I., *Collected Works,* Volume 31, 4th ed., pp. 461–534. Moscow: Progress Publishers.

Lenin, V. I. (1965b). Re the Monopoly of Foreign Trade. In: Lenin, V. I., *Collected Works,* Volume 33, 2nd English ed. Moscow: Progress Publishers.

Lenin, V. I. (1972a). Can the Bolsheviks Retain State Power? In: Lenin, V. I., *Collected Works,* Volume 26, pp. 87–136. Moscow: Progress Publishers.

Lenin, V. I. (1972b). Extraordinary Seventh Congress of the R.C.P.(B.). In: Lenin, V. I., *Collected Works,* Volume 27, pp. 85–158. Moscow: Progress Publishers.

Lenin, V. I. (1972c). A Great Beginning Heroism of the Workers in the Rear "Communist Subbotniks". In: Lenin, V. I., *Collected Works,* Volume 29, 4th ed., pp. 409–434. Moscow: Progress Publishers.

Lenin, V. I. (1974). The Proletarian Revolution and the Renegade Kautsky. In: Lenin, V. I., *Collected Works*, Volume 28, pp. 227–325. Moscow: Progress Publishers.

Lenin, V. I. (1977). The Impeding Catastrophe and How to Combat It. In: Lenin, V. I., *Collected Works*, Volume 25, pp. 323–369. Moscow: Progress Publishers.

Levcik, F., & Stankovsky, J. (1988). Eastern Europe's Trade Problems: Between the USSR and the West. Articles in Books: Hardt, J. P., & McMillan, C. H. (eds.). *Planned Economies: Confronting the Challenges of the 1980s*. Cambridge: Cambridge University Press.

Lipovská, H., Coufalová, L., & Žídek, L. (2018). Homo economicus in the shortage economy. *Danube: Law and Economics Review*. 9(4), pp. 207–226.

Maddison-Project, the. (2013). *Maddison Historical Statistics*. URL: www.ggdc.net/maddison/maddison-project/home.htm

Malý, V., & Herz, S. (1988). Příspěvek k pojetí systému plánovitého řízení v období intenzifikace. *Politická ekonomie*, 36(1), pp. 17–28.

Mandel, E. (1973). *An Introduction to Marxist Economic Theory*. 2nd ed., p. 80. New York: Pathfinder Press.

Marx, K. (1887). *Capital: A Critique of Political Economy: Volume I, Book One: The Process of Production of Capital*. Moscow: Progress Publishers.

Marx, K. (1970). Critique of the Gotha Programme. In: Marx, K., & Engels, F., *Selected Works*, Volume 3. Moscow: Progress Publishers.

Marx, K. (1976). Speech on the Question of Free Trade Delivered to the Democratic Association of Brussels at Its Public Meeting of January 9, 1848. In: Marx, K., & Engels, F., *Collected Works*, Volume 6. London: Lawrence & Wishart.

Marx, K., & Engels, F. (1969). Manifesto of the Communist Party. In: Marx, K., & Engels, F., *Selected Works*, Volume 1. Moscow: Progress Publishers.

Masarykův ústav a Archiv AV ČR, v.v.i. (2015). *CSAS Institute Fonds*. URL: www.mua.cas.cz/cs/pracoviste-csav-csas-institute-fonds-641

Melicher, A., & Procházka, M. (1986). *Plánovité riadenie zahraničného obchodu ČSSR*. Bratislava: Alfa.

Michal, J. Š (1994). *Komparativní hospodářské systémy*. Univerzita Karlova. Praha: Karolinum.

Mises, L. V. (1990). *Economic Calculation in the Socialist Commonwealth*. Auburn, Alabama: Ludwig Von Mises Institute.

Mises, L. V. (1991). *Two Essays by Ludwig von Mises: Liberty and Property; Middle-of-the-Road Policy Leads to Socialism*. Auburn, Alabama: Ludwig Von Mises Institute.

Mises, L. V. (1998). *Human Action*. Auburn, Alabama: Ludwig Von Mises Institute.

Mlčoch, L. (1990). *Chování československé podnikové sféry*. Výzkumná publikace Ekonomického ústavu ČSAV (VP) č. 348. Praha: Ekonomický ústav ČSAV.

Mlynář, Z. (1990). *Mráz přichází z Kremlu*. Praha: Mladá fronta.

Možný, I. (1991). *Proč tak snadno . . .: Některé rodinné důvody sametové revoluce*. 1st ed. Praha: Sociologické nakladatelství.

Municipal Council of Doubravice nad Svitavou. (1982). *Commemorative Book of Doubravice nad Svitavou, part XXVII*. URL: www.doubravicens.cz/cast-xxvii

Municipal Council of Letovice. (1971). *Town Chronicle of Letovice*, pp. 76–78. URL: www.letovice.net/mesto-1/kroniky-mesta/kroniky-mesta-z-let-1968-az-1977-961cs.html

Municipal Council of Velké Meziříčí. (1983–1987). *Town Chronicle of Velké Meziříčí*, p. 8. URL: www.velkemezirici.cz/kronika/1983-1987/files/assets/basic-html/page-12.html#

Nečasová, D. (2018). *Nový socialistický člověk: Československo 1948–1956*. Brno: Host.

Neveselý, K. (1977). Kritika revizionistického pojetí politického pluralismu za socialismu. In: *Sborník prací filozofické fakulty Brněnské univerzity*, G, 20/21, 1976–1977. Jan Evangelista Purkyně University.

North, D. C. (1990). *Institutions, Institutional Change and Economic Performance*. 1st ed. Cambridge: Cambridge University Press.

North, D. C. (1992). Institutions and Economic Theory. *The American Economist*, 36(1), pp. 3–6.

Nuti, D. M. (1981). Socialism on Earth. *Cambridge Journal of Economics*, 5(4), 1st December, pp. 391–403.

Nutter, W. G. (1968). Markets without Property: A Grand Illusion. In: *Market Mechanisms and Central Economic Planning, 1981, Collected Works of Milton Friedman Project Records*. Stanford: Hoover Institution Archives.

Nykryn, J. (1983). Úloha vnějších ekonomických vztahů v rozvoji čs. ekonomiky. *Politická ekonomie*, 31(9), pp. 975–986.

Nykryn, J. (1988). *Zahraniční obchod ČSSR*. Praha: Svoboda.

Oliva, F. (1952). *Socialistický výrobní způsob*. Praha: Osvěta.

Osterfeld, D. (1993). Marxism, Method, and Mercantilism. In: Maltsev, Y. N., *Requiem for Marx*. Auburn, Alabama: Ludwig Von Mises Institute.

Pacner, K. (2002). *Československo ve zvláštních službách: Pohledy do historie československých výzvědných služeb: 1914–1989*. Praha: Themis.

Pavlát, V., & Vojtíšek, J. (1959). *Předmět politické ekonomie; úvod do studia politické ekonomie*. Praha: Státní nakladatesví politické literatury.

Pawera, E., et al. (1985). *Stranické organizace a hospodářské vedení při zajišťování výrobních úkolů*. Praha: Svoboda.

Pellešová, P. (2002). Reflexe k hospodářské politice České republiky v procesu transformace. In: *Studia Oeconomica*. Karviná: Slezská univerzita v Opavě.

Petrov, M. (2013). *Retro ČS*. Brno: Jota.

Plocek, J. (2015). Gott za šest a půl tisíce aneb život muzikanta za socialismu. *Kulturní noviny*, 35. URL: www.kulturni-noviny.cz/nezavisle-vydavatelske-a-medialni-druzstvo/archiv/online/2015/35-2015/gott-za-sest-a-pul-tisice-aneb-zivot-muzikanta-za-socialismu

Procházka, V. (1962–1967). *Příruční slovník naučný*. Praha: Nakladatelství Československé akademie věd.

Průcha, V. (2000). Česká ekonomika: cesty staletím. In: *Ročenka HN 2000*. Praha: Economia.

Průcha, V., Chlumská, B., Kalinová, L., Šauer, P., Jedličková, E., Poláková, O., & Kudeříková, G. (1988). *Úvod do národohospodářského plánování*. Praha: VŠE, SNTL.

Pullmann, M. (2011). *Konec experimentu: přestavba a pád komunismu v Československu*. Praha: Scriptorium.

Půlpán, K. (1993). *Nástin českých a československých hospodářských dějin do roku 1990*. Praha: Institut ekonomických věd.

Raiser, M., Haerpfer, Ch., Nowotny, T., & Wallace, C. (2001). Social Capital in Transition: A First Look at the Evidence. *EBRD Working Paper* No. 61.

Read, L. E. (1999). *I, Pencil: My Family Tree*. New York: Foundation for Economic Education, Inc.

Rendl, V., Durdisová, J., Hájek, M., Janáček, K., Jírová, H., Kasan, J., . . . Vostrovská, Z. (1988). *Národohospodářské plánování*. 1st ed. Praha: VŠE, Státní pedagogické nakladatelství.

Robinson, J. (1942). *Essay on Marxian Economics*. London: Macmillan.

Rosenberg, J. (2017). *The History of Prohibition in the United States* [online]. URL: www.thoughtco.com/history-of-prohibition-1779250

Rothbard, M. N. (2009). *Man, Economy, and State: A Treatise on Economic Principles; with Power and Market: Government and the Economy*. Auburn, Alabama: Ludwig Von Mises Institute.

Rozental', M., & Judin, P. (1955). *Stručný filosofický slovník*. Praha: Státní nakladatelství politické literatury.

Rozsypal, K., Jírová, H., Sládková, J., Spěváček, V., & Vebrová, L. (1981). *Úvod do teorie a praxe národohospodářského plánování*. 2nd ed. Praha: SNTL.
Rudé Právo. (1986). Všichni kandidáti Národní fronty zvoleni. *Rudé právo*, 26th May.
Rutland, P. (1985). *The Myth of the Plan: Lessons of Soviet Planning Experience*. La Salle, IL: Open Court.
Rychlík, J. (2007). *Cestování do ciziny v habsburské monarchii a v Československu: Pasová, vízová a vystěhovalecká politika 1848–1989*. Praha: Ústav pro soudobé dějiny AV ČR.
Schönfelder, B. (2016). The Evolution of Law Under Communism and Post-Communism: A System-Theory Analysis in the Spirit of Luhmann. *Financial Theory and Practice*, 40(3).
Sitárová, Z., & Kliment, A. (1981). *Dějiny ekonomických teorií: stručný nástin*. Praha: Svoboda.
Sobek, V. (2011). *Pomohli jsme sestřelit Powerse: tajemství Vědeckotechnické rozvědky ČSSR*. Praha: Futura.
Soldát, M. (2015). *Dialogy o transformaci*. Praha: Institut pro péči o kulturní a intelektuální dědictví.
Soukup, M., & Žídek, L. (2019). *Growth Decomposition in the Social Czech Economy*. Acta Universitatis Agriculturae et Silviculturae Mendelianae Brunensis, Mendel Univerzity.
Soulsby, A., & Clark, E. (1996). Economic Restructuring and Institutional Change: Post-Communist Management in the Czech Republic. *Journal of Socio-Economics*, 25(4).
Stalin, J. V. (1953). *Spisy*. Volume 12. Praha: Svoboda.
Stalin, J. V. (1972). *Economic Problems of Socialism in the USSR*. Beijing: Foreign Languages Press.
Statistical Office. (1966–1993). *Statistické ročenky Československé socialistické republiky*. Praha: SNTL.
Šrein, Z. (1995). Rozpor mezi nominálním a reálným systémem centrálního plánovaní v Československu. In: Váňa, D., *Systém centrálně plánovaných ekonomik v zemích střední a jihovýchodní Evropy a příčiny jeho rozpadu: Praha, 24.–26. března 1994*. Praha: Vysoká škola ekonomická.
Stevens, J. N. (1985). *Czechoslovakia at the Crossroads: The Economic Dilemmas of Communism in Postwar Czechoslovakia*. Boulder: East European Monographs.
Štrougal, L. (2009). *Paměti a úvahy*. Praha: Epocha.
Šujan, I., & Šujanová, M. (1997). Makroekonomická situace v České republice. In: Švejnar, J., *Česká republika a ekonomická transformace ve střední a východní Evropě*. Praha: Academia.
Šulc, Z. (1995). O mechanismu fungování centrálně plánované ekonomiky se zvláštním zřetelem k čs. zkušenostem. In: Váňa, D., *Systém centrálně plánovaných ekonomik v zemích střední a jihovýchodní Evropy a příčiny jeho rozpadu: Praha, 24.–26. března 1994*. Praha: Vysoká škola ekonomická.
Šulc, Z. (2004). *Stát a ekonomika*. Praha: Karolinum.
Svěrák, V. (1983). Vnější kritéria efektivnosti: interakce cen a kursů měn. *Politická ekonomie*, 31(4), pp. 335–348.
Swain, N. J. (1998). The Visegrád Countries of Eastern Europe. In: Foley, B. J. (ed.). *European Economies Since the Second World War*. London: Macmillan Press.
Tanzi, V. (1995). Finanční trhy a veřejné finance v procesu transformace. In: Bulíř, A., & Jonáš, J., *Ekonomie reformy*. Praha: Management Press.
Teichová, A. (1995). Velké průmyslové podniky v Československu po roce 1948. Historický nástin strukturálních a organizačních změn. In: Váňa, D., *Systém centrálně plánovaných ekonomik v zemích střední a jihovýchodní Evropy a příčiny jeho rozpadu: Praha, 24.–26. března 1994*. Praha: Vysoká škola ekonomická.
Teplý, J. (1976). *Socialismus v čs. národním hospodářství*. Köln: Index.
Tíkal, S. (1990). Internacionalizace Československa a vyspělých tržních ekonomik. *Zahraniční obchod*, 1990(6), pp. 9–11.

Tooze, J. A. (2007). *The Wages of Destruction: The Making and Breaking of the Nazi Economy*. London: Penguin Books.

Tošovský, J. (2000). Po deseti letech: některé lekce z transformace. *Bankovnictví*, 7(11), pp. 11–14.

Tříska, D., Klaus, V., Holman, R., Rudlovčák, V., Hrubý, M., Mládek, J., ... Loužek, M. (2002). *Kupónová privatizace*. Sborník textů č. 13/2002. Praha: Centrum pro ekonomiku a politiku.

Turek, O. (1995). *Podíl ekonomiky na pádu komunismu v Československu*. Sešity Ústavu pro soudobé dějiny, Svazek 23. 1st ed. Praha: ÚSD.

Urbášek, P. (2008). *Vysokoškolský vzdělávací systém v letech tzv. normalizace*. Olomouc: Univerzita Palackého.

Ústav zdravotnických informací a statistiky & Ústav zdravotníckej štatistiky (1981). *ČSSR zdravotnictví 1981*. Praha: Ústav zdravotnických informací a statistiky.

Vácha, S. (1988). *Jak řídí Slušovice*. Praha: Novinář.

Vaněk, M., & Krátká, L. (2014). *Příběhy (ne)obyčejných profesí: česká společnost v období tzv. normalizace a transformace*. Praha: Karolinum.

Vaněk, M., Mücke, P., & Pelikánová, H. (2007). *Naslouchat hlasům paměti: teoretické a praktické aspekty orální historie*. Praha: Ústav pro soudobé dějiny AV ČR.

Vaněk, M., & Mücke, P. (2015). *Třetí strana trojúhelníku: teorie a praxe orální historie*. 2nd ed. Praha: Univerzita Karlova v Praze,

Vaněk, M., & Urbášek, P. (2005). *Vítězové? Poražení?: životopisná interview, II. díl, Politické elity v období tzv. normalizace*. Praha: Prostor.

Vassiliou, M. S. (2009). *The A to Z of the Petroleum Industry*. Lanham: The Scarecrow Press, Inc.

Večerník, J. (1992). Změny v příjmové nerovnosti v letech 1988–1992. *Sociologický časopis*, 28(5), pp. 666–684.

Večerník, J. (1998). *Občan a tržní ekonomika: Příjmy, nerovnost a politické postoje v české společnosti*. Praha: Nakladatelství Lidové Noviny.

Vencovský, F. (2003). *Vzestupy a propady československé koruny*. 1st ed. Praha: Oeconomica.

Veszeláková, M., et al. (1972). *Ekonomická encyklopedie*. Praha: Svoboda.

Vilímek, T. (2012). Mladoboleslavská Škodovka v období normalizace (1968–1989). In: Tůma, O., & Vilímek, T. (eds.). *Česká společnost v 70. a 80. letech: sociální a ekonomické aspekty*. Česká společnost po roce 1945, sv. 11, p. 288. Praha: Ústav pro soudobé dějiny AV ČR.

Vintrová, R. (2006). Historické předpoklady a reálné perspektivy konvergence české ekonomiky k Evropské unii. *Studie Národohospodářského ústavu Josefa Hlávky*. Study No. 7. Praha: Národohospodářský ústav Josefa Hlávky.

Vintrová, R. (2008). Česká a slovenská ekonomika 15 let po rozdělení. *Politická ekonomie*, 56(4), pp. 449–466.

Voráček, E. (1995). Konfrontace mocenských zájmů SSSR s nutností změny hospodářské strategie na přelomu 70.-80. let. In: Váňa, D., *Systém centrálně plánovaných ekonomik v zemích střední a jihovýchodní Evropy a příčiny jeho rozpadu: Praha, 24.–26. března 1994*. Praha: Vysoká škola ekonomická.

Vraný, J. (1995). Hospodářská stagnace a sociální napětí ve státně monopolních ekonomikách. In: Váňa, D., *Systém centrálně plánovaných ekonomik v zemích střední a jihovýchodní Evropy a příčiny jeho rozpadu: Praha, 24.–26. března 1994*. Praha: Vysoká škola ekonomická.

Wagner, R. E. (2014). James M. Buchanan and Me: Reminiscing about a 50-Year Association. *GMU Working Paper in Economics* No. 14–13.

Winiecki, J. (2000). Formal and Informal Rules in Post-Communist Transition. In: *A Liberating Economic Journey: Post-Communist Transition*, 1st ed. London: Centre for Research into Post-Communist Economies.

World Bank. (2018). *DataBank: World Development Indicators* [online]. URL: http://databank.worldbank.org/data/home

Zahraniční obchod. (1988). Statistika. *Zahraniční obchod*, 1988(4).

Žaloudek, K. (2004). *Encyklopedie politiky*. Prague: Libri.

Zeman, K. (1990). *Postavení ČSSR ve světové ekonomice v období osmdesátých let: Řešeno v rámci hlavního úkolu SPZV č. IX-2-4/06*. Praha: Ekonomický ústav ČSAV.

Zeman, M. (1989). Prognostika a přestavba. *Technický magazín*, August.

Žídek, L. (2017). *From Central Planning to the Market: The Transformation of the Czech Economy 1989–2004*. Budapest: CEU Press.

Zieleniec, J. (1990). *Československo na rozcestí: zpráva o stavu národního hospodářství a možnostech jeho nápravy*. Praha: Lidové noviny.

Zieleniec, J., Bulíř, A., Češka, R., Dvořák, P., Gavlas, I., Hlaváček, J., . . . Zemplinerová, A. (1990). Ekonomický subjekt. In: *Institucionální souvislosti fungování ekonomiky*. Praha: Ekonomický ústav ČSAV.

Zon, H. V. (2000). *The Political Economy of Indepedent Ukraine*. Basingstoke: Macmillan Press.

Acronyms

SBČS – Státní banka Československá (Czechoslovak State Bank)
VTR – Vědecko-technická rozvědka (Science and Technologies Secret Service)
PZO – Podnik zahraničního obchodu (Foreign trade enterprise)
SPK – Státní plánovací komise (State Planning Commission)
COCOM – Coordinating Committee for Multilateral Export Controls
COMECON – Council for Mutual Economic Assistance
StB – Státní Bezpečnost (State Security)
ROH – Revoluční odborové hnutí (Trade unions)
VHJ – Výrobně hospodářská jednotka (Production economic unit)
SoE – State-owned company
ÚKRK – Ústřední kontrolní a revizní Komise ÚV KSČ (The Central Control and Review Commission of the Central Committee of the Communist Party)
KSČ – Komunistická Strana Československa (Czechoslovak Communist Party)
JZD – Jednotné zemědělské družstvo (Agricultural cooperative)
ČSSR, ČSR, SSR – Československá Socialistická republika, Česká Socialistická republika, Slovenská Socialistická republika (Czechoslovak Socialist Republic, Czech Socialist Republic, Slovak Socialist Republic)
VRCV – Koeficient vnitřního cenového vyrovnání (Internal reproductive price compensation coefficient)
CPE – Centrálně plánovaná ekonomika (Centrally Planned Economy)
CZV – celozávodní výbor (all-enterprise committee)
ÚV KSČ – Ústřední výbor KSČ (Communist Party Central Committee)
ZO – základní organizace (basic organization)
GŘ VHJ – generální ředitelství VHJ (General Directory of VHJ)
OV KSČ – Okresní výbor KSČ (District Committee of KSČ)
KV KSČ – Krajský výbor KSČ (Regional Committee of KSČ)

Appendix

Fifth five-year plan and respective one-year plans, growth in percent

	5th five-year plan (years 1971–1975)		*1971*		*1972*		*1973*		*1974*		*1975*	
	[2]	*[18]*	*[1]*	*[4]*	*[5]*	*[7]*	*[5]*	*[9]*	*[11]*	*[13]*	*[14]*	*[18]*
	PLAN	*REALITY*	*PLAN*	*REALITY*	*PLAN*	*REALITY*	*PLAN*	*REALITY*	*PLAN*	*REALITY*	*PLAN*	*REALITY*
1) National income	28	32	5.2	5.2	5 [6]	5.9	5.1 [8]	5.3	5	6	2–3 [15]	6.2
2) Industry	34–36	38.5	5.7	6.9	5	6.8	5.8	6.9	5.8	6.3	6.4	7
a) mechanical engineering	45	50	8.1	8.2			7.6	8.8	7.5 [12]	7.9	9.8 [16]	9.3
b) chemical industry	55–60	61	7.1	11			8.6	10.7	7.7 [12]	8.2	8.1 [16]	10
3) Civil engineering	38	49	8.5	9.6	7.4	9.2	5	6.7	7.5	7.2	8.8 [15]	3.6
4) Agriculture	14	13.5	3	3.2	4.6	3.9	4.3	4.7	3.8	2.2	3.3	-1
5) Investments	35–37	48.4	4.3	5.7	4.8	8.7	6.8	9.2	9.6 [12]	9.3	7.4	8.3
a) civil engineering	33	46	4.7	6.6			4.6	6				
b) mechanical engineering	37	52.7	3.7	4			10.2	14.5				
6) Foreign trade – turnout	36–38	80					9.4 [8]	12	11.5 [12]	19.8		
Total imports			6.5	8.5	6.8	7	13.2 [8]	15.8			4 [17]	15.3
a) Capitalist states			12 [2]	8	2.9	2.9					12 [17]	0
b) Socialist states	70	92	7.9 [2]	8.7	9.7	8.9						
Total exports			8	10.2	7.1	8.3	★	8.4			6.4 [17]	13.2
c) Capitalist states			9.4 [2]	12	2.4	2					10 [17]	-1.2
d) Socialist states	56	73	5.3 [2]	9.4	10.6	10,9					9 [15]	20

Respective sources in square brackets. If not stated otherwise, each column's source in the column's header. ★ more than was planned, # less than was planned

5th five-year plan. Numbers [19] from 1976 wrote (ex-post) that the planned growth in agriculture was exceeded by 1.2% (which was not as can be seen in the table). It also claimed that the "investments in civil engineering grew by 35%, as was planned." In reality, they grew by 46 % as can be seen in the table.

1971. In Numbers [2], we found differences in both the plans and the reality. For example, the planned National income was 4.4% vs. 5% in reality. The Numbers [2] were published in 1972, i.e. after the results were known. That is, a lower plan was published ex post, perhaps so that the reality looked more favourable.

1973. Numbers [10] published in 1974 claimed that the plan in Civil engineering was exceeded by "more than 2%." Furthermore, according to the Numbers [10], the Investments grew "slightly more than was planned." Given the fact that the planned growth was 6.8 % and reality was 9.2 %, the investments grew, in our opinion, by a lot more than was planned.

Sixth five-year plan and respective one-year plans, growth in percent

	6th five-year plan (years 1976–1980)		*1976*		*1977*		*1978*		*1979*		*1980*	
	[21]	*[41]*	*[20]*	*[22]*	*[24]*	*[25]*	*[28]*	*[31]*	*[33]*	*[36]*	*[39]*	*[41]*
	PLAN	*REALITY*	*PLAN*	*REALITY*	*PLAN*	*REALITY*	*PLAN*	*REALITY*	*PLAN*	*REALITY*	*PLAN*	*REALITY*
1) National income	27–29	22	5	3.5	5.2	4.2	5 [29]	4.1	4.3	3	3.7	2.8
2) Industry	35	25,5	5.5	5.5	5.3	5.7	5.1	5	4.5	3.7	4	3.5
a) mechanical engineering			8	8.4	8.1	7.3	6.3 [30]	6.4	6.9	6.6	5.8	4.6
b) chemical industry			8.4	8.5	6.3	6.7	5.8	5.7	3.5	3.4	3.1 [40]	4.8
3) Civil engineering	44	25	8.5	7.5	6.2	4.4	6.1	5.6	5.8	3.7	3.8	1.3
4) Agriculture	15	11	4.5 [21]	−2.4	8.2	9.1	3.4 [30]	2.6	3.8	−4.2	7.2	6
5) Investments			6.4	3.6	5.8	5.7	5.6 [30]	4	2.9 [34]	1.8	2.4	1.4
a) civil engineering			#	3.3	6	3.2	7.2	2.1				
b) mechanical engineering			★	4	5.5	9.8	★	7.1	5.5 [37]	3.5		
6) Foreign trade – turnout	★	66			9.2	12.3	8	8.4				
Total imports							6.5	7.7				
a) Capitalist states									2	15	6	10.6
b) Socialist states			6.9	10.5			★	10.8			6.8	6.4
Total exports							7.9 [30]	9.2				
c) Capitalist states					#	15.3			7	15.5	10	25.5
d) Socialist states			7	16			10.1	9.4			7	10
7) SBČS credits			8.9 [82]	10.5 [83]								
a) operational credits					4.6 [83]	2.6 [84]	6.9 [84]	5.3 [85]	7.6 [85]	10.9 [86]	6.5 [86]	11.5 [87]
b) investment credits					13.9 [83]	11 [84]	22.7 [84]	4.4 [85]	2 [85]	1 [86]	5.3 [86]	4.6 [87]

Respective sources in square brackets. If not stated otherwise, each column's source in the column's header. ★ more than was planned, # less than was planned

6th five-year plan. It was considerably more difficult to find the plans. The main message that was given from the Act No. 69/1976 Coll. was that the effectivity must be increased.

1976. Numbers [23] from 1977 wrote that the decrease in agriculture was caused by the mostly dry weather. It gives the evidence that not everything is plannable.

1978. Numbers [32] from 1979 claim that "the plan in Civil engineering was exceeded by 0.5%." The opposite was true, as can be seen in the table – in 1978 the plan in Civil engineering was not met by 0.5%. Numbers from 1979 also claimed that the plan was met in both exports and imports – again, as can be seen, it was not, namely in exports.

Seventh five-year plan and respective one-year plans, growth in percent

	7th five-year plan (years 1981–1985)		*1981*		*1982*		*1983*		*1984*		*1985*	
	[64]	*[62]*	*[44]*	*[46]*	*[47]*	*[50]*	*[51]*	*[53]*	*[55]*	*[58]*	*[60]*	*[62]*
	PLAN	*REALITY*	*PLAN*	*REALITY*	*PLAN*	*REALITY*	*PLAN*	*REALITY*	*PLAN*	*REALITY*	*PLAN*	*REALITY*
1) National income	14–16	15	2.8	0	0.5	0	2	2.4	3 [56]	3.5	3.2	3.5
2) Industry	18–20	14	2.2	2.2	0.5 [48]	1.1	2.4	2.8	2.5 [57]	4	3	3.5
a) mechanical engineering	33–35	27	5.5	4.2	3	3.2	4.8	5	6.4	6.3	6	5.8
b) chemical industry	12	17	0.7	1.7	−0.1 [47]	1.3	0.8 [52]	3.3	2.4	4.5	3.3 [61]	5.1
3) Civil engineering			2.7 [45]	−1.8	−4.7 [48]	−3.8	2	2.8	0.5 [57]	1.8	1.2	1.3
4) Agriculture	10	9.2	2.6	−2.5	3.2	4.4	2.7	4.2	1.9	4.4	−1.1	−1.6
5) Investments	0	−5.4	0	−4.6	−3.3	−2.3	−2.9	0.6	★	4.2	2.7	5.4
a) civil engineering			2.8	−2.6			−3.2 [52]	1.4				
b) mechanical engineering			−1.8	−7.5								
6) Foreign trade – turnout	35–40 [47]	48.5	#	7.6							★	5.3
Total imports			#	5.8								
a) Capitalist states			#	3.5	#	−6.2					2 [91]	
b) Socialist states			11 [45]	9.8	15	15	9.9	13	★	12.4	4.5 [91]	6
Total exports			#	9.4								
c) Capitalist states			#	3.9	7.5	−1.4	4.6	5.7			2.3 [91]	
d) Socialist states			7.9 [45]	11.8	7.2	12.8	2.8	10	★	12.1	4.6 [91]	6.2
7) SBČS credits											2.9 [91]	2.7 [92]
a) operational credits					2.6 [88]	5 [89]	3.3 [89]	2.5 [90]	3.6 [90]	8.4 [91]		
b) investment credits					3.5 [88]	2.4 [89]	1.8 [89]	5.4 [90]	3.6 [90]	0 [91]		

Respective sources in square brackets. If not stated otherwise, each column's source in the column's header. ★ more than was planned, # less than was planned

7th five-year plan.

1982. The SBČS Bulletin [88] (published in English. i.e. for the foreign) reads: "New operational credits will be granted preferentially by the Bank to promote the expansion of export production, to adopt measures in production with the aim of attaining savings in the consumption of metals and imported raw materials, to support the growth of agricultural production and to extend services."

1984. The Bulletin SBČS [91] from 1985 read that the decrease in investment credits was "in harmony with the plan target." However as can be seen in the table, the plan (which was published in the SBČS Bulletin in 1984) was to increase the credits by 3.6%.

Part of the eighth five-year plan – one-year plans, growth in percent

	1986		*1987*		*1988*		*1989*	
	[67]	*[68]*	*[70]*	*[71]*	*[73]*	*[74]*	*[75]*	*[77]*
	PLAN	*REALITY*	*PLAN*	*REALITY*	*PLAN*	*REALITY*	*PLAN*	*REALITY*
1) National income	3.5	2.5	3	3	★	4	2.2	2.1
2) Industry	2.6	3.2	1.9	2.5	1.7	2.1	2	0
a) mechanical engineering	4.9	4.9	#	4				
b) chemical industry	2.7	4						
3) Civil engineering	3 [66]	2.6	1.3	2.1	0	0		
4) Agriculture	0.5	0.6	0.9	0.9	1.2	2.9		
5) Investments					−2.4	4	3.6	1.6
a) civil engineering					−5	1.8	1	0.9
b) mechanical engineering	#	6			1	6.7	6.5	2.3
6) Foreign trade – turnout								
Total imports			#	1.4				
a) Capitalist states								
b) Socialist states	★	3	−1	0.5	★	0.2	★	0
Total exports			#	3.4			3.6	6
c) Capitalist states							8.1 [76]	13.6
d) Socialist states	★	2.4	1.5	5.6	★	5.1	★	−4.7
7) SBČS credits	1.2 [92]	2.6 [93]						
a) operational credits								
b) investment credits								

Respective sources in square brackets. If not stated otherwise, each column's source in the column's header. ★ more than was planned, # less than was planned

1986. Numbers [69] from 1987 read that the plans in Civil engineering were fulfilled by 100.9 %.

1988. The SBČS Bulletin [95] from 1989 wrote that "It was possible to accomplish the planned targets set for exports and imports [the plans were not published], yet the planned proportions in the assortment of Czechoslovak exports failed to be maintained in full. Difficulties continued to remain in securing the planned growth of engineering product exports."

Dealing with the various sources was very complicated due to inconsistency in the numbers. Under each table for the respective five-year plans, we provide some examples of the inaccuracy, which, in our opinion, were partly caused by propaganda, partly by the effort to show that the plan was met. For obvious reasons, we consider the plans published in advance to be more trustworthy than those that were published ex post. However, we are aware that the Statistical yearbooks, from which we take the reality, were published by the state and thus could be made more favourable as well. An interesting publication in this sense was the "Numbers for Everyone" (Numbers) a pocketbook published by the statistical office which contained selected basic statistics along with short descriptions on their meaning. It was intended to be distributed (and read) among the citizens to be aware of the achievements of the socialist economy.

Overall plans

The plans gradually disappeared from the publications, as well as the notes that the "superb results were results of the KSČ economic policy." Furthermore, the planned growth rates were usually followed with a note that, for example, 90% of the planned increase will be covered with higher labour productivity.

Foreign trade

The Numbers [23] wrote that the main reason why the exports to capitalist states grew only slightly was "an insufficient supply of exports that would be possible to sell on the demanding markets." According to Čáp and Rybnikář (1983) [49], it was not possible to fulfil the plan in foreign trade in 1982 with capitalist countries, because "the deepening crisis in the capitalist world together with the discriminative measures against socialist countries influenced the development in foreign trade." [84] concludes similarly: "As a result of a sharper competition on the industrial production markets, the capitalist states increased the protectionist and discriminative measures against the imports from the socialist countries." Throughout the 7th five-year plan, the exports to the capitalist countries were "a lot lower than was planned. The drop would be even deeper were the planned value of industrial production exports not replaced with increased exports of raw materials, namely oil and metallurgy products" [56].

Investments

As can be seen in the tables, the plans were systematically lower than were the results. The regime was concerned – every source that mentioned the plans in investments also mentioned the problem of "the unfinished civil engineering projects and thus dispersed construction capacities, which held considerable amounts of money."

Agriculture

The structure of the plans differed from the structure of the reality – a few sources mentioned plans divided into plants and animal production. The plant production was always planned higher and resulted lower than the animal production.

SBČS credits

Are in fact total credits in the economy. Bulletin [83]: "By investment credit the bank is going to promote particularly the expansion of the fuels and energy base, construction of the Orenburg gas pipeline, the development of chemical industry and the housing construction. Through operational credit the Bank will back the creation of inventories for both the internal and external markets in the required assortment and quality, it will put pressure on the effectiveness and strict economy and will help secure the State plan tasks in accelerating the velocity of stocks, notably in industry and building."

References

[1] Pelc, et al. (1971). Nad úkoly plánu na rok 1971. *Plánované hospodářství*, 24(1).
[2] *Čísla pro každého: malá statistická ročenka*. (1972). Praha: SNTL.
[4] *Statistická ročenka ČSSR*. (1972). Praha: SNTL.
[5] *Čísla pro každého: malá statistická ročenka*. (1973). Praha: SNTL.
[6] Hůla, V. (1972). Základní úkoly a zaměření plánu v roce 1972. *Plánované hospodářství*, 25(1).
[7] *Statistická ročenka ČSSR*. (1973). Praha: SNTL.
[8] Hvorecký, J. (1973). Decembrové plénum ÚV KSČ a tohtoročný plan. *Plánované hospodářství*, 26(2).
[9] *Statistická ročenka ČSSR*. (1974). Praha: SNTL.
[10] *Čísla pro každého: malá statistická ročenka*. (1974). Praha: SNTL.
[11] Zasedání ústředního výboru KSČ ve dnech 27. a 28. listopadu. (1973). *O ekonomických otázkách*. Praha: Svoboda.
[12] Hůla, V. (1974). Zaměření plánu na rok 1974. *Plánované hospodářství*, 27(1).
[13] *Statistická ročenka ČSSR*. (1975). Praha: SNTL.
[14] *Čísla pro každého: malá statistická ročenka*. (1975). Praha: SNTL.
[15] Zasedání ústředního výboru KSČ ve dnech 27.–29. listopadu 1974. (1975). *O zabezpečování závěrů 14. sjezdu KSČ a o úkolech na rok 1975*. 2nd ed. Praha: Ústřední výbor KSČ.
[16] Hůla, V. (1975). Úspěšně splnit pátou a dobře připravit šestou pětiletku. *Plánované hospodářství*, 28(1).
[17] Címa, et al. (1975). Interview o letošním plánu. *Plánované hospodářství*, 28(2).
[18] *Statistická ročenka ČSSR*. (1976). Praha: SNTL.
[19] *Čísla pro každého: malá statistická ročenka*. (1976). Praha: SNTL.
[20] Rybnikář, K. (1976). K plánu rozvoje národního hospodářství na rok 1976. *Plánované hospodářství*, 29(1).
[21] Hůla, V. (1976). Na rozhraní dvou pětiletek. *Plánované hospodářství*, 29(1).
[22] *Statistická ročenka ČSSR*. (1977). Praha: SNTL.
[23] *Čísla pro každého: malá statistická ročenka*. (1977). Praha: SNTL.
[24] Hůla, V. (1977). Důsledně plnit program XV. sjezdu KSČ. *Plánované hospodářství*, 30(1).
[25] *Statistická ročenka ČSSR*. (1978). Praha: SNTL.
[28] Kop, R., & Rybníkář, K. (1977). K přípravě plánu na rok 1978. *Plánované hospodářství*, 30(8).
[29] Hůla, V. (1978). Úkoly třetího roku šesté pětiletky. *Plánované hospodářství*, 31(1).
[30] Zasedání Ústředního výboru Komunistické strany Československa dne 1. prosince 1977. (1978). *Hlavní úkoly rozvoje národního hospodářství v roce 1978*. Praha: Svoboda.
[31] *Statistická ročenka ČSSR*. (1979). Praha: SNTL.
[32] *Čísla pro každého: malá statistická ročenka*. (1979). Praha: SNTL.
[33] Zasedání ústředního výboru Komunistické strany Československa ve dnech 4. a 5. prosince 1978. (1978). *Hlavní úkoly rozvoje národního hospodářství: k výměně členských legitimací Komunistické strany Československa*. Praha: Svoboda.
[34] Hůla, V. (1979). Náročné úkoly v závěru pětiletky. *Plánované hospodářství*, 32(1).
[36] *Statistická ročenka ČSSR*. (1980). Praha: SNTL.
[37] *Čísla pro každého: malá statistická ročenka*. (1980). Praha: SNTL.
[39] Zasedání ústředního výboru Komunistické strany Československa ve dnech 10. a 11. prosince 1979. (1979). *Hlavní úkoly rozvoje národního hospodářství v roce 1980*. Praha: Svoboda.
[40] Hůla, V. (1980). Hlavní úkoly rozvoje čs. ekonomiky v roce 1980. *Plánované hospodářství*, 33(1).

[41] *Statistická ročenka ČSSR.* (1981). Praha: SNTL.
[44] Hůla, V. (1981). Rozvoj čs. ekonomiky v roce 1981. *Plánované hospodářství*, 34(1).
[45] *Čísla pro každého: malá statistická ročenka.* (1982). Praha: SNTL.
[46] *Statistická ročenka ČSSR.* (1982). Praha: SNTL.
[47] Potáč, S. (1981). 5. zasedání Ústředního výboru Komunistické strany Československa dne 9. prosince 1981. *O státním plánu hospodářského a sociálního rozvoje ČSSR na rok 1982 a návrhu zákona o 7. pětiletém plánu: zpráva přednesená Svatoplukem Potáčem dne 9. prosince 1981.*
[48] *Čísla pro každého: malá statistická ročenka.* (1983). Praha: SNTL.
[49] Čáp, V., & Rybnikář, K. (1983). K plnění plánu a k vývoji národního hospodářství v roce 1982. *Plánované hospodářství*, 36(2).
[50] *Statistická ročenka ČSSR.* (1983). Praha: SNTL.
[51] 7. zasedání Ústředního výboru Komunistické strany Československa ve dnech 24. a 25. listopadu 1982. (1982). *O státním plánu hospodářského a sociálního rozvoje ČSSR na rok 1983.* Praha: Svoboda.
[52] Potáč, S. (1983). Hlavní úkoly hospodářského a sociálního rozvoje na rok 1983. *Plánované hospodářství*, 36(1).
[53] *Statistická ročenka ČSSR.* (1984). Praha: SNTL.
[55] 9. zasedání Ústředního výboru Komunistické strany Československa ve dnech 23. a 24. listopadu 1983. (1983). K současné mezinárodní situaci; *O státním plánu hospodářského a sociálního rozvoje ČSSR na rok 1984.* Praha: Svoboda.
[56] Potáč, S. (1984). Státní plán hospodářského a sociálního rozvoje na rok 1984. *Plánované hospodářství*, 37(1).
[57] *Čísla pro každého: malá statistická ročenka.* (1985). Praha: SNTL.
[58] *Statistická ročenka ČSSR.* (1985). Praha: SNTL.
[60] Janza, V. (1985). Efektivnost plánu na rok 1985 – rozhodující zdroj růstu životní úrovně. *Plánované hospodářství*, 38(1).
[61] Ústřední výbor KSČ. zasedání ústředního výboru Komunistické strany Československa ve dnech 4. a 5. prosince 1984. (1984). *O státním plánu hospodářského a sociálního rozvoje Československé socialistické republiky na rok 1985.*
[62] *Statistická ročenka ČSSR.* (1986). Praha: SNTL.
[64] Ústřední výbor KSČ. (1981). *Hlavní směry hospodářského a sociálního rozvoje ČSSR na léta 1981–1985.*
[66] Věrtelář, V. (1986). Plán prvního roku 8. pětiletky. *Plánované hospodářství*, 39(1).
[67] Ježdík, V. (1987). Československá ekonomika v roce 1986. *Plánované hospodářství*, 40(3).
[68] *Statistická ročenka ČSSR.* (1987). Praha: SNTL.
[70] Ježdík, V. (1986). Československá ekonomika v roce 1987. *Plánované hospodářství*, 41(3).
[71] *Statistická ročenka ČSSR.* (1988). Praha: SNTL.
[73] *Čísla pro každého: malá statistická ročenka.* (1989). Praha: SNTL.
[74] *Statistická ročenka ČSSR.* (1989). Praha: SNTL.
[75] Rybnikář, K. (1988). Úkoly státního prováděcího plánu na rok 1989. *Plánované hospodářství*, 41(11).
[76] Věrtelář, V. (1989). Do závěru 8. pětiletky. *Plánované hospodářství*, 42(1).
[77] *Statistická ročenka Československé federativní republiky.* (1990). Praha: SNTL.
[82] *Bulletin – Státní banka československá.* (1976).
[83] *Bulletin – Státní banka československá.* (1977).
[84] *Bulletin – Státní banka československá.* (1978).
[85] *Bulletin – Státní banka československá.* (1979).
[86] *Bulletin – Státní banka československá.* (1980).
[87] *Bulletin – Státní banka československá.* (1981).

[88] *Bulletin – Státní banka československá.* (1982).
[89] *Bulletin – Státní banka československá.* (1983).
[90] *Bulletin – Státní banka československá.* (1984).
[91] *Bulletin – Státní banka československá.* (1985).
[92] *Bulletin – Státní banka československá.* (1986).
[93] *Bulletin – Státní banka československá.* (1987).
[95] *Bulletin – Státní banka československá.* (1989).

Table A Anonymized information about respondents

ID number	*Gender*	*Age*	*Education*	*Branch*	*Position*
ID001	M	65	higher	Food processing industry	production assistant director
ID002	M	82	higher	Water construction	director
ID003	M	61	higher	Engineering	chief designer
ID004	M	67	higher	Engineering	production assistant director
ID005	F	73	higher	Engineering	analyst and mathematician
ID006	M	63	higher	Engineering	director
ID007	M	N.A.	higher	Engineering	planner and supply manager
ID008	M	61	higher	Engineering	economic planner
ID009	M	67	higher	Transport	operating deputy in transport
ID010	M	66	higher	Agriculture	head of a production company
ID011	M	78	higher	Agriculture	production assistant director
ID012	M	71	secondary	Agriculture	designer
ID013	M	71	higher	State Planning Commission (SPC)	public relations
ID014	M	65	higher	Mining	power plant director
ID015	M	71	secondary	Engineering	foreman
ID016	M	82	higher	Mining	concern CEO
ID017	M	60	higher	Engineering + SPC	operative
ID018	M	54	higher	Agriculture	economist and planner
ID019	M	60	higher	SPC	operative
ID020	M	61	higher	Engineering	head of technical department
ID021	M	81	higher	Heavy engineering	CEO
ID022	M	67	higher	Engineering	CEO
ID023	M	77	higher	Construction	sectional construction manager
ID024	M	61	higher	Textile industry	head of human resources
ID025	M	67	higher	Communist Party	district committee chief secretary
ID026	M	59	higher	Communist Party	MP and district secretary
ID027	M	68	apprenticeship	Metallurgy	Leader of Associated Brigades
ID028	M	74	higher	Agriculture	chief economist
ID029	M	64	higher	Chemical industry	production leader
ID030	M	62	higher	Foreign trade	operative
ID031	F	60	higher	Construction	designer and leading worker
ID032	M	81	higher	Foreign trade, economic research	trade operative, scientist
ID033	M	74	higher	Transport	deputy, ministerial advisor
ID034	M	54	higher	Prognostic Institute	scientist
ID035	M	63	higher	Rolling mill	head of production
ID036	M	61	higher	Engineering	research department
ID037	M	79	secondary	Mechanical engineering	head of the department
ID038	M	79	higher	Engineering research	scientist
ID039	M	66	higher	Transport	ministerial officer

ID number	*Gender*	*Age*	*Education*	*Branch*	*Position*
ID040	M	68	higher	SPC	section chief
ID041	M	70	higher	Construction	technical director
ID042	M	79	secondary	Transport	stationmaster
ID043	M	57	higher	Engineering	assistant to the director
ID044	M	82	higher	Consumer electronics industry	head of economic department
ID045	M	72	higher	Agriculture	planner
ID046	M.	75	higher	Transport	manager
ID047	M	65	higher	Electrotechnical industry	CEO
ID048	M	85	secondary	Agriculture	head of company
ID049	M	82	higher	Automotive industry	director
ID050	M	68	higher	Investment engineering	head of trade department
ID051	M	73	higher	Automotive industry	economic director
ID052	M	71	higher	Catering industry	manager
ID053	M	54	secondary	Optical engineering	production controller
ID054	M	59	higher	Agriculture	production manager
ID055	M	67	higher	Textile industry	analyst
ID056	M	67	higher	Banking	managing clerk
ID057	M	79	higher	Textile industry	director, later deputy minister
ID058	M	88	higher	Construction	planner
ID059	M	79	higher	Engineering	price department representative
ID060	M	80	higher	Engineering research	head of department
ID061	M	78	higher	Research	economist and planner
ID062	M	65	higher	Agriculture	financial director
ID063	M	62	higher	Engineering	director
ID064	M	66	higher	Construction	investment methodologist
ID065	M	69	higher	Engineering	head of production planning department
ID066	M	65	higher	Metallurgy	head of project manager's office
ID067	M	65	higher	Power engineering	project head engineer
ID068	M	65	higher	Metallurgy	head designer
ID069	M	66	higher	Power engineering	assistant director for maintenance
ID070	M	65	higher	Electrical technology	head of control technology department
ID071	M	70	higher	Prognostic Institute	associate professor, head of department
ID072	M	66	higher	Transport, engineering	designer
ID073	M	75	higher	Knitting industry	CEO, deputy minister
ID074	M	66	higher	Mining	head of electrification
ID075	M	63	higher	Central Committee of the Com. Party	long-serving MP

Index